Programmer's Problem Solver

Second Edition

Robert Jourdain

Brady Publishing

New York   London   Toronto   Sydney   Tokyo   Singapore

Brady Publishing

Published by Brady Publishing
A Division of Prentice Hall Computer Publishing
15 Columbus Circle
New York, NY 10023

Manufactured in the United States of America

10   9   8   7   6   5   4   3   2

Library of Congress Cataloging-in-Publication Data

Jourdain, Robert, 1950-
    Programmer's problem solver / Robert Jourdain. – 2nd ed.
        p.   cm.
    Includes index.
    1. Electronic digital computers–Programming.   I. Title.
QA76.6.J685   1992
005.265–dc20   92-7980
    ISBN 0-13-720194-X   CIP

Limits of Liability and Disclaimer or Warranty

The author and publisher of this book have used their best efforts in preparing this book and the programs contained in it. These efforts include the development, research, and testing of the theories and programs to determine their effectiveness. The author and publisher make no warranty, express or implied, with regard to these programs or the documentation contained in this book. The author and publisher shall not be liable in any event for incidental or consequential damages in connection with, or arising out of, the furnishing, performance, or use of these programs.

All brand and product names mentioned herein are trademarks or registered trademarks of their respective holders.

Contents

8 Interpreting Keystrokes 219

9 Using a Mouse 241

10 Managing Disk Drives 287

14 Displaying Text 435

15 Displaying Graphics 463

16 Controlling a Printer 493

Introduction

By now, most people have figured out that The Information Age has done a great job of providing lots of information, but a pretty lousy job of organizing it. Computer programmers are in a better position than most to appreciate this observation, for their world consists of thousands upon thousands of diverse facts about hardware standards, operating system versions, and compiler libraries. A programmer's book shelf groans under the weight of the associated documentation. It's all there and it's all organized. It's just not organized in the way you usually need it.

This volume endeavors to bring together essential IBM PC programming information so that you can find what you want to know quickly and can see a working example written in the language you're using. It's amazing how hard it sometimes can be to find essential facts within voluminous documentation. Want to know how to send output to LPT2? Or to switch off the cursor? Or to find out whether expanded memory is installed? Don't waste your time looking in your compiler manual's index. You're not going to find what you need. But if you happen to have this reference on hand, take a look in the Contents and turn to page...

This book is organized around hardware, with chapters on printing, timing, disk operations, and so on. In many instances, you'll find explanations of how to perform tasks at three levels: at high level using compiler library functions, at middle level by calling the operating system, and at low level by directly accessing peripheral chips such as serial ports and video controllers. When high level compiler routines are lacking, you'll encounter examples of how to work at middle or low level in a high level language. By studying the different approaches, you can learn how high level languages call on the operating system, and how the operating system in turn manipulates hardware.

For nearly every programming task, you'll find examples in each of the four most commonly used programming languages. BASIC, Pascal, C, and 8086 assembler. Of course, compiler libraries vary from maker to maker, and so choices had to be made as to which compilers to use for program examples. The selection was not difficult for BASIC and Pascal, since Microsoft's BASIC and Borland's Turbo Pascal are the undisputed leaders. Selecting a C compiler was not so simple. At this writing, the King Kong versus Godzilla battle between the Borland and Microsoft C compilers continues unabated. And so examples are given for both when there are differences. The assembly language examples are universal and will work with any assembler, or as inline assembly code in compilers that accept it.

You may wonder whether this information is as relevant as it used to be. After a decade as the reigning PC operating system, DOS is showing its age. Now Microsoft Windows wants its turn. Is DOS worth this trouble? The answer is flatly yes. DOS-oriented programming is hardly about to go away. The tens of millions of PC's that lack the speed or memory to run Windows are going to go right on booting every morning for years to come. Microsoft knows this market is too large and lucrative to ignore, and plans to continue improving DOS. Meanwhile, Windows applications have raised user expectations about how easily software should be learned and operated. Many programmers now must develop nearly equivalent versions of their software for both DOS and Windows. This makes DOS programming all the harder and demands an even deeper appreciation of PC hardware to bring DOS applications up to Windows standards. This book can help you along.

Another trend is toward object oriented programming, especially in C. Ultimately, well-formed class libraries may replace the procedure libraries that accompany compilers today. But class libraries are in their infancy and are far from standardized. No attempt has been made to document them here. The procedures and functions described in this volume can readily be designed into object oriented routines, so the information in this volume is pertinent to programming in C++ as well.

There are, of course, lots of facts you won't find in this volume. No attempt has been made to include every function from every library, not every detail of every function that is treated here. That's what compiler documentation is for. Rather, this reference is intended to get you results as quickly as possible 95% of the time, and to teach you a lot about PC hardware along the way.

Prosperous computing!

Robert Jourdain

Program Organization

- Minitutorial: Managing Programs
- Intercept Command Line Parameters
- Read or Change DOS Environment Variables
- Run One Program from Within Another
- Return an Exit Code to DOS
- Make a Program Memory-Resident
- Convert Programs from .EXE to .COM Type

Minitutorial: Managing Programs

When a program is loaded, it finds itself in a complex environment where a number of factors determine how the program should behave. The program needs to find out whether any command line parameters were specified by the program user. It also may need to search the environment variables set up by DOS to communicate configuration information to all software running in the machine. Sometimes programs need to run other programs. And when programs terminate, they may need to stay memory-resident or return an error code to DOS.

DOS programs use one of two formats: EXE and COM. Unlike COM programs, EXE programs may be larger than 64K, but they require that DOS do some processing as it loads them into memory. COM programs, on the other hand, already exist in final form. COM programs are especially useful for short utilities. In either case, the code that comprises a program is preceded in memory by a *program segment prefix (PSP)*. This is an area 100h bytes large that holds special information DOS requires to operate the program. The PSP also provides a small buffer for file I/O operations.

For reference, here is a map of the PSP fields:

offset	field size	use
0h	dw	Machine code for calling an interrupt that terminates the program. Although the technique is now obsolete, programs can be designed so that the terminating RET instruction transfers control to this point.
2	dw	Segment address of the top of memory. This value can be used to calculate available conventional memory, as shown in Chapter 2, "Determining the Availability of Conventional Memory."
4	dw	Reserved.
6	dd	Long call to DOS function dispatcher.
A	dd	Terminate address (IP,CS). Specifies where control is passed when the program ends.
E	dd	Ctrl-Break exit address (IP,CS). The Ctrl-Break feature is discussed in Chapter 7, "Write a Ctrl-Break Routine."
12	dd	Critical error exit address (IP,CX). Critical error handlers are discussed in Chapter 10, "Detect and Recover from Disk Errors."
16	22 bytes	Reserved.
2C	dw	Paragraph # of program's environment. See "Read or Change DOS Environment Variables" below, for an explanation of how to use this value to get at a program's *current* or *master* environment.
2E	46 bytes	Reserved.
5C	16 bytes	Parameter area 1 (formatted as unopened FCB). This and the next field are provided for initializing the now-obsolete *file control blocks* discussed in the Chapter 12 *Minitutorial*.
6C	20 bytes	Parameter area 2 (formatted as unopened FCB).
80	128 bytes	Default disk transfer area. At start-up, this field receives command line data. It may optionally be used as a work area for disk I/O.

Intercept Command Line Parameters

When loaded, many programs allow the user to specify parameters on the DOS command line, often to indicate the name and path of the file that the program will first work on. This information is dumped into a 128-byte field in the program segment prefix (discussed in this chapter's *minitutorial*), beginning at offset 80h. This same field may also be used for disk transfer operations, so the command line information can be overwritten if it is not accessed in time. The information is written in the PSP exactly as it was typed. It is stored as a Pascal string with the first byte (at offset 80h) giving the string length.

BASIC

In Microsoft BASIC, the *COMMAND$* function returns the entire command line, converting it to uppercase letters and removing any leading spaces. You'll need to write a routine that divides the command line into its components.

```
TheLine$ = COMMAND$
```

Pascal

Turbo Pascal's *ParamCount* function reports how many parameters were passed on the command line, and the *ParamStr* function returns individual parameters. *ParamCount* returns an integer result. *ParamStr* takes an integer value that numbers the parameters, counting from 1 upward, and returns each parameter as a string. To see a listing of all parameters, you would write:

```
for I := 1 to ParamCount do Writeln(ParamStr(I));
```

C

In C, declare the *main* function this way:

```
main(int argc, char *argv[])
```

The compiler will initialize *argc* to hold the number of command line parameters, and it will fill the elements of *argv* with a pointer to each element of the command line in the order that they were typed in. The last element in the array, *argv[argc]*, is a null pointer. To see a listing of the command line parameters, you could write:

```
for(i=0; i<argc; i++) printf("%s\n",argv[i]);
```

3

Assembler

Assembly language programs must take the command line data directly from the PSP. EXE programs can use function 62h of interrupt 21h to return the PSP segment address in BX. In COM programs, CS always points to the PSP. This example moves the command line to the variable *COMMAND_LINE*, converting it to a C-style null-terminated string.

```
;---FETCH COMMAND LINE:

COMMAND_LINE   db 128 dup (?)


        mov   ax,seg COMMAND_LINE    ;point ES:DI to COMMAND_LINE
        mov   es,ax                  ;
        mov   di,offset COMMAND_LINE
        push  ds                     ;save DS
        mov   ah,62h                 ;function number
        int   21h                    ;find out the PSP
        mov   ax,bx                  ;shift PSP to AX
        mov   ds,ax                  ;now DS points to the PSP
        mov   si,80h                 ;offset to PSP field
        sub   cx,cx                  ;clear CX as counter
        mov   cl,[si]                ;get string length
        cmp   cl, 0                  ;test for no parameters
        je    NO_PARAMS              ;jump ahead if none
        inc   si                     ;forward ptr to first byte
        cld                          ;set direction flag
rep movsb                            ;transfer the command line
NO_PARAMS:                           ;
        mov byte ptr es:[di],0       ;null terminate the string
        pop   ds                     ;restore DS
```

Read or Change DOS Environment Variables

DOS maintains an *environment* in which it records information that any program may use. Certain DOS commands, such as PATH and COMSPEC, write or alter variables in the environment. When a program is started, DOS creates a copy of the environment for the program to use. For example, it might look up directory paths in the environment's PATH variable and use them when it searches for files.

The copy is called the *current environment,* while the original is called the *master environment.* The current environment ceases to exist when the program terminates. For this reason, there usually isn't much reason to change the current environment. However, various utility programs and software installation programs sometimes need to make lasting changes in the master environment.

The address of a program's current environment is found at offset 2Ch in the program's PSP (program segment prefix, discussed in the *minitutorial* at the beginning of this chapter). This address is a segment value within which the environment begins at offset 0. The location of the master environment is found at the same offset in the PSP of the *primary shell,* that is, of COMMAND.COM. This PSP is pointed to by interrupt vector 2Eh. An assembly language example below shows how it is accessed.

The DOS environment is one way in which you can configure your software. Instead of creating a configuration facility, you can have the user employ the DOS SET command to place configuration information in the environment. SET will accept variables of any name, so you can decide on one that only your program will use; you can devise any format you like for the information the variable will hold. This approach helps avoid keeping a separate configuration file for the program. However, many users are put off by the prospect of using unfamiliar DOS commands and editing their AUTOEXEC.BAT files. Also, the DOS environment can easily fill, and for the average user it is relatively difficult to enlarge, the environment using the SHELL command.

BASIC

In Microsoft BASIC, the *ENVIRON$* function returns variables from the environment. Its only parameter is a string naming an environment variable. The string must be uppercase; otherwise, *ENVIRON$* returns a null string. To find out the current setting for the PATH variable, write:

```
PathString$ = ENVIRON$("PATH")
```

5

Alternatively, you can use a numeric value for the parameter. *ENVIRON$* returns the first variable in the environment when this value is **1**, the second variable when it is **2**, and so on. A null string is returned when no variable corresponds to the number given. You can search the entire environment using this feature.

To modify or add to the program's copy of the environment, use BASIC's *ENVIRON* statement. If you were to write:

```
ENVIRON "PATH=C:\DOS"
```

the PATH variable in the environment would be changed to the specified string. If you want to add to the existing PATH specification, read it with *ENVIRON$*, append an additional directory path, and then reinsert the entire string using *ENVIRON*. To eliminate the PATH variable from the environment, write a semicolon instead of a specification:

```
ENVIRON "PATH=;"
```

Pascal

In Turbo Pascal, the *GetEnv* function returns a specified variable from the environment. To find out the current setting for the DOS PATH variable, write:

```
uses DOS;

var

  DOSPath: string[128];

  DOSPath := GetEnv('PATH');
```

The variable name may be written in either uppercase or lowercase letters, and it must not contain the "=" sign. An empty string is returned when the variable is not found.

You can use the *EnvCount* function to find out how many strings the environment contains. The integer returned by the function can be used in a loop to read the entire contents of the environment using *EnvStr*, which takes an integer parameter and returns the first string if the parameter is **1**, the second string if the parameter is **2**, and so on. To display the entire environment, you would write:

```
for I := 1 to EnvCount do Writeln(EnvStr(I));
```

Turbo Pascal does not provide a procedure for making changes in its copy of the environment. If you must do so, look up the environment's address in the program segment prefix. Turbo Pascal's *System* unit contains the global integer variable *PrefixSeg*, which reports the segment address of the PSP. Use it to find the segment of the program's environment, which is held at offset 2Ch.

C

Both the Borland and Microsoft compilers use the *getenv* function to read variables from the DOS environment. The function takes a single parameter — a pointer to a string naming the variable you want to fetch. This string may be in either uppercase or lowercase letters. A pointer to the variable is returned. It will be a null string if the variable was not found. To learn the current setting of PATH:

```
#include <stdlib.h>


char *return_string;


return_string = getenv("PATH");
```

Both compilers use the *putenv* function to alter the environment. Its only parameter is a string giving the new value for an environment variable. The function returns **0** when it succeeds in making the change. To add C:\DOS to the PATH variable:

```
putenv("PATH=C:\\DOS");
```

To alter an existing variable, first read it with *getenv*, modify it, and then reinsert it into the environment with *putenv*. To delete a variable, specify nothing at all when you use *putenv*. For example, to delete the PATH variable, you would write:

```
putenv("PATH=");
```

Assembler

To access a program's copy of the environment in assembly language, you'll need to find the environment and sort through it. First, find out the address of the program's PSP. In COM programs, CS always points to the PSP. In EXE programs, call function 62h of INT 21h. It returns the PSP segment in BX. You'll find the environment's segment address at offset 2Ch in the PSP.

The size of the environment, expressed in 16-byte paragraphs, is found in the two bytes that are at offset 0003h in the paragraph immediately preceding the environment segment. All variables in the environment consist of zero-terminated strings containing uppercase characters. The format for the variables is exactly as in a SET command: first the variable, then the "=" sign, and then the values assigned to the variables. This example points DS:SI to the first byte of the environment and leaves the environment length in CX:

```
;---POINT TO THE ENVIRONMENT:

        mov   ah,62h              ;function number
        int   21h                ;get the PSP segment
        mov   es,bx              ;place it in ES
        mov   ax,es:[2Ch]        ;get the environment segment
        dec   ax                ;pull back a paragraph
        mov   ds,ax              ;place it in DS
        mov   cx,[3]            ;get the environment size
        inc   ax                ;shift pointer back
        mov   dx,ax             ;
        sub   si,si             ;DS:SI pts to env, ready for MOVSB
```

As mentioned above, a program's master environment is found in the same way, but in the PSP of COMMAND.COM. The address of this PSP is held in interrupt vector 2Eh. This example locates the master environment:

```
        mov   ah,35h             ;function to get interrupt vector
        mov   al,2Eh             ;vector number
        int   21h                ;ES:BX (ES:0000) points to PSP
        mov   ax,es:[002Ch]      ;get environment address
        mov   es,ax              ;point ES to the environment
        sub   di,di              ;use DI as offset into the env
```

Run One Program from Within Another

DOS provides the EXEC function (number 4B of interrupt 21h) to run one program from within another. The first program is called the *parent process*, and the one that is loaded and run is called the *child process*. The child process can be a second copy of COMMAND.COM, in which case DOS commands can be run. An initial command may be appended to the specification, starting it with the symbol **/C**, as in the Pascal example below.

BASIC

BASIC's *SHELL* statement can load and run another program. The format is **SHELL command-string**. The command string may be just the name of a program, or it can be the name plus the parameters that would ordinarily follow the program name on the command line. If no command-string is named, a copy of COMMAND.COM is loaded and the DOS prompt appears. Any DOS commands may be used and, when finished, typing **EXIT** returns control to the BASIC program.

There are a number of restrictions on the use of SHELL. If the program that is loaded changes the screen mode, for example, the change will *not* be automatically remedied on return. All files must be closed before the program is loaded, and it must not be a program that stays resident after termination. See the BASIC manual for a discussion of several other problems.

In this example, SHELL loads the program C:\UTIL\TRASHER.COM:

```
Shell "C:\UTIL\TRASHER.COM"
```

Pascal

Turbo Pascal's *Exec* procedure loads and runs programs. It takes two string parameters. The first string gives the program's name and path, and the second specifies any command line parameters. This example loads a second copy of COMMAND.COM and requests a DIR command:

```
Exec('C:\COMMAND.COM', '/C DIR *.*');
```

A compiled program needs memory in which to run the EXECed process. So you must limit the heap size by beginning the program with a directive in the form:

```
{$M StackSize, MinimumHeap, MaximumHeap}
```

9

The heap may be eliminated when there are no heap allocations, as in this example, which provides for only a 4K stack:

```
{$M $1000, 0, 0}
```

C

In both the Borland and Microsoft compilers, the *execl* function loads and runs child processes. This function takes a variable number of parameters, all of them pointers to strings. The first parameter is the name and path of the program that will be loaded. The succeeding parameters are the command line arguments, one after another. A NULL character marks the end of the parameter list. This example runs a program called DSKDEATH.COM, and hands it the parameters "512" and "UNDO":

```
#include <process.h>

execl("C:\\UTIL\\DSKDEATH.COM","512","UNDO",NULL);
```

There are several variants on this function, some of which take the command line arguments as an array, or that can pass an environment to the child process. You also can control whether a DOS PATH search is made for the child process when it is loaded. See the documentation for details.

Assembler

Function 4Bh is more complicated than most, requiring four preparatory steps:

(1) Make space available in memory for the program.

(2) Create a parameter block.

(3) Build a drive, path, and program name string.

(4) Save the SS and SP registers in variables.

Space must be made in memory because DOS assigns the whole of memory to a program when it is loaded. Without freeing some memory there would be nowhere to load the second program. Chapter 3, "Allocate/Deallocate Conventional Memory," explains how it is done using the *SETBLOCK* function. Once memory is freed, you need merely place in BX the required number of 16-byte paragraphs of memory space, put 4Ah in AH, and execute interrupt 21h to shrink down the memory allocation so that only the number of paragraphs requested is available to the program.

The *parameter block*, to which ES:BX must point, is a 14-byte block of memory in which you place the following four pieces of information:

```
dw        segment address of environment string
dd        segment/offset of command line
dd        segment/offset of first file control block
dd        segment/offset of second file control block
```

The environment string must begin on a paragraph boundary. This is because the entry in the parameter block that points to the string holds only a two-byte segment value. All of this may be avoided if the new program can operate with the same environment string as the one that loads it. In that case, simply place ASCII 0 in the first two bytes of the parameter block.

The next four bytes of the parameter block point to a command line for the program being loaded. The command line begins with a byte holding the number of characters in the string, and ends the string with a byte of ASCII 13, (which is not counted in the string length).

The last eight bytes of the parameter block point to *file control blocks (FCBs)*. The FCBs hold information for the one or two files named in the command line. If no files are to be opened this way (as they virtually never are), fill the eight bytes with ASCII 0.

Finally, you must build a drive, path, and file name string. This is the string that names the program to be loaded. DS:DX points to the string when EXEC is executed. The string is a standard "*ASCII Z string*," which is nothing more than a drive specifier, a tree directory path, and the file name and extension, ending with an ASCII 0 byte.

Once all of the above information is set up, there remains one final task. All registers are altered by the program that is called. The stack segment and stack pointer must be saved so that they can be restored when control returns to the calling program. Set aside variables to do this. Since DS is also destroyed, these variables must be accessed relative to CS. Once SS and SP are saved, place 0 in AL to choose the "load and run" option. Then place 4Ah in AH and call interrupt 21h. At this point, essentially two programs are running, and the parent goes on "hold." DOS provides a way for the child program to pass a return code to the parent, so that errors and status may be reported. The section "Return an Exit Code to DOS," below, explains how this is done. Minimally, the carry flag is set on return if there has been an error; in this case AX returns 1 for an invalid function number, 2 if the file was not found, 5 for disk problems, 8 if insufficient memory, 10 if the environment string was invalid, and 11 if the format was invalid.

The example given here is the simplest possible, but often the EXEC procedure requires no more. Leave the entire parameter block as zeros, and do not create an environment string. This means that no command line is passed to the loaded program and that the environment will be the same as that of the calling program. You need only change the memory allocation, set up the file name and (empty) parameter block, and save SS and SP.

```
;---IN THE DATA SEGMENT:
FILENAME      db    'C:TRIAL.EXE',0;load TRIAL.EXE from drive C
;---REALLOCATE MEMORY:
         mov  bx,sp            ;SP points to top of stack
         mov  cl,4             ;divide by 16
         shr  bx,cl            ;
         mov  ax,S3            ;add in stack segment
         add  bx,ax            ;address of program end
         mov  ax,es            ;get paragraph # of start of program
         sub  bx,ax            ;calculate program size in paragraphs
         inc  bx               ;add 1 to be safe
         mov  ah,4Ah           ;function number
         int  21h              ;make the reallocation
;---POINT TO PARAMETER BLOCK:
         push CS               ;ES holds segment
         pop  es               ;
         mov  bx,offset PARAMETERS ;BX holds offset
;---STORE COPIES OF SS AND SP:
         mov  CS:KEEP_SS,ss    ;save SS
         mov  CS:KEEP_SP,sp    ;save SP
;---POINT TO FILE NAME STRING:
         mov  dx,offset FILENAME  ;offset in DX
         mov  ax,seg FILENAME     ;segment in DS
         mov  ds,ax            ;
;---LOAD THE PROGRAM:
         mov  ah,4Bh           ;EXEC function
         mov  al,0             ;choose "load and run" option
         int  21h              ;run it
;---AFTERWARDS, RESTORE REGISTERS:
         mov  ax,DSEG          ;restore DS
```

```
mov   ds,ax              ;
cli                      ;shut out interrupts
mov   ss,KEEP_SS         ;restore SS
mov   sp,KEEP_SP         ;restore SP
sti                      ;re-enable interrupts
ret                      ;end code, begin data
KEEP_SS dw 0             ;variables to hold SS:SP
KEEP_SP dw 0             ;
PARAMETERS equ this word ;begin parameter block
      dw 0
      dw offset COMMAND_LINE
      dw seg COMMAND_LINE
      dw 4 dup (?)
COMMAND_LINE db 10, 'myfile.doc', 13
```

Return an Exit Code to DOS

When programs terminate, they can return an *exit code* to DOS to report whether the program was able to complete its job successfully. Batch files can respond to these codes using the *ERRORLEVEL* command. A **0** code indicates successful completion. Other codes are up to you to define (**1** often indicates termination by Ctrl-Break). Your program's documentation should inform the user of the meaning of the codes the program returns. Programs run *by* your program can also return exit codes. See "Run One Program from Within Another," above, for a discussion of this topic.

BASIC

In Microsoft BASIC, a program can return an error code by terminating with an *END* statement followed by the number. *END* also closes all files. To return **0**:

```
END 0
```

Pascal

Turbo Pascal returns a specified exit code to DOS when you terminate a program with the *Halt* procedure. This integer code is the only parameter taken by *Halt* and it is an optional one. To return **1** as an exit code:

```
Halt(1);
```

C

Both Borland's C and Microsoft's C can return exit codes through the *exit* function. This function closes all files, outputs data waiting in buffers, and executes exit routines posted by the *atexit* function. The exit code is the only parameter. To return **0**:

```
exit(0);
```

Assembler

In assembly language, you can return an exit code by terminating the program by a call to function 4Ch of INT 21h. This is, in fact, the best way to end any program. The function flushes buffers associated with file handles, and restores the Ctrl-Break and critical-error interrupt vectors (other altered vectors must be restored by the program). The exit code is placed in AL. To return 1 to DOS, write:

```
;---TERMINATE PROGRAM AND RETURN EXIT CODE:
      mov   ah,4Ch            ;function number
      mov   al,1              ;exit code
      int   21h               ;quit
```

Make a Program Memory-Resident

Programs left resident in memory may serve as utilities to other programs, or as stand-alone applications accessed by hot keys. Memory-resident programs are normally accessed by interrupt vectors. When accessed through a hot key, code in the memory-resident program is chained into a keyboard input routine — either the *keyboard interrupt* (interrupt #9, which is discussed in the Chapter 7 *minitutorial*) or else the BIOS interrupt 16h routines that fetch key codes from the keyboard buffer. While it's easy to chain a program this way (see Chapter 4, "Chain into Existing Interrupts"), there are many pitfalls that make pop-up programs difficult to program. Most notably, you must be sure that no time-sensitive activities are taking place, such as disk operations or serial I/O. Matters become much more complicated when the memory-resident program swaps parts of itself into memory while temporarily setting aside current memory contents. Hardware interrupt calls to displaced drivers, such as a mouse driver, can wreck havoc. Writing a memory-resident program that can run on any hardware platform is a specialized programming skill beyond the scope of this book, and in most instances it is beyond the concern even of those who wish to write pop-up utilities. Instead, it is wiser to adopt one of the ready-made function libraries for creating pop-up programs.

Pascal

A Turbo Pascal program is made memory-resident just by terminating it with the *Keep* procedure:

```
Keep(0);
```

The only parameter is an exit code, normally 0 (see "Return an Exit Code to DOS," above, for a discussion of exit codes). The entire program remains in memory, including data, stack, and heap. You can use the $M compiler directive to limit the size of the heap. Its format is:

```
{$M stacksize,heapmin,heapmax}
```

C

In Borland's C, the *keep* function terminates a program and makes it memory-resident. An identical function in Microsoft's C is named *_dos_keep*. The function takes two parameters: first, an exit code, and second, a specification of the number of bytes the program should occupy when it is memory-resident. The exit code is normally 0. The program size must be calculated using constants defined by the compiler. These are **_SS**, **_SP**, and **_psp**, which represent the value of the stack segment, the stack pointer, and the program segment prefix (PSP), respectively. The PSP marks the beginning of the program, and the stack segment plus the stack pointer point to the start of the stack (that is, to the program's highest point in memory). Add an extra paragraph for safety's sake:

```
keep(0, (_SS, ((_SP + 16) / 16) - _psp));
```

Assembler

A program is made resident simply by terminating it with function 31h of interrupt 21h, instead of the usual function 4Ch of interrupt 21h. On entry, DX holds the program size expressed in 16-byte paragraphs. In addition, AL holds a return code. Resident programs are usually written in COM form, as discussed in "Convert Programs from .EXE to .COM Type," below. They are slightly more difficult to make resident as EXE files.

The examples below initialize interrupt vector 70h to point to the memory-resident program. The interrupt vector is set up using function 25h of interrupt 21h, as discussed in Chapter 4, "Write Your Own Interrupt Service Routine." Because it is executed as an interrupt, the routine ends with an IRET instruction. Apart from providing the routine, the set-up program does nothing more than initialize the interrupt vector, point DX to the end of the interrupt routine, and terminate.

Examples are given here for both COM and EXE files. Both set up the label "FINISH" to mark the end of the interrupt routine (recall that the $ sign gives the instruction pointer value at that point). In the COM file, FINISH gives the offset from the start of the PSP, as required by function 31h. In the EXE file, the offset is from the first byte following the PSP, and so 100h is added to this value so that this offset too starts from the bottom of the PSP. Note that by placing the routine first in the program, the set-up code can be excluded from the resident portion.

COM file case:

```
;---HERE IS THE INTERRUPT ROUTINE:
BEGIN:
      jmp   short SET_UP   ;jump over the resident routine
ROUTINE  proc far
      push ds              ;save altered registers
      .
      .
```

```
    (the routine)

        .

        .

    pop  ds              ;restore registers
    iret                 ;interrupt return
FINISH equ  $            ;mark end of routine
ROUTINE endp


;---SET UP THE INTERRUPT VECTOR:
SET_UP:mov  dx,OFFSET ROUTINE ;put offset of routine in DX
    mov    al,60h        ;interrupt vector number
    mov    ah,25h        ;function to set vector
    int    21h           ;set the vector
;---LEAVE THE PROGRAM, STAYING RESIDENT:
    lea    dx,FINISH     ;set offset of resident routine
    mov    ah,31h        ;function to terminate & stay resident
    mov    al,0          ;return code
    int    21h           ;quit, and routine stays resident
```

EXE file case:

```
;---HERE IS THE INTERRUPT ROUTINE:
    jmp  short SET_UP    ;jump over the resident routine
ROUTINE  proc far
    push ds              ;save altered registers

        .

        .

    (the routine)

        .

        .
```

```
        pop  ds              ;restore registers
        iret                 ;interrupt return
FINISH: equ  $               ;make end point of routine
ROUTINE endp


;---SET UP THE INTERRUPT VECTOR:
SET_UP:
        mov  dx,offset ROUTINE     ;put offset of routine in DX
        mov  ax,seg ROUTINE        ;put segment of routine in DS
        mov  ds,ax                 ;
        mov  al,60h                ;interrupt vector number
        mov  ah,25h                ;function to set vector
        int  21h                   ;set the vector
;---LEAVE THE PROGRAM, STAYING RESIDENT:
        mov  dx,FINISH+100h        ;set offset of end of resident routine
        mov  ah,31h                ;function number
        mov  al,0                  ;return code
        int  21h                   ;quit and stay resident
```

Convert Programs from .EXE to .COM Type

Assembly language programmers have the option of converting some programs from the usual EXE format to COM format. EXE files have a *header* field that contains information for a process called *relocation.* In relocation, DOS fills in segment addresses used by the program. In COM files, the processor's code segment and data segment registers are normally left pointing to the beginning of the program code, and all addresses of procedures and data are offsets from this point. Because offsets are limited to 64K, all code and data in COM programs must fit within 64K. Note that DS and ES can be redirected to dynamically allocated memory blocks or absolute memory addresses like the BIOS data area. But DS must be restored to its initial setting to use program variables.

EXE programs, on the other hand, may make *far* calls to procedures and may use *far* pointers to access data. In these cases, the program code must provide segment addresses as well as offsets. But there is no way for the linker that builds the program to know where in memory the program will reside. Consequently, the linker cannot determine what values to use for segment addresses (offsets pose no problem, however, since they remain relative to the segment addresses). The solution to this dilemma is to simply leave the segment addresses undetermined until an EXE program is loaded. At that time, DOS looks up the segment address locations in the program's header, calculates the proper segment values, and inserts them into the code. Figure 1-1 illustrates relocation.

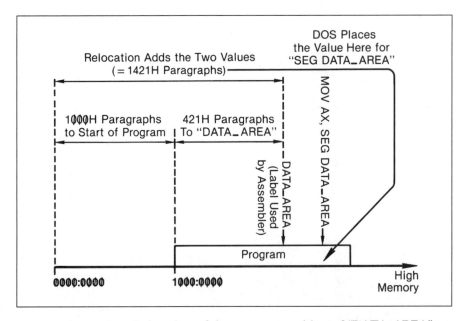

Figure 1-1   Relocation of the memory position of "DATA_AREA"

EXE files are slightly larger on disk than the COM equivalent, although they consume the same amount of RAM once loaded. By avoiding relocation, COM files also load more quickly than EXE files. Many programmers regard these advantages as being too trivial to matter.

Follow these rules when you design an assembly language program that will be converted to COM form:

(1) Make all procedures in the program *near* procedures.

(2) Place the line **ORG 100h** at the start of the code. This statement sets the point of origination of the code. Both EXE and COM programs begin with a standard *program segment prefix (PSP)* that is 100h bytes long. When an EXE program is loaded, the CS register points to the first byte following the PSP — that is, to the first byte of code. In COM programs, however, CS points to the start of the PSP.

(3) Include an ASSUME statement that sets DS — and usually ES and SS — to the same value as the code segment.

```
assume cs:CSEG, ds:CSEG, es:CSEG, ss:CSEG
```

This action keeps all parts of the program within the same 64K space, with the stack growing downward from the top of the 64K block. If required, the program can change SP to bring the top of the stack closer to the PSP, or can allocate memory for a larger stack or data work areas and change DS, ES, and SS, accordingly. Be aware that your linker may issue a warning that no stack segment has been created. Ignore it.

(4) The program's data can be placed anywhere in the program so long as it does not interfere with the code. It is best to begin the program with the data, since a macro assembler can create errors during its first pass if references are made to data items not yet encountered (recent assemblers overcome this problem). Start the program with a JMP instruction to jump over the data.

(5) Never use statements like **MOV AX,SEG NEW_DATA**. Only offsets are allowed. In particular, skip the usual code at the start of a program that sets up the data segment by **MOV AX,DSEG/MOV DS,AX**.

(6) Terminate the program by executing function 4Ch of INT 21h.

Once a program has been constructed in this way, assemble and link it as always. Then use the DOS EXE2BIN program to convert it to COM form using the command:

```
EXE2BIN MYPROG.EXE MYPROG.COM
```

Assembler

This example provides a short, complete program that fetches the BIOS equipment status byte and reports the number of serial ports in the machine. INT 11h returns the value in AX, placing it in bits 9 through 11.

```
        CSEG    segment

        org  100h

REPORT_SERIAL    PROC NEAR

        assume cs:CSEG, ds:CSEG, ss:CSEG  ;all segments set to CSEG
;    THE DATA:
        jmp  short BEGIN   ;jump over the data

MESSAGE1    db  'There are $'

MESSAGE2    db  ' serial ports(s) in this machine.$'
;    PRINT THE FIRST HALF OF THE MESSAGE:
BEGIN:  mov  ah,9          ;function 9 of INT 21h displays strings

        mov  dx,OFFSET MESSAGE1 ;point DS:DX to the string

        int  21h           ;write the first string
;    GET THE STATUS BYTE BIT FIELD:
        int  11h           ;place the byte in AX

        and  ax,111000000000b ;zero out all bits but 9 through 11

        mov  cl,9          ;will move bit field to bottom of AX

        shr  ax,cl         ;make the shift

        add  ax,48         ;turn into corresponding ASCII code
;    DISPLAY THE NUMBER OF SERIAL PORTS:
        mov  ah,2          ;use function 2 of INT 21h

        mov  dl,al         ;displays value in DL

        int  21h           ;display the number
;    NOW DISPLAY THE SECOND HALF OF THE MESSAGE:
        mov  ah,9          ;function to display string

        mov  dx,OFFSET MESSAGE2 ;get ready to write
```

```
        int   21h        ;write the string
        mov   ah,4Ch      ;function to exit program
        mov   al,0        ;exit code
        int   21h        ;end the program
REPORT_SERIAL   endp
CSEG    ends
        end   REPORT_SERIAL
```

2

Equipment Determination

- Minitutorial: Assessing System Resources
- Determine the DOS Version
- Determine the Number and Types of Video Adaptors
- Determine the Number and Types of Disk Drives
- Determine the Numbers and Types of I/O Ports
- Determine the Kind of Keyboard in Use
- Determine Whether a Mouse Is Present
- Determine the Availability of Conventional Memory
- Determine the Availability of Expanded Memory
- Determine the Availability of Extended Memory

Minitutorial: Assessing System Resources

When a program is loaded, its first job should be to find out where it is: Under what DOS version is the program running? What kinds of memory are present and how much is there of each? Is there a hard disk? What is the most advanced video mode available? Are all the required peripherals present? There are three ways to go about finding out this information. Least elegant is simply to prompt the program user for the information. This is a poor solution, because many users lack all conception of how a PC works, let alone whether the particular PC they use possesses certain components. A far better approach is to request configuration information from the system BIOS, information it garners during the machine's power-on self-test (POST). Unfortunately, this information is not always adequate, and it is not consistent between the various kinds of IBM

25

machines. And so usually the best option is to make direct access to the hardware in question, or to the device drivers that run the hardware.

This chapter shows how to detect many kinds of equipment. In most cases, it's as easy to search for equipment using a high-level language as it is in assembly language. Unfortunately, none of the four compilers discussed in this book provides a comprehensive set of functions for this purpose.

Determine the DOS Version

As PC DOS evolves, it adds new functions, some of which make it easier to create certain kinds of code. For instance, a more sophisticated system of error reporting was introduced with DOS 3.0. Before using these facilities, your program would need to be sure that it is running under DOS 3.0 or a later version. Many PCs continue to run under DOS 2.2.

DOS version numbers consist of two parts, a *major version number* and a *minor version number*. The **3** in 3.1 is a major version number. The minor version number, however, is reported as a two-digit value. For DOS 3.1 (3.10), the minor version number is **10**.

Function 30h of interrupt 21h returns the DOS version number, placing the major version number in AL and the minor version number in AH. Note that AL may return 0 to indicate a pre-DOS 2.0 version.

BASIC

In Microsoft BASIC, you'll need to call the DOS interrupt that returns the version number. This example finds out if the current version is at least DOS 3.0.

```
' $INCLUDE: 'QBX.BI'
DIM regs AS RegType   ' Define register array

regs.ax = &H3000      'function number in AH
CALL Interrupt(&H21, regs, regs)
DosVersion = regs.ax 'get the version number
DosVersion = DosVersion AND &HFF 'clear minor version #
IF DosVersion < 3 THEN WRITE "Pre-3.0 DOS version"
```

Pascal

Turbo Pascal's *DosVersion* returns an integer in which the high byte holds the major version number and the low byte holds the minor version number. Use *Hi* and *Lo* to obtain the two parts. For example

```
var
  Num: word;


Num := DosVersion;
Writeln('You are using DOS version ',Lo(Num),'.',Hi(Num));
```

C

Borland's C places the DOS major version number in the *char* global variable *_osmajor*, and the minor version number in *_osminor*. To access the variable, you'll need to declare them as external variables:

```
extern unsigned char _osmajor,_osminor;


printf("The DOS version is %d.%d",_osmajor,_osminor);
```

In the Microsoft compilers, call function 30h of INT 21h to return the major version number in AL and the minor version number in AH:

```
#include <dos.h>


union REGS regs;
char major_version, minor_version;


{
  regs.h.ah = 0x30;
  int86(0x21,&regs,&regs);
  major_version = regs.h.al;
  minor_version = regs.h.ah;
}
```

Assembler

```
;---DETERMINE THE DOS VERSION:
        mov  ah,30h        ;function number
        int  21h           ;get the version number
        mov  MAJ_VER,al    ;major version number
        mov  MIN_VER,ah    ;minor version number
```

Determine the Number and Type of Video Adaptors

To find out the active video system, begin by searching for a VGA or MCGA, then an EGA, then a CGA, and then an MDA. Call subfunction 0 of function 1Ah of interrupt 10h to find out VGA and MCGA status. AL will return 1Ah when one of these systems is present, in which case BL contains 7h for a VGA with a monochrome monitor, 08 for a VGA with a color monitor, Bh for an MCGA with a monochrome monitor, and Ch for an MCGA with a color monitor.

When no VGA or MCGA is present, search for an EGA by calling function 12h of interrupt 10h, with the value 10h in BL to specify that EGA information should be returned. On return, BL will hold 10h if an EGA is not present. To find the type of display, test bit 1 at 0040:0087; when it is 1 a monochrome display is attached, and when it is 0 a color display is attached. To find out the display resolution, a program must consult the EGA dip switch settings. These settings are returned in CL when function 12h of INT 10h is called. The pattern of the low four bits will be 0110 for the Enhanced Color Display. This same function reports the amount of memory on the EGA. On return, BL contains 0 for 64K, 1 for 128, 2 for 192K, and 3 for the full 256K of video RAM.

When no EGA is found, search for a monochrome or color adaptor by writing an arbitrary value to the cursor address register on their video controller chips and then read the value back to see if it matches. For the monochrome card, send 0Fh to port 3B4h in order to index the cursor register, and then read and write the cursor address from port 3B5h. The corresponding ports on the CGA are 3D4h and 3D5h. A Hercules monochrome graphics card can be distinguished by monitoring bit 7 at port 3B4h when a monochrome card is found. This bit, which is tied to vertical sync, changes on Hercules adaptors but is always set on MDAs.

The following assembly language routine provides an example. To set up a video determination routine in BASIC, Pascal, or C, see Chapter 4, "Call Interrupts from BASIC, Pascal, and C" and Chapter 13, "Program a Video Controller Chip," to learn how to call BIOS interrupts and program a video controller chip, and then follow the same basic recipe.

Assembler

```
;---SEARCH FOR A VGA OR MCGA:

      mov  ax,1A00h        ;function number
      int  10h             ;call video BIOS
      cmp  al,1Ah          ;is this a VGA/MCGA system?
```

```
        jne   TRY_EGA          ;jump if not
        cmp   bl,8             ;color VGA?
          .
          .


;---SEARCH FOR EGA
TRY_EGA:
        mov   ah,12h           ;function number
        mov   bl,10h           ;request EGA info
        int   10h              ;call EGA BIOS
        cmp   bl,10h           ;is there an EGA BIOS?
        je    TRY_CGA          ;jump if not
          .
          .


;---SEARCH FOR CGA:
        mov   dx,3D4h          ;point to 6845 address register
        mov   al,0Fh           ;request cursor register
        out   dx,al            ;index the register
        inc   dx               ;point to data register
        in    al,dx            ;get current reading
        xchg  ah,al            ;save the value
        mov   al,100           ;use 100 as test value
        out   dx,al            ;send it
        mov   cx,100h          ;must delay a bit
DELAY:  loop  DELAY            ;make the delay
        in    al,dx            ;read back the value
        cmp   al,100           ;compare
        jne   TRY_HGC          ;jump if no CGA
        xchg  ah,al            ;else there is CGA
```

```
        out  dx,al              ;…so restore initial reading

          .

          .


TRY_HGC:                        ;it's monochrome; test for Hercules
        mov  dx,3BAh            ;CRT status port
        in   al,dx             ;read the port
        and  al,80h            ;isolate bit 7
        mov  bl,al             ;save the value
        mov  cx,8000h          ;ready to loop
REPEAT:in   al,dx             ;read the port again
        and  al,80h            ;isolate bit 7
        cmp  bl,al             ;compare to saved value
        loope REPEAT           ;repeat if no change
        je   NOT_HGC           ;

          .

          .


NOT_HGC:                        ;it's an MDA
```

Determine the Number and Types of Disk Drives

To find out how many disk drives are in a machine, begin by obtaining the BIOS equipment status word, which reports the number of diskette drives. This is returned in the AX register by interrupt 11h. Bit 1 is set when diskette drives are present, in which case bits 6-7 report the number of diskette drives, with 0 indicating one drive, 1 indicating 2, and so on. With this information in hand, you can then begin searching for hard disk drives, starting from drive C if the machine has fewer than three diskette drives. Function 1Ch of interrupt 21h returns information about each drive. You can keep calling the function for ever higher drive numbers until there are no more.

Function 1Ch takes a drive number in DL on entry, with 0 as the current drive, 1 as drive A, 2 as drive B, and so on. On return, AL reports the number of sectors per cluster, CX the bytes per sector, and DX the clusters per disk. In addition, DS:BX points to a *media descriptor byte* that identifies the kind of disk. The value is F8h for a hard disk. Unfortunately, the descriptor byte is not very useful for identifying types of diskette drives. Because you know from the BIOS equipment list that a particular drive is a diskette drive, you can readily calculate the capacity from the information returned by function 1Ch. Take care not to apply this function to nonexistent diskette drives; a critical error will occur if the drive is "not ready."

BASIC

```
' $INCLUDE: 'QBX.BI'

DIM REGS AS RegType      ' Define register array

NumberDiskettes = 0

CALL Interruptx(&H11, REGS, REGS)  'get the equipment info

IF REGS.AX AND 1 = 1 THEN

NumberDiskettes = (REGS.AX AND &H00C0) \ 64 + 1

Write "There are",NumberDiskettes,"diskette drives."
```

Assuming there are fewer than three diskette drives, start searching for hard disks at drive #3:

```
NumberDrives = 0

DriveNumber = 3
```

```
LOOKAGAIN:
REGS.AX = &H1C00            'function number
REGS.DX = DriveNumber
CALL Interrupt(&H21, REGS, REGS)
DEF SEG = REGS.ES
DescriptorByte = PEEK(REGS.BX)
REGS.BX = 0
IF DescriptorByte = &HF8 THEN
   NumberDrives = NumberDrives + 1
   DriveNumber = DriveNumber + 1
   Goto LOOKAGAIN
ENDIF
PRINT "There are ",NumberDrives," hard disk drives");
```

Pascal

```
Uses DOS;

Var
 Regs: Registers;  {Registers type is declared in the DOS unit}
 NumberDrives,NumberDiskettes,DriveNumber: word;
 DescriptorByte: byte;

NumberDiskettes: = 0;
Intr($11,Regs);   {Call the interrupt}
if Regs.ax and 1 = 1 then
NumberDiskettes: = (REGS.ax AND $0000) div 64 + 1;
WriteIn ("There are;NumberDiskettes;diskette drives");
```

When there are fewer than three diskette drives, begin searching for hard disks at drive C:

```
NumberDrives = 0;

DriveNumber = 3;

LookAgain:

Regs.ah = $1C;          {function number}

Regs.dx: = DriveNumber;

Intr($21, Regs);

DescriptorByte: = Mem[Regs.es:Regs.bx];

Regs.bx: = 0';

if DescriptorByte = $F8 then

begin

 NumberDrives = NumberDrives + 1;

 DriveNumber = DriveNumber + 1;

 Goto LookAgain;

end;

Writeln('There are ',NumberDrives,' hard disk drives');
```

C

```
#include <dos.h>


union REGS regs;     /* declare the register array */
struct SREGS sregs;  /* struct for extra registers */
int number_diskettes,number_drives,drive_number;
char descriptor_byte;

number_diskettes = 0;
int86(0x11,&regs,&regs);    /* get BIOS equipment info */
```

35

```
number_diskettes = (regs.x.ax & 0x00C0) >> 6;
```

When there are fewer than three diskette drives, start searching for hard disks at drive C:

```
number_drives = 0;

drive_number = 3;

look_again:

regs.h.ah = 0x1C; /*function number*/

regs.x.dx = drive_number;

int86x(0x21,&regs,&regs,&sregs);

descriptor_byte = peekb(sregs.es,regs.x.bx)

regs.x.bx = 0;

if (descriptor_byte == 0xF8) {

  number_drives++;

  drive_number++;

  goto look_again;

}

printf("There are %d hard disk drives",number_drives);
```

Assembler

```
;---IN THE DATA SEGMENT:
NumberDrives db 0
NumberDiskette db 0
DriveNumber db 0

NextDrive:
;---COUNT DISKETTE DRIVES:
        mov  NumberDiskette, 0   ;default value
        int  11h                 ;get BIOS equipment list
```

```
        test ax,1              ;are these diskette drives?
        j2   NoDiskettes       ;jump ahead if not
        and  ax,0x00C0         ;isolate bit field
        mov  cl,6              ;prepare to shift
        shr  ax,cl             ;shift the field
        inc  ax               ;count from 1, not 0
        mov  NumberDiskette,al

NoDiskettes:
        mov  NumberDrives, 0
        mov  DriveNumber, 3


;---COUNT HARD DISK DRIVES:    ;assumes drive C is first hard disk
        mov  ah,1Ch           ;disk info function
        mov  dl,DriveNumber
        push ds               ;interrupt changes DS
        int  21h              ;get the info
        mov  al,ds:[bx]       ;get the descriptor byte
        pop  ds               ;restore DS
        mov  bx,0             ;clear BX for next time
        cmp  al,0F8h          ;is it a hard disk?
        jne  AllDone          ;jump if not
        inc  NumberDrives     ;else count the drive
        inc  DriveNumber      ;prepare for next
        jmp  short NextDrive
AllDone:
```

Determine the Numbers and Types of I/O Ports

During the power-on self-test (POST) that occurs whenever a computer is turned on, the BIOS determines how many serial ports and parallel ports are installed in the computer. BIOS interrupt 11h reports these findings in a 16-bit equipment status word that it returns in AX (there are no input registers). Bits 9 through 11 hold the number of serial ports in the machine, and bits 14 and 15 report the number of parallel ports. To isolate the bit field, AND the status word with 0E00h for serial ports, or with C000h for parallel ports. Then shift the field downward to obtain an integer value. In languages that have no shift instructions, divide the values by 512 or 16384, respectively, to achieve this effect.

There are a number of BIOS versions and some are better than others in finding ports, particularly serial ports. So the values returned in the equipment status word may fall short of the actual number.

In some machines, but not all, bit 12 of the status word indicates that a game port is installed. To be certain, it is better to search for game ports directly. This is done by writing any value to the game port address, 201h, and then immediately reading from the same address. When a game port is present, the four low bits of the byte read from the port will all be set.

BASIC

Use BASIC's *Interrupt* routine to fetch the BIOS status word:

```
' $INCLUDE: 'QBX.BI'
DIM REGS AS RegType      ' Define register array


CALL Interrupt(&H11, REGS, REGS)  'get the status word
NUMBERSERIAL = (REGS.AX AND &H0E00) \ 512;
LPT = 0
IF REGS.AX AND &H4000 = &H4000 THEN LPT = LPT + 1
IF REGS.AX AND &H8000 = &H8000 THEN LPT = LPT + 2
NUMBERPARALLEL = LPT
```

To check for a game port, write:

```
OUT &H201,1      'write an arbitrary value to the port
IF INP(&H201) AND &H0F = &H0F THEN WRITE "GAME PORT PRESENT"
```

Pascal

Use Turbo Pascal's *Intr* function to fetch the BIOS status word:

```
Uses DOS;
  Var
  Regs: Registers;  {Registers type is declared in the DOS unit}
  NumberSerial,NumberParallel: integer;


  Intr($11,Regs);   {Call the interrupt}
  NumberSerial := (Regs.AX And $0E00) div 512;
  NumberParallel := (Regs.AX And $C000) div 16384;
```

Use Turbo Pascal's *Port[]* array to search for a game port:

```
  Port[$201] := 1;  {write an arbitrary value to the port}
  If Port[$201] And $0F = $0F then Writeln('Game Port Present');
```

C

To return the BIOS equipment status word, the Borland compilers include the *biosequip* function and the Microsoft compilers, the *_bios_equiplist* function. Both functions take no parameters and return an unsigned integer value. Using Borland's C:

```
unsigned  number_serial,number_parallel;


number_serial = (biosequip() & 0x0E00) >>9
number_parallel = (biosequip() & 0xC000) >>14
```

Use the *inportb* function found in Borland's C, or the *inp* function provided in Microsoft's C, to find out whether a game port is present:

```
/* Borland */

outportb(0x201,1);  /* write an arbitrary value to the port */
if (inportb(0x201) & 0x0F == 0x0F) printf("Game Port Present");

/* Microsoft */
outp(0x201,1);  /* write an arbitrary value to the port */
if (inp(0x201) & 0x0F == 0x0F) printf("Game Port Present");
```

Assembler

In assembly language, just call INT 11h, isolate the relevant bit fields, and shift them.

```
;---FIND OUT THE NUMBER OF SERIAL AND PARALLEL PORTS:
        int   11h              ;get the equipment status word
        mov   ax,bx            ;make a copy
        and   ax,0E00h         ;isolate serial port field
        and   bx,0C000h        ;isolate parallel port field
        mov   cl,9             ;prepare to shift
        shr   ax,cl            ;now AX holds number of serial ports
        mov   cl,14            ;prepare to shift
        shr   bx,cl            ;now BX holds number of parallel ports


;---FIND OUT WHETHER A GAME PORT IS INSTALLED:
        mov   dx,201h          ;port number
        mov   al,1             ;arbitrary value
        out   dx,al            ;send the value to the port
        jmp   short $+2        ;give the port a moment to recover
        in    al,dx            ;read the port
        and   al,0Fh           ;zero out top four bits
        cmp   al,0Fh           ;are all four low bits set?
        jne   NO_GAME          ;if not, there is no game port
```

Determine the Kind of Keyboard in Use

Some programs need to know whether the machine they run on uses an 83- or 84-key keyboard or a 101-key *extended* keyboard. (The differences between keyboard models are explained in the Chapter 7 *minitutorial.*) This information is necessary if the program is to use features found only on the 101-key keyboards, such as the additional function keys <F11> and <F12>.

Machines that use extended keyboards have a modified keyboard interrupt in their ROM BIOS. The BIOS also provides additional routines for reading characters from the keyboard buffer and checking the status of the toggle and shift keys. These are functions 10h through 12h of interrupt 16h. The keyboard input functions provided in older machines that use 83- and 84-key keyboards are still found in machines with the more advanced BIOS. Software can use these older functions if it wants to avoid the advanced features of 101-key keyboards, thus ensuring compatibility with all machines.

Machines that support a 101-key keyboard also offer a function not found in earlier machines, one that allows a program to insert codes into the keyboard buffer just as if they had been typed in from the keyboard. This is function 5h of interrupt 16h. To test for an extended keyboard, a program attempts to use this function to write the value FFFFh into the keyboard buffer and then read it back. Function 5h returns 1 in AL when the buffer is full; in this case, you must remove a character from the buffer and try again. Because codes may already reside in the buffer, it may be necessary to request a character from the buffer as many as 16 times before you can be sure that you've exhausted all possibility that the code FFFFh is present. The examples found here for BASIC, Pascal, and C are simplified by emptying the buffer before the test begins. Note that an interrupt can insert additional characters in the buffer at any moment as the test is made.

BASIC

```
' $INCLUDE: 'QBX.BI'

DIM regs AS RegType          ' Define register array


DO                           'start by clearing the buffer
LOOP WHILE INKEY$ <> ""      'loop till null
REGS.AX = &H0500             'function to insert key code
REGS.CX = &HFFFF             'the pseudo code
```

```
CALL Interrupt(&H16, regs, regs)  'insert the code
DO
  C$ = INKEY$
  IF C$ = &HFF THEN WRITE "extended keyboard found"
  LOOP UNTIL C$ = ""
```

Pascal

```
Uses DOS;
var
  Regs: Registers;  {Registers type is declared in the DOS unit}
  TheKey: char;

while KeyPressed do TheKey := ReadKey;  {clear the buffer}
Regs.AH := $5;     {function number for inserting characters}
Regs.CX := $FFFF; {the pseudo key code}
Intr($16,Regs);    {insert the character}
while KeyPressed do if ReadKey = $FF then
  Writeln('Extended Keyboard Found');
```

C

```
#include <conio.h>
#include <dos.h>
union REGS regs;     /* declare the register array */

while(kbhit()) getch();    /* clear the buffer */
regs.h.ah = 5              /* function to insert keystroke */
regs.x.cx = 0xFFFF;        /* the pseudo key code */
int86(0x16,&regs,&regs);   /* insert the code */
  while(kbhit())
  if(getch() == 0xFF) printf("Extended keyboard found");
```

Assembler

```
try_again:
        mov  cx,0FFFFh          ;the pseudo key code
        mov  ah,5              ;BIOS function for inserting
codes
        int  16h              ;make the insertion
        or   al,al            ;buffer full?
        jz   try_next         ;jump ahead if not
        mov  ah,0             ;must remove a character from
buffer
        int  16h              ;fetch and discard character
        jmp  short try_again  ;now go and insert FFFF
try_next:
        mov  ah,1             ;function to test if keystroke
found
        int  16h              ;buffer empty?
        jz   no_extended_kybd ;if so, not an extended keyboard
        mov  ah,0             ;get ready to read a character
        int  16h              ;read it
        cmp  ax,0FFFFh        ;is it the pseudo key code?
        jne  try_next         ;if not, loop to next character
extended_kybd_found:          ;Eureka!

        .

        .


no_extended_kybd:             ;no luck
```

43

Determine Whether a Mouse Is Present

Before calling any of the mouse functions presented in Chapter 9, your program should check that a mouse driver is present in memory. This is done by testing the interrupt vector used by the driver, vector 33h, to see that it contains an address. When the vector is 0, it is uninitialized and no mouse driver is present.

Once a driver has been found, you may proceed to call mouse functions that return information about the mouse. Function 0 of interrupt 33h initializes the driver and returns –1 in AX when a physical mouse is detected by the driver, and 0 otherwise. Because this function switches off the mouse cursor, resets all parameters used by the mouse, and so on, you should make this check when your program starts. See Chapter 9, "Initialize the Mouse Driver," for more information about function 0.

You also can call function 24h of interrupt 33h to learn the driver version number. Version numbers are listed in two parts, the *major version number* (the **6** in **6.11**) and the *minor version number* (the **11**). Function 24h returns the major version number in BH and the minor version number in BL. In addition, CX returns a code number for the kind of mouse in use. The code numbers are **1** for a bus mouse, **2** for a serial mouse, **3** for an InPort mouse, **4** for a PS/2 mouse, and **5** for an HP mouse. Mouse driver documentation may report other codes that will be returned in this register.

BASIC

Microsoft BASIC does not provide a function that fetches interrupt vectors. Instead, use *Interrupt* (discussed in Chapter 4, "Write Your Own Interrupt Service Routine") to call DOS function 35h of INT 21h to fetch a vector. Place the vector number in AL and call the function. On return, ES:BX holds the specified vector.

```
' $INCLUDE: 'QBX.BI'

DIM REGS AS RegTypeX    ' Define register array


REGS.AX = &H3533        'function 35h, int vector 33h

CALL InterruptX(&H21, REGS, REGS)

IF REGS.ES = 0 THEN WRITE "No mouse driver installed"
```

When the vector is nonzero, call function 0 of interrupt 33h to find out whether a mouse is connected to the machine:

```
REGS.AX = &H0000                        'function number

CALL Interruptx(&H33, REGS, REGS)

IF REGS.AX = 0 THEN WRITE "No mouse installed"
```

Once you're sure that a driver and mouse are present, call function 24h of interrupt 33h to find out the driver version number:

```
REGS.AX = &H0024                        'function number

CALL Interruptx(&H33, REGS, REGS) 'get the version number

if REGS.BX = &H060B THEN WRITE "Mouse Driver Version 6.11"
```

Pascal

Turbo Pascal's *GetIntVec* function returns interrupt vectors. It takes two parameters: first, the interrupt number, and then a variable parameter of *Pointer* type in which the function deposits the interrupt vector.

```
Uses Dos;


TheVector: Pointer;


GetIntVec($33,TheVector);

if TheVector = nil then Writeln('No Mouse Driver');
```

Use *Intr* to find out whether a mouse is present and to determine the mouse driver version number:

```
Uses DOS;


Var

  Regs: Registers;   {Registers type is declared in the DOS unit}


  Regs.AX := 0;      {function to search for mouse}

  Intr($33,Regs);    {get the EMS version number}

  if Regs.AX = 0 then Write('No mouse connected');
```

```
Regs.AX := $0024;   {function to get version number}
Intr($33,Regs);    {get the driver version number}
if Regs.BX = $060A then Write('Driver version 6.11');
```

C

Both Borland's C and Microsoft's C use the *getvect* function to return an interrupt vector.

```
void interrupt(*the_vector)(); /*declare ptr of interrupt type*/

the_vector=getvect(0x33);      /*fetch vector 0x33*/
if (the_vector == 0) printf("No mouse driver");
```

Once you're sure a mouse driver is installed, use *int86* to call functions 0h to find out whether a mouse is connected to the machine and function 24h to find out the driver version number:

```
#include <dos.h>

union REGS regs;        /* declare the register array */

regs.x.ax = 0x0;        /* function to seek mouse */
int86(0x33,&regs,&regs);
if (regs.x.ax == 0x0) printf("No mouse installed");
regs.x.ax = 0x0024;     /* function to find version number */
int86(0x33,&regs,&regs);
if (regs.x.bx == 0x060B) printf("Driver Version 6.11");
```

Assembler

In assembly language, use DOS function 35h of interrupt 21h to fetch the vector used by the mouse driver. On entry, AL holds the vector number. On return, ES:BX holds the vector.

```
;---FIND OUT IF EXPANDED MEMORY DRIVER IS PRESENT:
        mov   ah,35h          ;function number
        mov   al,33h          ;mouse vector number
        int   21h             ;go fetch the vector
        cmp   ax,0            ;only need to test segment
        je    NO_MS_DRVR      ;no driver if vector is zero


;---IF A DRIVER IS PRESENT, SEEK THE MOUSE:
        mov   ax,0h           ;function number
        int   33h             ;call the interrupt
        cmp   ax,0            ;test for mouse
        je    NO_MOUSE        ;no mouse connected if zero


;---FIND THE DRIVER VERSION NUMBER:
        mov   ax,24h          ;EMS function number
        int   33h             ;get the version number
        cmp   BX,060Bh        ;test for version 6.11
```

Determine the Availability of Conventional Memory

Programs occasionally need to determine how much conventional memory is installed in a machine, and often need to know how much memory is available for their use. BIOS interrupt 12h reports installed memory, returning the number of 1K (1024-byte) blocks in AX. Finding "available" memory is not so simple. Compilers maintain one or more *heaps* from which they allocate memory blocks. Functions are provided that can tell the total amount of free memory in a heap, and also the size of the largest available block. BASIC automatically compacts the heap, but in other languages you must carefully think through the order in which objects are allocated and deallocated so that heap fragmentation will not become a problem.

BASIC

This example determines the total installed memory:

```
' $INCLUDE: 'QBX.BI'

DIM REGS AS RegType      ' Define register array


CALL Interrupt(&H12, REGS, REGS)

PRINT "There are ",REGS.AX," kilobytes installed"
```

BASIC's *FRE* function reports how much memory remains of the various categories into which BASIC divides memory. Write:

```
AvailableMemory = FRE(0)
```

to find out how much is left in the DGROUP, the general-purpose data segment. Use –1 as the parameter to obtain a value for far memory, –2 to determine stack space, and –3 to find out available expanded memory.

Pascal

To determine installed memory, write:

```
Uses DOS;

Var

  Regs: Registers;   {Registers type is declared in the DOS unit}
```

```
Intr($12,Regs);    {Call the interrupt}
Writeln('There are ',Regs.AX,' kilobytes installed');
```

Turbo Pascal's *MemAvail* routine reports total available memory in the heap, and *MaxAvail* tells the size of the largest available block:

```
Writeln('There are ',MemAvail,' bytes left in memory');


Writeln('The largest available block has ',MaxAvail,'
bytes');
```

C

Call interrupt 0x12 to determine installed memory:

```
#include <dos.h>


union REGS regs;    /* declare the register array */


int86(0x12,&regs,&regs);
printf("There are %d kilobytes installed",regs.x.ax);
```

In the Borland compilers, the *coreleft* function reports the space between the highest allocated block and the end of available memory, returning a *long* value:

```
largest_block = coreleft();
```

For the far heap, use the *farcorleft* function instead. In Microsoft's C, the *_memavl* function returns an unsigned integer giving the approximate available space in the near heap:

```
available_memory = _memavl();
```

The *_memmax* function reports the size of the largest available block.

Assembler

```
;---DETERMINE INSTALLED MEMORY:
        int   12h               ;call the interrupt
        mov   InstalledMem,AX   ;number of 1K blocks
```

At start-up, a program can find out how much memory is available for its use by asking function 48h of interrupt 21h for an impossibly large allocation (this function is discussed in Chapter 3, "Allocate/Deallocate Conventional Memory"). When the function fails to make the allocation, it sets the carry flag and returns the number of free paragraphs (16-byte units) in BX.

```
;---FIND OUT NUMBER OF AVAILABLE PARAGRAPHS:
        mov  ah,48h     ;function to allocate memory
        mov  bx,0FFFFh  ;request impossible allocation
        INT  21h        ;now BX holds number of free paragraphs
```

This technique works only if available memory is free for function 4Ah to allocate. COM programs, and most EXE programs, are given all free memory at start-up. So you must first shrink the program's memory allocation down to the size of its code and stack. Chapter 1, "Run One Program from Within Another," gives an example of how this is done.

Another way to determine available memory is to fetch the integer value held at offset 2 in the PSP. It tells the segment value of the last paragraph of memory. Available memory equals the difference between this value and the segment of the end of the program. Function 51h of interrupt 21h reports the PSP address. On return, BX holds the segment in which the PSP begins at offset 0.

Determine the Availability of Expanded Memory

A program must be certain that an expanded memory driver is present before calling any of the expanded memory routines that are discussed in Chapter 3. When no driver has been installed, the interrupt vector it uses (67h) is normally uninitialized, and the machine will crash the first time you make a call. The easiest way to find out whether a drive is present is to just fetch the segment part of interrupt vector and test that it is not a zero value (the start-up initialization value). However, to be absolutely certain that an EMS driver is pointed to by any nonzero vector setting, you should examine the driver itself. All EMS drivers have an identifying name located at offset 000Ah from the driver's starting segment in memory. This name is **EMMXXXX0.** Testing just the first three characters is adequate.

Once you are certain that an EMS driver is installed, you can find out the EMS version by calling function 46h of INT 67h. A version number consists of two parts—the *major version number* and the *minor version number*, such as the **3** and the **2** in **3.2.** Both parts are returned in the AL register using BCD (binary coded decimal) format. In BCD, a byte is divided into two four-bit fields, with each field holding a bit pattern from 0 to 9 — exactly as for a decimal digit. The major version number is found in the high four bits, the minor version number, the low four bits. Using hexadecimal numbers, AL will hold 30h for EMS Version 3.0, 32h for Version 3.2, and 40h for Version 4.0

Chapter 3, "Determine the Number of Available Expanded Memory Pages," explains how to find out how much of installed expanded memory is available for your program to use.

BASIC

Microsoft BASIC does not have a function that fetches interrupt vectors. Instead, use *Interrupt* (discussed in Chapter 4, "Call Interrupts from BASIC, Pascal, and C") to call DOS function 35h of interrupt 21h to fetch a vector. Place the vector number in AL and call the function. On return, ES:BX will hold the specified vector.

```
' $INCLUDE: 'QBX.BI'
DIM REGS AS RegTypex     ' Define register array


REGS.AX = &H3567         'function 35h, int vector 67h
CALL Interruptx(&H21, REGS, REGS)
```

```
TheSeg = REGS.ES
IF TheSeg = 0 THEN PRINT "No EMS Driver"
DEF SEG TheSeg
X = REGS.BX
IF PEEK(X)=69 AND PEEK(X+1)=77 AND PEEK(X+2)=77 THEN
   PRINT "EMS Driver Found"
ENDIF
```

To find out the EMS version number, call function 46h and then use AND to zero out the AH part of the AX register.

```
REGS.AX = &H4600              'function number
CALL Interruptx(&H67, REGS, REGS)  'get the version number
if REGS.AX AND &H00FF = &H40 THEN WRITE "EMS Version 4.0"
```

Pascal

In Turbo Pascal, it's easiest to fetch the interrupt vector using function 35h or interrupt 21h. AL holds the vector number on entry, and ES:BX holds the vector on return.

```
Uses Dos;

TheVector: Pointer;
S,O: word;

Regs.AH := $35;     {the interrupt function number}
Regs.AL := $67;     {the vector number}
Intr($21,Regs);     {get the vector}
S := Regs.es;
O := Regs.bx;
if S = 0 then
begin
  Writeln('No EMS Driver');
```

```
Halt;
end;
if (Mem[S:$A]=69) And (Mem[S:$B]=77) And (Mem[S:$C]=77)
then Writeln('EMS driver found');
```

You also can use *Intr* to call EMS function 46h to find out the EMS version number:

```
Regs.AH := $46;     {the interrupt function number}
Intr($67,Regs);     {get the EMS version number}
if Regs.AL = $40 then Write('EMS version 4.0 loaded');
```

C

Both the Borland and Microsoft compilers use the *getvect* function to return an interrupt vector.

```
char for *the_vector;


the_vector=getvect(0x67);        /*fetch vector 0x67*/
if (! the_vector) printf("No EMS drive present");
   if ((*the_vector == 'E') &&
        (*(the_vector+1) == 'M') &&
        (*(the_vector+2) == 'M') printf("EMS driver present");
```

Once you're sure an EMS driver is installed, use *int86* to call function 46h of interrupt 67h to find out the EMS version number:

```
#include <dos.h>


union REGS regs;     /* declare the register array */


regs.h.ah = 0x46;
int86(0x67,&regs,&regs);
if (regs.h.al == 0x40) printf("EMS 4.0 driver installed");
```

Assembler

In assembly language, use DOS function 35h of interrupt 21h to fetch the vector. On entry, AL holds the vector number. On return, ES:BX holds the vector.

```
;---FIND OUT IF EXPANDED MEMORY DRIVER IS PRESENT:
        mov  ah,35h          ;function number
        mov  al,67h          ;EMS vector number
        int  21h             ;go fetch the vector
        cmp  es,0            ;only need to test segment
        je   NO_EMS          ;no EMS if vector is zero
        mov  ax,es:[bx]      ;get first two bytes
        cmp  ax,'EM'         ;first two chars of EMM0000X
        jne  NO_EMS          ;no EMS if not a match
        mov  al,es:[bx+2]    ;get third byte
        cmp  al,'M'          ;third byte OK?
        jne  NO_EMS          ;no EMS if not
                             ;else EMS driver is installed


;---ONCE EMS PRESENCE IS CONFIRMED, FIND THE VERSION NUMBER:
        mov  ah,46h          ;EMS function number
        int  67h             ;get the version number
        cmp  al,40h          ;test for version 4.0
        je   VER_4           ;jump if found
```

Determine the Availability of Extended Memory

Function 88h of INT 15h reports how many 1K blocks of extended memory are installed in the machine, returning the value in AX. PCs that cannot have extended memory set the carry flag and return **80h** or **86h** in AH (notice that the high bit of AX is set in either case). In the following examples, the return value is converted to 0 when it is found that the machine does not support extended memory.

BASIC

```
' $INCLUDE: 'QBX.BI'
DIM regs AS RegTypex              ' Define register array


regs.ax = &H8800                 'function number
CALL Interruptx(&H15, regs, regs) 'call the interrupt
ExtendedMem = regs.ax            'get the return value
IF ExtendedMem AND &H8000 THEN ExtendedMem = 0  'detect pre-286
```

Pascal

```
Uses DOS;

Var
   Regs: Registers;  {Registers type is declared in the DOS unit}
   ExtendedMem: word; {holds the result}


Regs.AH := $88;     {the interrupt function number}
Intr($15,Regs);     {Call the interrupt}
ExtendedMem := Regs.AX; {Put the result in EstendedMem}
if ExtendedMem and $8000 <> 0 then ExtendedMem := 0; {pre-286}
```

C

```
#include <dos.h>

unsigned extended_mem;
union REGS   regs;

regs.h.ah = 0x88;           /* function number */
int86(15h,&regs,&regs);  /* call the interrupt */
extended_mem = regs.x.ax /* fetch the return value */
if (extended_mem & 0x8000) extended_mem = 0; {pre-286 case}
```

Assembler

```
;---DETERMINE AMOUNT OF EXTENDED MEMORY:
        mov  ah,88h          ;function number
        int  15h             ;call the interrupt
        jc   NO_EXTENDED     ;machine can't have extended memory
        mov  EXT_MEM,ax      ;otherwise, AX tells how many 1K blocks
```

3

Managing Memory

- Minitutorial: Kinds of Memory
- Allocate/Deallocate Conventional Memory
- Determine the Page-Frame Address of Expanded Memory
- Determine the Number of Available Expanded Memory Pages
- Allocate Expanded Memory Pages
- Switch between Expanded Memory Pages
- Get/Set an Expanded Memory Page Map
- Deallocate Expanded Memory Pages
- Integrate Expanded Memory into Your Programs

Minitutorial: Kinds of Memory

In the simplest case, a computer's memory is arranged as a single sequence of addresses numbered from 0 upward, with each address corresponding to one byte of storage. Unfortunately, IBM developed hardware in a way that made the organization of memory much more complicated. When the first IBM PCs were designed, state-of-the-art microprocessors had 16-bit registers. Binary arithmetic shows that a 16-bit number can represent a value from 0 to 65535 (to "64K," in computerese). Whenever a microprocessor accesses memory, one of its registers must hold the address the microprocessor will read from or write to. If the largest number a 16-bit register can hold is 64K, it would seem that the computer could have memory no greater than 64K.

In fact, early PCs made do with 64K of memory, or less. But by the time the first IBM PCs were designed, chips could address a full megabyte of data. This is done by a scheme called *segmentation*. In segmentation, two 16-bit registers are used to define an address. One register (a *segment register*) holds the address *segment,* and the second register (one of the CPU's general-purpose registers) holds the address *offset*. In theory, the two 16-bit numbers could be combined into a 32-bit number, and that would allow addresses as large as four and a quarter billion bytes. But segmentation does not work this way. A 32-bit address requires 32 lines throughout the computer's circuitry (through its *bus*), which is expensive to construct. So PC- and XT-style machines were designed with only 20 address lines. Twenty lines can represent a 20-bit number, and the largest number 20 bits can hold is 1,048,575. Thus, the address space of these machines is limited to about one megabyte.

This 20-bit value is constructed by multiplying the value of the segment register by 16 and then adding the value held in the offset register. For example, if a segment register holds the decimal value 10 and the offset holds 8, then the address is 168 (that is, 10 * 16 + 8). When the segment register holds the largest value possible — 65535 — then it is multiplied by 16 to make 1,048,560. This is the origin of the one-megabyte address space available to 8086 and 8088 processors.

To access memory above the one-megabyte limit, two requirements must be met. First, the processor must be able to generate numbers larger than 20 bits. And second, more than 20 address lines must be available to convey large addresses to memory circuitry. All 286, 386, and 486 machines fulfill these needs. 286 machines have 24 address lines, allowing addresses as high as 16 megabytes. 386 and 486 machines have 32 address lines to reach to four and a quarter gigabytes. Some addresses are occupied by read/write memory (RAM), some by read-only memory (ROM), and some go unused (when no memory chips are configured to cover a particular range of addresses).

Conventional memory begins from the bottom of the memory space and extends toward 640K as a solid block. RAM may then continue from the one-megabyte mark upward as *extended memory*. ROM, including the ROM holding the BIOS, tends to be placed at the high end of the first megabyte of memory space. However, expansion cards may place additional sequences of RAM or ROM at any place within the address ranges between 640K and 1M. ROM chips on these cards may provide routines for running the card, and RAM chips may provide special storage areas used by the card, such as video buffers.

In order to ensure software compatability across all machines, all processors from the 8086 to the 80486 support the basic 16-bit segmentation scheme. In order to generate addresses larger than 1 megabyte, processors from the 286 onward can switch into other addressing modes that generate addresses in different ways.

A 286 chip can function in either of two modes: *real mode* and *protected mode.* In real mode, the CPU operates just like an 8086 (or 8088) chip, limiting itself to one megabyte. In protected mode, the chip generates 24-bit addresses ranging up to 16 megabytes. You might guess that the chip generates large addresses simply by multiplying the contents of segment registers by 256 instead of 16. But a different scheme is employed, one that uses *selectors* instead of segments. The CPU maintains a table of 24-bit addresses. When a value (a selector) is placed in a segment register, the CPU uses it as an offset into a *descriptor table*, takes the address stored there, and uses it as the base address to which an offset is then added. Offsets are still limited to 16 bits, so memory can be allocated in blocks no larger than 64K.

One virtue of this scheme is that memory can be *protected*. In an unprotected memory scheme, such as exists in a PC running in real mode, malfunctioning software can accidentally write to parts of memory that it should not touch. It can overwrite parts of the operating system and cause the machine to subsequently crash, or it can write into disk buffers and corrupt files, directories, and file allocation tables. But when a CPU runs in *protected mode*, a program can access only those parts of memory that are specifically allocated to it. The table of descriptors tracks not only the starting location of any allocated memory block, but also the block's length. When an attempt is made to write outside of a permissable block, the CPU generates an *exception*—a kind of interrupt for which a recovery routine can be written. Memory protection is particularly useful in multitasking environments. Even when a program "crashes," other programs can go right on working because they and the operating system are unharmed.

While the 286 protected-mode scheme lets a program reach megabytes of memory, the limitation of offsets to 64K can make programming for large arrays difficult. 386 and 486 chips can overcome this limitation by generating 32-bit offsets when they operate in 32-bit mode. However, DOS is a 16-bit operating system, and special software must be employed in order to use the advanced features of these chips. Normally, these chips run in emulation modes in which they mimic 8086 and 80286 chips.

386 and 486 chips can manage memory with a process called *paging*. In this scheme, any 4K stretch of memory (a "page") can be assigned any range of addresses. Memory that physically starts at the 2-megabyte mark can be made to appear as if it starts at the 1-megabyte mark, or the 256K mark. What's more, the same addresses may be assigned to different blocks of memory. This feature provides the basis for the *virtual 86 mode* in which the processor divides extended memory into a number of blocks, each of which appears as a separate instance of conventional memory. Traditional applications may be multitasked, with one allocated to each memory block. From the application's point of view, it is merely running by itself in conventional memory, with all of conventional memory allocated to it.

Paging can also be used to fill in areas above the 640K usually devoted to conventional memory, and below the 1-megabyte mark. This area is called the *upper memory area*. The low end of this range of addresses is occupied by at least one video buffer, and the high end is filled by ROM chips. Between, large blocks may go unused. A 386 or 486 chips can reassign some extended memory pages so that they "fill" these blocks with usable memory addresses. Then, with proper memory-management software, the blocks can be occupied by device drivers, memory resident programs, or whatever, that would otherwise take up space below the 640K mark. Although the blocks are outside 640K, they are still within 1-megabyte, and so can be reached by a processor running in real mode.

Conventional memory is also expanded by using the *high memory area*. When a segment register is given the largest possible value in real mode, it points to a position just 16 bytes from the end of the first megabyte of memory. A 64K offset can be made from this point in all machines except 8086 or 8088 PCs. Thus, a processor operating in real mode is actually limited to a megabyte plus 64K, not a megabyte. Like the blocks above 640K, this area can be devoted to diverse purposes. DOS 5.0 can install itself in the high memory area.

Expanded Memory

Confronted with a large user-base of XT-class machines, and no common operating system for running the 286 chip in protected mode, three companies innovated the *LIM* (Lotus-Intel-Microsoft) *expanded memory standard* (EMS). This standard provides access to megabytes of extra memory for machines running in real mode, memory that is much better suited to holding data than code. It works by setting aside a 64K *page frame* (a 64K range of memory space) in the upper memory area. This frame is divided into four 16K *physical pages*. Software allocates as many 16K pages of expanded memory as it needs and then switches the ones it requires into view in the page frame. Thus, many data objects occupy the same memory addresses, and software must perform the extra work of switching the proper pages into view.

EMS memory is provided by special memory hardware in 8088 and 286 machines, hardware that is run by an EMS device driver called the *Expanded Memory Manager (EMM)*. The underlying hardware may vary in its characteristics, and so you never directly access the EMS hardware through port addresses. You always leave this job to the driver. Because they can page extended memory, 386 and 486 machines do not use special EMS hardware. Instead, special emulation software makes extended memory behave as if it were expanded memory. Whenever a particular expanded memory page is required, the processor changes the addresses assigned to the extended memory that holds the page, and the page appears within the expanded memory frame.

Two other kinds of EMS emulation software act like an EMS device driver, but actually store the EMS pages on disk or in extended memory. Those that use disk space appropriate a 64K block of conventional memory and use it as the page frame. The 16K pages are transferred to and from disk as required. Obviously, this technique can be slow, but it is the only alternative in 8088 machines. A second kind of emulator works the same way but stores the pages in extended memory in 286 machines, copying the pages back and forth between conventional and extended memory.

There are three EMS Versions: 3.0, 3.2, and 4.0. All the basic functionality is provided in 3.0. Version 3.2 adds a few functions to help applications share expanded memory. Version 4.0, however, greatly expands expanded memory capabilities. It allows multiple page frames in which pages may be of any size, and the page frame may be positioned anywhere in the first megabyte of memory. Version 4.0 also allows a maximum of 32M of expanded memory, instead of the 8M capacity of earlier versions. These modifications allow expanded memory to completely change the contents of the 640K conventional memory space so that operating environments can readily switch between applications. Unfortunately, more advanced EMS hardware is required to support 4.0, and it has been little used (nor is likely to ever be widely adopted now that the memory-management capabilties of 386 and 486 chips are widely available). For this reason, we confine the discussion in this chapter to EMS 3.0 and 3.2.

Extended Memory

To use extended memory with DOS, a programmer must turn to *DOS extenders*. There are two kinds of DOS extenders — 286 DOS extenders and 386 DOS extenders. Code developed with a 286 extender can run on a 286 chip, or a 386 or 486. In all cases, it treats the chip as having 16-bit registers. On the other hand, code developed for a 386 extender can run on a 386 or 386SX chip, or a 486 or 486SX chip, but not a 286. This code assumes 32-bit registers, and makes use of advanced memory management features found on these chips, but that are absent on the 286. There is no such thing as a 486 DOS extender, since the 486 is also a 32-bit chip, and its memory management system is almost identical to that of the 386 chip. Of course, there can be no such thing as an 8086 (or 8088) DOS extender for XT-class PCs, since these chips do not support extended memory.

Considering all the advantages of a 386 DOS extender, why bother with a 286 extender? One reason is that well over 12 million 286 machines have been sold worldwide, constituting a large part of the potential market for most software products. A second reason is that it is generally easier to port existing applications to a 286 extender. Taking full advantage of a 386 extender may entail substantial rewriting, especially of assembly language routines.

These days, several programs (including DOS) may make demands on extended memory at the same time. Some kind of memory manager is required to avoid conflicts. The *Extended Memory Specification (XMS)* is an industry standard that lets multiple *real mode* DOS applications share extended memory. A similar function is performed by the *DOS Protected Mode Interface (DPMI)*, which serves programs running in *protected mode* using a DOS extender. There is also the *Virtual Control Program Interface (VCPI)*, which allows EMS emulators working in extended memory to coexist with DOS extenders. VCPI is an extension of EMS Version 4.0. Ordinarily, these interfaces are only of concern to the designers of DOS extenders. DOS extenders are complicated, and vary in design. They are beyond the scope of this book. To learn more about them, consult the book *Extending DOS*, edited by Ray Duncan.

The complexities of memory management on IBM PCs has burdened programmers in several ways. Segmentation has made it difficult to work with data objects larger than 64K. Segmentation has also made compilers much more complicated to use by creating the need for various memory models. Expanded memory requires a complete reorganization of data access to allow for page switching, and makes it difficult to use both conventional memory and expanded memory for the same data set. Finally, by opting to use extended memory, programmers may be forced to write programs that can't work on millions of early machines.

Allocate/Deallocate Conventional Memory

A program can reserve memory for its data in several ways. *Local variables* are created on the stack while the routine that uses them functions, and then are destroyed, only to be recreated when the routine is called again. *Global variables* are placed in the program's *data segment* so that they are always available. Large data structures like arrays may also be placed in the data segment if they must always be on hand. However, many programs use data structures that are not always required, and it is wasteful to devote memory to them the entire time a program runs. It's better to allocate enough memory to hold the data, load the data from disk (or some other source), and then relinquish the memory allocated to the data when the program has finished with it. In this way, space is freed for further memory allocations.

Variable memory allocations are also useful when the amount of data that must be processed is variable. Consider a program that needs to create an array into which it will read an image file from disk. It can learn from the file size how large the array must be to hold the image. Allocating more memory would be wasteful. Similarly, a program may need to allocate all available memory to a data object, such as a text array. Because the program can find out how much memory is available when it starts up, it can then size the array and allocate memory for it.

DOS automatically allocates all available memory to COM programs. The same occurs with EXE programs unless a smaller allocation was specified at link time. The area from the end of program code to the end of allocated memory is available for program data. Languages like BASIC, Pascal, and C manage this area as one or more *heaps*. Assembly language programs can deallocate this memory and then use DOS functions to make transient allocations and deallocations of memory blocks.

BASIC

In Microsoft BASIC, all variables declared in subroutines are automatically allocated on the stack. The same can be done to other variables by preceding their first declaration with the line:

```
REM $DYNAMIC
```

To stop subsequent allocations from being dynamic, write:

```
REM $STATIC
```

Arrays are declared with a *DIM* statement, such as:

```
DIM MyVariable(100) as integer
```

They can be redimensioned, say to 200 elements, by writing:

```
REDIM MyVariable(200) as integer
```

Finally, to dispose of the array and free the memory allocated to it, write:

```
Erase MyVariable
```

Pascal

In Turbo Pascal, the *New* and *Dispose* procedures allocate blocks of memory. First, declare the *type* of data for which memory will be allocated. For example:

```
type
  MyPtr = ^MyRecord;
  MyRecord = record
     name: string[80];
     age:  byte;
     weight: word;
  end;
```

Next, declare an instance of the pointer:

```
var
  ThePtr: MyPtr;
```

Then use *New* to allocate a block:

```
New(ThePtr);
```

On return, *ThePtr* will have been filled with a pointer to the allocated block. Then you can assign values to the elements of the record by writing statements like:

```
ThePtr^.age := 87;
```

Later, to deallocate the block, use *Dispose*:

```
Dispose(ThePtr);
```

C

C compilers may use both *near* and *far* heaps, and different objects must be used to make or free allocations in each. There are several routines that can allocate memory, of which *malloc* is the most important. It allocates blocks in the near heap. Its counterpart, *free*, deallocates blocks from the near heap. For example, to allocate memory for a string, you could write:

```
char *my_string;

my_string = malloc(80);/* allocation for an 80-byte string*/

free(my_string);    /* later, deallocate the memory */
```

Allocations and deallocations on the far heap can be made with *farmalloc* and *farfree* in Borland's C, or *_fmalloc* and *_ffree* in Microsoft's C. These functions work just like *malloc* and *free*. You also can reallocate a block, normally to make it larger. This is done with *realloc* or *farrealloc* in the Borland compilers, and *realloc* or *_frealloc* in the Microsoft compilers. These functions take two parameters: first the pointer to which the block was first assigned, and then the new size for the block in bytes. The functions return a new pointer for the object. This is necessary in case the block's data has to be moved elsewhere in memory. To reallocate *my_string* to 100 bytes, you would write this in Borland's C:

```
my_string = realloc(my_string,100);
```

Assembler

DOS provides three memory allocation functions, numbers 48h-4Ah of interrupt 21h. Function 48h allocates memory, and 49h deallocates memory. The third function ("SETBLOCK") changes the size of memory currently allocated to a program: this is the function that must be executed before the others can be used. Then blocks may be allocated and deallocated freely. A program *must* deallocate all of the blocks it has allocated before terminating. Otherwise memory will be sequestered away from subsequent uses.

All three memory allocation functions of interrupt 21h use a 16-bit starting address for the memory block they operate upon. This address represents the *segment* in which the block begins (the block always starts at offset 0 in that segment). Thus the actual block starting location is at the memory address represented by this value multiplied by 16. Also, in all three functions, BX contains the number of 16-byte sections of memory ("paragraphs") that are to be allocated or freed. If the function fails, the carry flag is set and AX returns an error code explaining why. The three relevant codes are:

7	memory control blocks have been destroyed
8	there is insufficient memory available
9	the memory block address is invalid

The allocation function uses codes 7 and 9, the deallocation function uses codes 8 and 9, and the function that changes the allocation uses all three codes. The following code first allocates a 1024-byte block, saving its starting address in the variable BLOCK_SEG. BX holds the number of 16-byte paragraphs requested, and upon return the start address is found as AX:0 (that is, as a 0 offset within the segment value contained in AX). The second part of the code deallocates the same block, as is required at the end of a program. In this case, the value returned in AX above is placed in ES. DOS keeps track of the block size and knows how many paragraphs to deallocate.

```
;--- ALLOCATE A 1024-BYTE AREA:
      mov  ah,48h          ;function number
      mov  bx,64           ;request 64 16-byte paragraphs
      int  21h             ;attempt the allocation
      cmp  ax,8            ;error code for insufficient memory
      je   NO_ROOM         ;go to error handling routine
      mov  BLOCK_SEG,ax    ;else, AX holds block segment, save it
;--- DEALLOCATE THE SAME AREA:
      mov  ax,BLOCK_SEG    ;retrieve start address of the block
      mov  es,ax           ;place it in ES
      mov  ah,49h          ;function number to deallocate
      int 21h              ;make the deallocation
      ic Error Routine     ;respond to errors
```

Finally, here is an example in which function 4Ah resizes a previously allocated block. On entry, ES points to the block and BX tells the new size of the block in paragraphs. There are no return registers. The carry flag is set if an error occurs, in which case AX holds 7 if the block is nonexistent, 8 if memory was insufficient, or 9 if the pointer to the block was invalid. In addition, BX reports the size of the largest available block (again, in paragraphs).

```
;---RESIZE A PREVIOUSLY ALLOCATED MEMORY BLOCK:
     mov  ax,BLOCK_SEG     ;the block address
     mov  es,ax            ;point ES to the block
```

```
mov  ah,4Ah              ;function number
  mov  bx,128            ;change allocation to 128 paragraphs
  int  21h               ;give it a try
  jc   ErrorRoutine      ;respond to errors
```

Remember that COM programs and most EXE programs are automatically allocated all of available memory. They can request and release memory blocks only if they first pare down their own allocation using SETBLOCK. This is necessary when a program runs another program via the EXEC feature, which is discussed in Chapter 1, "Run One Program from Within Another."

Determine the Page-Frame Address of Expanded Memory

Function 41h of interrupt 67h returns the address of the first byte of the 64K page frame used by expanded memory. This address is set when the machine starts up and does not change thereafter. This function takes no input registers, and returns the segment address of the page frame in BX. The page frame begins at offset 0 in this segment. The function returns 0 in AH when it succeeds, or else one of the following error messages:

80h	when EMS software malfunctions
81h	when EMS hardware malfunctions
84h	when the specified function number is undefined

Before calling the expanded memory manager the first time, you should check that an expanded memory driver is present. You may also want to find out the driver version. See the discussion in Chapter 2, "Determine the Availability of Expanded Memory."

BASIC

```
' $INCLUDE: 'QBX.BI'
DIM regs AS RegType    ' Define register array
regs.ax = &H4100       'function to fetch page frame segment
CALL Interrupt(&H67, regs, regs)
IF regs.ax AND &HFF00 THEN
   GOSUB EMSError
   ELSE PageFrameAddr = regs.bx
ENDIF
```

Pascal

```
Uses DOS;
Var
    Regs: Registers;   {Registers type is declared in the DOS unit}

Regs.AH := $41;      {function to fetch page frame segment}
Intr($67,Regs);
if Regs.AH <> 0 then EMSErrorRoutine
    else PageFrameAddr := Regs.BX;
```

C

```
#include <dos.h>

union REGS regs;

regs.h.ah = 0x41;
int86(0x67,&regs,&regs);
if (regs.h.ah) EMS_error();
else page_frame_addr = regs.x.bx;
```

Assembler

```
;---FIND THE PAGE FRAME ADDRESS:
        mov  ah,41h          ;function number
        int  67h             ;get the frame address
        cmp  ah,0            ;test for errors
        jne  EMS_ERROR       ;jump if error
        mov  PAGE_FRAME,bx   ;save the frame address
```

Determine the Number of Available Expanded Memory Pages

Function 42h of interrupt 67h reports how many expanded memory pages are available for your program to use. The function takes no input registers, and returns the total number of 16K EMS pages found in the system in DX, and the number of available pages in BX. Remember that an operating environment or memory-resident program can appropriate expanded memory pages to itself at any time, so your program should not assume that the value returned in BX will be valid for as long as the program runs. The function returns 0 in AH when all has gone well, or else one of the following error codes:

80h   when EMS software malfunctions

81h   when EMS hardware malfunctions

84h   when the specified function number is undefined

BASIC

```
' $INCLUDE: 'QBX.BI'
DIM regs AS RegType     ' Define register array


regs.ax = &H4200        'function to report available pages
CALL Interrupt(&H67, regs, regs)
IF regs.ax AND &HFF00 THEN
 GOSUB EMSError
 ELSE AvailablePages = regs.bx
ENDIF
```

Pascal

```
Uses DOS;
Var
  Regs: Registers; {Registers type is declared in the DOS unit}
```

70

```
Regs.AH := $42;        {function to fetch page frame segment}
Intr($67,Regs);
if Regs.AH <> 0 then EMSErrorRoutine
   else AvailablePages := Regs.BX;
```

C

```c
#include <dos.h>

union REGS regs;

regs.h.ah = 0x42;
int86(0x67,&regs,&regs);
if (regs.h.ah) EMS_error();
   else available_pages = regs.x.bx;
```

Assembler

```
;---FIND OUT HOW MANY EMS PAGES ARE AVAILABLE:
        mov   ah,42h          ;function number
        int   67h             ;
        cmp   ah,0            ;test for errors
        jne   EMS_ERROR       ;jump if error
        mov   AVAIL_PAGES,bx  ;save the number of available pages
```

71

Allocate Expanded Memory Pages

Function 43h of interrupt 67h allocates EMS pages to your program, returning a 16-bit handle by which the pages are identified in other EMS functions. Although a 16-bit value, handle numbers range only from 00h to FEh, and the handle 00h is reserved. On entry, BX tells how many pages to allocate. If the function is successful, it returns 0 in AH and the handle in DX. Otherwise it returns one of the following error codes in AH:

80h   when EMS software malfunctions

81h   when EMS hardware malfunctions

84h   when the specified function number is undefined

85h   when no more handles are available

87h   when requested more pages than physically available

88h   when requested more pages than logically available

89h   when zero pages are requested

Once pages are allocated, they can be moved into view in the EMS page frame using function 44h of interrupt 67h, which is discussed in "Switch between Expanded Memory Pages," below.

Programming is usually simplified by allocating all pages required for a particular kind of data under one handle. Alternatively, you may wish to allocate only one page to a handle so that all pages are numbered 0, and then refer to each page by its handle number. You should check how many handles are available before doing this. Be sure to leave some handles available for other software.

A program can find out how many handles are currently active by calling function 4Bh of interrupt 67h. The function has no input registers. Similarly, function 4Ch reports how many pages have been allocated to a particular handle. Place 4Ch in AH, the handle in DX, and call interrupt 67h. Both functions return their result in BX. Alternatively, you can have the expanded memory manager fill an array with each handle and the number of pages allocated to it. Find out from function 4Bh how many handles are active and allocate memory to hold the array, allotting four bytes for each handle. Point ES:DI to the first byte of the array, place 4Dh in AH, and call interrupt 67h. Upon return, the first two bytes of the four allotted to each handle will contain the handle itself, and the second two bytes will contain the number of associated pages. All three of these functions return one of the following error codes:

80h   when EMS software malfunctions

81h   when EMS hardware malfunctions

83h   when the specified handle does not exist

84h   when the specified function number is undefined

BASIC

```
' $INCLUDE: 'QBX.BI'
DIM regs AS RegType      ' Define register array

regs.ax = &H4300        'function to allocate EMS pages
regs.bx = 10            'number of pages to allocate
CALL Interrupt(&H67, regs, regs)
IF regs.ax AND &HFF00 THEN
   GOSUB EMSError
   ELSE Handle1 = regs.dx
ENDIF
```

Pascal

```
Uses DOS;
Var
    Regs: Registers;   {Registers type is declared in the DOS unit}

Regs.AH := $43;      {function to fetch page frame segment}
Regs.BX := 10;       {number of pages to allocate}
Intr($67,Regs);
if Regs.AH <> 0 then EMSErrorRoutine
   else Handle1 := Regs.DX;
```

C

```
#include <dos.h>

union REGS regs;

regs.h.ah = 0x43;  /* function number */
regs.x.bx = 10;    /* number of pages to allocate */
int86(0x67,&regs,&regs);
if (regs.h.ah) EMS_error();
  else handle_1 = regs.x.dx;
```

Assembler

```
;---ALLOCATE 10 EXPANDED MEMORY PAGES:
        mov   ah,43h          ;function number
        mov   bx,10           ;number of pages to allocate
        int   67h             ;
        cmp   ah,0            ;test for errors
        jne   EMS_ERROR       ;jump if error
        mov   HANDLE_1,dx      ;save the handle
```

Switch between Expanded Memory Pages

Function 44h of interrupt 67h brings specified expanded memory pages into view in the page frame. The DX register is given the handle under which the desired page was allocated. BX receives the page number, counted from 0 upwards (thus, if you've allocated 10 pages, they are referred to as pages 0 through 9). Finally, the AL register is given the *physical page number*, that is, the position in the page frame to which the page is to be mapped. These four positions are numbered from 0 to 3, with 0 referring to the lowest address in the page frame. Any page can be brought into any position in the page frame.

Upon return, AH holds 0 if all has gone well, or else one of the following error codes is found in AH:

80h	when EMS software malfunctions
81h	when EMS hardware malfunctions
83h	when the specified handle does not exist
84h	when the specified function number is undefined
8Ah	when the specified page number is out of range
8Bh	when the page frame position is not from 0 to 3

Once a page is brought into the page frame, it is easiest to access it using hexadecimal numbers. Each window is 400h paragraphs large. When the base address of the page frame is E000h, then physical page 0 is at segment E000h, physical page 1 is at E400h, physical page 2 is at E800h, and physical page 3 is at EC00h.

The examples below switch page 3 into the physical page 1.

BASIC

```
' $INCLUDE: 'QBX.BI'
DIM regs AS RegType    ' Define register array


regs.ax = &H4401       'function to map pages, physical page 1
regs.dx = Handle1      'handle returned during allocation
regs.bx = 3            'page number
```

75

```
CALL Interrupt(&H67, regs, regs)
IF regs.ax AND &HFF00 THEN GOSUB EMSError
```

Pascal

```
Uses DOS;
Var

Regs: Registers;    {Registers type is declared in the DOS
                    unit}

Regs.AH := $44;     {function to map EMS pages}
Regs.AL := 1;       {physical page number}
Regs.BX := 3;       {logical page number}
Regs.DX := Handle1 {Handle under which pages allocated}
Intr($67,Regs);
if Regs.AH <> 0 then EMSErrorRoutine;
```

C

```
#include <dos.h>


union REGS regs;


regs.h.ah = 0x44;        /* function to map EMS pages */
regs.h.al = 1;           /* physical page */
regs.x.bx = 3;           /* logical page number */
regs.x.dx = handle_1     /* allocation handle */
int86(0x67,&regs,&regs);
if (regs.h.ah) EMS_error();
```

Assembler

```
;---MAP LOGICAL PAGE 3 TO PHYSICAL PAGE 1:
        mov   ah,44h           ;function number
        mov   al,1             ;physical page
        mov   bx,3             ;logical pagemov
        mov   dx,HANDLE_1      ;allocation handle
        int   67h             ;
        cmp   ah,0             ;test for errors
        jne   EMS_ERROR        ;jump if error
```

77

Get/Set an Expanded Memory Page Map

When a memory-resident program that uses expanded memory is activated, it must save the current state of the EMS hardware before switching its own expanded memory pages into the page frame. Otherwise, the wrong data will appear in the page frame when the memory-resident program returns control to the application it has interrupted.

Functions 47h and 48h of interrupt 67h, respectively, save and restore the state of the EMS driver. Your program must supply an arbitrary handle to function 47h. Later, function 48h will use the same handle to identify the saved information. Both functions return 0 in AH when they have succeeded, or else one of the following error codes:

80h   when EMS software malfunctions

81h   when EMS hardware malfunctions

83h   when the specified handle does not exist

84h   when the specified function number is undefined

8Ch   when the save area is full (function 47h)

8Dh   when the specified handle has already

      been used (function 47h)

8Eh   when the saved mapping is not found (function 48h)

There is no need to allocate storage for the saved data. Be aware that these functions can be relied on only when the expanded memory manager is limited to a 64K contiguous page frame. A much more complicated system of allocating and saving pages is allowed by Expanded Memory Manager Version 4.0. As explained in the *minitutorial* at the beginning of this chapter, these advanced EMS features are seldom used, and they are beyond the scope of the discussion here.

BASIC

```
' $INCLUDE: 'QBX.BI'
DIM regs AS RegType      'define register array
SaveHandle = 77          'arbitary handle
```

```
regs.ax = &H4700        'function to save EMS state
regs.dx = SaveHandle    'arbitrary handle
CALL Interrupt(&H67, regs, regs)
IF regs.ax AND &HFF00 THEN GOSUB EMSError


regs.ax = &H4800        'function to restore EMS state
regs.dx = SaveHandle    'use the handle again
CALL Interrupt(&H67, regs, regs)
IF regs.ax AND &HFF00 THEN GOSUB EMSError
```

Pascal

```
Uses DOS;
Var
 Regs: Registers;   {Registers type is declared in the DOS unit}
 SaveHandle: integer;


SaveHandle = 77;    {arbitrary handle}
Regs.AH := $47;     {function to save EMS state}
Regs.DX := SaveHandle;
Intr($67,Regs);
if Regs.AH <> 0 then EMSErrorRoutine;


Regs.AH := $48;        {function to restore EMS state}
Regs.DX := SaveHandle; {use the handle again}
Intr($67,Regs);
if Regs.AH <> 0 then EMSErrorRoutine;
```

C

```
#include <dos.h>

union REGS regs;
unsigned save_handle = 77;

regs.h.ah = 0x47;          /* function to save EMS state */
regs.x.dx = save_handle;   /* specify an arbitrary handle */
int86(0x67,&regs,&regs);
if (regs.x.ah) EMS_error();

regs.h.ah = 0x48;          /* function to restore EMS state */
regs.x.dx = save_handle;   /*use the handle again */
int86(0x67,&regs,&regs);
if (regs.x.ah) EMS_error();
```

Assembler

```
;---IN THE DATA SEGMENT:
SAVE_HANDLE dw ?

;---SAVE THE STATE OF THE EMS DRIVER:
        mov  ah,47h          ;function number
        mov  dx,77           ;arbitrary handle
        mov  SAVE_HANDLE,dx  ;save for later
        int  67h             ;save the driver state
        cmp  ah,0            ;test for errors
        jne  EMS_ERROR       ;jump if error
```

```
;---RESTORE THE STATE OF THE EMS DRIVER:
        mov  ah,48h            ;function number
        mov  dx,SAVE_HANDLE    ;recall the handle
        int  67h               ;save the driver state
        cmp  ah,0              ;test for errors
        jne  EMS_ERROR         ;jump if error
```

Deallocate Expanded Memory Pages

Function 45h of interrupt 67h deallocates all pages that were allocated to a particular handle. If a program has made multiple allocations, multiple deallocations are required. You cannot deallocate only some of the pages that have been allocated under a particular handle. On entry, DX holds the handle for the pages that will be deallocated. On return, AH holds 0 when the deallocation has been successful, or else one of the following error codes:

```
80h    when EMS software malfunctions

81h    when EMS hardware malfunctions

83h    when the specified handle does not exist

84h    when the specified function number is undefined

86h    when an error has occured in saving or

       restoring the page mapping
```

Many applications make the deallocation at the time they terminate, even though they might have been able to do so earlier. This approach is acceptable in a single-tasking environment, where no other application is likely to demand expanded memory pages while your application is running (device drivers and TSRs that require expanded memory normally allocate all they need upon loading — that is, before your application starts). However, in a multitasking environment like Windows or DesqView, other applications can demand expanded memory pages at any time. For this reason, it is good programming practice to relinquish expanded memory pages as soon as a program can. Keep this requirement in mind when first allocating pages. It may be better to allocate pages under several handles so that part can be deallocated and part retained.

Remember that DOS has no part in managing expanded memory. If your program fails to deallocate pages when it terminates, the pages will stay allocated to a nonexistent application and subsequently loaded applications will find little or no expanded memory available. For this reason, a program that uses expanded memory should always include routines for exiting through Ctrl-Break or through a critical error condition so that expanded memory pages can be deallocated when the application is abruptly terminated. If function 45h fails to deallocate pages when a program first asks it to, the program should try again. Otherwise, the pages will be unavailable until the computer is restarted.

BASIC

```
' $INCLUDE: 'QBX.BI'
DIM regs AS RegType      ' Define register array

regs.ax = &H4500         'function to deallocate pages
regs.dx = Handle1        'handle under which pages were allocated
CALL Interrupt(&H67, regs, regs)
IF regs.ax AND &HFF00 THEN GOSUB EMSError
```

Pascal

```
Uses DOS;
Var
   Regs: Registers;   {Registers type is declared in the DOS unit}

Regs.AH := $45;     {function to deallocate pages}
Regs.DX := Handle1  {handle under which pages were allocated}
Intr($67,Regs);
if Regs.AH <> 0 then EMSErrorRoutine;
```

C

```
#include <dos.h>

union REGS regs;

regs.h.ah = 0x45;        /* function to deallocate pages */
regs.x.dx = handle_1;    /* the allocation handle */
int86(0x67,&regs,&regs);
if (regs.x.ah) EMS_error();
```

Assembler

```
;---DEALLOCATE EXPANDED MEMORY PAGES:
        mov  ah,45h          ;function number
        mov  dx,HANDLE_1     ;allocation handle
        int  67h             ;
        cmp  ah,0            ;test for errors
        jne  EMS_ERROR       ;jump if error
```

Integrate Expanded Memory into Your Programs

Expanded memory is often used to hold large amounts of data. You'll have no help from DOS or from compilers in managing this data. Usually it takes just a little arithmetic to calculate the position of a particular data record within a large array. But, in accessing data held in expanded memory, your program needs not only to calculate a pointer, but also may need to call the expanded memory manager to switch pages. To do this, you need:

```
(1)   a handle

(2)   a page number

(3)   an offset within the page

(4)   the page frame address

(5)   the page position within the frame
```

As complicated as this sounds, it's often possible to work out a simple scheme for accessing data in expanded memory. You'll need to write a routine to which the program passes record numbers. The routine figures out which EMS page the record resides in, switches the page into view (if necessary), and returns a pointer to the data as an offset from the bottom of the expanded memory page frame. Obviously, this process is more time-consuming than just calculating a simple offset or taking a pointer from a pointer array. You can reduce the overhead of working with expanded memory by observing the following suggestions:

- Make sure that all pages that will be used by a single data object are allocated under a single handle. In doing so, you'll eliminate the handle from your calculations or, if you build a pointer array, you won't need to record each element's handle in it.

- To save time, do not have the expanded memory manager call a page into view if the page is already inview at the desired page frame position.

- Try to minimize the amount of page switching required. Expanded memory can be quite slow, particularly using early EMS boards. Design your data structures so that data that will be acted upon simultaneously can be brought into view on the same pages. For example, if you'll need to copy data from one EMS page to another, find some way of bringing both pages into view at once and then make the transfer. Don't read a word from page 1, switch to page 2 to write it, then go back to page 1 for the next word, and so on. If there isn't space available in the page frame to bring both pages into view at once, you may improve performance by copying the relevant data to a buffer in conventional memory, switching pages, and copying the data back.

- Avoid making disk transfers directly to expanded memory. DOS buffers or disk cache buffers may be positioned there too, confronting you with the chicken-or-egg problem of needing two sets of pages in view at the same time.

- If only one record needs to be in view at a time, you can eliminate the need to track a page's position within the page frame by always placing the page at the bottom of the page frame. In this case, if you want more than 16K of data in view at once, treat the pages as groups of two, three, or four, as if pages were allocated in blocks of 32K, 48K, or 64K. Then calculate offsets on the basis of that page size. For example, say that you allocate eight 16K expanded memory pages, and the record you want to access begins at the tenth byte of the last page. Then you could regard the allocation as consisting of two 64K pages, with the desired record being located at offset (3*16K)+10 on the "second" page.

  By working this way, the EMS page switching information is reduced to a single number — a (virtual) page for which the handle number, page frame address, and page frame offset are already known. Thus, a pointer array to the data record would need to contain only this page number and the offset within the page.

- Using a 32-bit pointer array, you can combine references to expanded memory and conventional memory by storing an EMS page number in place of a segment address. Then, when the program calls a routine that switches EMS pages and calculates pointers, the routine can test the range of the segment value. If the value is under, say, 500, the value would be understood to be an expanded memory page, and the routine would bring the page into view. Otherwise, the value would be considered a segment address pointing to conventional memory. There can be no confusion in this matter, since DOS will never allocate a memory block so low in memory that its segment would equal 500 or less.

- When space in the page frame is scarce, it's generally a bad idea to have data records span two expanded memory pages. If a little space is wasted at the end of each page, so be it. When a record spans two pages, you're forced to bring two pages into the frame when one might otherwise do the job, and the pages must be made adjacent.

There is another, entirely different approach to using expanded memory. Instead of accessing data directly in the EMS page frame, you can copy data from the frame down to conventional memory. Many TSRs work this way. They store most of their code in expanded memory, leaving just a kernel in conventional memory to detect the hotkey that activates the program. When the TSR comes into action, it exchanges part of the current contents of conventional memory with the code stored in expanded memory and then goes to work. Later, it reverses this process and returns control to whatever application was running when the TSR was started. All sorts of problems can arise when a TSR works this way, because the code can be laid down at memory locations occupied by device drivers or other resident code that may be activated at any moment.

An application program, on the other hand, can transfer data from expanded memory to *preallocated* portions of conventional memory without any risk of disruptions. Say that your program's data use a complicated record structure. You can declare a single instance of this structure as a global (static) variable in the program's data segment. Then the program can find out the address of that structure and transfer instances of the record from expanded memory. Once in place, a record can be accessed directly without numerous pointer operations, making for cleaner, tighter code. After work on a record is complete, it is transferred back to expanded memory. Obviously, there is overhead in transferring the data back and forth. But there are occasions when this approach works well.

4

Programming Interrupts

- Minitutorial: How Interrupts Work
- Program an Interrupt Controller Chip
- Allow/Disallow Particular Hardware Interrupts
- Call Interrupts from BASIC, Pascal, and C
- Write Your Own Interrupt Service Routine
- Chain into Existing Interrupts

Minitutorial: How Interrupts Work

Interrupts are signals to a computer's microprocessor that cause the processor to temporarily suspend what it is doing and perform a task that requires immediate attention. Many interrupts are devoted to common tasks that nearly all software requires, such as fetching keystrokes from the keyboard or opening files.

Interrupts are so named because they *interrupt* whatever the computer is doing. As a program runs, an interrupt breaks in and takes over the processor, does its job, quits, and then the program abruptly picks up where it left off. Hundreds, sometimes thousands of interrupts may occur in a second.

To successfully restart the program after an interrupt, the following information must be saved on the stack:

- The processor's *instruction pointer (IP)*, which points to the next instruction to be executed. The instruction pointer refers to an offset relative to the value in the processor's CS (code segment) register, and so both values (CS:IP) are pushed on to the stack, taking up four bytes.

- The processor's *flag register*, which must be preserved lest the interrupt's code makes changes in flags that later will be used by the program's code. This register takes up two bytes on the stack.

- Any other processor registers whose contents will be changed by the interrupt's code, each taking an additional two bytes of stack space.

The first two kinds of information—CS:IP and the flag register—are automatically pushed onto the stack when an interrupt occurs. Other processor registers are saved by the interrupt routine (commonly called an *interrupt handler* or *interrupt service routine (ISR)*. All registers are not saved automatically because many interrupt handlers alter only a few registers and would waste time by saving registers needlessly. When the interrupt service routine finishes, it restores the registers it has changed, and then executes an **IRET** (*Interrupt Return*) instruction, which pops the flag register and CS:IP off the stack and back into place on the processor. With CS:IP suddenly changed, the program that was interrupted begins functioning again.

There are two basic kinds of interrupts: *hardware interrupts* and *software interrupts.* A hardware interrupt is one that is initiated by hardware, whether by circuitry on the system board, by an expansion card, or through a port connected to an external device. Hardware interrupts may be initiated by events as diverse as a pulse of the computer's timer chip, a signal from a modem, or a press of a mouse button. These interrupts are managed by a *programmable interrupt controller chip* (*PIC*) which is discussed in "Program an Interrupt Controller Chip," below.

The *keyboard interrupt* is an example of a hardware interrupt. The interrupt starts up whenever a key code arrives from the keyboard. The interrupt analyzes the code and (in most cases) transforms it into an ASCII code that it places in the keyboard buffer. Then the keyboard interrupt terminates, and whatever software is running is free to read the keystroke from the buffer at its leisure. If the keyboard interrupt did not process the incoming key code the moment it arrived, the code could be lost when another key is pressed.

Software interrupts, on the other hand, are initiated by software rather than hardware. A program "calls" software interrupts in order to get a job done, such as to display a character on the screen. Actually, it's a bit of a misnomer to call them "interrupts." While a hardware interrupt like the keyboard interrupt can be activated at any moment, a software interrupt that passes character codes from the keyboard buffer to a program works only at the moment that the program asks it to—it doesn't really interrupt anything.

Hardware and software interrupts are related in that the same mechanism—a *vector table*—is used to start them. A *vector* is nothing more than the four-byte address of an interrupt handler, giving its segment and offset in memory. Interrupt handlers may be positioned anywhere in conventional memory. Some handlers are held on the ROM BIOS in upper memory, others are found within COMMAND.COM, and still others can be set up within device drivers or other memory-resident software, or even within application programs. The bottommost 1024 bytes of memory hold interrupt vectors, so there is room for 256 vectors in all. The lowest vectors in the table are used by hardware interrupts. These are numbered 8 higher than the actual interrupt number. Thus, the vector for interrupt 0 is at 0000:0020, interrupt 1 starts at 0000:0024, interrupt 2 is at 0000:0028, and so on. Figure 4-1 shows the path a program takes in executing interrupt 21h.

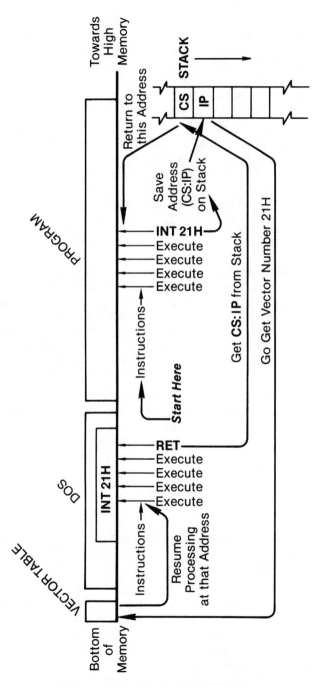

Figure 4-1   The Path of INT 21h

The lowest positions in the interrupt vector table are devoted to a special kind of interrupt: *exceptions*. An exception is essentially an interrupt initiated by the CPU itself when an error occurs that it cannot handle, as when a program attempts to divide a number by zero, or when it encounters a machine instruction that it does not recognize. Each kind of error is given its own interrupt vector that can be pointed to a recovery routine. Programmer's do not ordinarily need to write exception handlers, since compilers guard against the occurence of some kinds of errors and provide their own exception handlers for others.

Certain interrupts are available to any program. These include the BIOS interrupts, which are located in ROM in high memory, and thus are built into the machine. There are also the DOS interrupts found within COMMAND.COM. Interrupts that monitor a mouse or control expanded memory are provided by the device drivers that accompany these devices.

Interrupts are an inherent feature of PC hardware. The processor is designed to support them, and special circuitry extends to expansion card and I/O ports to support hardware interrupts. Interrupts are started up ("called") by executing the processor's INT instruction. For example, **INT 1Ah** executes interrupt number 1Ah. Before calling the interrupt, various processor registers are filled with data the interrupt requires. A register might point to a string that gives the name of a file that should be opened. These are the interrupt's *input registers*. Similarly, when the interrupt finishes, it may deposit information in particular registers. These are the *return registers*. Interrupts also leave status information in the processor's *flag register*. Many DOS interrupts set the *carry flag* when an error has occurred.

Some interrupts perform more than one task, and when they are called, you must specify a *function number*. For instance, function 0 of interrupt 1Ah returns the BIOS time-of-day count, and function 1 of the same interrupt sets the count. Function numbers are almost always placed in the processor's AH register before the interrupt is called. In assembly language, you would call function 0 of interrupt 1Ah by writing:

```
mov   ah,0
int   1Ah
```

The main DOS interrupts are all functions of INT 21H. To further organize interrupts, there may be *subfunction numbers* to specify tasks within a function. These numbers normally go in the processor's AL register.

Many interrupt routines employ variables and memory buffers that are allocated for their exclusive use. If a software interrupt service routine is at work and it is interrupted in some way — perhaps by activation of a memory-resident program (a TSR) — the same interrupt can be called again. When this happens, the variables used by the interrupt will be filled with new values. When control is returned to the first instance of the interrupt, it will attempt to finish the job it was doing. With its variables changed, it will make mistakes, and may crash the machine. It's possible to design interrupts that write their data on the stack, or that allocate memory buffers dynamically, so that one call to the interrupt does not interfere with another. Such interrupts are called *re-entrant*. The DOS interrupts, however, are *not* re-entrant.

Although interrupts are the domain of the assembly language programmer, it is easy to use them from BASIC, Pascal, and C. Indeed, many examples in this book use interrupts to give these languages capabilities that their libraries do not provide. See "Call Interrupts from Basic, Pascal, and C," below.

Here is a table of important interrupt vectors:

vector number	function
00h	Divide by zero error
01h	Processor single step
02h	Nonmaskable interrupt
03h	Processor break point
04h	Processor overflow
05h	Print screen
06h	Unused
07h	Unused
08h	Timer (time-of-day count)
09h	Keyboard
0Ah	Reserved
0Bh	COM2
0Ch	COM1
0Dh	Hard disk drive controller
0Eh	Diskette drive controller
0Fh	Printer controller
10h	Video driver
11h	Equipment configuration check
12h	Memory size check
13h	Disk I/O (PC/XT)
14h	Com port driver
15h	Network & miscellaneous services
16h	Keyboard buffer access

continues

vector number	function
17h	Printer access
18h	ROM BASIC
19h	System restart
1Ah	Timer & real-time clock access
1Bh	Ctrl-Break handler
1Ch	User defined timer tick routine
1Dh	Video parameter table
1Eh	Disk parameter table
1Fh	Graphics character table
20h	Program terminate
21h	DOS functions
22h	Terminate vector
23h	Ctrl-C vector
24h	Critical-error vector
25h	Absolute disk sector read
26h	Absolute disk sector write
27h	Terminate and stay resident

Program an Interrupt Controller Chip

Intel 8259 programmable interrupt controller (PIC) chips are used in all IBM PCs to manage *hardware* interrupts. A chip has eight interrupt channels. PC- and XT-style machines use one interrupt controller chip, and all others use two, or the equivalent of two combined on one custom chip. In the simplest case, each channel is connected to a single device. When a channel is activated, an *interrupt request* is made. These requests are numbered *IRQ0#* through *IRQ15#*.

As one interrupt is executed, requests for others may arrive. An interrupt controller chip keeps track of interrupt requests and decides which will be executed next on the basis of a priority scheme. Lower-numbered channels have the highest priority. Thus, IRQ0# takes precedence over IRQ1#. The priority scheme is complicated by the use of two chips. One chip acts as *master*, and one as *slave*. The eight channels of the slave chip work through channel 2 of the master chip, and so these eight channels hold highest priority after IRQ0# and IRQ1#. Interrupt requests 0 through 7 — those serviced by the master chip — are called from interrupt vectors 8h through Fh; interrupt requests 8 through 15 are serviced by the vectors 70h through 77h. Here are the standard interrupt assignments. They are listed in the order that the interrupt controller chip gives them priority, with interrupts 8 through 15 inserted between interrupts 2 and 3.

hardware interrupts by precedence

IRQ0	BIOS time-of-day update
1	Keyboard
2	Access to slave interrupt controller
8	Real-time clock
9	PS/2 video
10	General purpose
11	General purpose
12	PS/2 mouse
13	Math coprocessor error
14	Hard disk controller
15	General purpose
3	COM2

continues

hardware interrupts by precedence

4	COM1
5	LPT2
6	Diskette controller
7	LPT1

An 8259 chip has three one-byte registers that control and monitor the eight hardware interrupt lines. The *interrupt request register* (IRR) changes a bit to 1 when the corresponding interrupt line signals a request. The chip then checks whether another interrupt is in progress by consulting the *in service register* (ISR). Additional circuitry assures that the priority scheme is enforced. Finally, before invoking the interrupt, the *interrupt mask register* (IMR) is checked to see whether an interrupt of that level is currently allowed. Ordinarily, programmers access only the interrupt mask registers, which may be both read and written. The IMR register for the master controller chip is accessed through port address 21h, and through port address A1h for the slave controller chip.

There is another register that must be accessed by programmers who write hardware interrupt handlers. This is the *interrupt command register,* and it is used to tell an interrupt controller chip that a hardware interrupt has finished its job and is about to terminate. This register is accessed through ports 20h for the master controller, and A0h for the slave controller.

Interrupt controller registers are accessed by the *INP* and *OUT* statements in BASIC, the *Port[]* array in Turbo Pascal, *inportb* and *outportb* in Borland's C, *inp* and *outp* in Microsoft's C, and by the *IN* and *OUT* instructions in assembly language. The following examples merely test the interrupt mask register to see if the diskette interrupt (IRQ#6) is enabled. They AND the value read from the port with 64 — a number in which only bit 6 is set.

BASIC

```
IF INP(&H21) AND 64 THEN WRITE "DISKETTE INTERRUPT MASKED"
```

Pascal

```
if (Port[$21] And 64) <> 0 then Writeln('Diskette Int masked');
```

C

For Borland compilers:

```
if (inportb(0x21) & 64) printf("Diskette Interrupt masked");
```

For Microsoft compilers:

```
if (inp(0x21) & 64) printf("Diskette Interrupt masked");
```

Assembler

```
        in   al,21h        ;read the port
        test al,01000000b  ;is the bit set?
        jnz  INT_MASKED     ;if so, the interrupt is masked
```

Allow/Disallow Particular Hardware Interrupts

Programs can disable any or all hardware interrupts. This action is ordinarily required only when you write low-level code that accesses hardware directly. For example, if you write a routine that inserts codes into the keyboard buffer, you must shut out the keyboard interrupt while the routine is at work lest the keyboard interrupt break in and interfere. Hardware interrupts are also masked out to prevent delays from occurring during time-sensitive operations. A precisely timed I/O routine could not afford to be waylaid by a lengthy disk interrupt.

Ultimately, the execution of all interrupts depends upon the setting of the interrupt flag (bit 9) of the processor's flag register. When it is 1, the processor honors any interrupt request that the interrupt mask register permits. When it is 0, no hardware interrupt can occur. Assembly language programmers alter this flag by using the *CLI* instruction to disable interrupts and the *STI* instruction to re-enable them. Failure to follow *CLI* with *STI* usually locks up the machine since keyboard and mouse input is shut out.

To mask out particular hardware interrupts, simply send the appropriate bit pattern to an *interrupt mask register* (*IMR*). This 8-bit register is located at port address 21h for the master interrupt controller, and at A1h for the slave interrupt controller. Set those bits that correspond to the numbers of the interrupts you wish to mask. The example below first saves the current register setting, then blocks out the diskette interrupt, IRQ6#. This is done by setting bit 6 in the value read from the register. Later, the original port value is restored.

BASIC

```
KeepMask = INP &H21      'save current settings
OUT &H21,KeepMask AND 64 'mask the diskette interrupt
 .

 .

OUT &H21,KeepMask        'later, restore original settings
```

Pascal

```
var KeepMask: char;


KeepMask := Port[$21];              {save current settings}
Port[$21] := KeepMask And 64;   {mask the diskette interrupt}
.

.

Port[$21] := KeepMask;              {later, restore original settings}
```

C

For Borland compilers:
```
char keep_mask;


keep_mask = inportb(0x21);      /*save current settings*/
outportb(0x21,keep_mask & 64); /*mask the diskette interrupt*/
.

.

outportb(0x21,keep_mask);      /*later, restore original settings*/
```
For Microsoft compilers:
```
char keep_mask;


keep_mask = inp(0x21);          /*save current settings*/
outp(0x21,keep_mask & 64);     /*mask the diskette interrupt*/
.

.

outp(0x21,keep_mask);           /*later, restore original settings*/
```

Assembler

```
;---IN THE DATA SEGMENT:
KEEPMASK db ?


;---MASK OUT BIT 6 IN THE INTERRUPT MASK REGISTER:
    in   al,21h            ;fetch current IMR settings
    mov  KEEPMASK,al       ;save for later
    and  al,01000000b      ;set bit 6 (diskette interrupt)
    out  21h,al            ;send to the interrupt mask register
    .

    .

    mov  al,KEEPMASK       ;later, restore original settings
    out  21h,al            ;
```

Call Interrupts from BASIC, Pascal, and C

Many features offered by the BIOS and DOS interrupts are not available through the libraries that accompany high-level languages. Access to expanded memory or a mouse also usually requires direct calls to interrupts. Happily, any of the compilers discussed in this book can call any interrupt.

You need to understand a few facts about how microprocessors work in order to call an interrupt. The various processor models used in IBM PCs vary considerably in their design, but all share certain features. Microprocessors are built around *registers* — places that hold data as it is moved or transformed. All PC processors include four general purpose registers named AX, BX, CX, and DX. These are 16-bit registers, and their top and bottom halves may be referred to separately as AH and AL, BH and BL, CH and CL, and DH and DL. There are also a number of special purpose 16-bit registers, including BP, DI, and SI. Certain other registers are specialized for holding memory addresses. These include CS, DS, ES, and SS. These registers are always accessed as a whole register.

Normally, it is only the assembly language programmer's concern how registers are used. But if you want to call interrupts, you must be familiar with the register names so that you can load required input values into registers. In high-level languages, this is done by setting up an array in which there is an element corresponding to every register. You initialize the array elements used by the interrupt and then call the interrupt. For example, if the AH register takes the value 3, you must write a statement like **Regs.AH = 3**. After the interrupt has been executed, it may return results in particular registers, such as a file's attribute byte in the AL register. Your program would then read the value by a statement like **TheAttribute = Regs.AL**.

The exact form of the register array depends on the compiler. Some compilers use the same array for input values and return values. Others let you optionally declare a different array for return values. The compiler cannot know which registers are significant and which are not, so it initializes all registers before calling the interrupt, and returns all registers afterwards. This means that the compiler also preserves the contents of certain registers that it will need when the interrupt finishes, even when these registers are not used by an interrupt. All of this activity means that calling interrupts from a high-level language does not proceed as quickly as in assembly language. Usually the delay is insignificant. But it can make a difference in a few cases, such as when you call an interrupt repeatedly to draw on the screen pixel by pixel.

BASIC

Microsoft BASIC provides the *Interrupt* and *InterruptX* routines for calling interrupts. (These replace the *INT86* and *INT86X* routines found in earlier versions.) A program must be linked with the *QBX.LIB* file to use these routines or, when working in the QBX environment, you must load the **QBC.QLB** library by including **/L** in the command that starts up BASIC. The *QBX.BI* header file contains the required declarations, including structures that define an array for the processor registers. These include *RegType*, which is used with *Interrupt*, and *RegTypeX*, which is used with *InterruptX*. *RegType* looks like this:

```
TYPE RegType

    AX AS INTEGER

    BX AS INTEGER

    CX AS INTEGER

    DX AS INTEGER

    BP AS INTEGER

    SI AS INTEGER

    DI AS INTEGER

    FLAGS AS INTEGER

END TYPE
```

The *RegTypeX* structure is exactly the same, except that it adds two more elements at the end:

```
    DS AS INTEGER

    ES AS INTEGER
```

A statement like:

```
    DIM Regs AS RegType
```

would create an array in the form of *RegType*, naming it *Regs*.

The only difference between *Interrupt* and *InterruptX* is the use of the DS and ES address registers by the latter routine. For most BIOS and DOS interrupts, *Interrupt* will do the job. But occasionally you may need to change DS or ES, and so will require *InterruptX*.

Both *Interrupt* and *InterruptX* take the same three parameters. First, you specify the interrupt number, normally using a hexadecimal number. Then you specify the name of the register array used for loading registers, and then the array that returns values from the interrupt. Usually, it's best to use the same array. To call a function in DOS's interrupt 21h, you might write

```
INTERRUPT(&H21,Regs,Regs)
```

BASIC presents two problems in loading the registers. First, you often need to load just half of one of the general purpose registers (AX through DX). For instance, you may need to place 7 in AH and 3 in AL. The easiest way to load these registers is by using four-digit hexadecimal numbers. The high two digits in such a number would represent the contents of AH, and the low two bits, AL. Since both registers must be initialized at the same time, you would write:

```
Regs.AX = &H0703
```

If the two values were held in variables, you could assemble this number by multiplying the value that goes in AH by 256 and then adding it to the value that goes in AL. Of course, you must use integer arithmetic in this calculation.

The second problem in loading registers is in filling registers with addresses that point to variables, particularly string variables. This is done with BASIC's *VARSEG* and *VARPTR* functions, which return a variable's segment and offset in memory. If an interrupt requires that ES:DI point to a buffer you have set up named *MyBuffer*, you would initialize the registers by writing:

```
Regs.ES = VarSeg(MyBuffer)
```

```
Regs.DI = VarPtr(MyBuffer)
```

DOS interrupt routines require strings formatted as they are in the C language. In C, the string ends with a byte of ASCII 0. To set up a string in BASIC for use by an interrupt, append a byte of 0:

```
MyString$ = MyString$ + CHR$(0)
```

The following example finds out a file's attribute byte through subfunction 0 of function 43h of DOS interrupt 21h. As always, when they are required, function numbers go in AH and subfunction numbers go in AL. For this interrupt, DS:DX must point to a path string giving the name and location of the file. Because DS is changed, the *InterruptX* routine is required. On return from the interrupt, the CL register holds the attribute byte. Because you need to fetch CH and CL together (as CX), you must zero out the high byte of the value returned in case CH contains a value other than 0. Do this by ANDing the value with **00** for the part of the CX register you want cleared, and **FF** for the part you want preserved. When you clear the lower part of the register, divide the result by 256 to shift the value down by eight bits. Here is the code:

```
' $INCLUDE: 'QBX.BI'

DIM Regs AS RegTypeX      ' Define register array


PathString$ = "C:\PRIMATES\CHIMP.DOC"+CHR$(0)

Regs.AX = &H4300
```

```
Regs.DS = VARSEG(PathString$)

Regs.DX = VARPTR(PathString$)

CALL InterruptX(&H21, regs, regs)

TheAttribute = Regs.CX

TheAttribute = TheAttribute AND &H00FF
```

Pascal

Turbo Pascal's *Intr* procedure calls interrupts. It defines a *Registers* record (found in the DOS unit) that takes the form:

```
Type

  Registers = record

    case Integer of

      0: (AX, BX, CX, DX, BP, SI, DI, DS, ES, Flags: Word);

      1: (AL,AH,BL,BH,CL,CH,DL,DH: Byte);

    end;
```

Pascal conveniently lets you access a register like AX as either AX, AH, or AL. The same register array is used for both input registers and return registers. The *Intr* procedure takes two parameters: first, the interrupt number, and then a pointer to the register array.

Some DOS interrupts require string arguments for which a pointer to the string is placed in a register pair, such as DS:DX. These interrupts use zero-terminated strings that do not begin with a descriptor. However, Pascal strings begin with a one-byte descriptor that tells the string's length, and they do not end with a byte of zero. To use a Pascal string, add a zero byte at its end. Then employ the *Seg* and *Ofs* functions to fetch the string's address, and increase the value returned by *Ofs* by 1 to point to the first byte of the string rather than to its descriptor.

The following example reads a file's attribute using subfunction 0 of function 43h of INT 21h. On entry, DS:DX points to a file name and path. On return, the attribute is deposited in CL.

```
uses Dos;
```

```
Var

  Regs: Registers;   {Registers type is declared in the DOS unit}

  FilePath: string[64];

  Attribute: Byte;


  FilePath := Concat('C:\PRIMATES\CHIMP.DOC',Chr(0));

  Regs.AH := $43;        {function number}

  Regs.AL := $00;        {subfunction number}

  Regs.DS := Seg(FilePath);  {point DS:DX to the path string}

  Regs.DX := Ofs(FilePath) + 1;

  Intr($21,Regs);        {Call the interrupt}

  Attribute := Regs.CL; {Put the result in Attribute}
```

C

Both the Borland and Microsoft compilers provide the *int86* and *int86x* functions to call interrupts. They differ in that *int86x* can alter the DS and ES registers, while *int86* cannot. Both functions use a union named *regs* that is defined in *dos.h*. Its form is as follows:

```
struct WORDREGS {

  unsigned int  ax, bx, cx, dx, si, di, cflag, flags;

};


struct BYTEREGS {

  unsigned char  al, ah, bl, bh, cl, ch, dl, dh;

};


union REGS {

  struct WORDREGS x;

  struct BYTEREGS h;

}
```

Note that Microsoft's C lacks the *flags* field in WORDREGS.

The *int86* function takes three parameters: first the interrupt number, then a pointer to the input registers, and then a pointer to the return registers. The same array may be used for both. The *int86x* function adds a fourth parameter that points to a list of the four segment registers:

```
struct SREGS {

    unsigned int  es;

    unsigned int  cs;

    unsigned int  ss;

    unsigned int  ds;

};
```

The following example returns a file's attribute byte by calling subfunction 0 of function 0x43 of interrupt 0x21. On entry, DS:DX points to a path string naming the file. DOS uses C strings for this purpose, so no adjustments are required. The file's attribute is returned in CL.

```
#include <dos.h>


union REGS regs;        /* declare the register array */
struct SREGS sregs;     /* declare struct for extra registers */
char file_attribute;    /* will hold the return value */
char *path_string = "C :\\PRIMATES\\CHIMP.DOC";


{
   regs.h.ah = 0x43;    /* function number */
   regs.h.al = 0;       /* subfunction number */
   regs.x.dx = FP_OFF(path_string);
   sregs.ds = FP_SEG(path_string);
  int86x(0x21,&regs,&regs,&sregs);
   file_attribute = regs.h.cl;
```

Write Your Own Interrupt Service Routine

There are several reasons for writing an interrupt service routine. Certain interrupt vectors are intended to be redirected to routines of your making. These include the critical-error handler, the Ctrl-Brk handler, and extensions to the time-of-day interrupt. Printer interrupts and communications interrupts allow the computer to rapidly switch back and forth between I/O operations and other processing. You may also want to write an interrupt to replace an existing handler, or you may want to add features to an existing handler.

An interrupt handler is not much more than an ordinary subroutine. It does its job and quits. It differs from ordinary subroutines in that it ends with an IRET instruction and saves any processor registers that it changes (except the flag register, which is saved automatically). Once the routine is written, the routine's address must be placed in the appropriate vector slot. If nonzero, the value currently found in the slot should be saved. Later, when the program quits, it must see to it that the original vector is restored. If the vector is not restored, the interrupt can be called with the vector pointing to whatever code happens to have filled the space previously occupied by the interrupt handler. Note that vectors for Ctrl-break and critical error handler routines (vectors 23h and 24h) are automatically reinitialized when a program terminates.

BASIC

Microsoft BASIC offers little support for writing your own interrupt service routines, but it does provide the *ON event* statements to respond to hardware interrupts. For example, the statement:

```
ON COM(1) GOSUB ProcessComBuffer
```

causes control to jump to the *ProcessComBuffer* subroutine whenever a COM1 interrupt occurs. Here are the other options:

- **ON KEY(n%) GOSUB TheRoutine** invokes *TheRoutine* whenever a specified key is pressed. The key number $n\%$ is 1 to 10 for <F1> to <F10>, 11 through 14 for cursor-up, left, right, and down, and 30-31 for <F11> and <F12>. In addition, codes 15 through 25 can be made to represent any other keys by using the *KEY* statement to assign the key's scan code to the code number.

- **ON PEN GOSUB TheRoutine** branches to *TheRoutine* when a lightpen is activated.

- *ON PLAY(bufferposition)TheRoutine* turns control over to *TheRoutine* when the buffer used for playing background music empties to a specified point. This option lets a program refill the buffer so that music can continue without interruption.

- *ON STRIG(eventtype) GOSUB TheRoutine* invokes *TheRoutine* when a specified joystick event has occured.

- *ON TIMER(numberseconds) GOSUB TheRoutine* branches to *TheRoutine* when a specified number of seconds have passed.

In all cases, event trapping must be enabled before a statement can be used. Trapping can be switched off or suspended at any moment. For example, *TIMER ON* switches on event trapping for the *TIMER* statement. *TIMER OFF* causes timer events to be ignored. And *TIMER STOP* suspends trapping. In the latter case, events are sensed, but the associated routine is not activated until another *TIMER ON* statement is encountered. Event trapping requires considerable background activity that slows programs. It can be disabled at any time by inserting *EVENT OFF* statements, and then reenabled by inserting *EVENT ON*. Examples are found in Chapter 5, (Control Real-Time Operations,) and Chapter 9, (Take Digital Input from a Game Port).

Pascal

Turbo Pascal makes it easy to write interrupt handlers. Use this format to set up the handler:

```
procedure MyHandler(Flags,CS,IP,AX,BX,CX,DX,SI,DI,DS,ES,BP:Word);

interrupt;

begin

   .

   .    {interrupt code here}

   .

end;
```

The registers are passed as pseudoparameters, and can be used or modified as your code requires. For example, the routine can test AH for a function number, or return a result in CL. Fewer registers may be declared, but they must be eliminated in order, starting from the left side of the declaration (from *Flags*). All registers are automatically saved on entry and restored on return. When writing a handler for a hardware interrupt, avoid using Turbo Pascal's I/O and memory-management functions, because these are not re-entrant.

Once the routine has been written, you'll need to point an interrupt vector to it. This is done with the *SetIntVec* procedure, which takes two parameters: first the interrupt number, and then the service routine address, which is of *pointer* type. Assemble the pointer using Turbo Pascal's *Addr* function:

```
SetIntVec($62,Addr(MyHandler));
```

You can test whether the vector is free for use, and can chain and restore vectors, by using the *GetIntVec* function. It also takes a vector number as its first parameter, and then a *pointer* variable in which the function deposits the vector:

```
var TheVector: pointer


GetIntVec($62,TheVector);
```

C

To declare the C function *my_handler* as an interrupt routine, write:

```
void interrupt my_handler()
{
   .
   .            /* interrupt code */
   .
}
```

Then install a vector to the handler using *setvect* in Borland's C or *_dos_setvect* in Microsoft's C. Using vector 0x62, you would write:

```
setvect(0x62,my_handler);          /* Borland */
```

or:

```
_dos_setvect(0x62,my_handler);     /* Microsoft */
```

To find out whether a vector is in use, or to chain interrupts, use the *getvect* function in the Borland compilers, or the *_dos_getvect* function in the Microsoft compilers. You can declare a variable in which the functions can return a vector by writing:

```
void interrupt (*keepvector)();
```

To fetch the vector, write:

```
keepvector = getvect(0x62);        /* Borland */
```

or:

```
keepvector = _dos_getvect(0x62);   /* Microsoft */
```

Assembler

Function 25h of interrupt 21h sets an interrupt vector to a specified address. On entry, DS:DX holds the interrupt handler's segment and offset, and AL holds the number of the interrupt vector that will point to the handler. Remember that an interrupt routine must end with **IRET** rather than the usual **RET** instruction. (IRET pops three words off the stack — the flag register is included — whereas RET pops only two words. If you attempt to test your handler as an ordinary procedure, but as one ending with IRET, the stack will be thrown off balance.) Note that function 25h automatically disables hardware interrupts when it changes the vector, so there is no danger that a hardware interrupt could break in midway and attempt to use the vector.

```
;---TO SET UP THE INTERRUPT:
        push  ds                    ;save DS
        mov   dx,offset ROUTINE     ;offset of the int routine in DX
        mov   ax,seg ROUTINE        ;segment of the interrupt routine
        mov   ds,ax                 ;place in DS
        mov   ah,25h                ;function to set up a vector
        mov   al,60h                ;the vector number (INT 60h)
        int   21h                   ;change the interrupt
        pop   ds                    ;restore DS


;---THE INTERRUPT ROUTINE:
ROUTINE                     proc far
        push ax                     ;save all changed registers
          .
          .
          .
        pop   ax                    ;restore all changed registers
        mov   al,20h                ;these two lines for
        out   20h,al                ;  hardware interrupts only
        iret
ROUTINE     endp
```

As the example shows, you should place the following two lines of code at the end of any hardware interrupts you write:

```
mov  al,20h
out  20h,al
```

It is coincidental that the numbers (20h) are the same in the two lines. If a hardware interrupt does not end with this code, the 8259 chip will not clear its *in service register* so that it reenables interrupts at lower levels than the one just completed. Failure to add this code can easily crash a program, since the keyboard interrupt is likely to be shut out (even Ctrl-Alt-Del will be useless). Note that this code is not required by handlers that add extensions to existing hardware interrupts, such as those that use vector 1Ch to chain into the time-of-day interrupt (discussed in Chapter 5, "Set/Read the BIOS Time-of-Day Count").

When a program ends, the original interrupt vectors should be restored. Otherwise a subsequent program may call the interrupt and jump to a place in memory where your routine no longer resides. Function 35 of INT 21h returns the current value of a vector, placing the segment value in ES and the offset in BX. Before setting up your own interrupt, use this function to fetch the current vector, save the value, and then restore it using function 25h (as above) just before terminating your program. For example:

```
;---IN THE DATA SEGMENT:

KEEP_CS   dw   0           ;holds segment for replaced inter-
rupt

KEEP_IP   dw   0           ;holds offset for replaced interrupt


;---AT THE BEGINNING OF THE PROGRAM:
      mov  ah,35h          ;function number to get vector
      mov  al,1Ch          ;number of the vector (the timer
INT)
      int  21h             ;now segment is in ES, offset in BX
      mov  KEEP_IP,bx       ;store offset
      mov  KEEP_CS,es       ;store segment


;---AT THE END OF THE PROGRAM:
      push ds              ;preserve DS
      mov  dx,KEEP_IP       ;prepare to restore offset
      mov  ax,KEEP_CS       ;
```

```
        mov   ds,ax        ;prepare to restore segment
        mov   ah,25h       ;function to set an interrupt vector
        mov   al,1Ch       ;number of the vector
        int   21h          ;now the interrupt vector is reset
        pop   ds           ;restore DS
```

There are a couple of pitfalls to look out for when you write an interrupt service routine. If the new interrupt routine needs to access variables it declares, take care that DS is properly set. Set up a stack segment if the interrupt makes heavy demand on the stack, lest it overwhelm the stacks provided by the programs it interrupts. And, finally, remember to include code in your Ctrl-Break or Critical-Error exit procedures to restore vectors.

Chain into Existing Interrupts

There are occasions when a program must *chain* into an interrupt vector. The program redirects the vector so that, when the corresponding interrupt occurs, control transfers to your routine instead of the original interrupt service routine. At some point during the execution of your routine, the routine calls the original ISR, *chaining* into it. One routine after another can chain into an interrupt vector in this way.

The easiest way to call the displaced interrupt service routine is by a *far* CALL instruction. This instruction pushes a segment and offset onto the stack because there will be a *far* return instruction at the end of the routine it calls. However, the original interrupt service routine ends with an IRET instruction, which pops an offset, a segment, and a flag register from the stack. To keep the stack in balance, you must push the flag register onto the stack with a PUSHF instruction just before executing the CALL instruction.

The CALL instruction uses a *dword ptr* (double word pointer) directed to the original ISR. This pointer is stored in memory and the CALL instruction must be able to find it when the procedure in which it resides is activated. In many cases, particularly with memory-resident programs, there is no way of knowing the offset of this pointer relative to DS, ES, of the stack segment. And so it is best to place it relative to CS, as in the example below.

The example below sets up a routine that chains into the BIOS keyboard interrupt, INT 16H. In this case, the BIOS ISR is called immediately upon entry to the new service routine. The new routine can then examine the results returned by the BIOS ISR, such as key codes, and alter them as it sees fit. The BIOS ISR could just as well be called *after* the new routine finishes its work. For example, a new function could be added to the interrupt, say, function 7. On entry, the new routine would examine AH for the number 7 and execute a special routine if it finds this value. In this case, it would not bother to call the BIOS routine, but would return its own function results instead.

You must take great care to see that all significant registers are preserved. For example, interrupt 16h both receives and returns values in AX, and the code used by your routine must not alter these values (unless this is the routine's purpose). Be sure to save the flag register also. Survey an interrupt's documentation to find out the input and return registers for *all* functions of the interrupt.

Finally, be sure to restore the original interrupt vector if your program is not going to remain memory-resident. Keep this in mind when designing Ctrl-Break or critical-error exit routines.

Assembler

Here is the new routine that is chained into the interrupt vector:

```
the_routine  proc  far
        pushf                           ;get ready to call the chained interrupt
        call    dword ptr cs:keep_ofs   ;call the chained interrupt
        push    ax                      ;save return values
        push    bx                      ;
        pushf                           ;save return flags also
        .                               ;
        .                               ;
        .                               ;your routine now does its work
        .                               ;
        .                               ;
        popf                            ;restore BIOS function's return flags
        pop     bx                      ;restore BIOS function's return values
        pop     ax                      ;
        iret                            ;terminate as an ordinary ISR
keep_ofs        dw ?                    ;storage for chained interrupt's offset
keep_seg        dw ?                    ;storage for chained interrupt's segment
the_routine  endp
```

This procedure installs the new routine:

```
install_routine     proc
        mov     ah,35h                  ;function to fetch interrupt vector
        mov     al,16h                  ;will chain into INT 16h (BIOS keyboard)
        int     21h                     ;fetch the vector
        mov     keep_seg,es             ;save the segment
        mov     keep_ofs,bx             ;save the offset
        mov     ax,seg the_routine      ;point DS:DX to the_routine
        mov     ds,ax                   ;
```

```
        mov    dx,offset the_routine
        mov    ah,25h          ;function to set interrupt vector
        mov    al,16h          ;will replace vector for INT 16h
        int    21h             ;replace the vector
        ret                    ;
install_routine    endp
```

Finally, this routine restores the original interrupt vector:

```
deinstall_routine    proc
        mov    ax,keep_seg     ;point DS:DX to the original INT 16h
        mov    ds,ax           ;
        mov    dx,keep_ofs     ;
        mov    ah,25h          ;function to set interrupt vector
        mov    al,16h          ;will restore INT 16h vector
        int    21h             ;restore the vector
        ret                    ;
deinstall_routine    endp
```

5

Clocks and Timers

- Minitutorial: How PCs Measure Time
- Program a Timer Chip
- Set/Read the BIOS Time-of-Day Count
- Set/Read the Time
- Set/Read the Date
- Set/Read the Real-Time Clock
- Time or Delay Program Operations
- Control Real-Time Operations

Minitutorial: How PCs Measure Time

PCs keep track of time in two ways. First, all PCs have a timer chip that is initialized to pulse roughly 18.2 times per second. These pulses are tallied by the operating system to form the *BIOS time-of-day count*, a four-byte value held in the BIOS data area at 0040:006C.

Timer chips pulse at the same rate in all machines, no matter how fast the machine's processor runs. The rate deviates only when software has reprogrammed the timer chip, or when someone has changed the computer's clock crystal to make the machine run faster. Whenever the timer chip pulses, the *timer interrupt* is invoked to increment the time-of-day count. The chip operates independently of the main processor, and it keeps its beat no matter what else happens in the computer. However, software can temporarily disable the timer interrupt and throw off the time-of-day count.

The second way PCs measure time is by a *real-time clock*—a clock that counts hours, minutes, and seconds. A PC's real-time clock is powered by a battery, so it keeps on running when the machine is turned off. Of course, just like a wristwatch, a real-time clock can be set to the wrong time, and it is not perfectly accurate and gradually deviates from the actual time.

When a PC is booted, DOS reads the time from the machine's real-time clock and converts the values it finds into the BIOS time-of-day reading. A setting of 0 corresponds to midnight. Thereafter, the value is incremented 18.2 times per second (which is to say that it increases by 182 in ten seconds). When DOS needs to know the time, it converts the time-of-day count back to the hour/minutes/seconds format.

PC- and XT-type machines do not have built-in real-time clocks, although many machines have a clock installed on an expansion card. When no clock is available, DOS prompts the user to input the time when the machine boots. However, this information is not requested when an AUTOEXEC.BAT file is used, as is normally the case. In this instance, DOS simply initializes the BIOS time-of-day count to 0. Software can easily change the time-of-day count, although this is seldom advisable.

At boot time, DOS also obtains the current date from the computer's real-time clock, or by prompting the user, and stores it in a variable. This value is updated after the time-of-day passes midnight. At that time the BIOS sets a flag — the "midnight flag." Certain DOS functions watch the flag, waiting for it to change. Be aware that two BIOS functions — functions 0 and 1 of interrupt 1Ah — clear the flag. If they are called after the flag is set and before DOS detects the change, DOS will miss the date change.

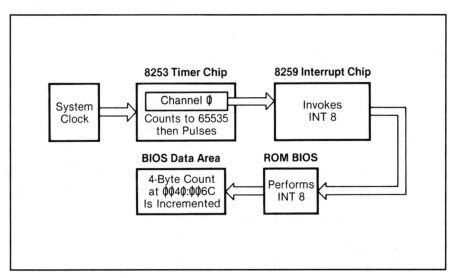

Figure 5-1   Updating the BIOS time-of-day count

Program a Timer Chip

All PCs use a variant of the Intel 8253 timer chip to time certain operations. Early PCs used a three-channel chip; later models employ a timer chip that has a fourth channel. Each channel is accessed through its own port address, numbered 40h, 41h, 42h, and 44h. A channel consists of three registers, all of which are accessed through the same port. Each channel has an eight-bit I/O register that sends and receives data. Generally speaking, when a channel is programmed, a two-byte value is sent through its port, low byte first. The number is passed to a 16-bit *latch register*, which keeps the number, and from there a copy is placed in a 16-bit *counter register*. In the counter register, the number decrements by 1 each time a pulse from the system clock enters the channel. When the number reaches zero, the channel issues an output pulse and then a new copy of the latch register's number is moved into the counter register and the process repeats. The smaller the number in the counter register, the faster the channel counts down and pulses. The current value of any counter register may be read at any time without disturbing the count. All channels are always active.

Each channel has two lines going into it, and one line coming out. The *out* line conducts the pulse that occurs when a channel counts down to zero. These pulses initiate different kinds of activity in the machine. Here are the roles for the channels:

Channel 0 is used by the BIOS time-of-day clock. It is initialized at start-up so that it issues a pulse roughly 18.2 times a second. A four-byte tally of these pulses is kept in memory at 0040:006C. Each pulse invokes the timer interrupt (INT 8); it is this interrupt that increments the tally. This is a *hardware* interrupt, and so it continues to occur no matter what the CPU is doing, so long as hardware interrupts are enabled. Diskette drives use this channel to time the period between finishing drive operations and turning off the drive motor. In addition, software other than your own may expect this channel to pulse at the standard rate. So you should avoid reprogramming the channel unless you have a compelling reason to do so, and then only for short periods.

Channel 1 controls memory refresh. Dynamic RAM chips use capacitors that gradually lose their charge. The chips must be constantly recharged ("refreshed") or they will lose the data they hold. Each pulse from this channel triggers the refresh logic. This channel should never be tampered with. In fact, PS/2 machines are designed in a way that the channel cannot be reprogrammed by software.

Channel 2 is connected to the computer's speaker, and it produces simple square-wave signals for making sound. Simple tones may be made to occur simultaneously with other program operations, or more complex sounds can be produced with the full attention of the CPU. Channel 2 may also be disconnected from the speaker and used for timing operations.

119

Channel 3 is the *watchdog timer.* It sees to it that no software running in the machine is allowed to shut out interrupts for too long. The timer interrupt constantly resets this channel so that the channel normally does not count down to zero. When the timer interrupt is shut out for too long, the channel counts to zero and issues a nonmaskable interrupt that can be used by operating systems to retake control of the machine. This feature is implemented only on 386-based systems.

The two lines going into each channel consist of a *clock* line that feeds the system clock signal from the system clock chip, and a line called the *gate* that can shut out the system clock signal. Except in Channel 2, the gate is always open for the clock signal. On Channel 2, the gate can be opened and closed; this feature lets you program sound. The Channel 2 gate is closed by setting the lowest bit at port address 61h; changing the bit back to 0 reopens the gate. Figure 5-2 diagrams a timer chip.

Because its channels time very short intervals, a timer chip is seldom useful for timing program operations. The chip receives 1.19318 million pulses per second from the system, and its channels count down at this rate. Because the largest number held by 16 bits is 65,535, and because that number divides into the clock pulse rate 18.2 times, the longest possible period between pulses is scarcely a twentieth of a second. Most timing operations instead use the BIOS time-of-day count, which tallies these eighteenth-second units. An interval is timed by reading the time-of-day value and comparing it to some earlier reference value to see how many pulses have passed. Interrupt-driven techniques described later in this chapter use the time-of-day count for *real-time* operations.

Timer chips offer six modes of operation for each channel. Programmers ordinarily confine themselves to mode 3. In this mode, once a latch register is given a number, it immediately loads a copy into the counter register. When the number reaches 0, the latch instantly reloads the counter, and so on. During half of the count the *out* line is "on" and during half it is "off." The result is a square wave pattern that is equally useful for making sound and for counting.

An eight-bit *command register* controls how a number is loaded into any of the three or four channels. This register is located at port address 43h. The command register is sent a byte that tells which channel to program, in what mode, and whether one or both of the bytes of the latch will be sent a number. It also shows whether the number will be in binary or BCD (binary coded decimal) form. The bit pattern is as follows:

```
bits        0     if 0, binary data, else BCD

          1-3     mode number, 0-5

          4-5     kind of operation:

           00 =   move counter value into latch

           01 =   read/write high byte only
```

```
        10 = read/write low byte only
        11 = read/write high byte, then low byte
6-7    number of channel to program 0-3
```

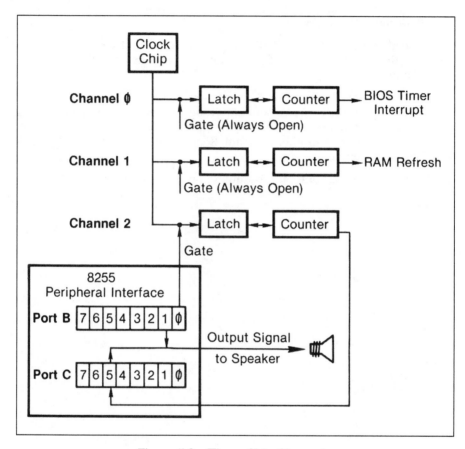

Figure 5-2   Timer Chip Channels

In summary, here are the three steps for programming a channel. Once step 3 is completed, the programmed channel immediately begins to function at the new setting.

(1) Send a byte to the command register (43h) that holds the bit pattern that selects the channel, the read/write status, the mode of operation, and the numerical type.

(2) If Channel 2, enable the clock signal by setting bit 0 at port address 61h. (When bit 1 of this register is set, Channel 2 drives the speaker. Set it to 0 for timing operations.)

(3) Calculate a counter from 0–65535, place it in AX, and send the low byte and then the high byte to the channel's I/O register (42h for the sound channel).

Because the timer channels are never at rest, programs should restore the original settings of the registers before quitting. Remember that if sound is in progress when a program terminates, the sound will continue even after DOS takes control and loads another program. Keep this in mind when designing a Ctrl-Break exit routine.

See Chapter 6, "Play a Tone," for examples of programming a timer chip.

Set/Read the BIOS Time-of-Day Count

At start-up, DOS consults the computer's real-time clock (or queries the computer user) to learn the time of day. This value is converted into the number of seconds that have passed since midnight. It is then multiplied by 18.2068 so that it corresponds to the number of times the computer's timer chip would have pulsed during the same time period. This value is stored in four bytes starting at 0040:006C. The figure 18.2068 results from dividing the timer chip clock rate (1,193,180 pulses per second) by the maximum timer divisor (65,535).

Any program can read the time-of-day value directly from memory, although it is considered good programming practice to use an interrupt for this purpose. This is interrupt 1Ah, which is devoted to setting and reading the time in various ways. Function 0 causes the interrupt to return the time-of-day reading, and function 1 causes the interrupt to set the time-of-day. In either case, the two high bytes of the reading go in CX and the two low bytes in DX. Changing the time-of-day count has no effect on the current real-time clock settings. Remember that if you change this value, DOS will report an incorrect time-of-day to software, and will use incorrect values when it time-stamps files.

In addition to the time-of-day reading, function 0 of interrupt 1Ah also returns (in AL) a flag telling whether midnight has passed since the reading was first set. There is no way of finding out whether more than one midnight has passed. The midnight flag is reset when this function is called.

DOS uses the midnight flag to update its calender settings. Certain DOS functions check the flag when they are called. If your software happens to call interrupt 1Ah *after* midnight but *before* DOS checks the flag, the flag will be reset and DOS will miss the passage of a day. This design flaw is not significant in machines that are turned on and off each day. But machines that run continuously can end up placing inaccurate date stamps on files, and so on. For this reason, it's a good idea to avoid interrupt 1Ah and read the time-of-day count directly from memory. For the sake of completeness, the examples below show how to access this interrupt in any of the four languages. But in most cases it's wiser to go straight to memory for the timer count.

BASIC

BASIC's *TIMER* function returns the time-of-day count as a floating-point value that reports the value in seconds. Don't be fooled by the apparent high accuracy of the numbers it returns. They may appear to measure time in thousandths of a second, but the real accuracy is no better than that of the time-of-day clock. To learn the current reading:

```
      TimeOfDayCount = TIMER
```

There is no companion routine to set the count. If you must change the count, you can use BASIC's *Interrupt* routine to call function 1 of interrupt &H1A (Chapter 4, "Call Interrupts from BASIC, Pascal, and C," explains how it works). To set the count to midnight:

```
 ' $INCLUDE: 'QBX.BI'
 DIM regs AS RegType       ' Define the processor registers


 regs.ax = &H0100          ' place &H01 in AH
 regs.cx = &H0000          ' the new reading goes in DX:CX
 regs.dx = &H0000          '
 CALL Interrupt(&H1A, regs, regs)   ' set the time-of-day
```

Pascal

Turbo Pascal has no facilities for accessing the time-of-day count. But you can use the *Intr* procedure to call interrupt $1A. Because the interrupt returns a 32-bit value in two 16-bit registers, you need to assemble the two parts into a long value by using a shift instruction.

```
uses dos.h
Regs: Registers              {declare the processor registers}
CurrentTime: longint;
MidnightFlag: byte;


Regs.ah := 0;                {function to read time-of-day count}
Intr($1A,Regs);
CurrentTime := Regs.cx;
CurrentTime := CurrentTime shl 16; {shift high word up 16 bits}
CurrentTime := CurrentTime + Regs.dx;
MidnightFlag := Regs.al;
```

To set the time-of-day count to midnight:

```
Regs.ah := 1;              {function to set time-of-day count}

Regs.cx := 0;              {CX:DX equals 0 for midnight}

Regs.dx := 0;

Intr($1A,Regs);            {Set the time-of-day}
```

C

Both Borland's C and Microsoft's C provide functions that return the time-of-day reading or set it, but the functions have different names and work differently. In Borland's C, the function is called *biostime*. It takes two parameters, the first of which is either **0** when you want to read the time, or **1** when you want to set it. The second parameter is a *long* value that holds the new time-of-day count when it is set. This second parameter is ignored when you read the time-of-day, so you can write any value in its place. In this case, the function returns the count as a *long* value. To read the time-of-day:

```
#include <bios.h>


long  current_time;

current_time = biostime(0,0L);
```

To set the time-of-day to midnight:

```
current_time = 0;

biostime(1,current_time);
```

Microsoft's C provides the *_bios_timeofday* function for this purpose. It takes the same parameters as Borland's C, but when it returns the time, it places it in whatever variable was specified as the second parameter. In this case, the function also returns an unsigned value telling the status of the midnight flag. To read the time-of-day:

```
#include <bios.h>


long  current_time;

unsigned  midnight_flag;


midnight_flag = _bios_timeofday(0,current_time);
```

To set the time-of-day to midnight:

```
current_time = 0;
_bios_timeofday(1,current_time);
```

Assembler

To fetch the current time-of-day count:

```
mov   ah,0     ;function to read the count
int   1Ah      ;call the interrupt
               ;now CX:DX holds the count
               ;and AL holds the midnight flag
```

To set the time-of-day to midnight:

```
mov   ah,1     ;function to set the count
sub   cx,cx    ;clear CX
mov   cx,dx    ;now DX:CX = 0
int   1Ah      ;set the count
```

Set/Read the Time

When a PC starts running, it fetches the time from its real-time clock and converts it into the BIOS time-of-day count discussed in the *minitutorial* at the start of this chapter. Thereafter, whenever DOS needs to know the time, it converts the current time-of-day reading back to hours, minutes, and seconds.

When a PC user sets the time with the DOS *TIME* command, both the real-time clock and the BIOS time-of-day reading are reset. However, early PCs that used the 8088 processor did not have a built-in real-time clock. While many of these machines have a real-time clock installed through an expansion slot, the clock must be read and set by utility software, not by DOS. In these machines, the DOS *TIME* command only changes the time-of-day reading.

BASIC

BASIC's *TIME$* function sets and retrieves the time as a string variable that uses the format **hh:mm:ss**, with the hours counted from 0 to 23, starting from midnight. The value for hours is always given as two bytes, with a leading zero if one is required. For 5:10 PM:

```
TIME$ = "17:10:00"          'set the time

PRINT "The time is ",TIME$   'display the time
```

Use the *MID$*, *LEFT$*, and *RIGHT$* functions to isolate a part of the string. Then convert the substrings to numeric form with *VAL*. Conversely, you can use the *STR$* function to convert numeric values into substrings. These may then be combined into a string that *TIME$* can use to set the time.

Pascal

The Turbo Pascal *GetTIme* and *SetTIme* procedures get and set the time. Both functions take the same four *word*-length parameters: hours, minutes, seconds, and hundredths of a second. For *GetTIme*, the parameters must be variables so that the function has a place to return the information. The hour of the day is counted from 0 to 23, with 0 as midnight. Minutes and seconds are counted from 0 to 59, and hundredths of a second from 0 to 99. Begin by initializing the parameters:

```
Var

Hours,Minutes,Seconds,Hundredths : word;
```

127

To set the time to 7:21 in the evening:

```
Hours := 19;

Minutes := 21;

Seconds := 0;

Hundredths  := 0;

SetTime(Hours,Minutes,Seconds,Hundredths);
```

To display the time:

```
GetTime(Hours,Minutes,Seconds,Hundredths);

Writeln("The time is ",Hours,":",Minutes,":",Seconds);
```

C

Borland's C uses the *gettime* and *settime* functions, and Microsoft's C uses the *_dos_gettime* and *_dos_settime* functions, to get and set the time. All four take a single parameter: a pointer to a structure that is declared in *dos.h*. This structure is named *time* in Borland's C and *dostime_t* in Microsoft's C. Here is the structure in the Borland compilers:

```
struct time

{

 unsigned char ti_min;          /* minutes */

 unsigned char ti_hour;         /* hour of the day */

 unsigned char ti_hund;         /* hundredths of a second */

 unsigned char ti_sec;          /* seconds */

};
```

And here is the structure in the Microsoft compilers:

```
struct dostime_t

{

 unsigned char hour;            /* hour of the day */

 unsigned char minute;          /* minutes */

 unsigned char second;          /* seconds */
```

```
        unsigned char hsecond;      /* hundredths of a second */
  };
```

This example uses Borland's C to read the time and then set the hour of the day to noon.

```
#include <dos.h>


struct time time_struct;


gettime(&time_struct);
time_struct.ti_hour = 12;
time_struct.ti_min = 0;
  settime(&time_struct);
```

Assembler

DOS interrupts nominally set the time with an accuracy of 100ths of a second. But the time-of-day count in which the time is stored is updated at only a fifth this rate, so the 100ths-second reading is really only an approximation. Function 2Ch of INT 21h retrieves the time, and function 2Dh sets it. In both cases, CH holds the hour (0-23, where 0 = midnight), CL holds minutes (0-59), DH holds seconds (0-59), and DL holds "hundredth-seconds" (0-99). When you set the time, AL returns 0 when the input values were in range and the time could be set, or FFh otherwise. AL does not return an error code when you retrieve the time, since nothing can go wrong.

```
;---TO RETRIEVE THE TIME:
        mov   ah,2Ch              ;function number for get time
        int   21h                ;get the time
        mov   HOURS,ch           ;move hours reading to a variable


;---TO SET THE TIME:
        mov   ch,HOURS           ;enter the time values
        mov   cl,MINUTES         ;
        mov   dh,SECONDS         ;
```

```
mov  dl,HUNDREDTHS    ;
mov  ah,2Dh           ;function number for set time
int  21h              ;sets the time
cmp  al,0FFh          ;check that time value was correct
je   ERROR            ;go to error routine if not
```

Set/Read the Date

Like the time, the current date is read from the computer's real-time clock when the computer boots. The value is stored in memory and updated by DOS after the BIOS time-of-day count passes midnight. Be aware that calling functions 0 or 1 of interrupt 1Ah, which, respectively, read and set the time-of-day count, can cause DOS to fail to update its date reading (as explained in this chapter's *minitutorial*).

BASIC

DATE$ sets or retrieves the date as a string in the format mm-dd-yyyy. You may use slashes instead of dashes, and the first two digits of the year may be omitted. For June 21, 1992:

```
DATE$ = "06/21/92"          'set the date


PRINT "The data is ",DATE$ 'display the date
```

Use BASIC's *MID$*, *LEFT$*, and *RIGHT$* functions to obtain any part of the string returned by *DATE$*. *VAL* converts strings to numeric form, and *STR$* does the reverse.

Pascal

Turbo Pascal provides the *GetDate* and *SetDate* procedures. Years are counted from 1980 to 2099, months from 1 to 12, and the day of the month from 1 to 31. The parameters are listed in this order. For *GetDate*, the parameters must be variables, and there is a fourth parameter that returns the day of the week as well, counted from 0 to 6, with 0 corresponding to Sunday. First initialize the parameters:

```
var TheYear, TheMonth, TheDay, TheDayOfWeek : word;
```

To set the date to June 21, 1991:

```
TheYear := 1991;
TheMonth := 6;
TheDay := 21;
SetDate(TheYear, TheMonth, TheDay);
```

To display the day of the week:

```
GetDate(TheYear,TheMonth,TheDay,TheDayOfWeek);

Write('Today is ',TheDayOfWeek);
```

C

The Borland C compilers use the *getdate* and *setdate* functions to get and set the date. Microsoft uses similar functions named *_dos_getdate* and *_dos_setdate*. All four functions use a structure defined *dos.h*. The structure is named *date* in Borland's C and *dosdate_t* in Microsoft's C. A pointer to this structure is the only parameter the functions require. Here is the structure in Borland's C:

```
struct date
{
  int  da_year;   /* year */
  int  da_day;    /* day of the month */
  int  da_mon;    /* month */
};
```

And here is the structure in Microsoft's C:

```
struct dosdate_t
{
  unsigned char day;        /* day of the month */
  unsigned char month;      /* month */
  unsigned int year;        /* year */
  unsigned char dayofweek;  /* day of the week */
};
```

The *_dos_setdate* function returns 0 when the function has been able to set the time; otherwise it returns a nonzero value. None of the other functions return error codes. In this example, which uses Borland's C, the current year is displayed and then the date is set to June 21, 1992:

```
#include <dos.h>

struct date date_struct;
getdate(&date_struct);
```

```
printf("The year is %d",date_struct.da_year);
```

```
date_struct.da_day = 21;

date_struct.da_mon = 6;

date_struct.da_year = 1992;

  setdate(&date_struct);
```

Assembler

Functions 2Ah and 2Bh of DOS interrupt 21h get and set the date. To find out the date, place 2Ah in AH and execute the interrupt. On return, CX contains the year as a number from 1980–2099. DH holds the number of the month, and DL holds the day. In addition, AL reports the day of the week, counted from 0 to 6, with Sunday as 0.

```
mov   ah,2Ah            ;function number to retrieve date

int   21h               ;get the date

mov   DAY,dl            ;day returned in DL

mov   DAYOFWEEK,al      ;day of week returned in AL

mov   MONTH,dh          ;month returned in DH

mov   YEAR,cx           ;year returned in CX
```

To set the date, place the day, month, and year in the same registers and execute function 2Bh. If the values for the date are invalid, AL returns FF; otherwise it returns 0.

```
mov   dl,DAY            ;place day in DL

mov   dh,MONTH          ;place month in DH

mov   cx,YEAR           ;place year (eg. 1985) in CX

mov   ah,2Bh            ;function number to set date

int   21h               ;set the date

cmp   al,0FFh           ;check if operation successful

je    ERROR             ;date out of range, go to error routine
```

Set/Read the Real-Time Clock

A real-time clock (RTC) uses an independent processor to count the time without interference from other computer operations. It also has a battery power supply that keeps it running when the computer is turned off. When the machine starts up, the operating system reads the real-time clock and converts its time reading into the BIOS time-of-day reading that is discussed in "Set/Read the BIOS Time-of-Day Count," above. At that time, DOS also reads the current data from the clock and stores it in internal variables. Thereafter, DOS uses these values when it needs to know the time or date; it does not read the real-time clock again until the machine is restarted. Software can change the real-time clock settings, but the time-of-day reading will not be automatically updated when this occurs, and the DOS time and date readings will not match the real-time clock settings.

Real-time clocks became standard in PCs with the advent of the IBM AT. Prior to that, PCs could have a real-time clock installed on an expansion board, but they would require that special utility software be called from the machine's AUTOEXEC.BAT file to initialize the time-of-day reading.

Because PC- and XT-style machines lack a built-in real-time clock, no provision was made in the BIOS to support the clock. Starting with the AT, BIOS interrupt 1Ah was expanded to set and read the real-time clock. Because the readings are never more than two decimal digits, the time values are given in binary coded decimal (BCD) format in which a byte is divided in half, with each half holding a decimal digit from 0 to 9.

On all IBM machines, functions 0 and 1 of interrupt 1Ah read and set the BIOS time-of-day count. Six additional functions were added to service the real-time clock:

```
    Function 2:     Read the time from the real-time clock
    On return: CH = hours in BCD

               CL = minutes in BCD

               DH = seconds in BCD

    Function 3:     Set the time on the real-time clock
    On entry:  CH = hours in BCD

               CL = minutes in BCD

               DH = seconds in BCD

               DL = 0 if daylight savings, else 1
    Function 4:     Read the date from the real-time clock
```

On return: CH = century in BCD (19 or 20)

CL = year in BCD (offset from 1980)

DH = month in BCD

DL = day of month in BCD

Function 5:   Set the date on the real-time clock

On entry: CH = century in BCD (19 or 20)

CL = year in BCD (offset from 1980)

DH = month in BCD

DL = day of month in BCD

Function 6:   Set the alarm on the real-time clock

On entry: CH = hours in BCD

CL = minutes in BCD

DH = seconds in BCD

Function 7:   Reset the alarm

(no input registers)

The "alarm" is an interrupt that is invoked at the specified time. The setting is made as an offset from the time the setting is made. The maximum period is 23:59:59. Interrupt vector 4Ah is pointed to the alarm routine. Note that if the clock is not operating (most probably as the result of a dead battery) then functions 2, 4, and 6 set the carry flag.

None of the compilers discussed in this book provide routines for reading the real-time clock directly. Instead, the functions discussed in "Set/Read the Time," above, work through DOS and operate only on the BIOS time-of-day reading. To access the clock directly, you'll need to call interrupt 1Ah. The examples below find out the time by calling function 2 of this interrupt.

BASIC

```
' $INCLUDE: 'QBX.BI'
DIM REGS AS RegType     ' Define register array


REGS.AX = &H0200     'function to read the time
CALL Interrupt(&H1A, REGS, REGS)
```

```
TheTime = REGS.CX        'CH = hour, CL = minutes
TheHour = TheTime \256 'clear CL, shift down CH
WRITE((TheHour\16)*10) + (TheHour AND &HF)
```

Pascal

```
Uses DOS;

Var

   Regs: Registers;   {Registers type is declared in the DOS unit}
   Hour: byte;


Regs.AH := 2;        {function to read the time}
Intr($1A,Regs);      {Call the interrupt}
Hour := Regs.CH;     {get the hour}
 Writeln('The hour is ',(Hour Shr 4 * 10)+(Hour and $F));
```

C

```
#include <dos.h>

 union REGS regs;                  /* declare the register array */
 char hour


 regs.h.ah = 2;                    /* function to read the time */
 int86(0x1A,&regs,&regs);
 hour = regs.h.ch;     /* save the hour reading */
 printf("The hour is %d",((hour >> 4)*10)+(hour & 0xF));
```

Assembler

```
;---READ THE TIME FROM THE REAL-TIME CLOCK:
    mov   ah,2                  ;function number
    int   1Ah                   ;call the BIOS time interrupt
    mov   THE_HOUR,ch           ;save the hour reading(BCD)
    mov   THE_MINUTES,cl        ;save the minutes reading(BCD)
```

Low-Level Access

A real-time clock is accessed through the same port addresses in both AT-style machines and PS/2 machines. The clock uses 14 registers:

register number	function
00h	Seconds
01	Seconds alarm
02	Minutes
03	Minutes alarm
04	Hours
05	Hours alarm
06	Day of the week
07	Day of the month
08	Month
09	Year
0A	Status register A
0B	Status register B
0C	Status register C
0D	Status register D

The registers are accessed by first sending a register number to port address 70h and then reading the register value from 71h. Bits in the four status registers perform various functions, of which only the following are of much concern to programmers:

Register A:

    bit 7   1 = time update in progress (wait

               until 0 before reading)

Register B:

    bit 6   1 = *periodic* interrupt is enabled

       5   1 = *alarm* interrupt is enabled

       4   1 = *update-ended* interrupt is enabled

       1   1 = hours counted by 24, 0 = counted by 12

       0   1 = daylight savings time enabled

Note that the interrupt handler pointed to by interrupt vector 4Ah can be invoked in three ways, all of which are disabled at start-up. The *periodic* interrupt occurs at regular intervals. The period is initialized to roughly one millisecond. The *alarm* interrupt occurs when the settings in the three alarm-related registers match their corresponding timing registers. The update-ended interrupt occurs after every update of the register settings on the chip. See Chapter 4, "Write Your Own Interrupt Service Routine," to learn how to write an interrupt service routine that can use these features.

Time or Delay Program Operations

A program times operations exactly as people do: It takes an initial reading of the time and later compares it to a subsequent reading. The readings can be taken in hours-minutes-seconds format, but it is unwieldly to calculate the difference between two such readings because the counting system is not decimal. Instead, programs normally consult the BIOS time-of-day reading, which gives the time as a single integer. Once a program has obtained the difference between the beginning and ending times, it divides the value by 18.2 to obtain the number of seconds that have passed.

The time-of-day reading is also used to delay program operations for a specified period. The number of seconds of delay is multiplied by 18.2, and the resulting value is added to an initial time-of-day reading. Then the program continually reads the time-of-day and compares it to the value it has calculated. When the values match, the delay is complete.

Compiler functions in Pascal and C provide delays accurate to 1 millisecond. This is achieved by calibrating a software loop against the BIOS time-of-day reading. By determining that the loop is executed n times between increments of the BIOS clock, the compiler can multiply the result by 18.2 and then divide it by 1000 to calculate how many passes through the loop equal a thousandth of a second. Any program can set up code to obtain this level of accuracy.

The four bytes that hold the time-of-day count start at 0040:006C. Timings or delays under 14 seconds can be made by reading the lowest byte alone. The lowest two bytes can time up to an hour (actually, one second short of an hour). In these cases, be sure to allow for a "turnover" condition in which the initial reading is higher than the second reading.

Rather than access the BIOS data area directly, you can call interrupt 1Ah with the AH register set to 0 to fetch the time-of-day value. The interrupt returns the time-of-day count in the CX and DX registers (with the low part of the value in DX). As this chapter's *minitutorial* explains, using this function can cause DOS to lose track of the correct date, and so direct access to the time-of-day count is preferred.

BASIC

Use BASIC's *TIMER* function to time or delay program operations. It returns the time-of-day count as a floating point value giving the number of seconds that have passed since midnight (assuming the count has been initialized to the correct value). You can measure fractions of a second with this function, but remember that the values returned by *TIMER* are no more accurate than the time-of-day reading. To take a reading:

```
TimeReading = TIMER
```

Pascal

Turbo Pascal's *Delay* procedure causes a delay that is measured in thousandths of a second. To delay for one half second (500 milliseconds), write:

```
Delay(500);
```

Delay cannot be used to time program operations. Instead, the BIOS time-of-day must be read at the beginning and conclusion of the timed period. "Set/Read the BIOS Time-of-Day Count," above, shows how.

C

Borland's C provides the *delay* function for program delays. It's only parameter is the number of milliseconds the delay should last. For a half-second delay, you would write:

```
delay(500);
```

The Microsoft C compilers do not offer a *delay* function. However, you can readily apply the *_bios_timeofday* function to make delays. Use the same function for timing operations (or the equivalent function in the Borland compilers — *biostime*). "Set/Read the BIOS Time-of-Day Count," above, gives examples of how these functions are used.

Assembler

This example makes a five-second delay. Note that only the least significant byte of the time-of-day count is used. The value 91 (5 * 18.2) is added to the initial reading.

```
;---TAKE THE INITIAL TIME-OF-DAY READING:
        mov  ax,40h        ;segment of BIOS data
        mov  es,ax         ;point ES to it
        mov  dl,es:[6Ch]   ;get the count (low byte to DL)
        add  dl,91         ;add the time offset
;---LOOP UNTIL THE DELAY IS OVER:
```

```
TRYAGAIN:

      cmp  dl,es:[6Ch]   ;is it time yet?

      jne  TRYAGAIN      ;loop if not
```

The loop continues until the value at 40:006Ch exactly equals the first reading. If a lengthy interrupt or a memory-resident program breaks in during the loop, the BIOS count may have passed the target value when control is returned to your code. This situation is usually not serious when only the low byte of the count is used, but when two bytes are used, it would take an hour for the correct count to come up again. Be careful.

As a second example, here is code that times a program operation. The example assumes that the timed interval will be under one hour, and so only the low two bytes of the time-of-day count are used.

```
;---IN THE DATA SEGMENT:

STARTTIME   dw 0            ;holds initial time-of-day reading

;---GET THE INITIAL TIME-OF-DAY COUNT:

      mov  ah,0             ;set function number

      int  1Ah             ;get the count (low word in DX)

      mov  OLDCOUNT,dx      ;save the initial count

      .

      .  (the timed process moves along)

      .

;---LATER, TO CALCULATE THE ELAPSED TIME:

      mov  ah,0             ;set the function number

      int  1Ah             ;get the count

      mov  bx,OLDCOUNT      ;retrieve the first reading

      cmp  bx,dx           ;check for "turn over"

      jg   ADJUST          ;jump to adjust routine if "turn over"

      sub  dx,bx           ;else, find difference (=elapsed pulses)

      jmp  short FIGURE_TIME ;jmp to time calculation

;---ADJUST FOR TURN OVER:

ADJUST:

      mov  cx,0FFFFh        ;place largest number (65535) in CX
```

```
        sub  cx,bx      ;subtract first reading
        add  dx,cx      ;add second reading, leave elapsed time in DX
        mov  dx,cx      ;as above, leave elapsed time in DX
;---BEGIN TIME CALCULATION ROUTINE:
FIGURE_TIME:            ;now divide DX by 18.2 for seconds
                        ;etc.
```

Control Real-Time Operations

In *real-time* operations, a program executes instructions at specified points in time, rather than as quickly as possible. This technique is often associated with robotics, but it has more mundane applications, as when a communications program "wakes up" and transfers data at a preset time, or a time-scheduling program automatically reminds the computer user of appointments.

Real-time operations are necessarily tied to some kind of clock. As we explained in the *minitutorial* at the beginning of this chapter, most PCs have two kinds of clocks: the BIOS time-of-day clock run by the machine's timer chip, and the computer's real-time clock, which is used to make the initial setting of the BIOS clock when the computer is booted. Because many early PCs lack a true real-time clock, it is best to rely on the time-of-day count.

Real-time programs work in two basic ways. In programs that have little or nothing to do between the real-time instructions, the program merely needs to idle along, doing nothing but checking the BIOS time-of-day count to sense when it is time to become active. This technique is little more than a series of delay loops.

The second approach is more difficult. It is used when a program is constantly busy and the real-time event scheduler needs to interrupt the program at specific times in order to carry out some task. That is done by hooking the scheduler on to the timer interrupt, which normally is executed 18.2 times per second. Each time the interrupt occurs, control is passed to the scheduler and it checks the new value of the time-of-day count, compares it to the time the next event should begin, and then initiates the event if the proper moment has arrived. Otherwise, the routine returns having done nothing. Figure 5-3 illustrates this process.

The timer interrupt is pointed to by interrupt vector 8h. When it occurs, a routine in the BIOS code is executed and it increments the time-of-day count — a four-byte value kept at 0040:006C in the BIOS data area. You may read or change the time-of-day count through interrupt 1Ah, as shown in "Set/Read the BIOS Time-of-Day Count," above, or better, read it directly from memory (interrupt 1Ah can throw off the DOS date reading).

Once the BIOS code has done its work, it calls interrupt 1Ch. The code pointed to by this interrupt vector is executed, then control returns to the timer interrupt, which in turn terminates. Thus, interrupt 1Ch is chained to interrupt 8h. At start-up, interrupt 1Ch points to nothing more than an *IRET* (*Interrupt Return*) instruction, so it does nothing at all until the interrupt vector is redirected. Many programs use this interrupt vector — particularly memory-resident programs — so you should always chain your routine into this vector and not simply replace it. Chapter 4, "Chain Into Existing Interrupts," shows how interrupts are chained.

When timing must be precise, you should keep in mind that the time-of-day clock can miss ticks when the timer interrupt is somehow momentarily prevented from occurring. This may happen when the timer interrupt handler executes code that takes longer to perform than the time between ticks. This should never happen. To avoid it, have the handler set a flag notifying your program that a particular event must be performed. Then let the handler immediately terminate to avoid delaying the timer interrupt. Structured this way, your program must constantly poll the flags and initiate events on the basis of the flag settings.

Even with the best of efforts at keeping the BIOS time-of-day count on target, timing may be thrown off when other programs have chained handlers into the timer interrupt. There is nothing you can do about ill-behaved software that throws off the count. If you are concerned about the accumulation of clock delays, consider having your event scheduler periodically check the machine's real-time clock and readjust the BIOS time-of-day reading, if necessary.

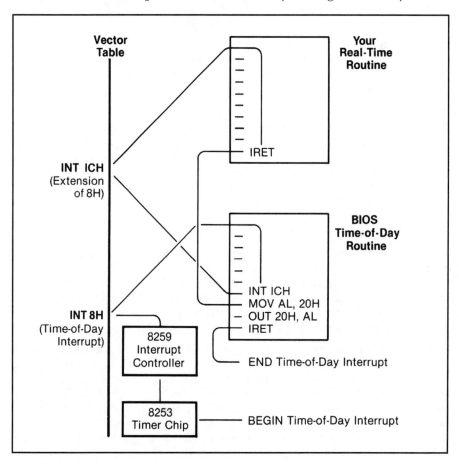

Figure 5-3   Extending the timer interrupt

Only BASIC has built-in support for real-time operations. In Pascal and C, it is your job to point the timer interrupt vector to the event schedule you have devised. Chapter 4, "Write Your Own Interrupt Service Routine," shows how this is done. The BASIC and assembly language examples below create an alarm clock that prints a message when a particular moment arrives. The message is directly displayed by the interrupt handler.

BASIC

BASIC provides primitive control over real-time operations by the **ON TIMER(n) GOSUB** statement. When a program comes upon this statement, it begins to count to the number of seconds given by *n*. Meanwhile, program operations continue. When *n* seconds have passed, the program jumps to the subroutine beginning at the specified line number, performs the subroutine, and then returns to where it left off. The counting then starts anew from 0, and the subroutine will be called again after *n* seconds more.

ON TIMER will not function until it is enabled by a **TIMER ON** statement. It may be disabled by **TIMER OFF**. In cases where the timing should continue but transfer to the subroutine must be delayed, use **TIMER STOP**. In this case it is remembered that *n* seconds have passed, and the program jumps to the subroutine as soon as another *TIMER ON* statement is encountered.

In this example, ON TIMER is used to update a clock on the screen:

```
TIMER ON                        'enable the timer
ON TIMER(60) GOSUB DisplayTime 'change the clock every 60 secs
    .

    .


Displaytime:
LOCATE 1,35:PRINT"TIME: ";LEFT$(TIME$,5) 'print the time
Return
```

Assembler

In the example below, a routine (unshown) requests from the program user a value no larger than 60 for the number of minutes that should pass before an alarm goes off. The number, which is stored in MINUTES, is multiplied by 1092, giving the equivalent in time-of-day pulses that must pass (1092 = 60 seconds * 18.2 pulses per second). The number of pulses is added to a copy of the low word

145

of the current time-of-day reading, which is saved as ALARMCOUNT. A one-hour period fits into 16 bits — longer periods require more complicated 32-bit operations.

Next, the vector for interrupt 1Ch is changed to point to a procedure called ALARM. Remember that once the vector is changed, ALARM will immediately begin to be invoked 18.2 times a second. When it is called, it fetches the current time-of-day reading via interrupt 1Ah and compares the value to ALARMCOUNT. If the two values match, the routine calls a procedure that displays a screen message (also unshown). Otherwise, the routine simply returns. The usual return code for hardware interrupts (**MOV AL,20h/OUT 20h,AL/IRET**) is not required, since it is handled by the timer interrupt. Be very careful about saving changed registers. See Chapter 4 to learn how to share the Interrupt vector with other software.

```
;---IN THE DATA SEGMENT:

MINUTES     dw  0            ;holds number of minutes until alarm

ALARMCOUNT  dw  0            ;holds time-of-day for alarm setting


;---SET ALARMCOUNT TO THE AWAITED BIOS TIME-OF-DAY VALUE:
        call REQUEST_MINUTES ;get from user the minutes until alarm

        mov  ax,MINUTES      ;move number of minutes to AX

        mov  bx,1092         ;number of time-of-day pulses/minute

        mul  bx              ;multiply - result now in AX
     ;GET CURRENT TIME-OF-DAY VALUE:
        mov  ah,0            ;function number for time-of-day read

        int  1Ah             ;get count, low word in DX
     ;ADD THE TWO VALUES:
        add  ax,dx           ;add alarm time to current time-of-day

        mov  ALARMCOUNT,ax   ;set time-of-day value for the alarm
;---CHANGE THE DUMMY INTERRUPT VECTOR:
        push ds              ;save the data segment

        mov  ax,seg ALARM    ;get segment of the alarm routine

        mov  ds,ax           ;place segment in DS
```

```
        mov   dx,offset ALARM  ;get offset of the alarm routine

        mov   al,1Ch           ;number of interrupt vector to change

        mov   ah,25h           ;DOS function that changes vectors

        int   21h             ;change the vector

        pop   ds              ;restore the data segment

                              ;
;---PROGRAM CONTINUES ALONG...NEW INTERRUPT OCCURS 18.2 TIMES/SEC
                              ;
;---PROCEDURE TO SOUND ALARM:
ALARM   proc far              ;create a far procedure

        push ax               ;save changed registers

        push cx               ;

        push dx               ;


;---READ THE TIME-OF-DAY COUNT:
        mov   ah,0            ;function number for time-of-day read

        int   1Ah            ;get count, low word in DX
;---GET THE COUNT CORRESPONDING TO ALARM TIME:
        mov   cx,ALARMCOUNT   ;get variable that signals "time's up"

        cmp   dx,cx           ;does the current reading match?

        jne   NOT_YET         ;if not, leave the routine
;---SOUND ALARM IF THE TWO COUNTS MATCH:
        call SETALARMFLAG     ;set flag so that alarm starts on return
;---OTHERWISE, RETURN FROM INTERRUPT:
NOT_YET:
        pop   dx             ;restore changed registers

        pop   cx             ;

        pop   ax             ;

        iret                 ;return from interrupt
ALARM   endp                 ;end of the procedure
```

6

Programming Sound

- Minitutorial: How PCs Make Sound
- Beep the Speaker
- Play a Tone
- Play a Sequence of Tones in the Foreground
- Play a Sequence of Tones in the Background
- Make Sound Effects

Minitutorial: How PCs Make Sound

Sounds are remarkably complex phenomena. When a musical instrument plays a Middle A, it produces much more than a simple 440 cycles-per-second waveform that defines the frequency of Middle A. There are also myriad *overtones* — multiples of the fundamental frequency that sound at lesser intensity. Each overtone has its own pattern of *onset* (appearance) and *offset* (cessation), some rising quickly and then disappearing, others appearing slowly and lasting as long as the fundamental tone. In addition, the instrument produces all sorts of *nonharmonic* waveforms that function as dissonance or noise. All of these sounds combine to form a single note from an instrument, and the characteristics of the aggregate sound will vary with the note's frequency and the loudness at which it is played. The sound of a full orchestra entails the assemblage of dozens of these complex tones.

That you've never head such sounds emanating from a PC speaker is not because programmers have not wanted to create them. It simply can't be done with ordinary PC circuitry. Computers that produce rich sounds do so by meticulously calculating the waveforms of each component of every note and adding them together. This process is called *additive synthesis*, and the principles on which it relies are still being devised. No one has yet worked out a recipe for synthesizing

149

a completely natural oboe, violin, or French horn. Only the synthesized sounds of a few percussion instruments can pass for the real thing. Once the composite waveform has been synthesized, it is played back using special circuitry that translates the computer-generated digital patterns into analog waveforms that can drive a speaker.

Another way computers can make music is to use a *sound synthesis chip*, which can be programmed to produce multiple waveforms that can be combined to create music with multiple voices. Some of these chips can only produce simple waveforms. The resulting sound is "thin" and toylike. It can be grating on the ears. The best sound synthesis chips can create waveforms of moderate complexity by modulating basic waveforms. The extra modulation can sometimes be applied in ways that produce rough approximations of the sounds of familiar musical instruments. Even when the sound is unfamiliar, at least it is richer and less "electronic sounding" than a simple waveform.

Mainstream PCs support neither approach to producing sound. They contain circuitry for generating a single simple tone, and that's all. Technically, the circuitry produces a *square wave* — a wave that abruptly rises and falls instead of following the rolling pattern on a sine wave. Square waves contain a number of overtones of the fundamental tone, but the speakers found in most PCs are of poor quality and tend to round out the sound into a sine wave, resulting in a thin sound that is predominantly of one frequency. This is why PCs don't do much more than beep at you. But clever programming can create richer sounds (or the illusion of richer sounds), as we show in this chapter.

If you want to perform more elaborate sound programming on an IBM-type computer, you have three options:

(1) You can program a PCjr (now a dinosaur) or a PS/1 machine, both of which are equipped with sound synthesis chips. Because few programmers want their programs to be restricted to these machines, we don't discuss these chips here. Documentation for the chips is available in the *Technical Reference Manuals* for these machines.

(2) You can acquire a MIDI port for your PC. *MIDI* stands for *Musical Instrument Digital Interface.* It is a worldwide standard for controlling music synthesizers with PCs. You insert a MIDI expansion card in one of your computer's slots and connect it to any of dozens of commercially available synthesizers. Then you write programs that send commands to the MIDI interface, which in turn controls the devices connected to it. The synthesizers are connected to their own speakers, so the computer's speaker goes unused.

(3) You can buy special expansion boards for additive synthesis. These minimally contain a *digital-to-analog converter* for converting digitally encoded sound into analog waveforms. Many also include an *analog-to-digital converter* by which you can record ("sample") sounds, encode them digitally, and place them in the computer's memory. Output from

one of these expansion cards goes to an external amplifier and then on to external speakers. Some boards may directly drive earphones. Sometimes these expansion boards are built around *digital signal processor (DSP)* chips, which are optimized for creating or analyzing waveforms. DSP chips are usually programmed in assembly language (each chip has its own), or sometimes in C. DSP programming is not a project to be taken lightly.

PCs produce sound using the same timer chip that constantly updates the time-of-day clock. The *minitutorial* at the beginning of Chapter 5 describes how timer chips are designed. You'll need to read that section to understand many of the discussions here. Timer Channel 2 is connected to the computer's speaker. The channel can be programmed to turn on and off at a regular rate. In doing so, the speaker's magnetic coil is pulsed on and off to produce a sound of a given frequency. Unfortunately, the timer chip cannot alter the amplitude of the wave it produces, so there is no control over the volume of sound coming from the speaker.

All channels on the timer chip continuously pulse; they cannot be shut off. Software can do no more than change a channel's pulse rate or interrupt the connection between the chip and the computer's speaker. For this reason, it is a simple matter to have sound played while the computer performs other functions. This is referred to as playing sound *in the background.* Playing a *sequence* of sounds in the background is more difficult, because the program must return to reprogramming the timer chip at exactly the right moment. Of course, sound may also be played *in the foreground,* with software waiting for the sound to finish before moving on to the program's next task. The sound is made in the same way in both cases.

Of the compilers we discuss in this book, only Microsoft BASIC is adept at making sounds. It includes a *PLAY* command that takes coded strings for playing melodies or sound effects. Most important, BASIC can play these sequences in the background. The other compilers are much less capable. The sound routines for Turbo Pascal and Borland's C only make single tones in the foreground. And Microsoft's C has no facilities for sound at all. Nonetheless, elaborate sound sequences can be produced in any language by directly programming the timer chip. In addition, all of these compilers can turn to the operating system to make a simple beep.

Beep the Speaker

A program can sound a simple beep by outputting the ASCII 7 character (the "bell" control code) just as if you were writing it to the screen. No symbol is actually displayed.

BASIC

In BASIC, just write *BEEP*:

```
BEEP      'beeps the speaker
```

Pascal

Use *Write* to output the character. The *Writeln* procedure will cause the cursor to wrap even though no character is actually printed on the screen.

```
Writeln(Chr(7));
```

C

In C, use *putch* to write ASCII 7.

```
putch(7);              /* beep the speaker */
```

Assembler

Any of the DOS screen functions will cause the speaker to beep when they encounter ASCII 7. This example uses function 2 of INT 21h.

```
mov   ah,2      ;function to write character on screen
mov   dl,7      ;send ASCII 7
int   21h       ;the speaker beeps
```

You can also use the BIOS "teletype" routine, which is discussed in Chapter 14, "Write a Single Character on the Screen." This is function Eh of interrupt 10h. Place the "bell" character (ASCII 7) in AL and call the function. Normally, this functions also takes input values in BH and BL, but they are irrelevant in this application.

152

```
mov  ah,0Eh     ;teletype function
mov  al,7       ;"bell" character
int  10h        ;the speaker beeps
```

Avoid BIOS function Ah of INT 10h for this purpose. Instead of beeping, it displays the ASCII 7 symbol.

Play a Tone

Most compilers discussed in this book provide routines for making single tones, although only BASIC can play the tone in the background as other operations proceed. In Microsoft's C, and in assembly language, you must directly program the timer chip to start and stop the desired sound.

Here's how the chip is programmed. The speaker receives not one, but two, inputs to make sound. As Figure 5-2 shows, in addition to the signal from Channel 2 of the timer chip, a signal is received from bit 1 of a general-use port address called System Control Port B. The two signals are ANDed and the result goes to the speaker. Normally, the timer chip drives the speaker and the System Control Port is used just to enable the speaker (that is, to provide a continuous **1** value so that all timer chip output is preserved as it is ANDed). But the pulse rate of either can be changed, and combining the actions of the two inputs can produce special sound effects, as "Making Sound Effects," below, demonstrates.

In addition, bit 0 of System Control Port B needs to be set in order to "open the gate" between the timer chip and the speaker. Both bits 0 and 1 of this port are reset to 0 in order to stop the sound. Thereafter, the timer chip will continue to pulse at the rate it was last programmed, but nothing will be heard because the signal is effectively disconnected. Here are the steps to making a sound:

(1) Calculate a countdown value to send to the timer chip by dividing 1.19 million (the chip's clock rate) by the number of cycles per second desired. The frequencies of the octave starting at middle C are:

Middle	C	523.3
	D	587.3
	E	659.3
	F	698.5
	G	784.0
	A	880.0
	B	987.7

Frequencies an octave higher are roughly twice these values, and two octaves higher they are twice as great again. Conversely, frequencies an octave lower are about half of these values. For Middle A, the value would be 1190000/440, which equals 2705.

(2) Send the value B6h to the timer chip command register at port 43h. This action causes Channel 2 to operate in timer mode 3, which is appropriate for making sound.

(3) Transmit the countdown value to timer Channel 2 by outputting it to port address 42h. Send first the low byte (least significant byte), and then the high byte (most significant byte).

(4) Enable the speaker by turning on bits 0 and 1 of System Control Port B, which is found at port address 61h. First read the value from this port, then OR it with the binary value 00000011, which equals 3 in decimal. Finally, send the value back to the port. The sound will begin immediately.

(5) Make a delay or go on to other activities.

(6) When you want the sound to stop, change bits 0 and 1 in Port B back to 0. If you forget to do this, the sound will continue indefinitely — even after your program has terminated. As in step 4, begin by reading the value from port 61h. Then AND the eight-bit value with binary 11111100 (decimal 252) to reset the bits, and send the value back to the port.

You can also produce sound by toggling back and forth bit 1 of System Control Port B. When a program changes the bit back and forth as rapidly as possible, the frequency produced is far too high to be useful. Thus, delay loops must be inserted between the on-off actions. Because bit 0 of Port B controls the gate to Channel 2 of the timer chip, which in turn is connected to the speaker, this bit should be turned off to disconnect the timer channel. Figure 6-1 shows how this method sets the sound frequency.

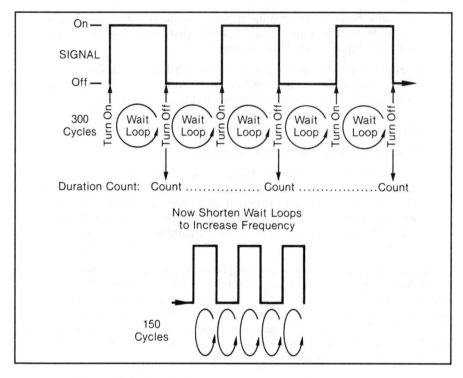

Figure 6-1   Producing sound by System Control Port B

BASIC

The BASIC SOUND statement plays a tone over a wide range of frequencies and durations. The frequency is given in cycles per second (37-32767), and the duration is counted in pulses of the BIOS time-of-day reading (0-65535), where there are 18.2 such pulses per second. For example:

```
SOUND 440,91
```

plays Middle A for five seconds (5 * 18.2 = 91).

The *SOUND* statement in BASIC cannot make simultaneous sound, but the *PLAY* statement can if it is especially instructed to do so. *PLAY* is followed by a string that tells what notes (and rests) are to be played, their durations, and other characteristics. The details of PLAY strings are discussed in "Play a Sequence of Tones in the Foreground," below. When the string contains the letters *MB* ("music background"), the string is placed in a buffer and is performed while other program operations proceed. Conversely, *MF* ("music foreground") stops all other program operations until the string is finished. Here a single tone A is played in the background:

```
PLAY "MB A"        'plays A...
   .               '...while doing this

   .
```

<hr>

Pascal

The Turbo Pascal *Sound* procedure starts up a sound of a given frequency. The sound continues until you execute a *NoSound* command. In the interim, you can perform other operations, or can simply make a delay. A succession of *Sound* commands can be made without placing *NoSound* commands between them.

```
uses Crt;

Sound(523);
Delay(500);
Sound(784);
Delay(2000);
NoSound;
```

<hr>

C

Like Turbo Pascal, Borland's C uses its *Sound* function to start up a sound and *NoSound* to end the sound. Other operations may proceed while the sound continues, or a program can make a delay until the sound is finished. There's no need to use *NoSound* between *Sound* commands when one sound follows immediately upon the previous one.

```
#include <dos.h>

Sound(523);
Delay(500);
Sound(784);
Delay(2000);
NoSound;
```

Microsoft's C has no sound functions. Here is an example of programming the timer chip directly in C. A middle A (440 Hz) is played for one second while a delay is made. The example assumes a routine named *Delay* is available for making timed delays. It uses the *inp* and *outp* functions found in Microsoft's C; Borland's C provides the *inportb* and *outportb* instead. The two-byte latch value is sent by first zeroing out the high byte to send the low byte, and then shifting the high byte eight bits left to output it.

```
unsigned latch_value = 2705;


outp(0x43,182); /* initialize the timer command register */

outp(0x42,latch_value & 0xFF); /* send low latch value */

outp(0x42,latch_value >> 8);   /* send high latch value */

outp(0x61,inp(0x61) ¦ 3);      /* enable the speaker */

delay(1000);                   /* delay 1000 milliseconds */

outp(0x61,inp(0x61) & 252);    /* shut off the sound */
```

Assembler

This assembly language example programs timer chip Channel 2 to produce a middle A. A delay is made by waiting for a random keystroke. To precisely time the duration of the tone, use the BIOS time-of-day count, as discussed in Chapter 5, "Set or Read the BIOS Time-of-Day Clock."

```
;---ENABLE CHANNEL 2 BY SETTING Port B of the 8255 chip:
PORT_B equ  61h          ;set address of PB on the 8255 chip
       in   al,PORT_B    ;get Port B
       or   al,3         ;turn on 2 low bits (3=00000011B)
       out  PORT_B,al    ;send changed byte to Port B
;---SET UP I/O REGISTER:
COMMAND_REG   equ  43h   ;set address of command register
CHANNEL_2     equ  42h   ;set address of channel 2
       mov  al,10110110b ;bit pattern for channel 2, 2 bytes,
                         ;mode 3, binary number
       out  COMMAND_REG,al;send byte to command register
```

```
;---SEND COUNTER TO LATCH:
        mov   ax,2705        ;the counter: 1190000/440
        out   CHANNEL_2,al   ;send LSB
        mov   al,ah          ;shift MSB, since must send from AL
        out   CHANNEL_2,al   ;send MSB
;---DELAY BY WAITING FOR KEYSTROKE:
        mov   ah,1           ;function number of INT 21h
        int   21h            ;call interrupt
;---TURN OFF THE SOUND:
        in    al,PORT_B      ;get the byte in Port B
        and   al,11111100b   ;force the two low bits to 0
        out   PORT_B,al      ;send changed byte to Port B
```

Finally, here is an example in which sound is produced through System Control Port B. In the following example, there are two variables. The one labeled *FREQUENCY* is used as the counter in the delay loops between the on-off actions. The smaller the number, the quicker the alternation, and the higher the frequency. The variable *NUMBER_CYCLES*, on the other hand, sets the duration of the tone. It tells how many times the whole on-off process should be cycled through. The larger the number, the longer the tone lasts.

```
NUMBER_CYCLES  equ  1000
FREQUENCY      equ  300
PORT_B         equ  61h
        mov   dx,NUMBER_CYCLES  ;DX counts the length of the tone
        in    al,PORT_B         ;get Port B
        and   al,11111110b      ;disconnect speaker from timer chip
NEXT_CYCLE:
        or    al,00000010b ;turn on speaker
        out   PORT_B,al         ;send the command to Port_B
        mov   cx,FREQUENCY      ;move the delay for 1/2 cycle to CX
FIRST_HALF:
        loop FIRST_HALF   ;make delay while speaker is on
        and   al,11111101b;turn off speaker
```

```
        out   PORT_B,al      ;send the command to Port_B
        mov   cx,FREQUENCY ;move the delay for 2nd half of cycle
SECOND_HALF:
        loop SECOND_HALF;make delay while speaker is off
        dec   dx                 ;subtract 1 from the number of cycles
        jnz   NEXT_CYCLE   ;if 0, then duration is exhausted
```

The frequent occurence of the timer interrupt adds a buzz to a sound produced this way. The buzz can be eliminated by shutting off interrupts with the CLI instruction (and later re-enabling them with STI). Doing so throws off the BIOS time-of-day count — an outcome that is not acceptable.

Play a Sequence of Tones in the Foreground

This section shows how to make a timed string of sounds while the computer does nothing else. In the next section we'll see how sound sequences are performed while the computer is busy with other operations. When the sound is nonsimultaneous, the computer's processor is free to reprogram the timer chip at short intervals. Frequent reprogramming is necessary when sound is to be distorted to create slides, warbles, and other sound effects.

BASIC provides a *PLAY* statement for playing sound sequences. Pascal and C provide no facilities of this kind at all, so you'll need to build your own sound routines in these languages. There is no "best way" to construct such a routine, since some approaches are better for music and others for sound effects. The assembly language example given below is oriented toward playing pure tones, much like BASIC's *PLAY* statement.

BASIC

The PLAY statement is one of BASIC's most complex features. A statement is comprised of a string of notes that is interspersed with information about how the notes are to be played. The notes are written as the letters A – G, and signs for sharps and flats ("accidentals") follow. Sharps are shown by # or +, and flats by –. **PLAY"CC#D"** (c, c-sharp, d) and **PLAY"CD-D"** (c, d-flat, d) are equivalent (but you should not use accidentals to specify nonblack-key notes, such as c-flat). A second way of naming notes is to calculate a code number from 0 to 84, where 0 equals a rest, and 1 through 84 correspond to the 84 possible notes in the seven octaves, starting from the bottom. Precede the number with the letter N, as in **PLAY"N3N72N44"**.

A seven-octave range is allowed, each octave reaching from C to B. The octaves are numbered from 0 to 6, and middle C starts octave 3. The current octave may be changed at any point in the string by inserting **O** (the letter "O," not zero) followed by the octave number. All notes that follow are played in that octave until another octave setting is made. When none is initially set, octave 4 is used. **PLAY"O3CO4CO5CO6C"** plays progressively higher Cs. Another way to change the octave is to place the symbols > or < in the string; these respectively move a tune up or down one octave. Thus, **PLAY"O3C>C>C>C"** also plays progressively higher Cs.

Notes may be given different lengths by inserting a code number preceded by the letter L. All notes that follow are given that length until another length code appears. The code is a number from 1 to 64, where 1 is a whole note and 64 is a 64th note. Write **L4** to make quarter notes. The tempo at which the notes are played is set by a tempo code, which is the letter T followed by a number from 32 to 255, giving the number of quarter notes per minute. When left unspecified,

161

the note length defaults to L4, and 120 is used for the tempo. To change the length of only a single note and not all that follow, place the value of the length *after* the note, and without the letter L. **PLAY "L4CDE16FG"** plays E as a 16th note and all others as quarter notes.

Rests are counted in the same way as note lengths are counted. Place a number from 1 to 64 after the letter P (for "pause"). **P1** gives a whole note pause, and **P64** gives a 64th note pause. Placing a period after a note has the same effect as it does in ordinary music notation: the length of the note is extended by half. A second period extends the length by half as much again.

By default, notes are played for 7/8th of their specified duration. To play them for their full duration (*legato*), put **ML** in the string. To play them at 3/4th duration (*staccato*), put **MS** in the string. And to return the texture to normal, write **MN**.

Normally, all other program activity stops until the string has been completed. Use **MB** to cause the string to be played in the background while statements that follow the PLAY statement are executed. To restore the normal situation, write **MF**.

Finally, the PLAY statement allows *substrings* to be played from within a larger string. This means that a part of a string can be set up as an ordinary string variable, and then that variable can be called from within the string that forms the PLAY statement. This is done by inserting a pointer to the substring in a command and preceding it with **X**. For example, if **S$="EEEEE"**, then in the statement:

```
PLAY"CDX"+VARPTR$(S$)+"FG"
```

the note E is repeated five times so that the sequence becomes: c, d, e, e, e, e, e, f, g.

This example plays the familiar grandfather clock chimes. The string first sets the melody to play in legato, then sets the tempo and starting octave, and finally lays out the four notes, a pause, and then the same four notes in reverse. The spaces between the codes are entirely for the convenience of the programmer— BASIC ignores them.

```
PLAY "ML T40 O3 ECD<G P32 G>DEC"
```

Assembler

This assembly language example programs the timer chip to produce pure sounds. It does no more than play a scale of eight notes, but with a little modification it could be made quite versatile. There are three data strings. The first sets the duration of each note as a multiple of an arbitrary delay period (changing the arbitrary period changes the tempo). The second string holds frequencies for each of the eight notes; the values are those that, when placed in the latch register of Channel 2 of the 8253 chip, result in the desired tones. The third string holds the melody in the form of code numbers from 1 to 8 that correspond to the eight frequencies. This string terminates with FF to flag its end. The routine does nothing more than read each note of the melody, look up the corresponding frequency, and place it in Channel 2. Then the duration assigned to that note is fed into a delay loop that uses the time-of-day count. When the delay is finished, the next note is processed. Figure 6-2 diagrams the routine.

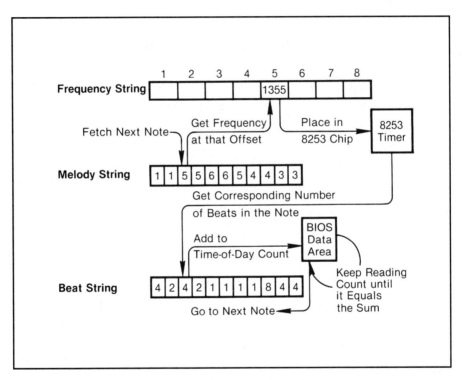

Figure 6-2   Playing a string of notes

```
;---IN THE DATA SEGMENT:

BEAT        db    10,9,8,7,6,5,4,3,2      ;duration of each note

FREQUENCY   dw    2280,2031,1809,1709     ;table of frequencies

            dw    1521,1355,1207,1139

MELODY      db    1,2,3,4,5,6,7,8,0FFh  ;frequency code of each note
```

```
;---INITIALIZATION:
PORT_B        equ  61h
COMMAND_REG   equ  43h
LATCH2        equ  42h
      mov  ax,0040h        ;point ES to BIOS data area
      mov  es,ax           ;
      in   al,PORT_B       ;get current status of Port B
      or   al,00000011b    ;enable the speaker and timer
                            channel 2
      out  PORT_B,al       ;replace the byte
      mov  si,0            ;initialize ptr to melody/beat
                            strings
      mov  al,0B6h         ;initialize channel 2 for mode 3
      out  COMMAND_REG,al ;send byte to command register

;---LOOK UP A NOTE, GET ITS FREQUENCY, PLACE IN CHANNEL 2:
NEXT_NOTE:
      lea  bx,MELODY       ;get offset of melody string
      mov  al,[bx][si]     ;get code for nth note of the string
      cmp  al,0FFh         ;is it FF? (end of string marker)
      je   NO_MORE         ;if so, jump to end of routine
      mov  ah,0            ;convert AL to word-length operand
;GET THE FREQUENCY:
      mov  bx,OFFSET FREQUENCY;get offset of the frequency table
      dec  ax             ;AX - 1 so that counting starts from 0
      shl  ax,1           ;double AX, since word-length table
      mov  di,ax          ;mov to DI for addressing
      mov  dx,[bx][di]    ;get the frequency from the table
;START THE NOTE PLAYING:
      mov  al,dl          ;prepare to send low byte of frequency
```

```
        out   LATCH2,al       ;send to latch register (via I/O reg)

        mov   al,dh           ;prepare high byte

        out   LATCH2,al       ;send high byte

;---CREATE DELAY LOOP:

        mov   bx,OFFSET BEAT  ;get offset of beat string

        mov   cl,[bx][si]     ;get beat value for not number SI

        mov   ch,0            ;clear high half of CX to use as word

        mov   bx,es:[6Ch]     ;get low word of BIOS count

        add   bx,cx           ;add beat count to current BIOS count
STILL_SOUND:

        mov   dx,es:[6Ch]     ;get low word of BIOS count

        cmp   dx,bx           ;cmp count with end-of-note count

        jne   STILL_SOUND     ;if not equal, continue sound

        inc   si              ;else, point to next note

        jmp   NEXT_NOTE       ;go get the next note

;---FINISH UP:

NO_MORE:

        in    al,PORT_B       ;get the byte in Port_B

        and   al,0FCh         ;turn off the speaker bits

        out   61h,al          ;replace the byte in Port_B
```

Play a Sequence of Tones in the Background

Simultaneous, *background* sound is a tricky bit of *real-time* programming. Real-time routines hook into the BIOS timer interrupt, which is activated 18.2 times per second. A background sound routine starts a sound and then, every time it is awakened, checks to see if it is yet time to stop the current sound, and possibly to start a new one.

Usually only a few lines are executed when the interrupt service routine is called — just enough to determine that no change of sound is required. The duration of each note is measured in ticks of the BIOS clock. Whenever a change is made from one note to another, the duration of the new note is calculated as a number of pulses of the BIOS time-of-day count, and that value is added to a reading of the current count. The time-of-day value is checked each time the routine is invoked, and when the awaited value finally comes up, a chain of events looks up the next note, programs its frequency into Channel 2 of the timer chip, and sets up a new duration counter. Extra code is required for the special cases of the first and last notes of the strings.

BASIC makes it easy to program real-time sound. In Pascal, C, or assembly language, you'll need to build the routines from the bottom up. See Chapter 5, "Set/Read the BIOS Time-of-Day Count" and "Control Real-Time Operations" to learn about the BIOS timer interrupt and about how real-time routines are set up.

BASIC

A simultaneous tone string is just another option within Microsoft BASIC's very elaborate *PLAY* statement, which is discussed at length in "Play a Sequence of Tones in the Foreground," above. Simply add **MB** ("Music Background") to the beginning of the control string. Replace it with **MF** ("Music Foreground") to cause *PLAY* to revert to stopping all other program operations until the melody is finished. This example plays a scale while drawing and filling a box while the screen is in a graphics mode.

```
PLAY "MB T100 O3 L4;CDEFGAB>C"    'play a scale from middle C
LINE(10,10)-(80,80),1,BF          'draw a box at the same time
```

Make Sound Effects

Despite its primitive sound system, a PC can produce impressive sound effects. This is done by continuously altering the frequency of the sound coming from the computer's speaker. As always, it's possible to play the sound in the background as other operations proceed. But sound effects take more processor time than pure tones because the timer chip must be reprogrammed constantly. For video game authors, there can be a trade-off between stimulating sound and interesting events on the screen. Good sound effects are discovered by experimentation. In this section, we'll look at four simple effects: slides, warbles, clicks, and double-tones.

Sliding tones are made by continuously changing frequency. These effects can be made more dramatic by slightly shortening the duration of each segment of the tone as it rises, or by slightly lengthening the duration as the tone falls. Slides can be nested within other slides, as Figure 6-3 shows. This effect is familiar from video games.

Another approach is to alternate between two frequencies. *Vibrato* occurs when frequencies are only a step or two apart. A further separation leads to a buzz. More separation still produces a warbling sound. And when the frequencies are widely separated, the sound is piercing and can be used as an alarm.

Clicks are ordinary tones that are sounded for too short a time for the ear to define a frequency. They're produced just like any simple tone, but using a short duration. Although the ear hears a click and not a tone, the quality of the clicks still varies by the frequency of the tone used. Interesting, if somewhat subtle, effects can be achieved by producing a sequence of clicks using different frequencies.

Finally, it's possible to create the illusion of two tones sounding at once. As the *minitutorial* at the beginning of this chapter explains, sound can be produced either through Channel 2 of the timer chip, or through System Control Port B. These two methods may be combined to simulate the production of two simultaneous sounds. The pulse rates combine to create the effect of a complex wave form. The two sounds are each of diminished intensity, and if they are not widely separated, the result is more like a buzz than like two voices. You can get some interesting sound effects this way, but it's no way to write a duet.

To produce a double-tone, start sound from Channel 2 of the timer chip. Then modulate output to the speaker from bit 1 of Port B of the peripheral interface. You'll find an example of this technique below.

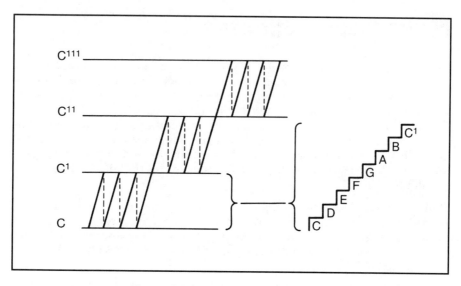

Figure 6-3   Nested sliding sounds

BASIC

This code produces an ascending sliding tone:

```
FOR N=1 TO 500 STEP 15
SOUND 400 + N,1
NEXT
```

and here are slides within slides:

```
FOR I=1 TO 3              'set number of repetitions
FOR J=0 TO 6              'repeat scale 6 times
PLAY"MBL64T2550="+VARPTR$(J)+";ba#ag#gf#fed#dc#cc#
                            dd#eff#gg#aa#b"
NEXT                      'repeat at higher octave (o=j)
NEXT                      'repeat the whole sequence
```

This code produces a vibrato:

```
FOR N=1 TO 50             'set duration
SOUND 440,1               'play an A
SOUND 445,1               'play the A slightly sharped
NEXT                      'repeat
```

168

and these lines create a piercing buzz:

```
FOR N=1 TO 100          'set duration
PLAY"l64t255"           'fastest possible tempo
PLAY"O1A"               'play a low A
PLAY"O5A"               'play a high A
NEXT                    'repeat
```

Finally, this command produces a click:

```
PLAY"L64T25501A"        'click
```

Pascal

This code produces an ascending sliding tone:

```
var
   Frequency,i: word;

Frequency := 0;
for i := 1 to 90 do
begin
   Sound(Frequency);
   Delay(50);
   Frequency := Frequency + 15;
end;
NoSound;
```

and here are slides within slides:

```
var
   BaseFrequency,Frequency,i,j: word;

BaseFrequency := 0;
```

```
for j := 1 to 10 do
begin
  Frequency := BaseFrequency;
  for i := 1 to 15 do
  begin
    Sound(Frequency);
    Delay(15);
    Frequency := Frequency + 50;
  end;
BaseFrequency := BaseFrequency + 100;
end;
NoSound;
```

This example produces a vibrato:

```
for N:= 1 to 50 do       {set duration}
begin
  Sound(840);            {play a note}
  Delay(30);             {30 milliseconds}
  Sound(850);            {play the note slightly sharped}
  Delay(30);             {30 milliseconds}
end;
NoSound;
```

whereas this code generates a piercing warble:

```
for N := 1 to 50 do      {set duration}
begin
  Sound(440);            {play a middle A}
  Delay(30);             {30 milliseconds}
  Sound(1760);           {play A two octaves higher}
  Delay(30);             {30 milliseconds}
end;
```

```
NoSound;
```

Finally, this statement makes a click:

```
Sound(200);
Delay(5);
NoSound;
```

C

These examples employ the *sound* and *delay* functions found in Borland's C. You'll need to write equivalent functions when using one of the Microsoft compilers ("Play a Tone," above, and Chapter 5, "Time or Delay Program Operations" explain how). The first example generates an ascending sliding tone:

```
int  frequency,i;

frequency = 0;
for (i = 1; i < 300; i++)
{
   sound(frequency);
   delay(50);
   frequency = frequency + 15;
}
nosound();
```

Here are slides within slides:

```
int basefrequency,frequency,i,j;

basefrequency = 0;
for (j = 1; j<=10; j++)
{
  frequency = basefrequency;
```

```
for (i = 1; i <= 15; i++)
{
   sound(frequency);
   delay(15);
   frequency = frequency + 50;
}
basefrequency = basefrequency + 100;
}
nosound();
```

This example produces a vibrato:

```
for (i = 1; i < 50; i++) /* set duration */
{
 sound(840);              /* play a note */
 delay(30);              /* 30 milliseconds */
 sound(850);              /* play the note slightly sharped */
 delay(30);              /* 30 milliseconds */
}
nosound();
```

This example makes a piercing warble:

```
for (i = 1; i < 50; i++) /* set duration */
{
 sound(440);              /* play a middle A */
 delay(30);              /* 30 milliseconds */
 sound(1760);              /* play A two octaves higher */
 delay(30);              /* 30 milliseconds */
}
nosound;
```

Finally, this statement makes a click:

```
sound(200);

delay(5);

nosound;
```

Assembler

To make sliding tones in assembly language, it's easiest to use the method of sound production controlled from the 8255 peripheral interface chip. Simply modulate bit 1 of Port B between 1 and 0. For simplicity, this example uses empty timing loops. Each time the timing loop is restored by placing a value in CX, slightly increase or decrease that value. Here, the tone rises:

```
;---DISABLE THE TIMER CHIP

PB      equ   61h           ;set PB equal to address of 8255 port B

        in    al,PB         ;get the byte at PB

        or    al,1          ;turn off bit 0

        out   PB,al         ;put the changed byte back in PB

;---SET THE SOUND FREQUENCY AND DURATION

        mov   bx,1000       ;initial counter value, decreased below

        mov   dx,1000       ;sound will continue for 1000 cycles

REPEAT:                     ;return here after each cycle

;---TURN THE SPEAKER BIT ON

        or    al,00000010b ;force bit 1 "on"

        out   PB,al         ;place "on" byte in PB

        mov   cx,bx         ;set counter for 1st half of cycle

CYCLE1:

        loop  CYCLE1        ;idle at loop

;---TURN THE SPEAKER BIT OFF

        and   al,11111101b ;force bit 1 "off"

        out   PB,al         ;place "off" byte in PB
```

```
        mov  cx,bx              ;set counter for 2nd half of cycle
CYCLE2:
        loop CYCLE2             ;idle at loop for 1000 repetitions
;---GO ON TO NEXT CYCLE
        dec  bx                 ;decrement counter, increase frequency
        dec  dx                 ;decrement the remaining duration
        jnz  REPEAT             ;do another cycle if DX not 0
                                ;else, the sound ends...
```

This simple method results in the high range passing considerably more quickly than the low range. Over short intervals this effect is actually desirable; when not, code must be added so that as the tone rises DX is given ever higher values when it is reloaded (sixth line of the example).

As a second example, here is a routine that creates the "double_tone" discussed above. Note that interrupts are disabled because the timer interrupt audibly interferes.

```
;---START SOUND OUTPUT FROM CHANNEL 2 OF 8253 TIMER CHIP:
        in   al,61h             ;get byte from Port B
        or   al,3               ;turn on bottom 2 bytes
        out  61h,al             ;send byte back to PB
        mov  al,10110110b       ;bit pattern for 8253 command register
        out  43h,al             ;send to register
        mov  ax,600h            ;counter for channel 2
        out  42h,al             ;send low byte
        mov  al,ah              ;ready to send high byte
        out  42h,al             ;send high byte
;---GENERATE A SECOND FREQUENCY FROM THE 8255 CHIP:
NUMBER_CYCLES equ  9000         ;number of times to cycle on-off
FREQUENCY     equ  150          ;delay time for 1/2 cycle
        cli                     ;disable interrupts
```

```
        mov   dx,NUMBER_CYCLES ;DX counts the length of the tone
        in    al,61h           ;get Port B
        and   al,11111111b     ;disconnect speaker from timer chip
NEXT_CYCLE:
        or    al,00000010b     ;turn on speaker
        out   61h,al           ;send the command to Port_B
        mov   cx,FREQUENCY     ;move the delay for 1/2 cycle to CX
FIRST_HALF:
        loop  FIRST_HALF       ;make delay while speaker is on
        and   al,11111101b     ;turn off speaker
        out   61h,al           ;send the command to Port_B
        mov   cx,FREQUENCY     ;move the delay for 2nd half of cycle
SECOND_HALF:
        loop  SECOND_HALF      ;make delay while speaker is off
        dec   dx               ;subtract 1 from the number of cycles
        jnz   NEXT_CYCLE       ;if 0, then duration is exhausted
        sti                    ;reenable interrupts
;---SHUT OFF CHANNEL 2 OF TIMER CHIP:
        in    al,61h           ;get byte from Port B
        and   al,11111100b     ;turn off bottom 2 bits
        out   61h,al           ;replace the byte
```

Intercepting Keystrokes

- Minitutorial: How Keyboards Work
- Clear the Keyboard Buffer
- Check the Keyboard Buffer for Keystrokes
- Insert Keystrokes into the Keyboard Buffer
- Intercept Keystrokes Without Displaying Them
- Intercept Keystrokes and Display Them Automatically
- Intercept a Keystroke Only If One Is Available
- Intercept a String of Keystrokes
- Write a General-Purpose Keyboard Input Routine
- Write a Ctrl-Break Routine

Minitutorial: How Keyboards Work

IBM has created three keyboard standards: the 83-key keyboard found on early PCs and XTs, an 84-key keyboard shipped with early ATs, and a 101-key *extended* keyboard used with later ATs, XTs, and PS/2s. The 84-key model uses a slightly different arrangement of the keys, and adds the <Sys-Req> key. The 101-key model adds new keys, including more function keys and separate keypads for numbers and cursor control. These keyboards also rearrange certain keys, most notably by moving the function keys from the left side of the keyboard to the top.

A keyboard contains a microprocessor that senses each keystroke and deposits a *scan code* in System Control Port A (port address 60h). A scan code is a one-byte number that represents an identification number assigned to each key. A table of scan codes is found in Chapter 8, "Look Up a Scan Code."

A keystroke occurs in two parts — a *press* and a *release* — and a scan code results from each action. To distinguish between the two kinds of events, each scan code is tailored to be either a *make code* (when a key goes down) or a *break code* (when a key is released). In most machines, a break code consists of two bytes. The first byte is always **F0h** and the second is the scan code itself. Make codes consist of only the one-byte scan code.

In PC- and XT-class machines, both make codes and break codes are one byte long. The high bit of the code tells whether the key has just been pressed (bit #7=0) or released (bit #7=1). For example, the seven-bit scan code of the <B> key is 48, which is 110000 in binary. When the key goes down, the code sent to System Control Port A is **00**110000, and when the key is released, the code is **10**110000.

When a scan code is deposited in System Control Port A, the keyboard interrupt (IRQ#9) is invoked. The processor momentarily sets aside its work and executes the routine associated with this interrupt. When the scan code originates from a shift or toggle key, a change in the key's status is recorded in memory (more on this in Chapter 8, "Check/Set the Status of the Toggle and Shift Keys"). In most other cases, the scan code is transformed into a character code, except when the scan code results from a key release, in which case it is discarded. Of course, the routine first checks the settings of the shift and toggle keys to get the character code right (is it "a" or "A"?). Then the code is placed in the *keyboard buffer* — a holding area in memory from which programs can fetch the codes at their leisure. The next section, "Clear the Keyboard Buffer," explains how the buffer is constructed. For a few special cases, such as <PrtSc>, the keyboard interrupt handler directly invokes a routine pointed to by an interrupt vector instead of placing a code in the buffer. Figure 7-1 shows the path a keystroke takes to travel to your programs.

In most machines, the keyboard interrupt handler calls function 4Fh of BIOS interrupt 15h, placing the scan code of the pressed key in AL. Normally, this function does nothing at all, returning the same code in AL. But a program can chain a routine into the interrupt, intercept the function number, and then change or discard the scan code that will be interpreted by the keyboard interrupt handler. This mechanism lets you reprogram keyboard keys. Unfortunately, function 4Fh is not found on early PCs, nor on XTs for which the BIOS date is 11/8/82 or earlier.

The keyboard interrupt handler inserts two kinds of codes in the keyboard buffer, *ASCII codes* and *extended codes*. ASCII codes are one-byte numbers that correspond to the IBM extended ASCII character set. The characters include the usual typewriter symbols, plus foreign language characters and graphics symbols. The ASCII codes also include 32 *control codes* that ordinarily are used to send commands to peripheral devices like printers or modems. You'll find a complete listing of the ASCII character set and its symbols in Chapter 8, "Look Up an ASCII Code," and a discussion of the control codes in Chapter 17, "Look Up a Communications Control Code."

Extended codes are assigned to keys or key-combinations that have no ASCII symbol to represent them, such as the function keys or combinations of the <Alt> and alphabet keys. Extended codes are two bytes long, with the first byte always 0. The second byte is a code number that is usually identical to the scan code of the associated key. The code **0;30**, for example, represents <Alt-A>, and **30** is the scan code for the "A" key. The initial 0 flags that the code is an extended code and not an ASCII code. Chapter 8, "Look Up an Extended Code." lists the extended codes.

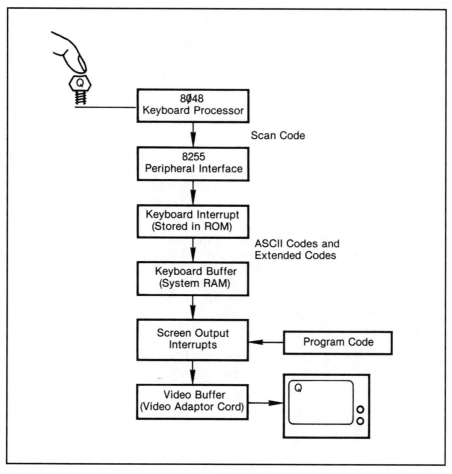

Figure 7-1   From keyboard to screen

The computer's built-in BIOS supplies routines for fetching codes from the keyboard buffer. DOS also provides routines for this purpose, which work by calling the BIOS functions. There are two versions of these BIOS routines, those intended for 83-key keyboards and those intended for 101-key keyboards. No special versions of these routines were devised for 84-key keyboards, since these keyboards added only the Sys-Req key, which does not place a code in the keyboard buffer.

Early machines have only the 83-key versions of the BIOS routines. For this reason, software must be able to determine which kind of keyboard the computer uses before the software can use the features of the 101-key keyboards, such as the extra function keys. Chapter 2, "Determine the Kind of Keyboard in Use," explains how to do this. Computers that have a BIOS that supports the extended-keyboard functions also provide the 83-key functions, even though such machines work with a 101-key keyboard. In this case, the 83-key functions filter out the additional codes that normally would be placed in the keyboard buffer by the 101-key keyboard. Thus, software can be written to use only the 83-key codes and can still run on any machine without adding code to adapt it to keyboard differences.

Except for a few special-purpose keys like <Pause> and <PrtSc>, no keystroke directly controls PC hardware. Each code deposited in the keyboard buffer must be interpreted by your program; if a key has a special role, such as to move the cursor leftward or to delete a character, your program must provide code to achieve that effect.

Both the BIOS and DOS provide routines for fetching codes from the keyboard buffer. The DOS functions call the BIOS functions, adding Ctrl-Break checking. In turn, keyboard functions provided in high-level languages tend to call on the DOS functions. There are functions for testing whether the keyboard buffer holds any codes and what the next code will be. Functions that actually extract a code from the buffer may either wait for a keystroke if the buffer is empty or return without a code in order to avoid suspending the system. Valuable processor time can be wasted waiting for keystrokes, and so, starting with the IBM AT, BIOS functions call function 90h ("Device Busy") of interrupt 15h when the buffer is empty. An operating system can use this feature to multitask between keystrokes.

Clear the Keyboard Buffer

Sometimes it's a good idea to have a program clear the keyboard buffer when prompting the user for input. This is especially true when the user's response can lead to irreversible loss of data or damage to data, as when a program asks, *"Should the file be saved before closing?"* In such a case, clearing the buffer eliminates any inappropriate or accidental keystrokes that might be waiting in the buffer and that could signal the wrong response. It's generally not a good idea to clear the keyboard buffer in other cases, since doing so undermines the type-ahead feature and makes it impossible to use keyboard macros.

The buffer holds up to 15 keystrokes, no matter whether the keystroke results in a one-byte ASCII code or a two-byte extended code. For this reason, the buffer provides two bytes in memory for each keystroke. For one-byte codes, the first byte holds an ASCII code, and the second, holds the key's scan code. For extended codes, the first byte holds ASCII 0 and the second byte holds the extended code number, which is usually the key's scan code but not always, since some keys—such as the function keys — combine with shift keys to produce more than one extended code.

The buffer is designed as a *circular queue*, also known as a *first-in first-out (FIFO) buffer*. Like any buffer, it occupies a range of contiguous memory addresses. But no particular memory location marks the beginning of data in the buffer. Rather, two pointers keep track of the "head" and "tail" of the string of codes currently in the buffer. The head pointer points to the first character in line, and the tail pointer points to the buffer position *following* that last character.

When a program reads a code from the buffer, the head pointer is adjusted to point to the next code in line. The tail pointer is adjusted similarly when a new character is added to the buffer. Once the highest memory position in the buffer is filled, the insertion of new characters wraps around to the low end of the buffer. In this way, the head will sometimes be at a higher memory location than the tail. Additional incoming characters are discarded when the buffer fills; the keyboard interrupt handler beeps the computer's speaker when this happens. Figure 7-2 diagrams some possible configurations of data in the buffer.

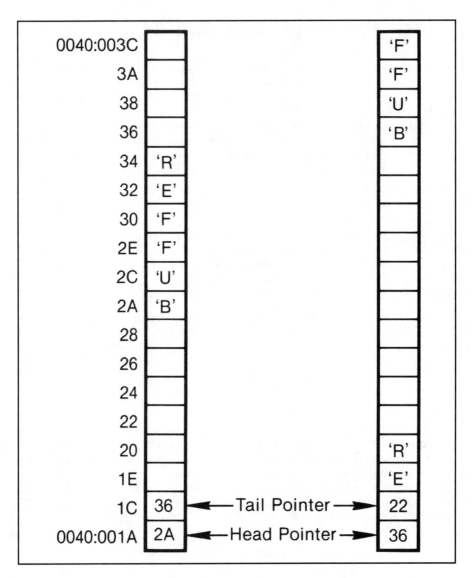

Figure 7-2   Keyboard buffer configurations

The keyboard buffer is held in the BIOS data area, which begins at 0040:0000. The 32 bytes of the buffer start at memory location 0040:001E. The head and tail pointers are found at 0040:001A and 0040:001C, respectively. Although the pointers are two bytes long, only the low byte is significant. The values of the pointers vary from 30 to 60 (1Eh to 3Ch), corresponding to offsets within the BIOS data area.

One way to clear the keyboard buffer is to make the value of the head pointer equal to that of the tail pointer. You need to momentarily shut off hardware interrupts if you do this. Otherwise, the keyboard interrupt might break in and change the tail pointer between the time your program reads one pointer and changes the other. It's risky to directly access the buffer pointers because utility software or an operating environment can modifying the buffering scheme. A better way to clear the buffer is by reading and discarding characters from the buffer until no more appear. In doing this, there's no need to differentiate between ASCII codes and extended codes. Just keep reading from the buffer until no more input appears.

BASIC

BASIC's *INKEY$* routine returns a null string ("") when the buffer is empty. Just loop until a null string is returned.

```
DO

LOOP WHILE INKEY$ <> ""    'loop till null
```

Pascal

In Turbo Pascal, repeatedly execute first the *KeyPressed* function to find out if at least one keystroke is present in the buffer, and then the *ReadKey* function to fetch the code. *KeyPressed* returns a *boolean* value, and *ReadKey* returns a *char*.

```
var

   TheKey: char;


while KeyPressed do TheKey := ReadKey;
```

C

In both Borland's C and Microsoft's C, you can use the *kbhit* function to find out if any keystrokes are present in the buffer, and *getch* to remove each keystroke in turn.

```
#include  conio.h


while(kbhit()) getch();
```

Assembler

Subfunction FFh of function 6 of interrupt 21h returns keystrokes without waiting if none is available. The zero flag is set when no keystroke is found. Keep calling the interrupt until no keystroke is returned:

```
;---CLEAR THE KEYBOARD BUFFER:

KEY_FOUND:
        mov  ah,6           ;function number
        mov  dl,0FFh        ;subfunction number goes in DL
        int  21h            ;seek a keystroke
        jnz  KEY_FOUND      ;loop if a keystroke is returned
```

Function C of interrupt 21h performs any of the DOS keyboard input functions 1, 6, 7, 8, and Ah (described elsewhere in this chapter), but clears the keyboard buffer first. Simply place the number of the input function in AL (here it is 1):

```
;---CLEAR BUFFER BEFORE AWAITING KEYSTROKE:

        mov  ah,0Ch         ;select DOS function 0Ch
        mov  al,1           ;select which key input function
        int  21h            ;clears buffer, waits for keystroke
```

Check the Keyboard Buffer for Keystrokes

You can check whether or not there has been keyboard input without actually removing a character from the keyboard buffer. As "Clear the Keyboard Buffer" above, explains, the buffer uses two pointers to keep track of the beginning and end of the queue of characters currently in the buffer. When the two pointers are equal, the buffer is empty.

BASIC

Microsoft BASIC does not provide a function for determining whether the keyboard buffer holds a character. Instead, use the *Interrupt* routine to call function Bh of INT 21h. It returns FFh in AL when the buffer holds a character.

In this example, the value returned in AX is ANDed with &HFF to zero-out the high-eight bits of the register, and the result is then compared to &HFF. If a keystroke is present, a routine called *GetKeystroke* is called. (See Chapter 4, "Call Interrrupts from BASIC, Pascal, and C," for a discussion of how BASIC calls interrupts.)

```
' $INCLUDE: 'QBX.BI'
DIM regs AS RegType      ' Define register array


regs.ax = &H0B00
CALL Interrupt(&H21, regs, regs)
Result = regs.AX AND 8HFF
IF Result = 8HFF THEN GOTO Getkeystroke
```

Pascal

In Turbo Pascal, the *KeyPressed* function returns *True* when a code is present in the keyboard buffer. For example, the line:

```
if KeyPressed then FetchKeystroke;
```

sends the program to the *FetchKeystroke* routine if a keystroke has arrived.

C

The *kbhit( )* function, which is found in both Borland's C and Microsoft's C, returns 0 when the buffer is empty, or a nonzero value otherwise. This example calls the *fetch_keystroke( )* routine if the buffer holds a code:

```
if(kbhit()) fetch_keystroke();
```

Assembler

Function Bh of INT 21h returns FFh in the AL register when the keyboard buffer holds one or more characters, or returns 0 when the buffer is empty:

```
;---CHECK IF A CHARACTER IS IN THE BUFFER:
        mov   ah,0Bh          ;function number
        int   21h             ;call interrupt 21
        cmp   al,0FFh          ;compare to FFh
        je    GET_KEYSTROKE   ;jump to input routine if char present
```

Function 1 of BIOS interrupt 16h provides the same service, and it also returns a copy of the next character without actually removing it from the buffer. The zero flag is cleared if a character is waiting, or set if there is none. When a character is present, it is reported in AX, with AL returning the character code for one-byte ASCII characters, or ASCII 0 for extended codes, in which case the code number appears in AH. Here is an example:

```
;---FIND OUT IF THERE IS A CHARACTER:
        mov   ah,1            ;set function number
        int   16h             ;check for character in buffer
        jz    NO_CHARACTER    ;jump if zero flag is set
;---THERE IS A CHARACTER, SO SEE WHAT IT IS:
        cmp   al,0            ;is it an extended code?
        je    EXTENDED_CODE   ;if so, go to extended code routine
                              ;otherwise, take character from AL
```

Instead of function 1, use function 11h of interrupt 16h when working with a 101-key extended keyboard. This function can report codes generated only by this kind of keyboard. See Chapter 2, "Determine the Kind of Keyboard in Use," to learn how a program can find out whether an extended keyboard is present.

Insert Keystrokes into the Keyboard Buffer

On machines that support a 101-key extended keyboard, the BIOS includes a routine for inserting codes into the keyboard buffer. Ordinarily, such codes would match those inserted by the keyboard interrupt — that is, they would act as "make believe" keystrokes. However, any two-byte code is allowed.

Programs seldom have reason to send themselves messages in this way, but this feature can be useful when memory-resident programs, such as keyboard macro programs, need to send control codes or data to application software. Unfortunately, software that uses this feature cannot run on any machine, since those that use 83- or 84-key keyboards do not support the feature. In these cases, a program would need to access the keyboard buffer directly. See Chapter 2, "Determine the Kind of Keyboard in Use," to learn how to find out whether a machine supports this function.

It is function 5h of interrupt 16h that inserts codes into the keyboard buffer. On entry, CH:CL holds the two bytes that are returned in AH:AL by other BIOS keyboard functions. Usually, CL holds a character's ASCII code and CH holds the scan code of the key associated with the character. For extended codes, CL is 0 and CH holds the extended code number (which sometimes, but not always, is the corresponding scan code). On return, AL holds 0 if no error has occurred, and 1 if the keyboard buffer was full and no code could be inserted. The following examples insert the extended code 15;0 (the backtab character) into the buffer.

BASIC

```
' $INCLUDE: 'QBX.BI'
DIM REGS AS RegType     ' Define register array


REGS.AX = &H0500        'function to insert codes into buffer
REGS.CX = &H1500        'code is 15;0
CALL Interrupt(&H16, REGS, REGS) 'insert the char
IF REGS.AX AND 1 THEN... '...then an error has occurred
```

Pascal

```
Uses DOS;

Var

   Regs: Registers;   {Registers type is declared in the DOS unit}


Regs.AH := $05;          {function number}
Regs.CX := $1500;        {code is 15;0}
Intr($16, Regs);         {insert the character}
if Regs.AL = 1 then...   {...then an error has occurred}
```

C

```
#include <dos.h>

union REGS regs;                    /* declare the register array */

regs.h.ah = 0x05;                   /* function number */
regs.x.cx = 0x1500;                 /* code is 15;00 */
int86(0x16,&regs,&regs);            /* set the ratio */
if (regs.h.al = = 1)...;            /* ...then error */
```

Assembler

```
;---INSERT 15;0 into the keyboard buffer:
        mov   ah,5             ;set function number
        mov   ch,15            ;extended code number for backtab
        mov   cl,0             ;extended code flag
        int   16h             ;insert the code
        cmp   al,1             ;test that all went well
        je    INSERT_ERROR     ;jump if error
```

Intercept Keystrokes Without Displaying Them

Programs usually display ("echo") incoming keystrokes to show what has been typed. Most programming languages have functions that automatically echo characters, particularly routines that input an entire string of characters followed by <Enter>. But automatic echoing is usually undesirable. Instead, each keystroke must first be examined to find out whether or not it should be displayed. Tests are performed to determine whether the character is within the range of characters appropriate to the work the software is performing. For example, at a given moment, a program might discard all characters except numerals. In addition, keystrokes used to issue commands to the software must be identified and processed without displaying their associated characters.

BASIC

BASIC provides the *INKEY$* function to fetch codes from the keyboard buffer without displaying them. *INKEY$* does not wait for a character when none is waiting in the keyboard buffer, but returns an empty string (" ") instead. The function returns a *string* value that is one byte long for ASCII characters and two bytes long for extended characters. You can use the *LEN* function to test the string length, and the *RIGHT$* function to remove the first (zero) character of extended codes. Use BASIC'S *ASC* function to convert the code to a numeric value for range checking and so on. In this example, *INKEY$* waits for character, determines whether it is an extended code, and then converts the code to numeric type.

```
KEYLOOP:

  C$=INKEY$                  'try for a code

  IF C$="" THEN GOTO KEYLOOP    'loop if none is present

  IF LEN(C$)=2 THEN GOTO EXTENDEDCODE 'jump if extended

  KEYCODE=ASC(C$)            'convert to numeric value

     .

     .

EXTENDEDCODE:               'extended code case
```

189

```
C$=RIGHT$(C$,1)               'eliminate 1st byte of code
KEYCODE=ASC(C$)               'convert to numeric value

   .

   .
```

Pascal

In Turbo Pascal, the *ReadKey* routine returns a *char* value from the keyboard buffer without displaying it. *ReadKey* waits for a keystroke if the buffer is empty. When the value is **0**, an extended code has arrived, and *ReadKey* must be called a second time to fetch the extended code number.

```
var
   TheChar: char;


TheChar := ReadKey;
if TheChar <> Chr(0) then
   begin                 {ASCII code case}

     .

     .

   end else
   begin                 {extended code case}
     TheChar := ReadKey;

     .

     .

   end;
```

C

The *getch* function fetches a code from the keyboard buffer without echoing, and waits for one if none is present. This function returns an integer value. When the value is 0, an extended code has been found and *getch* must be called a second time to obtain the code number.

```
#include  <conio.h>
```

190

```
int  the_char;

the_char = getch();

if(the_char){                    /* ASCII code case */

    .


    .

} else {                         /* extended code case */

the_char = getch();

    .


    .

}
```

C also offers the *ungetch* function for *returning* a character to the keyboard buffer. The character is not actually returned to the buffer, but nonetheless it will be the next one returned by *getch* or a related function. *Ungetch* can be useful when your program encounters a keystroke of the wrong kind as it reads in a sequence of keystrokes. For example, a keyboard input routine may be assembling a sequence of digits into a number. When it reads a character other than a digit, the routine can return that character to the buffer and go about finishing the work at hand. Later, the program can return to reading keyboard input without needing to be concerned that a character has been read from the buffer but not yet processed. The *ungetch* function takes an integer parameter specifying the character. It returns this value if the character has been successfully reinserted into the keyboard buffer; otherwise, it returns *EOF*. This example first reads a character and then returns it.

```
#include <conio.h>


int  the_char;


the_char = getch();

if (ungetch(the_char) == EOF) error_routine;
```

Note that *ungetch* cannot insert more than one character into the keyboard buffer after each read from the buffer. So you can't use this function to write data into the buffer for later use.

Assembler

Functions 7 and 8 of INT 21h wait for a character if none is in the keyboard buffer; when one arrives, they return the character without echoing it on the screen. Function 8 detects the Ctrl-Break condition, while function 7 does not. In both cases, the character is returned in AL. An extended code has arrived when AL contains ASCII 0. Repeat the interrupt and the second byte of the code appears in AL.

```
;---GET A KEYSTROKE:

        mov   ah,7          ;set function number

        int   21h           ;wait for character

        cmp   al,0           ;see if extended code

        je    EXTENDED_CODE  ;go to extended code routine if so

        .                   ;otherwise, take character from AL

        .



;---EXTENDED CODE ROUTINE:

EXTENDED_CODE:

        mov   ah,7          ;function number again

        int   21h           ;now the extended code number is in AL

        cmp   al,75         ;check if "cursor-left"

        jne   C_R           ;if not, check next possibility

        jmp   CURSOR_LEFT   ;if so, go to routine

C_R:    cmp   al,77         ;...etc...
```

You can also use function 0h of the BIOS interrupt 16h. The function waits for a character and returns it in AL. In this function, extended codes require calling the interrupt only once. If 0 appears in AL, the extended code number is found in AH. The Ctrl-Break condition is not detected.

```
;---GET A KEYSTROKE:

        mov   ah,0          ;function number to intercept keystroke

        int   16h           ;get the keystroke
```

```
        cmp  al,0              ;is it an extended code?
        je   EXTENDED_CODE     ;if so, go to special routine
          .                    ;otherwise, take ASCII char from AL

          .


;---EXTENDED CODE ROUTINE:
EXTENDED_CODE:
        cmp  ah,75             ;take extended code from AH
          .                    ;...etc...

          .
```

On machines using a 101-key extended keyboard, you can use function 10h of interrupt 16h instead. It can return the codes for keys not found on the 83- and 84-key keyboards served by function 0. Function 0 is still at your disposal in these machines and it will translate or filter out keystrokes not found on older keyboards. See Chapter 2, "Determine the Kind of Keyboard in Use," to learn how to determine the kind of keyboard a computer uses.

Intercept Keystrokes and Display Them Automatically

Automatic display of keystrokes ("echoing") descends from a time when most software behaved like a teletype machine. Today's programs seldom use this feature. Instead, they examine each keystroke as it arrives to determine whether it should be displayed or not, and if so, they precisely control where and how the keystroke is displayed. By comparison, a simple keyboard loop with automatic echoing might display (or attempt to display) inadmissable keystrokes, and might allow input to spill over to areas of the screen where it should not intrude. Note that when extended codes are echoed, they are displayed as two separate codes, with the first character (ASCII 0) appearing as a blank.

Of the compilers discussed in this book, only the C compilers provide a function that inputs a single character from the keyboard and echos it automatically. BASIC and Pascal programs must provide the code that displays each character as it arrives.

C

The *getche* function displays each character that it returns, and waits for a keystroke when none is present in the keyboard buffer. When the return value is 0, an extended code has been found and *getche* must be called a second time to fetch the code number. In this case, *getche* displays a blank for the first character, and then the ASCII symbol associated with the extended code number.

```c
#include  <conio.h>


int  the_char;


the_char = getche();
if(the_char){             /* ASCII code case */

  .

} else {                  /* extended code case */
the_char = getche();

  .

}
```

194

Assembler

Function 1 of INT 21h fetches a character from the keyboard buffer, waiting for one if none is found, and then echos the character on the screen at the current cursor position. Text wraps around from one line of the screen to the next. There is no *word wrap*, and individual words may be broken in two.

Characters are returned in AL. AL receives **0** when an extended code is intercepted, in which case you should repeat the interrupt to bring the second byte of the code into AL. In this case, the function displays the 0 character as a blank, and then follows it with the ASCII symbol associated with the extended code. This function detects the Ctrl-Break condition, which is discussed in "Write a Ctrl-Break Routine," below.

```
;---GET A KEYSTROKE:

        mov   ah,1           ;set the function number
        int   21h            ;wait for a character
        cmp   al,0           ;extended code?
        je    EXTENDED_CODE   ;if so, jump to special routine
        .                    ;else, take ASCII character from AL

        .

;---EXTENDED CODE ROUTINE:

        mov   ah,1           ;prepare to call function again
        int   21h            ;bring the code number into AL
        cmp   al,77          ;check if "cursor-right"
        jne   C_R            ;if not, check next possibility
        jmp   CURSOR_RIGHT   ;if so, go to routine
C_R:    cmp   al,75          ;...etc...
```

This function ignores the escape key. It interprets a <Tab> keystroke normally. The <Backspace> key causes the cursor to move back one space, but the character in that position is not erased and it will be overwritten by the next incoming character. The <Enter> key makes the cursor move to the start of the current line — there is no "line feed" to the next line of the display.

Intercept a Keystroke Only If One Is Available

Some real-time applications cannot stop to wait for incoming keystrokes. A video game, for example, would need to stop all action on screen while waiting for keystrokes. Such applications test for the presence of a keystroke before attempting to take one from the buffer, or they use a routine that immediately returns either a code from the buffer or a flag telling that no code is available.

BASIC

BASIC's *INKEY$* function returns a one- or two-byte string if it finds a character in the keyboard buffer, or a null string (two quotation marks with nothing between) if it does not. This function does not wait for a keystroke. A one-byte string holds an ASCII code, and a two-byte string holds an extended code. You can use *LEN* to find out the string length, *RIGHT$* to eliminate the first, zero character of an extended code, and *ASC* to convert the string to a numeric value in order to perform error-checking and conversions. In this example, *C$* holds the string returned by *INKEY$*, and *KEYCODE* holds an integer conversion of this value.

```
C$=INKEY$                      'try for a code
IF C$="" THEN GOTO NOKEYSTROKE 'jump ahead if no keystroke
IF LEN(C$)=2 THEN GOTO EXTENDEDCODE 'jump if extended
KEYCODE=ASC(C$)                'convert to numeric value
   .
   .


EXTENDEDCODE:                  'extended code case
  C$=RIGHT$(C$,1)              'eliminate 1st byte of code
  KEYCODE=ASC(C$)              'convert to numeric value
   .
   .
```

```
NOKEYSTROKE:                    'no keystroke case

     .

     .
```

Pascal

In Turbo Pascal, call the *KeyPressed* function to find out if the keyboard buffer holds a code. It returns TRUE when a code is present, and FALSE otherwise. Then call *ReadKey* only if a code is available. It returns a *char* value that is 0 for extended codes, in which case you must call *ReadKey* a second time to fetch the extended code number.

```
var
   TheChar: char;


if KeyPressed then
begin
   TheChar := ReadKey;
   if TheChar <> Chr(0) then
     begin                  {ASCII code case}

        .

        .

     end else
     begin                  {extended code case}
       TheChar := ReadKey;

        .

        .

     end;
```

C

In both Borland's C and Microsoft's C, call the *kbhit* function to see if the buffer holds a keystroke, and then *getch* to fetch the keystroke if one is present. When the return character is 0, an extended code has been found, and you can get the code by using *getch* a second time without calling *kbhit* first.

```
int the_key;   /* holds the keystroke */


if (kbhit)
{
  the_key = getch();
  if (the_key)     /* ASCII code case */
  {

    /* process ASCII codes here */

  } else {
    the_key = getch();

    /* process extended codes here */

  }
}
```

Assembler

Function 6 of INT 21h is the only interrupt that intercepts keystrokes without waiting. The function does not echo characters on the screen, nor does it sense Ctrl-Break. FFh must be placed in AL before calling this interrupt. Otherwise function 6 serves an entirely different purpose — it displays at the current cursor position whatever character is found in DL. The zero flag is set if there are no characters in the buffer. When a character is intercepted, it is placed in AL. Should the character be 0, an extended code is indicated, and a second call is needed to fetch the code number.

```
    mov  ah,6        ;DOS function 6
    mov  dl,0FFh     ;request function for keyboard input
    int  21h         ;get character
    jz   NO_CHAR     ;jump to NO_CHAR if no keystroke
```

```
        cmp   al,0            ;see if character is ASCII 0
        je    EXTENDED_CODE   ;if so, go to extended code routine
         .                    ;ASCII character now in AL

         .

EXTENDED_CODE:
        int   21h             ;get 2nd byte of extended code
         .                    ;code number now in AL

         .
```

Although there is no BIOS routine that returns a keystroke only if one is present in the keyboard buffer, you can easily combine BIOS functions 0 and 1 of interrupt 16h to achieve the same effect. Function 1 checks whether a keystroke is present in the buffer and clears the zero flag if so. There are no input registers. If a character is present, function 0 can then be called to fetch it from the buffer. For ASCII codes, this function returns the code in AL and the scan code of the key that produced the character in AH. For extended codes, AL holds 0 and AH holds the extended code number.

```
;---Intercept a keystroke only if one is waiting:
        mov   ah,1            ;function to check for keystroke
        int   16h             ;
        jnz   NoChar          ;jump ahead if no character
        mov   ah,0            ;function to fetch a character
        int   16h             ;and now the char is in AH:AL

         .

         .

NoChar:                       ;continue without a character

         .

         .
```

For 101-key extended keyboards, use function 11h of interrupt 16h instead of function 1, and function 10h of interrupt 16h instead of function 0. These capture keystrokes that don't occur on earlier 83- and 84-key keyboards. Chapter 2, "Determine the Kind of Keyboard in Use," explains how software can find out the kind of keyboard a machine is using.

Intercept a String of Keystrokes

Most compilers include a library function that returns an entire string from the keyboard, echoing each character as it arrives. When the <Enter> key is pressed, the function returns the input in a string variable (the <enter> character (ASCII 13) is not appended to the string). DOS also includes such a function, although it is not necessarily used by compilers. The screen echo occurs at the current cursor position and wraps around to the next screen row without performing any sort of word wrap.

These input routines descend from a time when software behaved like a teletype machine, displaying both input and output as an unending sequence of left-justified lines much like the DOS command line. Typically, such routines discard extended codes, but accept control codes (ASCII 0 through 31), displaying them as a two-character sequence like ^G. Such routines are of little use in today's "user-friendly" software, but they still may play a role in simple utility programs, or in software developed for in-house use.

BASIC

BASIC's *INPUT* function intercepts and echos strings. INPUT incorporates certain line-editing features so that typing errors may be corrected before the string is entered. The cursor keys work normally, as do the <Del> and <Back-space> keys. A number of other editing commands, such as for deleting to the end of the line, are listed in the compiler's documentation.

INPUT may optionally display a message to prompt the user for input. This message is displayed at the current cursor position, and the input is echoed immediately thereafter. The input string may be up to 254 characters long. The excess characters are ignored when this length is exceeded. To ask a user to input his or her name, you might write:

```
INPUT "Enter your name: ",NAME$  'assign string to NAME$
```

Specify a null string when no message is required:

```
INPUT "",NAME$
```

INPUT can automatically convert numbers into numeric form. This is done when the specified variable is of numeric type, rather than string type. For example:

```
INPUT "Enter your age: ",AGE%  'input age, return as an integer
```

Several values may be elicited by a single INPUT statement. For example:

```
INPUT "Enter day, month, and year: ",DAY%,MONTH%,YEAR%
```

The data is separated by commas as it is input, not by pressing the <Enter> key. The cursor wraps to the start of the next line after each INPUT statement. To stop this from happening, place a semicolon after the word *INPUT*:

```
INPUT; "Enter your telephone number: ",TELNUMBER$
```

Pascal

Pascal's *Readln* function inputs strings from the keyboard, echoing each character as it arrives, starting from the current cursor position. In its simplest use, the function takes a single string variable as a parameter:

```
var

    TheString: string[65];



Readln(TheString);   {input the string}
```

If you specify a numeric variable instead, *Readln* will convert the incoming string to that value:

```
var

    TheNumber: word;



Readln(TheNumber);   {input an unsigned integer}
```

This function can take several parameters at once:

```
Readln(TheNumber,TheString);
```

The logic of how multiple parameters are defined is a bit complicated. When two or more *numeric* values are input, the end of each is marked by either a space character, or by pressing <Enter>. In either case, the function returns only when <Enter> is pressed after all parameters have been input. Because strings may contain spaces, multiple strings must each be terminated by <Enter>. Strings and numbers can be combined in one statement.

Readln can edit input by the <Backspace> key, but <Del> doesn't work. The <Esc> key clears the line and restarts input from the beginning, or from whatever point the <Enter> key was last pressed. Additional characters are ignored when the user attempts to input more characters than the variables have been declared to hold.

C

C programs can input and convert strings of data using the *scanf* function, or variants of this function. *Scanf* is much like the familiar *printf* function that displays data. The first parameter for the function is a string containing specifiers for the kind of input that will be received. Additional parameters point to the variables where the corresponding input will be placed by *scanf*. For example, to input a string variable, write:

```
char the_string[80];


scanf("%s",&the_string);
```

The incoming string is displayed as it is typed, and it is deposited in the variable *the_string*. By preceding the variable name with the "&" sign, you tell scanf the variable's address. As in a *printf* statement, the symbol %s means "a variable of string type." Other symbols include %c for a character (byte), %d for integers, %l for long values, and %f for a floating point value. To input an integer, write:

```
int the_integer;


scanf("%d",&the_integer);
```

To input first a string and then an integer, write:

```
scanf("%s%d",&the_string,&the_integer);
```

As they are typed in, multiple values are separated by either spaces or carriage returns (this means that you cannot input strings that contain space characters using *scanf*). When carriage returns are used instead of spaces, display wraps to the next line. Tab keystrokes are interpreted normally, and functionally tabs act like spaces. The <Esc> key displays a backslash, wraps the cursor to the next line, and starts input all over again. A carriage-return terminates the function, but only when enough individual data items have been input. The *scanf* function can behave erratically when the wrong kind of data is received. These characteristics make *scanf* unsuitable for mass-market software.

Because input is buffered, the <cursor-right> and <cursor-left> keys work in an unusual way — one that is familiar from the DOS command line. The <cursor-left> key acts as a backspace, while the <cursor-right> key reintroduces whatever was last written at the position to which the key moves the cursor. By holding down <cursor-right>, the user can recall the string that was typed the last time the function was used.

The *scanf* function is one of the most elaborate offered by standard C libraries. There are a number of ways in which you can limit the kind of input, the length of input, and how the input is formatted. For example, you can restrict input to the characters A through Z by specifying **%[A-Z]** in the input string. There also are related functions, such as *cscanf*, which formats input according to a specification string to which it receives a pointer. See the extensive documentation that accompanies the *scanf* function for more information.

In addition to *scanf*, C offers the *gets* function for inputting strings with automatic screen echo. It takes buffered input from *stdin* (that is, from the keyboard buffer). A single *gets* statement can input only one string, and no conversions are performed. Unlike *scanf*, the string can include spaces. Input ends when the <Enter> key is pressed. Extended codes are ignored and control codes are represented as two-character sequences like **^A**. The left and right cursor keys work in the same way as in *scanf*. Here is an example:

```
char the_string[80];


gets(&the_string);
printf("Here is the string: %s\n",the_string);
```

Assembler

Function 0Ah of INT 21h inputs strings of up to 254 characters, echoing the input onto the display. On entry, DS:DX points to the place in memory where the string will be deposited. The first byte at this location must be initialized with the maximum number of bytes allocated to the string. After the string is entered, the second byte is given the number of characters actually received. The string itself begins from the third byte.

The code originating from the terminating carriage return (ASCII 13) is entered as the final character of the string. Allocate just enough memory for the desired string length plus the initial two bytes and one extra byte for the carriage return. When you set the maximum string length in the first byte, you must add 1 for the carriage return character. However, the carriage return is *not* counted in the character tally placed by the function in the second of the two leading bytes. Thus, to receive a 50-character string, allocate 53 bytes of memory and place 51 in the first byte. If 50 characters are entered, on return the second byte will contain 50 and the 53rd byte of allocated memory will hold ASCII 13.

```
;---IN THE DATA SEGMENT:
STRING db   53 dup(?)    ;space for 50 char string
                         ;  (2 chars for descriptor, 1 for CR)
```

203

```
;---RECEIVE A STRING FROM THE KEYBOARD:
        lea  dx,STRING     ;DS:DX points to string space
        mov  bx,dx         ;make BX also point to string
        mov  al,51         ;set string length (+1 for CR)
        mov  [bx],al       ;place in first byte of descriptor
        mov  ah,0Ah        ;function number of string routine
        int  21h           ;receive the string
;---CHECK THE LENGTH OF THE STRING:
        mov  ah,[bx]+1     ;length now in AH
```

This interrupt uses the DOS line editing functions. Striking the backspace or cursor-left keys deletes the prior character on the screen, and eliminates it from memory as well. The tab key works, extended codes are ignored, and empty strings are permitted (that is, a carriage return without any preceding keystrokes). On the monitor, strings wrap at the end of a line, and the screen scrolls upward when a string reaches the bottom right corner. When keystrokes exceed the allotted length of the string, they are ignored and the speaker beeps.

DOS provides a second way of receiving a string. Function 3Fh of interrupt 21h is a general purpose input function that is most commonly used in disk operations. It requires a predefined *handle*, which is a code number used by the operating system to designate an I/O device. The handle for the keyboard is the number 0, and on entry it is placed in BX. Point DS:DX at the place where the string is to reside, place the maximum string length in CX, and call the function:

```
;---INPUT STRING:
STRING_BUFFER DB 102 DUP (?)


;---INPUT STRING: READ STRING WITHOUT ECHOING:
        mov  ah,3fh              ;function number
        mov  bx,0               ;handle number
        lea  dx,STRING_BUFFER   ;DS:DX points to buffer
        mov  cx,100             ;maximum length of string
        int  21h                ;wait for input
```

String input terminates when the Enter key is struck, and DOS adds two characters to the end of the string: a carriage return and line feed (ASCII 13 and ASCII 10). Because of these additional characters, when the length of a string is specified as 100 characters, it may occupy up to 102 bytes of memory. The length of the string entered is returned in AX, and this value includes the two terminating characters.

Write a General-Purpose Keyboard Input Routine

The system of codes used by the keyboard defies simple interpretation. The codes may be one or two bytes long, and there is no simple correspondence between the code length and whether it is for a character or for hardware control. Not all keystroke combinations even produce a unique code, and extra care must be taken to differentiate them. Neither the ASCII codes nor the extended codes are consistently numbered in a fashion that optimizes testing and error checking. Consequently, keyboard input routines can be messy.

When your program is controlled by a mouse as well as the keyboard, the keyboard input routine must be expanded into a general-purpose *event loop.* The program no longer just waits for the next keystroke and then responds. Instead, it calls a keyboard input routine only after ascertaining that a keystroke is available. Otherwise, it continually watches for changes in the mouse position and changes in the status of the mouse buttons.

Normally, once a mouse button is pressed, the input loop watches only the mouse until the button activity has finished (sometimes the loop also watches the shift key status registers discussed in Chapter 8, "Check/Set the Status of the Toggle and Shift Keys," to decode *shift-clicks* or *shift-drags*). Only after the mouse button is released is another pass made to see if a keystroke has arrived. Note that the keyboard interrupt will continue to insert codes into the buffer no matter what is happening with the mouse — the two devices are completely independent. Actual mouse input code is not included here because it depends entirely on the screen design, menuing system, and so on. See Chapter 9, "Intercept Clicks, Double-Clicks, and Drag Events," for a discussion of mouse input code design.

Sometimes the input loop can be simplified by converting mouse actions, such as menu selections, into the corresponding keyboard control codes and passing those codes through the keyboard input loop for interpretation and execution. The examples found in this section are designed this way.

The examples also use flags to tell the routine whether or not to accept certain kinds of input at any moment. These flags let a program customize the input routine for the task at hand. For instance, all extended codes could be rejected while a file name is elicited. An actual input routine will use a more elaborate system of checks to keep input in range. Figure 7-3 diagrams the input loop design.

In these examples for BASIC, Pascal, and C, a BIOS keyboard interrupt is called to obtain keystrokes instead of using the compiler's own input functions. This is function 0 of INT 16h. Its virtue is that it lets the routine test the scan codes of incoming ASCII codes so that the routine can differentiate between keystrokes that produce the same code, such as <Backspace> and <Ctrl-H>. The function returns an ASCII code in AL and the scan code in AH. For extended codes, AL is 0 and the extended code number is returned in AH. Machines that support a 101-key keyboard can use BIOS function 10h instead. It captures keystrokes not found on 83- and 84-key keyboards, and which are filtered out by function 0 on these machines. The examples below confine themselves to function 0. See Chapter 2, "Determine the Kind of Keyboard in Use," to learn how to determine whether a machine uses a 101-key keyboard.

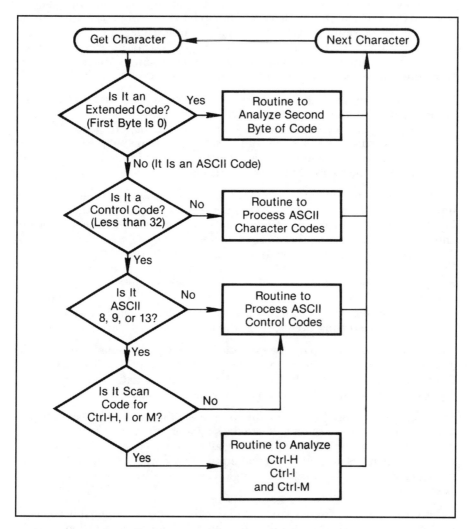

Figure 7-3 Flow chart for a general input routine

Function 0 of interrupt 16h (and function 10h as well) waits for a keystroke if none is found in the buffer. Software that uses a mouse should not suspend operations this way, since it must constantly poll the mouse driver to look for changes in the mouse coordinates or buttons. Accordingly, before calling the keyboard input function, the examples in this section call function 1 of interrupt 16h (or optionally function 11h for 101-key keyboards) to find out if a keystroke is waiting. If not, the call to function 0 is skipped over and control moves on the mouse input code. Functions 1 and 11h clear the processor's zero flag (bit 6 of the flag register) when a character is found in the keyboard buffer.

BASIC

```
' $INCLUDE: 'QBX.BI'
DIM REGS AS RegType      ' Define register array for interrupt

AcceptAlpha = TRUE
AcceptExtended = TRUE
AcceptControl = TRUE
NextInput:
   KeyCode = &HFF        '&HFF flags that no event has arrived
   REGS.AX = &H0100      'test to see if a char is available
   CALL Interrupt(&H16,REGS,REGS)    'call the interrupt
   ZeroFlag = REGS.FLAGS AND &H40
   If ZeroFlag = 0 THEN 'if character is present...
        REGS.AX = &H0000      'function to fetch character
        CALL Interrupt(&H16, REGS, REGS) 'get the character
        KeyCode = Regs.AX AND &HFF       'isolate the key code
        ScanCode = (Regs.AX AND &HFF00) \ 256 'isolate/shift scan code
   ELSE
             'mouse input routine
      .
      . 'If mouse activity is detected, this routine loops until
```

207

```
    .    'mouse input has finished.
    .    'When a menu selection is made, the corresponding
    .    'keystroke codes are placed in KeyCode and ScanCode.
    .
  ENDIF
  IF KeyCode = &HFF THEN GOTO NextInput 'loop when no input
  IF (KeyCode = 0) AND AcceptExtended = TRUE THEN GOTO ExtendedCode
  IF (KeyCode < 32) AND AcceptControl = TRUE THEN GOTO ControlCode
  IF KeyCode > 122 THEN GOTO NextInput 'out of range
  IF NOT AcceptAlpha THEN GOTO NextInput 'accept alpha?
    .
    .    'process alphabetic data
    .
  GOTO NextInput  'go get next char


ExtendedCode:    'ScanCode holds the extended code number
  IF ScanCode=15 THEN CALL BackTabRoutine:GOTO NextInput
  IF ScanCode=72 THEN CALL CursorUpRoutine:GOTO NextInput
    .
    .      'etc.
    .
  GOTO NextInput    'ignore extraneous extended codes


ControlCode:    'control codes are 1-byte ASCII codes in KeyCode
  IF KeyCode = 8 THEN
    IF ScanCode = 14 THEN '<backspace> scan code
    CALL BackspaceRoutine:GOTO Nextinput
    ELSE CALL CtrlHRoutine:GOTO Nextinput
     ENDIF
  ENDIF
  IF KeyCode = 9 THEN
```

```
    IF ScanCode = 15 THEN '<tab> scan code
    CALL TabRoutine:GOTO Nextinput
    ELSE CALL CtrlIRoutine:GOTO Nextinput
    ENDIF
  ENDIF
  IF KeyCode = 13 THEN
    IF ScanCode = 28 THEN '<enter> scan code
    CALL EnterKeyRoutine:GOTO Nextinput
    ELSE CALL CtrlMRoutine:GOTO Nextinput
    ENDIF
  ENDIF
  IF KeyCode = 27 THEN
    IF ScanCode = 1 THEN '<esc> scan code
    CALL EscKeyRoutine:GOTO Nextinput
    ELSE CALL Ctrl[Routine:GOTO Nextinput
    ENDIF
  ENDIF

    .

    .  'now test other control codes
    .  'without scan code comparisons


    .

  If KeyCode = 26 THEN END 'Quit if Ctrl-Z

  GOTO NextInput    'ignore extraneous command codes
```

Pascal

```
uses DOS;
Var
  Regs: Registers;          {declare interrupt register array}
  KeyCode,ScanCode: Byte;
  AcceptAlpha,AcceptExtended,AcceptControl: Boolean;
```

209

```
   Label                        {flags to control input types}

   NextInput, ExtendedCode, ControlCode;

   AcceptAlpha := TRUE;      {Initialize flags}
   AcceptExtended := TRUE;
   AcceptControl := TRUE;
NextInput:
   KeyCode := $FF;              {FF flags that no event has arrived}
   if KeyPressed = TRUE then
   begin
     Regs.AH := 0;            {BIOS function number}
     Intr($16,Regs);          {get the keystroke}
     KeyCode := Regs.AL;
     ScanCode := Regs.AH;
   end else
   begin                   {mouse input routine}

     .
     . {If mouse activity is detected, this routine loops}
     . {until mouse input has finished.}
     . {When a menu selection is made, the corresponding}
     . {keystroke codes are placed in KeyCode and ScanCode}

     .
   end;
   if KeyCode = $FF then goto NextInput; {loop when no input}
   if (KeyCode = 0) and AcceptExtended then goto ExtendedCode;
   if (KeyCode < 32) and AcceptControl then goto ControlCode;
   if KeyCode > 122 then goto NextInput; {out of range}
   If not AcceptAlpha then goto NextInput; {accept alpha?}

   .
   . {process alphabetic data}
```

```
        .
     goto NextInput;  {go get next char}


ExtendedCode:    {ScanCode holds the extended code number}
     if ScanCode=15 then begin BackTabRoutine;goto NextInput;end;
     if ScanCode=72 then begin CursorUpRoutine;goto NextInput;end;

        .
        .    {etc.}
        .

     goto NextInput; {ignore extraneous extended codes}


ControlCode:    {control codes are 1-byte ASCII codes in KeyCode}
     if KeyCode = 8 then if ScanCode = 14  {<backspace> scan code}
       then begin BackspaceRoutine;goto Nextinput;end
       else begin CtrlHRoutine;goto Nextinput;end;
     if KeyCode = 9 then if ScanCode = 15  {<tab> scan code}
       then begin TabRoutine;goto Nextinput;end
       else begin CtrlIRoutine;goto Nextinput;end;
     if KeyCode = 13 then if ScanCode = 28 {<enter> scan code}
       then begin EnterKeyRoutine;goto Nextinput;end
       else begin CtrlMRoutine;goto Nextinput;end;
     if KeyCode = 27 then if ScanCode = 1  {<esc> scan code}
       then begin EscKeyRoutine;goto Nextinput;end
       else begin Ctrl[Routine;goto Nextinput;end;

        .
        .   {now test other control codes}
        .   {without scan code comparisons}
        .

     If Keycode = 26 then Exit;    {Quit program if Ctrl-Z}
     goto NextInput; {ignore extraneous command codes}
```

211

C

```c
#include <dos.h>

union REGS regs;          /* declare the register array*/
unsigned char keycode,scancode;
unsigned char accept_alpha,accept_extended,accept_control;
                          /*flags to control input types*/

accept_alpha = 0xFF;      /* initialize flags */
accept_extended = 0xFF;
accept_control = 0xFF;
next_input:
  keycode = 0xFF;         /*0xFF flags that no event has arrived*/
  if (kbhit())
  {
    regs.h.ah = 0;              /*BIOS function number*/
    int86(0x16,&regs,&regs); /*get the keystroke*/
    keycode = regs.h.al;
    scancode = regs.h.ah;
  } else {                      /* begin mouse input routine*/
    .
    . /*If mouse activity is detected, this routine loops*/
    . /*until mouse input has finished*/
    . /*When a menu selection is made, the corresponding*/
    . /*keystroke codes are placed in keycode and scancode*/
    .
  }
  if (keycode == 0xFF) goto next_input; /*loop when no input*/
```

```
    if (keycode == 0 && accept_extended) goto ExtendedCode;
    if (keycode < 32 && accept_control) goto ControlCode;
    if (keycode > 122) goto next_input; /*out of range*/
    if (! accept_alpha) goto next_input; /*accept alpha?*/
        .
        .   /*process alphabetic data*/
        .
    goto next_input;   /*go get next char*/


ExtendedCode:    /*scancode holds the extended code number*/
    if (scancode==15){BackTabRoutine();goto next_input;}
    if (scancode==72){CursorUpRoutine();goto next_input;}
        .
        .    /*etc.*/
        .
    goto next_input; /*ignore extraneous extended codes*/


ControlCode:    /*control codes are 1-byte codes in keycode*/
    if (keycode == 8){
        if (scancode == 14){ /*<backspace> scan code*/
        BackspaceRoutine();goto next_input;}
        else {CtrlHRoutine();goto next_input;}
    }
    if (keycode == 9){
        if (scancode == 15){   /*<tab> scan code*/
        TabRoutine();goto next_input;}
        else {CtrlIRoutine();goto next_input;}
    }
    if (keycode == 13){
        if (scancode == 28){ /*<enter> scan code*/
```

```
    EnterKeyRoutine();goto next_input;}
    else {CtrlMRoutine();goto next_input;}
}
if (keycode == 27){
   if (scancode == 1){   /*<esc> scan code*/
   EscKeyRoutine();goto next_input;}
   else {CtrlBracketRoutine();goto next_input;}
}

  .
  .   /*now test other control codes*/
  .   /*without scan code comparisons*/

  .
If (keycode == 26) exit();   /* quit on Ctrl-Z */
goto next_input; /*ignore extraneous command codes*/
```

Assembler

```
;---GET A KEYSTROKE AND DETERMINE ITS TYPE:
NEXT:
        mov   ah,01h         ;function to test for keystrokes
        int   16h            ;
        jz    MOUSEMONITOR   ;jump to mouse routine if no char
        mov   ah,0           ;select BIOS keyboard input function
        int   16h            ;go get the keystroke
        cmp   al,0           ;check if extended code
        je    EXTENDED_CODE  ;if so, jump to its routine
        cmp   al,32          ;check if control code
        jl    CONTROL_CODE   ;if so, jump to its routine
        cmp   al,122         ;see if above range of typewriter chars
        jg    NEXT           ;if so, get another character
```

214

```
;---NOW PROCESS CHARACTER IN AL: (assumes ES:DI -> input buffer)
        stosb                   ;save character in memory at ES:DI ptr
        mov  ah,2               ;choose DOS function to display char
        mov  dl,al              ;put character in DL, as required
        int  21h               ;display character (cursor forwards)
          .                     ;etc.

          .

          .

        jmp  NEXT               ;get next character


MOUSEMONITOR:                   ;process mouse code here

          .

          .

          .

        jmp  Next
;---ANALYZE EXTENDED CODES (2nd byte of code is in AH):
EXTENDED_CODE: cmp  ah,71  ;check number against bottom of range
        jl   REJECT            ;if below, get next char via REJECT
        cmp  ah,81             ;check number against top of range
        jg   REJECT            ;if above, get next char via REJECT
;---AH HAS A CURSOR CODE -- ANALYZE IT:
        cmp  ah,72             ;see if 'cursor up'
        je   C_U               ;if so, go to 'cursor up' routine
        cmp  ah,80             ;see if 'cursor down'
        je   C_D               ;if so, go to 'cursor down' routine

          .

          .
```

```
C_U:    call CURSOR_UP       ;perform 'cursor up' routine
        jmp  NEXT            ;get next keystroke
C_D:    call CURSOR_DOWN     ;perform 'cursor down' routine
        jmp  NEXT            ;get next keystroke


;---ANALYZE CONTROL CODES (start with special cases)
CONTROL_CODE: cmp  al,13    ;is the code ASCII 13?
        jne  TAB            ;if not, check next special case
        cmp  ah,28          ;it's 13 -- was scan code for CR?
        jne  C_M            ;if not, go to Ctrl-M case
        call CARRIAGE_RETURN ;perform carriage return routine
        jmp  NEXT           ;go get next keystroke
C_M:    call CTRL_M         ;perform Ctrl-M routine
        jmp  NEXT           ;go get next keystroke
TAB:    cmp  al,9           ;check whether TAB or Ctrl-I...
             .
             .
        cmp  al,10          ;after special cases, check others
             .
             .
REJECT: jmp  NEXT           ;default: go get another keystroke
```

Write a Ctrl-Break Routine

When the keyboard interrupt detects the Ctrl-Break key combination, the interrupt sets a flag indicating that there is need for the Ctrl-Break routine to come into action. Control is given to the Ctrl-Break routine only at the time that the program uses a DOS function that is capable of sensing this flag. Normally, only the standard DOS input-output functions can detect Ctrl-Break (functions 1 through C of interrupt 21h except for functions 6 and 7). However, the computer user can configure DOS so that all DOS functions check for Ctrl-Break whenever they are called. This is done by placing the line **BREAK = ON** in a computer's AUTOEXEC.BAT or CONFIG.SYS files. This action slightly slows program execution.

The Ctrl-Break routine exists as a way of exiting a program at any time, particularly when the program has run into trouble and cannot terminate normally. When a DOS function senses the Ctrl-Break status, control is directed to the routine pointed to by interrupt vector 23h. DOS sets up the routine to quit the program in progress. But the routine may be rewritten to any specifications you like.

A programmable routine is required so that a program can clean up after itself before terminating. The routine can query the user as to whether he or she really wants to quit the program. Files can be saved, and changed interrupt vectors restored. Any direct control over hardware must also be relinquished. For example, the program may need to turn off sound, or send a form-feed to the printer. Once these tasks have been taken care of, the Ctrl-Break routine must execute a command to terminate the program. If the routine just returns using an IRET (interrupt return) instruction, control is given back to the program.

The following example shows a Ctrl-Break routine rendered in assembly language. It terminates a program using function 4Ch of interrupt 21h. A routine can be written in high-level languages using the techniques shown in Chapter 4, "Write Your Own Interrupt Service Routine," which explains how to write an interrupt handler.

Assembler

This example exits a program after executing a sequence of Ctrl-Break instructions.

```
;---HERE IS THE NEW CTRL-BREAK ROUTINE:

C_B     proc far

          .
```

```
          .
          .                      ;Ctrl-Break exit code goes here
          .
          .

     mov  ah,4Ch                 ;function to terminate
     mov  al,0                   ;return code
     int  21h                    ;quit the program
C_B  endp


;---THIS CODE SETS THE INTERRUPT VECTOR:
     push ds                     ;preserve DS
     lds  dx,C_B                 ;point DS:DX to the Ctrl-Break routine
     mov  ah,25h                 ;function to change interrupt vector
     mov  al,23h                 ;number of the vector
     int  21h                    ;change the vector
     pop  ds                     ;restore DS
```

DOS automatically reinitializes the Ctrl-Break vector when a program terminates, so there is no need for the Ctrl-Break routine to do this job itself.

Note that a program can check at any time if a "request" for the Ctrl-Break routine has been made. Place 0 in AL and call function 33 of INT 21h. On return, DL will hold 1 if the status is "on" and 0 if it is not. Placing 1 in AL at entry *sets* the status. In this case, before calling the function, place 1 or 0 in DL to turn the status "on" or "off."

8

Interpreting Keystrokes

- Minitutorial: Kinds of Keystrokes
- Check/Set the Status of the Toggle and Shift Keys
- Use the Numeric Keypad and Cursor Keys
- Use Special-Purpose Keys
- Look Up a Scan Code
- Look Up an ASCII Code
- Look Up a Box-Graphic Code
- Look Up an Extended Code

Minitutorial: Kinds of Keystrokes

Every time a keyboard key is pressed or released, the keyboard sends a scan code to the computer. The keyboard interrupt interprets each scan code and performs one of the following actions:

- When the scan code is associated with a *shift key* (<Shift>, <Ctrl>, or <Alt>) or a *toggle key* (<Caps Lock>, <Num Lock>, <Scroll Lock>, or <Ins>) the keyboard interrupt alters settings in two status bytes held in the BIOS data area. Individual bits in these bytes report whether a toggle key is "on" or "off," or whether a shift or toggle key is currently held down.

- When the scan code is associated with an ordinary character key like <A> or <#>, the keyboard interrupt consults the shift/toggle status registers to see whether the key is being used in lower- or uppercase, and then it deposits a one-byte ASCII code in the keyboard buffer.

- When the scan code comes from a special-purpose key, the code may result in either an ASCII or extended code, depending on whether the ASCII character set provides a symbol for the keystroke. For example,

<Enter> and <Esc> are both associated with one-byte ASCII codes. <Cursor-down> and <F1> are not supported by the ASCII set, so extended codes are used.

- A few keystrokes or keystroke combinations, such as <Ctrl-Alt-Del>, <PrtSc>, and <Sys Req>, cause the keyboard interrupt handler to directly call another interrupt routine.

- Finally, certain keystroke combinations, including <Ctrl-Brk> and <Ctrl-PrtSc>, set flags that may subsequently be used by the operating system. For example, the <Ctrl-Brk> flag tells DOS to exit the current application, and to execute an associated software interrupt before doing so. However, the interrupt service routine is not actually executed until the program calls a DOS routine.

This chapter lists the various key groupings, gives their codes, and explains any anomalies. You'll also find tables of ASCII codes, extended codes, and scan codes. You'll find that not all keys are logically grouped by the kind of code they issue. <Tab>, for example, generates a one-byte ASCII code, but <Back Tab> creates a two-byte extended code. These irregularities result from the limitations of the ASCII character set. Your keyboard input routines should take into account the following anomalies:

- There are four ASCII codes that can be produced in two ways. ASCII 8 is produced by both the Backspace key and by Ctrl-H, ASCII 9 by the Tab key or Ctrl-I, ASCII 13 by the Enter key or Ctrl-M, and ASCII 27 by the Esc key or Ctrl-[.

- The Ctrl key combines with the letters of the alphabet to produce one-byte (ASCII) codes. All other Ctrl combinations produce two-byte (extended) codes.

- The symbols that correspond to the 32 ASCII *control codes* are not displayed by those key input functions that automatically *echo* characters. However, they can be displayed by function 10h of INT 10h or by mapping the code directly into the video buffer.

- The <5> key on the numeric keypad is not operational when the <NumLock> key is set for cursor control.

- The <Ins> key is the one key that, when struck, both places a code to the keyboard buffer *and* makes a change in the shift and toggle key status registers. The bits in the status bytes are not toggled however, but are set only so long as the key is held down.

There are many keystroke combinations that are rejected by the keyboard interrupt handler. For example, combinations of <Alt> and the cursor keys do not leave any code at all in the keyboard buffer. Short of rewriting the keyboard interrupt handler (no small undertaking!) there's no way of using such key combinations that will work on all machines. However, on most machines you can use the "keyboard intercept" feature to detect unsupported keystrokes and report them as supported keystrokes.

This is function 4Fh of interrupt 15h, which is called by the keyboard interrupt every time that interrupt is activated. On both entry and exit, the AL register holds the scan code that was received by the interrupt and will be processed by the interrupt when function 4Fh returns. The function normally does nothing. Your programs can chain a routine into interrupt 15h (using the technique shown in Chapter 4, "Chain into Existing Interrupts") to act as function 4Fh and translate or discard incoming scan codes. Unfortunately, this feature was introduced only with the IBM AT and is not found in earlier machines.

Check/Set the Status of the Toggle and Shift Keys

The two bytes found at memory locations 0040:0017 and 0040:0018 hold bits showing the status of the shift and toggle keys.

position	bit	key	meaning when bit=1
0040:0017	7	Insert	Insert mode "on"
	6	CapsLock	CapsLock mode "on"
	5	NumLock	NumLock mode "on"
	4	ScrollLock	ScrollLock mode "on"
	3	Alt shift	key down
	2	Ctrl shift	key down
	1	Lefthand shift	key down
	0	Righthand shift	key down
0040:0018	7	Insert	key down
	6	CapsLock	key down
	5	NumLock	key down
	4	ScrollLock	key down
	3	Ctrl-NumLock	Ctrl-NumLock mode "on"

101-key keyboards have two Alt keys and two Ctrl keys. You can find out which key is down by looking at the appropriate bits at the following addresses:

position	bit	key	meaning when bit=1
0040:0018	1	Left Alt	key down
	0	Left Ctrl	key down
0040:0096	3	Right Alt	key down
	2	Right Ctrl	key down

The keyboard interrupt updates these status bytes immediately when a toggle or shift keystroke occurs. Note that the "key down" status of the <Ins> key is changed even when there is no room in the keyboard buffer for the code left by this keystroke.

The keyboard interrupt checks these status bits before interpreting incoming keystrokes, so when a program changes one of the bits, the effect is the same as physically striking the corresponding key. A program can set the state of any of these keys, particularly <NumLock>, to assure that input is of the desired kind. Conversely, your programs may need to read the status of the keys, perhaps to echo their current status on the screen. Most keyboards have indicator lights that show the current settings for <NumLock>, <CapsLock>, and <ScrollLock>. The indicator lights respond to changes your programs make in the status bytes.

The Shift Keys

The three kinds of shift keys cause only some of the other keys of the keyboard to generate different codes. Shift key combinations generate ASCII codes when character keys are upshifted or when <Ctrl> is combined with the letters <A> through <Z> (resulting in ASCII codes 1-26). All other shift key combinations produce extended codes.

Inadmissible shift key combinations produce no code at all. Except in the case of the special Ctrl-Alt combinations, only one shift key will be effective when more than one is pressed, with priority given to <Alt>, then <Ctrl>, and then <Shift>.

The ability to tell when a shift key is held down can occasionally be used as a way of sending signals to software without going through the keyboard buffer. Many memory-resident programs use shift key combinations as hotkeys by which the program is "awakened." The keys can also be used within a running application to signal an urgent message, such as "stop the printer." While a key code could do the same thing, the code might not be read from the buffer for quite some time as other commands are interpreted and executed.

Another advantage is that the shift keys can give fine control over certain kinds of operations. For example, consider a video game in which one spaceship continuously fires rounds at another. The spaceship guns might be controlled by a joystick button or by a keyboard key. The buttons on a joystick act like momentary contact switches; at any moment, the computer can find out whether the button is up or down. But when a keyboard key like <Ctrl-F> is used for the same purpose, a code would be repeatedly inserted into the keyboard buffer at a rate dictated by the computer's BIOS (the "typematic" rate). The keyboard's repeat rate is slow, and the keyboard input routine would need to test for an incoming keystroke for quite a while until it became clear that <Ctrl-F> was no longer held down. The result would be a noticeable delay between the time a key is released and the time the spaceship gun stops firing. By using shift keys instead, software can continuously examine the shift/toggle status registers and respond instantly to the release of a key.

The Toggle Keys

There are four toggle keys: <CapsLock>, <NumLock>, <ScrollLock>, and <Ins>. <CapsLock> works like the CapsLock on a typewriter keyboard. Note that the two <Shift> keys reverse the function of keys, so when Caps Lock is set to "on," the combination of, say, a <Shift> key and the <A> key will produce a *lowercase* "A." Num Lock toggles the function of the numeric keypad keys, which are also reversed by the Shift keys.

<ScrollLock> is intended to toggle the cursor keys in and out of a state where they scroll the screen rather than move the cursor. However, this key has no control over the screen or over operating system functions that write to the screen. It's up to you to write the code that makes the cursor keys work this way.

Finally, the <Ins> key is intended to toggle software in and out of a mode where text is inserted in the middle of other text. Again, it is the programmer's responsibility to endow the key with this role. Programmers have used this key in a variety of ways, but users tend to expect the key to have its traditional function. <Ins> is unique among all keys in that it places a code (0;82) in the keyboard buffer. It also sets bits in the status bytes shown above, but these last only as long as the key is held down. The other toggle keys make lasting changes in the status bytes, but leave nothing in the keyboard buffer.

All of the examples below test and set the status of the <Caps Lock> key. They do this by fetching the status byte at 0040:0017 and testing the high bit (whose value equals 128). Only the C compilers offer functions that can fetch this status byte, and none provides a way of changing the status byte.

BASIC

To find out the <Caps Lock> key status:

```
DEF SEG = &H40          'set memory segment to BIOS data area
STATUSBYTE=PEEK(&H17)   'get status byte
PRINT "Caps Lock is ";
IF STATUSBYTE AND 64 THEN PRINT "on" ELSE PRINT "off"
```

To toggle <Caps Lock> on, no matter the current setting:

```
DEF SEG = &H40
POKE &H17,PEEK(&H17) OR 64
```

Alternatively, you can find out the status of individual shift keys by calling the *GetShiftState* function found in the BASIC Toolbox. The function takes only one argument: the number of a bit in the status byte at 0040:0017. The function returns TRUE when the bit is set, and FALSE otherwise. For example, to find out if the <Ctrl> key is currently held down, you would write:

```
Result = GetShiftState(2)
```

Pascal

Use an absolute variable to read or write the status byte. First, declare the variable:

```
KeyboardStatus: byte absolute $0040:$0017;
```

Then AND the variable with the appropriate bit number. To test the status of the Caps Lock, write:

```
if KeyboardStatus and 64 <> 0

   then writeln('<Caps Lock> is ON')

   else writeln('<Caps Lock> is OFF');
```

To toggle <Caps Lock> on:

```
KeyboardStatus := KeyboardStatus or 64;
```

C

Both Borland and Microsoft C compilers provide functions that return the shift/toggle status byte at 0040:0017. The function is called *bioskey* in Borland's C and *_bios_keybrd* in Microsoft's C. Both functions return an integer value with the status byte in the low eight bits. The only parameter required is the interrupt function number **2**.

```
#include <bios.h>

int   status_byte;


status_byte = bioskey(2);       /* Borland */
```

or

```
status_byte = _bios_keybrd(2);  /* Microsoft */


if (status_byte & 64) printf("The <Caps Lock> mode is ON");
```

To turn on the <Caps Lock> mode, no matter the current setting, write:

```
char far *status_ptr = 0x00400017;


status_ptr = 0x00400017;
*status_ptr = *status_ptr ¦ 64;
```

Assembler

Function 2 of interrupt 16h gives access to the status byte at 0040:0017, returning it in AL.

```
;---CHECK STATUS OF CAPS LOCK MODE
        mov  ah,2          ;set function number
        int  16h           ;get the status byte
        test al,01000000b  ;test bit 6
        jz   caps_lock_off ;if bit is 0 then Caps Lock is off
```

Machines with 101-key keyboards can also use function 12h of interrupt 16h. Like function 2, it returns the status byte at 0040:0017 in AL. It returns a second status byte in AH that reports the status of the individual Alt and Ctrl keys:

bit	key	meaning when bit is set
7	Insert	Insert "on"
6	Caps Lock	Caps Lock mode "on"
5	Num Lock	Num Lock mode "on"
4	Scroll Lock	Scroll Lock mode "on"
3	Right Alt	key down
2	Right Ctrl	key down
1	Left Alt	key down
0	Left Ctrl	key down

Before using this function, you must ascertain whether a 101-key keyboard is in use. Chapter 2, "Determine the Kind of Keyboard in Use," explains how this is done.

Alternatively, you can access the status bytes directly. In this example, the Caps Lock mode is forced on by turning on bit 6 of the status byte at 0040:0017 (here addressed as 0000:0417).

```
sub   ax,ax                 ;set ES to 0
mov   es,ax                 ;
or    es:[417h],1000000b    ;set bit 6 in the status byte
```

Use the Numeric Keypad and Cursor Keys

The numeric keypad includes number keys that may double as cursor-control keys, the <Ins> and <Del> keys, and the <+> and <-> keys. Many keyboards have separate keypads for the cursor keys and number keys, but the ASCII codes or extended codes originating from the two keypads are the same as those from a combined keypad (scan codes differ, however). The <NumLock> key toggles most of the keypad keys between their two functions of moving the cursor and entering numbers. The <+> and <-> keys issue the same codes no matter how <NumLock> is set. The <5> key in the center of the keypad is not associated with cursor movements and is active only when <NumLock> is "on."

The keypad's number keys issue the same one-byte codes as the number keys at the top row of the keyboard — ASCII codes 48 through 57 for the numerals 0 through 9. Your programs can differentiate between the two key sets by checking the key scan codes. Chapter 7, "Write a General-Purpose Keyboard Input Routine," shows how this is done, and "Look Up a Scan Code," below, provides a table of scan codes. Note that either of the <Shift> keys shifts the keypad keys to the mode opposite that set by the <NumLock> key. The setting of the CapsLock key has no effect on the keypad. When <Num Lock> is "off," most keypad keys generate extended codes. Some of the keys, but not all, may be combined with <Ctrl> to generate additional codes. Unfortunately, <Ctrl-cursor-up> and <Ctrl-cursor-down> are not supported. The "keyboard intercept" function (function 4Fh of interrupt 15h, discussed in this chapter's *minitutorial*) can be used to detect these key combinations and transmit them to the keyboard interrupt handler as a supported keystroke combination, but the BIOS in early PCs does not provide this facility.

There is no connection whatsoever between the cursor keys and video hardware. Your programs must provide the code that causes the cursor to move, or the screen to scroll, when a cursor key is pressed.

Here is a summary of the keypad codes:

```
ASCII codes:

43                      +

45                      -

46                      .

48 - 57                 0 - 9
```

```
Extended codes:
72, 75, 77, 80          Cursor Up, Left, Right, & Down
71, 73, 79, 81          Home, PgUp, End, PgDn
82, 83                  Ins, Del
115, 116                Ctrl-cursor left, -cursor right
117, 118, 119, 132      Ctrl-end, -PgDn, -Home, -PgUp
```

Use Special-Purpose Keys

In addition to the numeric keypad keys, a keyboard has several special-purpose keys, some of which have no equivalent on a typewriter. These include <Enter>, <Escape>, <Backspace>, <Delete>, <Tab>, <Backtab>, <PrtSc>, and the function keys. All are discussed in this section.

The Enter, Escape, Backspace and Tab Keys

The <Enter>, <Escape>, <Backspace>, and <Tab> keys are the only four non-character keys that generate one-byte ASCII codes. Their codes are among the *control codes* that comprise the first 32 numbers of the ASCII character set. These four codes may also be produced by combinations of letter keys and <Ctrl>:

```
ASCII  8     Backspace      <Ctrl-H>
       9     Tab            <Ctrl-I>
      13     Enter          <Ctrl-M>
      27     Escape         <Ctrl-[>
```

Chapter 7, "Write a General-Purpose Keyboard Input Routine" shows how your software can tell the difference between the single keystrokes and the <Ctrl> key combinations.

The Delete and BackTab Keys

You might think that the <Delete> key would be related to the <Backspace> key. Both keys are used to delete characters from the screen, the difference being that <Delete> removes the character under the cursor, while <Backspace> removes the character to the left of the cursor. Similarly, it's natural to expect <BackTab> (the combination of <Shift> and <Tab>) to be related to <Tab>, since the only difference in their usual function is to tab the cursor in opposite directions. However, neither <Delete> nor <BackTab> are included among the 32 control codes that begin the ASCII character set. And so they are given the following extended codes:

```
Delete          0;83
BackTab         0;15
```

The Function Keys

Early PC keyboards had 10 function keys. More recent models usually use 101-key keyboards that have 12 function keys. In order to ensure that software will work with all machines, programmers seldom employ the additional keys. When these keys are used, their codes must be read from the keyboard buffer using the

BIOS *extended keyboard* functions (or keyboard input routines that use these functions). The functions are discussed in Chapter 7, "Check the Keyboard Buffer for Keystrokes," and "Interpret Keystrokes Without Displaying Them."

The function keys issue different codes in combinations with the <Shift>, <Ctrl>, and <Alt> keys, giving at least 40 possible keystrokes. In all cases, the resulting code is a two-byte extended code, in which the first byte is always ASCII 0 and the second byte is an arbitrary number. As you can see, the addition of the extra keys disrupts the numbering scheme used for these codes.

Function key combination	Extended Code		
<F1> to <F10> (unshifted)	0;59	to	0;68
<F11> to <F12> (unshifted)	0;133	to	0;134
<Shift> + <F1> to <F10>	0;84	to	0;93
<Shift> + <F11> to <F12>	0;135	to	0;136
<Ctrl> + <F1> to <F10>	0;94	to	0;103
<Ctrl> + <F11> to <F12>	0;137	to	0;138
<Alt> + <F1> to <F10>	0;104	to	0;113
<Alt> + <F11> to <F12>	0;139	to	0;140

The PrtSc Key

The PrtSc key varies from keyboard to keyboard. On some, it exists as a single-purpose key; on others, the key has two functions, and it must be used in combination with a <Shift> key to invoke the PrtSc routine. This routine is pointed to by interrupt vector 5, which is initialized at start-up. If you don't mind disabling the PrtSc feature, you can redirect this vector to a routine you have written and use the PrtSc key as a hotkey. This is a hardware interrupt, and you must be very careful about how you handle it. See Chapter 4, "Write Your Own Interrupt Service Routine," for further discussion.

Look Up a Scan Code

Every keyboard key bears a unique code number called a scan code. As the *minitutorial* at the beginning of Chapter 7 explains, the keyboard interrupt converts scan codes into codes that are placed in the keyboard buffer, or into settings in the shift/toggle key status bytes. Although the operating system handles this work for you, there are still occasions when you may need to know a scan code. In a few cases, different keystrokes result in the same ASCII code, and the only way to learn the keystroke's origin is to find out its scan code. For example, ASCII codes 8, 9, 13, and 27 result from <Backspace> or <Ctrl-H>, <Tab> or <Ctrl-I>, <Enter> or <Ctrl-M>, or <Esc> or <Ctrl-[>. Armed with the information in this table, you can use certain keyboard input functions to learn the scan code associated with an ASCII code. See Chapter 7, "Write a General-Purpose Keyboard Input Routine," for examples.

Typewriter Keys

"1" - 2	"T" - 20	"L" - 38
"2" - 3	"Y" - 21	";" - 39
"3" - 4	"U" - 22	"'" - 40
"4" - 5	"I" - 23	"`" - 41
"5" - 6	"O" - 24	"\" - 43
"6" - 7	"P" - 25	"Z" - 44
"7" - 8	"[" - 26	"X" - 45
"8" - 9	"]" - 27	"C" - 46
"9" - 10	"A" - 30	"V" - 47
"0" - 11	"S" - 31	"B" - 48
"-" - 12	"D" - 32	"N" - 49
"=" - 13	"F" - 33	"M" - 50
"Q" - 16	"G" - 34	"," - 51
"W" - 17	"H" - 35	"." - 52
"E" - 18	"J" - 36	"/" - 53
"R" - 19	"K" - 37	space bar - 57

Control Keys

Esc - 1	Ctrl - 29	Alt - 56
Backspace - 14	left shift - 42	CapsLock - 58
Tab - 15	right shift - 54	NumLock - 69
Enter - 28	PrtSc - 55	ScrollLock - 70

Function Keys

F1 - 59	F5 - 63	F9 - 67
F2 - 60	F6 - 64	F10 - 68
F3 - 61	F7 - 65	F11 - 217
F4 - 62	F8 - 66	F12 - 218

Keypad Keys

"7" - 71	"5" - 76	"3" - 81
"8" - 72	"6" - 77	"0" - 82
"9" - 73	"+" - 78	"." - 83
"-" - 74	"1" - 79	Sys Req - 132
"4" - 75	"2" - 80	

Look Up an ASCII Code

This table gives all 256 ASCII codes in decimal, hex, and binary form, and the symbols associated with the codes. Code numbers 0 - 31, the *control codes,* are explained in greater detail in Chapter 17, "Look Up a Communications Control Code."

symbol	decimal	hex	binary	symbol	decimal	hex	binary
(null)	0	00	00000000	0	48	30	00110000
☺	1	01	00000001	1	49	31	00110001
☻	2	02	00000010	2	50	32	00110010
♥	3	03	00000011	3	51	33	00110011
♦	4	04	00000100	4	52	34	00110100
♣	5	05	00000101	5	53	35	00110101
♠	6	06	00000110	6	54	36	00110110
•	7	07	00000111	7	55	37	00110111
◘	8	08	00001000	8	56	38	00111000
○	9	09	00001001	9	57	39	00111001
◙	10	0A	00001010	:	58	3A	00111010
♂	11	0B	00001011	;	59	3B	00111011
♀	12	0C	00001100	<	60	3C	00111100
♪	13	0D	00001101	=	61	3D	00111101
♫	14	0E	00001110	>	62	3E	00111110
☼	15	0F	00001111	?	63	3F	00111111
►	16	10	00010000	@	64	40	01000000
◄	17	11	00010001	A	65	41	01000001
↕	18	12	00010010	B	66	42	01000010
‼	19	13	00010011	C	67	43	01000011
¶	20	14	00010100	D	68	44	01000100
§	21	15	00010101	E	69	45	01000101
▬	22	16	00010110	F	70	46	01000110
↨	23	17	00010111	G	71	47	01000111
↑	24	18	00011000	H	72	48	01001000
↓	25	19	00011001	I	73	49	01001001
→	26	1A	00011010	J	74	4A	01001010
←	27	1B	00011011	K	75	4B	01001011
∟	28	1C	00011100	L	76	4C	01001100
↔	29	1D	00011101	M	77	4D	01001101
▲	30	1E	00011110	N	78	4E	01001110
▼	31	1F	00011111	O	79	4F	01001111
(space)	32	20	00100000	P	80	50	01010000
!	33	21	00100001	Q	81	51	01010001
"	34	22	00100010	R	82	52	01010010
#	35	23	00100011	S	83	53	01010011
$	36	24	00100100	T	84	54	01010100
%	37	25	00100101	U	85	55	01010101
&	38	26	00100110	V	86	56	01010110
'	39	27	00100111	W	87	57	01010111
(	40	28	00101000	X	88	58	01011000
)	41	29	00101001	Y	89	59	01011001
*	42	2A	00101010	Z	90	5A	01011010
+	43	2B	00101011	[	91	5B	01011011
,	44	2C	00101100	\	92	5C	01011100
-	45	2D	00101101	]	93	5D	01011101
.	46	2E	00101110	^	94	5E	01011110
/	47	2F	00101111	__	95	5F	01011111

symbol	decimal	hex	binary	symbol	decimal	hex	binary
`	96	60	01100000	É	144	90	10010000
a	97	61	01100001	æ	145	91	10010001
b	98	62	01100010		146	92	10010010
c	99	63	01100011	ô	147	93	10010011
d	100	64	01100100	ö	148	94	10010100
e	101	65	01100101	ò	149	95	10010101
f	102	66	01100110	û	150	96	10010110
g	103	67	01100111	ù	151	97	10010111
h	104	68	01101000	ÿ	152	98	10011000
i	105	69	01101001	Ö	153	99	10011001
j	106	6A	01101010	Ü	154	9A	10011010
k	107	6B	01101011	¢	155	9B	10011011
l	108	6C	01101100	£	156	9C	10011100
m	109	6D	01101101	¥	157	9D	10011101
n	110	6E	01101110	Pt	158	9E	10011110
o	111	6F	01101111	ƒ	159	9F	10011111
p	112	70	01110000	á	160	A0	10100000
q	113	71	01110001	í	161	A1	10100001
r	114	72	01110010	ó	162	A2	10100010
s	115	73	01110011	ú	163	A3	10100011
t	116	74	01110100	ñ	164	A4	10100100
u	117	75	01110101	Ñ	165	A5	10100101
v	118	76	01110110	ª	166	A6	10100110
w	119	77	01110111	º	167	A7	10100111
x	120	78	01111000	¿	168	A8	10101000
y	121	79	01111001	⌐	169	A9	10101001
z	122	7A	01111010	¬	170	AA	10101010
{	123	7B	01111011	½	171	AB	10101011
¦	124	7C	01111100	¼	172	AC	10101100
}	125	7D	01111101	¡	173	AD	10101101
~	126	7E	01111110	«	174	AE	10101110
⌂	127	7F	01111111	»	175	AF	10101111
Ç	128	80	10000000	▓	176	B0	10110000
ü	129	81	10000001	▒	177	B1	10110001
é	130	82	10000010	▓	178	B2	10110010
â	131	83	10000011	│	179	B3	10110011
ä	132	84	10000100	┤	180	B4	10110100
à	133	85	10000101	╡	181	B5	10110101
å	134	86	10000110	╢	182	B6	10110110
ç	135	87	10000111	╖	183	B7	10110111
ê	136	88	10001000	╕	184	B8	10111000
ë	137	89	10001001	╣	185	B9	10111001
è	138	8A	10001010	║	186	BA	10111010
ï	139	8B	10001011	╗	187	BB	10111011
î	140	8C	10001100	╝	188	BC	10111100
ì	141	8D	10001101	╜	189	BD	10111101
Ä	142	8E	10001110	╛	190	BE	10111110
Å	143	8F	10001111	┐	191	BF	10111111

symbol	decimal	hex	binary	symbol	decimal	hex	binary
∟	192	C0	11000000	α	224	E0	11100000
⊥	193	C1	11000001	β	225	E1	11100001
⊤	194	C2	11000010	Γ	226	E2	11100010
⊢	195	C3	11000011	π	227	E3	11100011
—	196	C4	11000100	Σ	228	E4	11100100
+	197	C5	11000101	σ	229	E5	11100101
╞	198	C6	11000110	μ	230	E6	11100110
╟	199	C7	11000111	τ	231	E7	11100111
╚	200	C8	11001000	Φ	232	E8	11101000
╔	201	C9	11001001	Θ	233	E9	11101001
╩	202	CA	11001010	Ω	234	EA	11101010
╦	203	CB	11001011	δ	235	EB	11101011
╠	204	CC	11001100	∞	236	EC	11101100
═	205	CD	11001101	Ø	237	ED	11101101
╬	206	CE	11001110	∊	238	EE	11101110
╧	207	CF	11001111	∩	239	EF	11101111
╨	208	D0	11010000	≡	240	F0	11110000
╤	209	D1	11010001	±	241	F1	11110001
╥	210	D2	11010010	≥	242	F2	11110010
╙	211	D3	11010011	≤	243	F3	11110011
╘	212	D4	11010100	⌠	244	F4	11110100
╒	213	D5	11010101	⌡	245	F5	11110101
╓	214	D6	11010110	÷	246	F6	11110110
╫	215	D7	11010111	≈	247	F7	11110111
╪	216	D8	11011000	°	248	F8	11111000
┘	217	D9	11011001	•	249	F9	11111001
┌	218	DA	11011010	·	250	FA	11111010
█	219	DB	11011011	√	251	FB	11111011
▄	220	DC	11011100	ⁿ	252	FC	11111100
▌	221	DD	11011101	²	253	FD	11111101
▐	222	DE	11011110	■	254	FE	11111110
▀	223	DF	11011111	(blank 'FF')	255	FF	11111111

Look Up a Box-Graphic Code

For convenience, these diagrams summarize the ASCII code numbers of the symbols used to construct lines and boxes.

Look Up an Extended Code

Extended codes — those for keystrokes that the ASCII character set does not provide for — are returned as two-byte values, with the first byte always 0. The second byte is usually the scan code of the associated key. This is not always the case, however, because some keys, including the function keys and some cursor keys, combine with shift keys to produce more than one non-ASCII code.

value of 2nd byte	corresponding keystroke
15	Shift + Tab (backtab)
16-25	Alt + Q to Alt + P (the top row of letters)
30-38	Alt + A to Alt + L (the middle row of letters)
44-50	Alt + Z to Alt + M (the bottom row of letters)
59-68	Function keys 1 to 10 (unshifted)
71	Home
72	Cursor-up
73	PgUp
75	Cursor-left
77	Cursor-right
79	End
80	Cursor-down
81	PgDn
82	Ins
83	Del
84-93	Function keys 1 to 10 with the Shift key down
94-103	Function keys 1 to 10 with the Ctrl key down
104-113	Function keys 1 to 10 with the Alt key down
114	Ctrl + PrtSc
115	Ctrl + Cursor-left
116	Ctrl + Cursor-right
117	Ctrl + End
118	Ctrl + PgDn

continues

value of 2nd byte	corresponding keystroke
119	Ctrl + Home
120-131	Alt + 1 to Alt + = (top row of the keyboard)
132	Ctrl + PgUp
133-134	Function keys 1 to 10 (unshifted)
135-136	Function keys 11 and 12 with the Shift key down
137-138	Function keys 11 and 12 with the Ctrl key down
139-140	Function keys 11 and 12 with the Alt key down

9

Using a Mouse

- Minitutorial: Programming for a Mouse
- Initialize the Mouse Driver
- Show or Hide the Mouse Cursor
- Set the Shape of a Text Mouse Cursor
- Set the Shape of a Graphics Mouse Cursor
- Get or Set the Mouse Cursor Position
- Confine the Mouse Cursor to a Portion of the Screen
- Define a Screen Region in Which the Mouse Cursor Will Not Appear
- Track Mouse Movements
- Set the Ratio Between Motions of the Mouse and Cursor
- Monitor the Mouse Buttons
- Intercept Clicks, Double-Clicks, and Drag Events
- Set Up a Mouse Interrupt Routine
- Take Analog Input from a Game Port
- Take Digital Input from a Game Port

Minitutorial: Programming for a Mouse

All mice work through a mouse driver. The driver tracks mouse movements and the state of the mouse buttons. Mouse movements are reported to the driver as changes in relative position. The driver creates the mouse cursor and converts the relative mouse movements into absolute screen positions. In order to do this, the driver determines the current screen mode so that it can create the appropriate kind of cursor and can keep the cursor in view. The driver also sets up a number of special facilities, such as the ability to change the cursor appearance or position, the ability to maintain the cursor within a particular part of the screen, and so on.

Once loaded, a mouse driver is always active, even when applications that do not use a mouse are running. A mouse will have no effect on a program until the program makes the cursor visible and monitors the cursor position and button status.

Every mouse manufacturer ships its own driver. Some drivers offer a few more features than others, but all follow the same system of calls used by the Microsoft mouse, which is the **de facto** industry standard. To ensure compatability, software rarely uses nonstandard calls.

The most obvious difference between mice is that some have two buttons and some have three. Since many mice lack a third (middle) button, this button is seldom used. Each button is given a number, with the left button as **0**, the right button as **1**, and the middle button as **2**. Thanks to this numbering scheme, no confusion arises when a three-button mouse is used instead of a two-button mouse. As a practical matter, most applications really only use the left mouse button. When the right button is employed, it often is for "escape" or "undo" commands. For instance, in some programs the left mouse button takes the user deeper into a hierarchy of windows, while the right button "undoes" these actions by returning the user to the next-higher level.

Mouse support is rapidly becoming obligatory in commercial applications. Many programers have been slow to modify existing applications to use a mouse. This is not because it is difficult to monitor the status of the mouse cursor and mouse buttons. Rather, the inclusion of mouse support sometimes requires radical restructuring of programs. It all depends on how much control the mouse is given.

Some applications have been designed (or revised) to support no more than menu selections by a mouse. In this case, you only need to devise a system of pull-down menus, and to intercept the menu selections. Normally, most menu selections are paralleled by a keyboard control code. For each menu selection, your program can generate a code identical to the one that would result from a keystroke. For example, say that files are saved by typing <Ctrl-S>, which generates ASCII 19. This value is assigned to a variable that is then passed through a keyboard input loop for interpretation. The loop does range testing on the value to decide whether it should be accepted or not, and then calls the associated subroutine that actually saves a file. In this scheme, when a mouse is used to select "Save File" from a menu, the menu-based command can be converted to ASCII 19 and passed through the keyboard input loop exactly as if it had originated from a keystroke.

Pull-down menus tend to complicate software design because, in the simplest case, anything the program can do can be called upon at any moment by the user. By comparison, traditional applications tend to limit the user to a small range of actions at any moment by using hierarchies of menus. Say that the user is in the midst of setting Tab positions in a document. It's easy to design code that expects the next few keystrokes (or mouse movements) to be information about Tabs, and that interprets the keystrokes or movements that way. It's another matter altogether to design a program that can abruptly switch tasks and, by a menu choice, suddenly begin setting page margins for printing, only to return to Tab settings a moment later.

In practice, no software allows users access to all features at all times. Some dialog boxes require that the user complete the task at hand before any further menu selections can be made. Often, certain menu choices are disabled until they make sense, or until they can be handled. Yet, even when you deal with the problems of mouse-driven menus by disabling menu selections, your programs can be made considerably more complex by the need to monitor what can and cannot be allowed at any moment.

Beyond menu selections, the most common application of a mouse is in setting the cursor position, and in selecting blocks of text. These kinds of mouse events also can sometimes be converted into corresponding keyboard events. But a mouse cursor can behave differently from a conventional text cursor. A press of the <cursor-right> key may be converted into a single rightward movement of the cursor by one character. The mouse cursor, however, can abruptly jump several characters or lines, perhaps to a screen position unoccupied by text. Code that works well with keyboard input may need to be thoroughly reworked to handle these sorts of mouse motions.

The most complex mouse programming of all occurs when a mouse is used to draw graphics on the screen and to edit those graphics. Usually, these kinds of programs are built from the ground up to support a mouse, since this kind of input is unwieldly from the keyboard.

It's important to understand how the screen position of the mouse cursor is defined. In text modes, the cursor jumps between discrete row and column positions, and the entire cursor is contained within a character cell. But in graphics modes, the cursor moves continuously across the screen, and sometimes it may reside half inside a specified boundary, half outside. Accordingly, in graphics modes a *hot spot* must be defined for the cursor — a single pixel within the pattern of pixels that make up the cursor. The position of the hot spot is equivalent to the position of the cursor. Locating the cursor at pixel 100,50 means that the cursor's hot spot falls on that point. Similarly, the cursor is regarded as being within a given screen region only when its hot spot enters the region. The mouse driver can move the hot spot to any position on the screen. When a hot spot resides on the left edge of a cursor, and the cursor is moved to the right edge of the screen, the mouse driver will display only part of the cursor so that the hot spot can move all the way to the screen edge. The default graphics cursor is an arrow, with the tip of the arrow set as the hot spot.

The mouse driver always reports screen positions as if it were operating in a graphics mode. For example, when the display operates in a 640 x 200 CGA mode, coordinates between 0 and 639, and 0 and 199 are returned. The same range of coordinates are used by the driver when a CGA screen operates in a text mode. In this case, you must divide the positions returned by the driver by 8 in order to convert them into row and column coordinates.

To make matters more complicated, the mouse driver may return coordinates in this range even when the screen does not use a 640 x 200 pixel mode. For example, the driver uses a 640 by 200 matrix (a "virtual screen") for a 640 x 350 monochrome display running in text modes. In this case, your program would need to multiply and divide vertical coordinates by 8, just as for a 200-line screen. The following table shows the virtual resolutions of the various screen modes. The *cell size* indicates how many pixels the mouse cursor moves between character positions (in text modes) or pixel positions (graphics modes).

screen mode	type	virtual screen	cell size
0h	text	640 x 200	16 x 8
1h	text	640 x 200	16 x 8
2h	text	640 x 200	8 x 8
3h	text	640 x 200	8 x 8
4h	graphics	640 x 200	2 x 1
5h	graphics	640 x 200	2 x 1
6h	graphics	640 x 200	1 x 1
7h	text	640 x 200	8 x 8
Dh	graphics	640 x 200	2 x 1
Eh	graphics	640 x 200	1 x 1
Fh	graphics	640 x 350	1 x 1
10h	graphics	640 x 350	1 x 1
11h	graphics	640 x 480	1 x 1
12h	graphics	640 x 480	1 x 1
13h	graphics	640 x 200	2 x 1

Mouse drivers always work through interrupt 33h. The various mouse functions are called by placing a function number in the AX register (and not in AH, as is usually the case for interrupt function numbers). Of the compilers discussed in this book, only Microsoft BASIC offers any mouse support at all. The BASIC Toolbox includes routines for a half dozen of the most important mouse calls.

For most other calls, you can use the *MouseDriver* subroutine, which takes arguments for the AX, BX, CX, and DX registers, and then calls interrupt 33h. For Turbo Pascal and the C compilers, you must directly call the interrupt.

This chapter concludes with two sections that show how to monitor input from a *game port*. Like a mouse, a device connected to a game port inputs data about device coordinates and about the status of buttons located on the device. As their name implies, game ports were devised to support joysticks and other devices used with video games. But these ports are used with other devices, such as graphics tablets. There is no standard driver for game ports. Your programs must monitor the hardware directly.

Initialize the Mouse Driver

Function 0 of interrupt 33h reinitializes a mouse driver so that all of its internal variables are set to their start-up values. This leaves the mouse cursor hidden and set to the middle of the screen. The function also does an equipment check, returning -1 in AX when a mouse is installed, and 0 otherwise. BX returns the number of mouse buttons.

Memory-resident programs that use a mouse must save the current state of the mouse driver so that it may be restored when the memory-resident program quits. Otherwise, the program that is interrupted may malfunction. Functions 16h and 17h of interrupt 33h save and restore the driver state. Before using them, call function 15h, which returns in BX the size in bytes of the buffer required to hold the driver state. Then point ES:DX to the buffer and call function 16h to save the state. Later, call function 17h to transfer the saved data back to the driver, again with ES:DX pointed to the buffer.

BASIC

```
' $INCLUDE: 'QBX.BI'
DIM REGS AS RegType                  ' Define register array


REGS.AX = &H0000
CALL Interrupt(&H33, REGS, REGS)   'initialize the driver
```

Alternatively, use the BASIC Toolbox *MouseInit* subroutine:

```
MouseInit
```

Pascal

```
Uses DOS;
Var
  Regs: Registers; {Registers type is declared in the DOS unit}


Regs.AX := 0;      {the interrupt function number}
Intr($33,Regs);    {initialize the driver}
```

246

C

```c
#include <dos.h>

union REGS regs;            /* declare the register array */

regs.x.ax = 0;              /* function number */
int86(0x33,&regs,&regs);   /* initialize the driver */
```

Assembler

```asm
;---INITIALIZE THE MOUSE DRIVER
        sub   ax,ax               ;function number = 0
        int   33h                 ;initialize the driver
```

Show or Hide the Mouse Cursor

Functions 1 and 2 of interrupt 33h turn the mouse cursor "on" and "off," respectively. A mouse driver always keeps track of mouse movements, updating its pointers to the screen whenever the mouse is moved. But the driver displays the mouse cursor only when software requests that it do so. Unless you reset the mouse (see "Initialize the Mouse Driver," above) or specifically position the mouse cursor (see "Get or Set the Mouse Cursor Position," below), the cursor may appear at any screen position when it is turned on.

Programs that use a mouse usually turn on the cursor when they start, and leave it on until the program finishes. Be sure to turn off the cursor before quitting. Otherwise, it may continue to appear on the screen in other applications that do not offer mouse support. A program also must turn the cursor off each time it writes to the screen and then turn it back on immediately afterward. This is necessary because the mouse driver constantly records the screen image at the place where the mouse cursor resides so that it can restore the image when the cursor is moved elsewhere. If your program writes *over* the cursor, the previous screen image at that point will be restored when the cursor is moved away. But if you turn off the cursor and then write the data, the new data will be saved when the cursor is turned back on, and the data will be properly restored when the cursor moves.

The mouse driver employs a *cursor flag* for a leveled approach to showing and hiding the cursor. Before the cursor is initially turned on, the cursor flag is set to −1. Function 1 increments the flag to 0, causing the cursor to appear. Function 2 decrements the flag by 1. Function 2 may be called any number of times to set the cursor flag to larger negative numbers. When the flag is -3, it takes three calls to Function 1 to bring the cursor back into view. However, once the flag is set to 0, additional calls to Function 1 will not increase the flag to a value greater than 0. Most programs just switch the flag back and forth between -1 and 0, but the cursor-level feature sometimes comes in handy when several layers of objects obscure the cursor. One drawback of the feature is that you must carefully design your code so that Function 2 is not called unnecessarily. Otherwise, calls to Function 1 may fail to turn the cursor on.

Both functions 1 and 2 of INT 33h have no input registers, except for the function number, which goes in AH. There are no return registers.

BASIC

```
' $INCLUDE: 'QBX.BI'
DIM REGS AS RegType      ' define register array



REGS.AX = &H0001         ' function to display the cursor
CALL Interrupt(&H33, REGS, REGS)    ' display the cursor


REGS.AX = &H0002         ' function to hide the cursor
CALL Interrupt(&H33, REGS, REGS)    'the the cursor
```

Alternatively, call the *MouseShow* and *MouseHide* subroutines found in the BASIC Toolbox:

```
MouseShow                'increment the cursor flag


MouseHide                'decrement the cursor flag
```

Pascal

```
Uses DOS;
Var
  Regs: registers;


Regs.AX := 1;        {function to display mouse cursor}
Intr($33,Regs);      {display the cursor}


Regs.AX := 2;        {function to hide mouse cursor}
Intr($33,Regs);      {hide the cursor}
```

249

C

```c
#include <dos.h>

union REGS regs;              /* declare the register array */

regs.x.ax = 1;                /* function to display cursor */
int86(0x33,&regs,&regs);      /* display the cursor */

regs.x.ax = 2;                /* function to hide cursor */
int86(0x33,&regs,&regs);      /* hide the cursor */
```

Assembler

```asm
;---DISPLAY THE MOUSE CURSOR:
      mov   ax,1h              ;function to display cursor
      int   33h                ;display the cursor

      mov   ax,2h              ;function to hide cursor
      int   33h                ;hide the cursor
```

Set the Shape of a Text Mouse Cursor

When working in a video text mode, a mouse driver can create two kinds of cursor. One option is a *hardware cursor*. This is the normal screen cursor generated by video hardware. It is composed of horizontal scan lines. Normally, only one of two lines are shown in order to underline characters. But the mouse driver can program the cursor to fill all or part of a text-screen character cell. (Any program can also program the cursor shape, see Chapter 13, "Change the Cursor Shape.")

The second option is a *software* or *attribute* cursor. In this case, the mouse driver writes data at the screen position at which the cursor appears. In so doing, the driver can change the character displayed at that position, or the attribute of the character so that it blinks, its background color is changed, and so on.

Function Ah of interrupt 33h sets the text cursor type. On entry, AX holds the function number and BX holds 1 to select a hardware cursor, and 0 to select an attribute cursor. When selecting a hardware cursor, CX holds the starting scan line and DX holds the ending scan line. Scan lines are numbered from 0 upward, depending on the video display and screen mode. Line 0 is at the top of a character cell, line 1 is at the next line down, and so on.

Attribute cursors are more complicated. Like the graphics mouse cursors discussed in "Set the Shape of a Graphics Mouse Cursor," below, attribute cursors are created using a pair of 16-bit masks — the *screen mask* and the *cursor mask*, which are placed in CX and DX, respectively. A mask is applied to the combined character byte and attribute byte that hold the data for a particular screen position. The low eight bits of the mask affect the character, and the high eight bits affect the attribute byte.

The screen mask is ANDed with the character-attribute pair. This action determines which bits in the two bits will be preserved. When all bits in the screen mask are set, the character and attribute are maintained as they were. When all bits are 0 in the mask, the character and attribute are both set to zero. Of course, the mask can have any bit pattern in order to change particular aspects. For example, the mask can switch off the high bit of the attribute byte to discontinue character blinking.

The cursor mask is then XORed over the result of the AND operation with the screen mask. Recall that an XOR operation produces a 1 when one of the input values is a 1 and the other a 0. When the cursor mask is set to 0, no changes are made in the character or attribute. This is because, when a bit in the character or attribute is set, it XORs with 0 to make 1; conversely, bits that are not set XOR with 0 to make 0. When all bits in the cursor mask are set, the bit patterns for the character and attribute are inverted.

In itself, the act of inverting characters is not very useful, because wherever the cursor travels, characters change to different symbols and attributes jump from one color to another. But when the screen mask is first applied with zeros for the character or attribute, the character or attribute is "cleared," and the cursor mask can then XOR any character or attribute it wishes. Thus, to make the text cursor be ASCII character FEh, you would use FF00h as the screen mask to preserve the attribute and clear the character, and then would use 00FEh as the cursor mask, again to preserve the attribute, and also to write FEh as the character.

Do just the opposite to change the attribute to a particular color but leave the character unchanged. In an eight-color screen mode, to make the cursor write a blue background and make no other changes, you'd need to set bits 4 through 7 of the attribute byte to 001. In this case, the screen mask would be FFh for its high byte in order to leave the character unchanged. The low byte would need to have bits 4 through 7 zeroed out, and so it would have the bit pattern 01110000, which is 70h. Thus, the screen mask would be FF70h. The cursor mask would have all zeros except in the three bit field, in which the third bit would be set to make a blue background. The bit pattern for the mask would be 0000000001000000, which is 0040h.

To set an attribute cursor, call function Ah of interrupt 33h with the function number in AX, 0 in BX to specify an attribute cursor, the screen mask in CX, and the cursor mask in DX. There are no return registers.

These examples set the mouse cursor as an attribute cursor. The cursor leaves the character unchanged, but changes the background to blue, as described in the text above.

BASIC

```
' $INCLUDE: 'QBX.BI'
DIM REGS AS RegType      'Define register array

REGS.AX = &H000A         'function to set text mode cursor
REGS.BX = &H0000         'subfunction to set attribute cursor
REGS.CX = &HFF70         'screen mask
REGS.DX = &H0040         'cursor mask
CALL Interrupt(&H33, REGS, REGS)
```

Pascal

```
Uses DOS;
Var
  Regs: Registers;    {Registers type is declared in the DOS unit}

Regs.AX := $000A;    {function to set text mode cursor}
Regs.BX := $0000;    {subfunction to set attribute cursor}
Regs.CX := $FF70;    {screen mask}
Regs.DX := $0040;    {cursor mask}
Intr($33,Regs);
```

C

```c
#include <dos.h>
union REGS regs;        /* declare the register array */

regs.x.ax = 0x000A;     /* function to set text mode cursor */
regs.x.bx = 0x0000;     /* subfunction to set attribute cursor */
regs.x.cx = 0xFF70;     /* screen mask */
regs.x.dx = 0x0040;     /* cursor mask */
int86(0x33,&regs,&regs);
```

Assembler

```
;---SET AN ATTRIBUTE TEXT CURSOR:
        mov   ax,000Ah        ;function to set text mode cursor
        mov   bx,0000h        ;subfunction to set attribute cursor
        mov   cx,FF70h        ;screen mask
        mov   dx,0040h        ;cursor mask
        int   33h
```

253

Set the Shape of a Graphics Mouse Cursor

Function 9h of INT 33h sets the shape of the mouse cursor in graphics modes and defines a point in the cursor that is the hot spot (the *hot spot* is the point in the cursor that corresponds to the cursor's "position" on the screen). The cursor is composed from a 16 x 16 bit *screen mask* and a 16 x 16 bit *cursor mask*. It's important to understand how these masks work.

A graphics cursor can be any size and shape within the 16 x 16-pixel boundaries. The standard arrow cursor, for example, covers only about half of the 16 x 16-pixel area. In a monochrome video mode, the cursor works in such a way that the arrow is always black. To prevent the cursor from blending in with a black background, the margin around the cursor is made to appear white. Other pixels within the 16 x 16-pixel area go unchanged. A single mask could not create this effect, because there are three kinds of pixels: those made black, those made white, and those that are unchanged.

The screen mask determines which parts of the 16 x 16-pixel area are preserved. It does this by ANDing the mask with the screen image. In an AND operation, a pixel is left on only if the mask pixel and the screen pixel are *both* on. For an arrow cursor, the screen mask would have all bits set that are outside the arrow or the margin about the arrow. When one of these bits is ANDed with a screen pixel that is "on," the pixel will stay on (1 AND 1 = 1). When one of the bits is ANDed with a pixel that is "off," the pixel will stay off (1 AND 0 = 0). Pixels in the arrow and arrow-margin parts of the mask are all set to 0, and so they will erase the pixels at that part of the screen (0 AND 1 = 0 and 0 AND 0 = 0).

Once the screen mask has done its job, the cursor mask draws the actual cursor. For an arrow cursor, this mask would set all pixels within the arrow image, but not within the arrow's margin and not elsewhere in the 16 x 16-pixel block. This mask is XORed with the screen image. In an XOR operation, a bit is set when only one of the two compared bits is set. Because the pixels holding the arrow have been cleared (set to 0) by the screen mask, the arrow is drawn (1 XOR 0 = 1). Other areas, including the pixel margin, are unchanged. This is because, when a screen pixel is on (set to 1), it XORS with 0 to make 1, and so it remains on. But when a screen pixel is off (set to 0), it XORS with 0 to make 0, and so it remains off.

Not all cursors work like the standard arrow cursor. When the cursor mask has pixels set in a part of the 16 x 16-pixel block that was not cleared by the screen mask, screen pixels at that point are *inverted*. Matters can become quite complicated in color modes when the AND and XOR operations can alter screen colors.

The screen and cursor masks are written in memory as two 32-byte bit arrays. The first two bytes hold the bit pattern for the top row of the mask, the next two bytes hold the second row, and so on. Both masks are stored together, with the cursor mask immediately following the screen mask. Before calling function 9h, point ES:DX to the first byte of the screen mask. In addition, BX is given the horizontal hot spot position, and CX is given the vertical position. The values are expressed as numbers between –16 and 16.

BASIC

```
' $INCLUDE: 'QBX.BI'
DIM REGS AS RegTypeX     ' Define register array
DIM CURSORDATA(32) AS INTEGER


REGS.AX = &H0009           'function number
REGS.BX = &H0004           'horizontal hot spot position
REGS.CX = &H0004           'vertical hot spot position
REGS.ES = VARSEG(CURSORDATA)   'point ES:DX to the masks
REGS.DX = VARPTR(CURSORDATA)
CALL InterruptX(&H33, REGS, REGS)
```

Pascal

```
Uses DOS;
Var
  Regs: Registers;   {Registers type is declared in the DOS unit}
  CursorData: array [1..32] of word;

Regs.AX: = $0009;          {function number}
Regs.BX: = $0004;          {horizontal hot spot position}
Regs.CX: = $0004;          {vertical hot spot position}
Regs.ES: = Seg(CursorData);   {point ES:DX to the masks}
Regs.DX: = Ofs(CursorData);
Intr($33,Regs);
```

C

```
union REGS regs;      /* declare the register array */
unsigned int cursor_data[32];



regs.x.ax = 0x0009;              /* function number */
regs.x.bx = 0x0004;              /* horizontal hot spot position */
regs.x.cx = 0x0004;              /* vertical hot spot position */
regs.x.es = FP_SEG(cursor_data)   /* point ES:DX to the masks */
regs.x.dx = FP_OFS(cursor_data)
int86(0x33,&regs,&regs);
```

Assembler

```
;---SET A GRAPHICS MOUSE CURSOR:
        mov  bx,0004h                ;horizontal hot spot position
        mov  cx,0004h                ;vertical hot spot position
        mov  ax,seg CURSORDATA  ;point ES:DX to the mask data
        mov  es,ax                   ;
        mov  dx,ofs CURSORDATA  ;
        mov  ax,0009h                ;function number
        int  33h                     ;call the interrupt
```

Get or Set the Mouse Cursor Position

Function 4 of interrupt 33h sets the mouse cursor position, and function 3 reports it. In both cases, AX takes the function number. For setting the position, CX is given the *x* (horizontal) coordinate and DX is given the *y* (vertical) coordinate. Function 3 returns the current position in the same registers. This function also reports the mouse button settings, which are discussed in "Monitor the Mouse Buttons," below. Function 4 has no return registers.

If you specify a coordinate outside the screen, the driver will convert it to the nearest available point. For instance, if you specify that the cursor belongs on column 800 of a 640-column screen, the cursor will be fixed at column 640.

The examples below assume that the screen is operating in text mode 7. As the *minitutorial* at the beginning of this chapter explains, *x* and *y* coordinates must be multiplied or divided by 8 for this screen mode.

BASIC

```
' $INCLUDE: 'QBX.BI'
DIM REGS AS RegType        ' Define register array


REGS.AX = &H0003          'function to get the cursor position
CALL Interrupt(&H33, REGS, REGS)  'get the position
Column = REGS.CX \8        'get text column
Row = REGS.DX \8           'get text row
REGS.AX = &H0004          'function to set the cursor position
REGS.CX = NewColumn * 8   'new text column
REGS.DX = NewRow * 8      'new text row
CALL Interrupt(&H33, REGS, REGS)  'set the position
```

Alternatively, the BASIC toolbox provides the *MousePoll* subroutine to report on the mouse cursor coordinates and button settings. Its format is as follows:

```
MousePoll row%, col%, leftbutton%, rightbutton%
```

The function returns the row and column coordinates in the first two variables, and TRUE or FALSE in the second two variables, depending on whether the corresponding button is currently pressed (TRUE) or not (FALSE).

Pascal

```
Uses DOS;
Var
  Regs: registers;
  Row,Column: word;

Regs.AX := 3;              {function to get cursor position}
Intr($33,Regs);           {get the coordinates}
Column := Regs.CX div 8   {get text column}
Row := Regs.DX div 8      {get text row}

Regs.AX := 4;              {function to set cursor position}
Regs.CX := Column * 8;     {new text column}
Regs.DX := Row * 8;        {new text row}
Intr($33,Regs);           {set the position}
```

C

```
#include <dos.h>
union REGS regs;           /* declare the register array */
int  column, row;

regs.x.ax = 3;             /* function to get cursor position */
int86(0x33,&regs,&regs);   /* get the coordinates */
column = regs.x.cx >> 3    /* text column */
row = regs.x.dx >> 3       /* text row */
```

```
regs.x.ax = 4;              /* function to set cursor position */
regs.x.cx = column << 3     /* text column */
regs.x.dx = row << 3        /* text row */
int86(0x33,&regs,&regs);    /* set the coordinates */
```

Assembler

```
;---GET THE MOUSE CURSOR POSITION:
        mov   ax,3              ;function number
        int   33h              ;call the interrupt
        mov   bx,cx            ;save column position
        mov   cl,3             ;get ready to shift
        shr   bx,cl            ;adjust column
        shr   dx,cl            ;adjust row
        mov   MOUSE_X,bx       ;get column
        mov   MOUSE_Y,dx       ;get row


;---SET THE MOUSE CURSOR TO ROW 12, COLUMN 40:
        mov   ax,4             ;function number
        mov   bx,40            ;horizontal position
        mov   dx,12            ;vertical position
        mov   cl,3             ;prepare to shift
        shl   bx,cl            ;adjust column
        shl   dx,cl            ;adjust row
        mov   cx,bx            ;column to CX
        int   33h             ;set the cursor
```

Confine the Mouse Cursor to a Portion of the Screen

The mouse cursor can be restricted to a rectangular area of the screen. This feature can be used to keep the cursor within menus, dialog boxes, and so on. Function 7h of interrupt 33h sets the horizontal limits of mouse cursor motion. On entry, CX holds the left column and DX the right column. Function 8h does the same for vertical cursor motion, with the top row in CX and the bottom row in DX. The screen positions are numbered using the same system employed for positioning the mouse cursor (see the table in this chapter's *minitutorial*). The maximum and minimum positions are included within the area the mouse can travel. Remember that a graphics cursor may wander outside this area; the restriction applies to the cursor's hot spot, not the entire cursor.

The following examples limit the mouse to the top left corner of the screen, keeping it within columns 0 and 300, and rows 0 and 200. The examples assume a screen mode that does not require translation of the screen coordinates.

BASIC

```
' $INCLUDE: 'QBX.BI'
DIM REGS AS RegType      ' Define register array


REGS.AX = &H0007         'function to set horizontal limits
REGS.CX = 0              'left column
REGS.DX = 300            'right column
CALL Interrupt(&H33, REGS, REGS)   'set the limits
REGS.AX = &H0008         'function to set vertical limits
REGS.CX = 0              'top row
REGS.DX = 200            'bottom row
CALL Interrupt(&H33, REGS, REGS)   'set the limits
```

Alternatively, use the *MouseBorder* subroutine that is found in the BASIC Toolbox. It takes two pairs of coordinates as parameters — first, the row and column of the top-left corner of the area in which the mouse is to be confined, and second, the row and column of the bottom-right corner.

```
MouseBorder toprow%,leftcol%,bottomrow%,rightcol%
```

Pascal

```
Uses DOS;
Var
    Regs: Registers;    {Registers type is declared in the DOS unit}


Regs.AX := $0007;       {function to set horizontal limits}
Regs.CX := 0;           {left column}
Regs.DX := 300;         {right column}
Intr($33,Regs);         {set the limits}
Regs.AX := $0008;       {function to set vertical limits}
Regs.CX := 0;           {top row}
Regs.DX := 200;         {bottom row}
Intr($33,Regs);         {set the limits}
```

C

```
#include <dos.h>


union REGS regs;        /* declare the register array */


regs.x.ax = 0x0007h;    /* function to set horizontal limits */
regs.x.cx = 0;          /* left column */
regs.x.dx = 300;        /* right column */
int86(0x33,&regs,&regs);  /* set the limits */
regs.x.ax = 0x0008h;    /* function to set vertical limits */
regs.x.cx = 0;          /* top row */
regs.x.dx = 200;        /* bottom row */
int86(0x33,&regs,&regs);  /* set the limits */
```

Assembler

```
;---CONFINE THE MOUSE CURSOR TO 0,0 - 300,200
        mov   ax,0007h          ;function to set horizontal limits
        mov   cx,0              ;left column
        mov   dx,300            ;right column
        int   33h              ;set the limits
        mov   ax,0008h          ;function to set vertical limits
        mov   cx,0              ;top row
        mov   dx,200            ;bottom row
        int   33h              ;set the limits
```

Define a Screen Region in Which the Mouse Cursor Will Not Appear

Function 10h of interrupt 33h defines a rectangular area on the screen within which the mouse cursor automatically turns off when it enters. On entry, CX holds the left column of the protected area, SI holds the right column, DX holds the top row, and DI holds the bottom row. These columns and rows are included in the protected area.

Unfortunately, this function does not automatically turn the cursor back on when it leaves the specified rectangle. You must continue to monitor the cursor position and turn it back on with function 1 of interrupt 33h (discussed in "Show or Hide the Mouse Cursor," above).

The examples below protect a rectangle between columns 10 and 50 and rows 5 and 30.

BASIC

```
' $INCLUDE: 'QBX.BI'

DIM REGS AS RegType      ' Define register array


REGS.AX = &H0010          'function number

REGS.CX = 10              'left column

REGS.SI = 50              'right column

REGS.DX = 5               'top row

REGS.DI = 30              'bottom row

CALL Interrupt(&H33, REGS, REGS)   'set the protected area
```

Pascal

```
Uses DOS;

Var

  Regs: Registers;   {Registers type is declared in the DOS unit}
```

263

```
Regs.AX := $10;        {the interrupt function number}

Regs.CX := 10;         {left column}

Regs.SI := 50;         {right column}

Regs.DX := 5;          {top row}

Regs.DI := 30;         {bottom row}

Intr($33,Regs);        {set the protected area}
```

C

```c
#include <dos.h>

union REGS regs;       /* declare the register array */


regs.x.ax = 0;         /* function number */

regs.x.cx = 10;        /* left column */

regs.x.si = 50;        /* right column */

regs.x.dx = 5;         /* top row */

regs.x.di = 30;        /* bottom row */

int86(0x33,&regs,&regs);   /* set the protected area */
```

Assembler

```
;---SET THE PROTECTED AREA:
        mov  ax,10h               ;function number

        mov  cx,10                ;left column

        mov  si,50                ;right column

        mov  dx,5                 ;top row

        mov  di,30                ;bottom row

        int  33h                  ;set the protected area
```

Track Mouse Movements

Function Bh of interrupt 33h reports the actual distance traveled by the mouse since the last call to the function. The unit of measurement is the *mickey*, which is equal to roughly 1/200th of an inch. The function returns the relative horizontal motion in CX, and the relative vertical motion in DX. For horizontal motions, a negative value indicates movement to the left, a positive value, movement to the right. Similarly, negative and positive values in DX indicate motions away from and toward the user ("up" and "down"), respectively. The step count is automatically reinitialized to 0 each time a program calls the function.

BASIC

```
' $INCLUDE: 'QBX.BI'
DIM REGS AS RegType          ' Define register array


REGS.AX = &H000B              'function number
CALL Interrupt(&H33, REGS, REGS)
HORZ_MOVEMENT = REGS.CX  'get the relative horizontal movement
VERT_MOVEMENT = REGS.DX  'get the relative vertical movement
```

Pascal

```
Uses DOS;
Var
  Regs: Registers;   {Registers type is declared in the DOS unit}
  HorzMovement,VertMovement: integer;


Regs.AX := $000B;          {the interrupt function number}
Intr($33,Regs);            {call the interrupt}
HorzMovement := Regs.CX; {get the relative horizontal movement}
VertMovement := Regs.DX; {get the relative vertical movement}
```

C

```
#include <dos.h>

union REGS regs;      /* declare the register array */
int horz_motion,vert_motion;

regs.x.ax = 0x000B;        /* function number */
int86(0x33,&regs,&regs);   /* call the interrupt */
horz_motion = regs.x.cx    /* get the horizontal motion */
vert_motion = regs.x.dx    /* get the vertical motion */
```

Assembler

```
;---FIND OUT THE RELATIVE MOUSE CURSOR MOVEMENT:
        mov  ax,000Bh           ;function number
        int  33h                ;call the interrupt
        mov  HORZ_MOTION,CX      ;get the horizontal motion
        mov  VERT_MOTION,DX      ;get the vertical motion
```

Set the Ratio Between Motions of the Mouse and Cursor

Programs can change the ratio of mouse movement to mouse cursor movement. Mouse movement is measured in *mickeys*. Most mice have a resolution of 200 mickeys per inch. A certain number of mickeys moved in a particular direction translates into one pixel of mouse cursor movement. By default, it takes 8 mickeys to move the cursor horizontally by one pixel, and 16 mickeys to move vertically by one pixel. The ratios are different because the screen is not square, but the mouse is assumed to track equal distances in all directions.

Function Fh of interrupt 21h can change the mickey-to-pixel ratio. On entry, CX takes the number of mickeys required to move the mouse cursor one pixel horizontally. DX takes a like value for vertical cursor movements. The minimum value is 1, which would make the mouse extremely sensitive (moving the mouse a fraction of an inch would take the cursor all the way across the display). The larger the value, the more lethargic the mouse cursor.

Mouse drivers provide an acceleration feature by which the mouse moves a greater distance per mickey when the mouse is moved quickly. This approach lets you move the mouse cursor across the screen without large mouse motions, but still lets you do precise work at slow speeds. Mouse drivers vary in how they accelerate the cursor; typically they double the mouse speed when a certain speed (measured in mickeys-per-second) is achieved. Function 13h of INT 33h lets you change the threshold at which the doubling of speed occurs. Just place the mickeys-per-second value in DX and call the function. The default value is 64 mickeys per second; you can turn off acceleration by using a very large value.

The following examples reduce the default mickey-to-pixel ratios by half, making the mouse more sensitive. As compensation, they undo the acceleration effect by using a large value for the threshold.

BASIC

```
' $INCLUDE: 'QBX.BI'
DIM REGS AS RegType      ' Define register array


REGS.AX = &H000Fh        'function to set mickeys-per-pixel
REGS.CX = 4              '4 mickeys-per-pixel horizontally
REGS.DX = 8              '8 mickeys-per-pixel vertically
CALL Interrupt(&H33, REGS, REGS) 'set the ratio
```

267

```
REGS.AX = &H0013h        'function to set mouse acceleration
REGS.DX = 10000          'acceleration threshold
CALL Interrupt(&H33, REGS, REGS) 'set the new acceleration
```

Pascal

```
Uses DOS;

Var

    Regs: Registers;    {Registers type is declared in the DOS
unit}


Regs.AX := $000Fh;       {function to set mickeys-per-pixel}

Regs.CX := 4;            {4 mickeys-per-pixel horizontally}

Regs.DX := 8;            {8 mickeys-per-pixel vertically}

Intr($33, Regs);         {set the ratio}

Regs.AX := $0013h;       {function to set mouse acceleration}

Regs.DX := 10000;        {acceleration threshold}

Intr($33, Regs);         {set the new acceleration}
```

C

```
#include <dos.h>

union REGS regs;         /* declare the register array */

regs.x.ax = 0x000F;      /* function to set mickeys-per-pixel */

regs.x.cx = 4;           /* 4 mickeys-per-pixel horizontally */

regs.x.dx = 8;           /* 8 mickeys-per-pixel vertically */

int86(0x33,&regs,&regs); /* set the ratio */
```

```
regs.x.ax = 0x0013;       /* function to set acceleration */
regs.x.dx = 10000;        /* acceleration threshold */
int86(0x33,&regs,&regs);  /* set the new acceleration */
```

Assembler

```
;---ALTER MOUSE MOTION PARAMETERS:
    mov  ax,000Fh        ;function to set mickeys-per-pixel
    mov  cx,4            ;4 mickeys-per-pixel horizontally
    mov  dx,8            ;8 mickeys-per-pixel vertically
    int  33h             ;set the ratio
    mov  ax,0013h        ;function to set acceleration
    mov  dx,10000        ;acceleration threshold
    int  33h             ;set the new acceleration
```

Monitor the Mouse Buttons

Functions 5h and 6h of interrupt 33h report information about the mouse buttons. Both functions return a button status byte in AX that tells the current state of the two or three buttons. Bit 0 is set when the left mouse button is down; otherwise, it is zero. Similarly, bit 1 shows the status of the right mouse button, and bit 2 shows the status of the middle button if a mouse has one.

This status byte is also returned by function 3h of interrupt 21h, which reports the mouse cursor position (discussed in "Get or Set the Mouse Cursor Position," above). The status byte is not always reliable because a button click can occur while the program is busy with other matters between calls to the mouse functions; in this case, the program might miss a button click. To circumvent this problem, functions 5h and 6h report whatever button activity has occurred since the functions were last called. Function 5h tracks button presses and function 6h tracks button releases.

On entry, BX holds a value that indicates which button you want information for. The value is 0 for the left button, 1 for the right button, and 2 for the center button. On return, BX reports the number of button presses or releases since the last call to the particular function. CX and DX report the horizontal and vertical cursor positions, respectively, at the last button press or release. Using this data, you can determine not only that the mouse has been "clicked," but also the cursor position at the time of the click. Unfortunately, the mouse driver does not time intervals between button presses and releases and decide which events should be considered a click and which should be disregarded. For this kind of analysis, your program needs to repeatedly monitor the button status byte and make the necessary timings. See "Intercept Clicks, Double-Clicks, and Drag Events," below for more on this topic.

The following examples use function 06h to find out where the cursor resided when the left button was last released.

BASIC

```
' $INCLUDE: 'QBX.BI'
DIM REGS AS RegType      ' Define register array

REGS.AX = &H0006         'function number
REGS.BX = 0              'button number
CALL Interrupt(&H33, REGS, REGS)
```

```
IF REGS.BX THEN          'if the left button has been released…
   CURSORCOL = REGS.CX   'get the cursor column
   CURSORROW = REGS.DX   'get the cursor row
ENDIF
```

Pascal

```
Uses DOS;

Var
   Regs: Registers;   {Registers type is declared in the DOS unit}
   CursorCol,CursorRow: word;   {will hold the return values}

Regs.AX := 6;      {the interrupt function number}
Regs.BX := 0;      {button number for left button}
Intr($33,Regs);    {Call the interrupt}
if Regs.BX <> 0 then    {if the button has been released…}
begin
   CursorCol := Regs.CX;  {get the cursor column}
   CursorRow := Regs.DX;  {get the cursor row}
end;
```

C

```
#include <dos.h>

union REGS regs;        /* declare the register array */
int cursorcol,cursorrow; /* will hold the results */
```

```
regs.x.ax = 6;        /* function number */
regs.x.bx = 0;        /* code for left button */
int86(0x33,&regs,&regs);
if(regs.x.bx) {        /* if the button has been released… */
  cursorcol = regs.x.cx;  /* cursor column */
  cursorrow = regs.x.dx;  /* cursor row */
}
```

Assembler

```
;---GET THE CURSOR POSITION AT LAST LEFT BUTTON RELEASE:
        mov   ax,6h              ;function number
        mov   bx,0              ;button number
        int   33h               ;call the interrupt
        cmp   bx,0              ;button released?
        je    NOT_RELEASED      ;jump if not
        mov   CURSORCOL,cx      ;get the column
        mov   CURSORROW,dx      ;get the row
```

Intercept Clicks, Double-Clicks, and Drag Events

Many programs that use a mouse need to detect mouse clicks and double-clicks, and to track button-down events (*drag* events). A single mouse click consists of a mouse-down event followed by a mouse-up event. Most mouse drivers offer no support for detecting these events. Instead, you must write code that monitors the two events and times the interval between. When the interval is short enough, the combined event is regarded as a click. Otherwise, the two component events are usually ignored (unless, of course, the mouse cursor moves while the mouse button is held down, in which case a program may treat the mouse-down and mouse-up events as a drag operation).

Click duration is measured by the BIOS time-of-day clock, which is discussed in Chapter 5, "Set or Read the BIOS Time-of-Day Count." This four-byte value is incremented by the PC's timer chip 18.2 times per second. When a program learns that a mouse button has been pressed, it records the current time-of-day reading and then watches for a button-up event, or for a change in the mouse cursor position. If the cursor starts moving, control jumps to a routine that tracks drag events, or perhaps to a routine that pulls down menus. Otherwise, the program waits for the button release and then reads the time-of-day again. If not too many 18ths of a second have passed since the button-down event, the program decides that a mouse click has occurred and responds accordingly. Otherwise, the two events are ignored, just as an inadmissable keystroke would be.

Double-clicks make matters more complicated. After a single click has been detected, the program must postpone jumping to the appropriate routine until it is certain that another click is not about to arrive to make a double-click. Again the BIOS time-of-day reading is consulted. A program must make three timings to detect a double-click, clocking the periods within the two clicks and the period between the two.

In reality, all sorts of combinations of click timings and cursor movements can occur, and your mouse input routine must be prepared to sort out what should be accepted as a legitimate event from what should be considered an input error. One problem is that the mouse position may be slightly shifted when a click or double-click is made. These events should not be considered as a very short drag operation nor as a user error. Rather, a mouse input routine should require that the mouse cursor move a minimum distance before an event will qualify as a drag operation.

You also need to provide for the case where one click occurs and a second button-down event happens within the time allowed for a double-click, but the second button-up event occurs too late to define a second click. Should you treat the combined events as a single click? Or should you discard them all as an input error? It all depends on what effects the mouse clicks will have, and on how you foresee the user working with the program. There are no hard and fast rules. In fact, a click-then-drag operation would be a perfectly acceptable form of mouse input.

Once a program has detected a click, double-click, or the beginning of a drag, it needs to learn the object on the screen with which the event is associated. There are two general approaches to this problem. Either a program can run through some calculations that figure out what object is located at the mouse cursor, or the program can maintain a list of all screen objects and their locations, and simply run through the entire list to see if the mouse cursor is over one of the objects. Let's look at some examples of the two approaches.

Say you've constructed a pull-down menu system, with the menus listed on a menu bar on the top row of a text screen. The menu bar is always in view, and nothing ever covers any part of it. In addition, the names of the menus are written within 15 column-wide fields that are contiguous, and that begin at the left edge of the screen. When a mouse-down event occurs in this situation, a program would immediately check the mouse cursor position. If the cursor is found on the top row of the screen, its column number would be divided by 15 to find out what menu-name field it resides in. Then a routine would be called to pull down the associated menu. The menu-management code would then follow the mouse-cursor movements, move a bar cursor across the menu selections as the cursor changed rows, and perhaps switch to a different menu if the cursor strayed to the left or right. The program would keep a table of values that tell it how many entries each menu contains and codes for the routines associated with each menu choice. All the while, the menu-management routine would keep an eye on the mouse button to see whether it has been released. Once the button goes up, the routine restores the screen to as it was before the menu was pulled down and calls the procedure associated with the menu selection.

Now, consider an entirely different kind of mouse programming in which a number of moveable graphic objects are located on the screen and can be selected and perhaps edited by the mouse. In this case, it's usually not possible to calculate which object resides at any particular point on the screen because the user is free to resize objects or move them to any location. So an array or linked list must be set up that lists each object and its position. When a mouse-down event occurs, the entire array is searched to see if the cursor hot spot falls within one of the objects. This is not a particularly efficient approach, but the inefficiency does not usually matter because the search is conducted at a time when the program is idling within an input loop.

Sometimes one mouse-selectable screen object lies entirely inside another. For example, you might create a dialog box with a button in it and want to discern when a mouse click has occurred within either object. This situation is handled simply by drawing larger objects before overlapping smaller ones, and successively entering the coordinates of each into the tracking array. Then, when a mouse-down event occurs, the array is searched "backward" from end to beginning so that tests are made for the smaller, overlapping objects before tests are made for the larger ones. Note that you can use this technique to define regions that are not physically drawn on the screen, such as a three-pixel wide margin around an object. Another trick is to make the first element in the array the boundary rectangle of the window in which the objects are drawn. This element is selected when no other element in the array corresponds to the coordinates of a mouse-down events, and thus signifies a mouse-down event within the window's content region but outside any object.

Set Up a Mouse Interrupt Routine

You can set up a routine that will be activated by the mouse driver whenever specified mouse events occur. This feature saves your program the trouble of constantly polling the mouse driver. Function Ch of interrupt 33h sets up the routine. On entry, ES:DX points to the routine, and CX holds a bit pattern specifying the kinds of events for which the routine should be called. The pattern is:

bit	meaning when bit is set
0	Mouse has moved
1	Left button pressed
2	Left button released
3	Right button pressed
4	Right button released
5	Middle button pressed
6	Middle button released

When the routine is called by the driver, the processor registers contain the following information:

register	contents
AX	A mask like above, in which the only bit set indicates the event that has started up the routine.
BX	The button state, using the same bit patterns listed in "Monitor the Mouse Buttons," above.
CX	The cursor's horizontal coordinate using the system explained in this chapter's *minitutorial*.
DX	The cursor's vertical coordinate.
DI	Mouse horizontal motion in mickeys, as explained in "Set the Ratio Between Motions of the Mouse and Cursor," above.
SI	Mouse vertical motion in mickeys.

276

You can change the mask settings at any time by calling function 0Ch again with a different value in CX. Remember that the mouse driver operates independently of your program, so you must unlink the routine when your program quits. This is done by calling function 0h of interrupt 33h, which initializes the mouse driver (as discussed in "Intialize the Mouse Driver," above). Be sure to include this code in your Ctrl-Break and critical-error handlers.

Take Analog Input from a Game Port

A game port can support up to four analog inputs. These are usually paired to represent *x* and *y* coordinates. In this way, the coordinates for two joysticks can be monitored simultaneously. Other devices, such as graphics tablets, may also be connected to a game port. They send information through a game port in the same way as joysticks. This section discusses how to read joystick coordinates, and the next section discusses how to find out the status of joystick buttons.

Information for all four analog channels is communicated by just one byte that is found at port address 201H. The bit assignments are:

bit	joystick
0	X-axis of stick A
1	Y-axis of stick A
2	X-axis of stick B
3	Y-axis of stick B

A single bit describes a coordinate by means of *timing*. A program sends a byte of any value to the port. This causes the four low bits to be set to 1. Then the program continuously reads the value of the port, timing how long it takes for the bit in question to return to 0. The elapsed time is proportional to the joystick position on that axis. The bit transitions from 1 to 0 are longest for the down-position on the Y-axis, and the right-position on the X-axis. Thus, the shortest bit timing for game port bits 0 and 2 correspond to the left edge of the screen, and the longest to the right edge. Similarly, the shortest timings for bits 1 and 3 correspond to the top edge of the screen, and the longest, to the bottom.

Timings vary by joystick design, and between individual joysticks of the same design. For this reason, software that uses joysticks usually provides a routine that measures the joystick timings and correlates them to screen coordinates.

The timings represent static positions, not motions. They have nothing to do with the speed at which a joystick is being moved. No matter what the joystick position, the bits change from 1 to 0 very quickly relative to the speed at which the joystick is moved mechanically. A program has time to check the coordinates many times during a single movement of a joystick. Reasonably good accuracy can be obtained by testing the Y-axis and X-axis positions in succession; there is usually no need to write more complicated routines that watch two channels simultaneously.

BIOS function 84h of Interrupt 15h returns joystick coordinates. This function is not found in the original IBM PCs and early XTs. On entry, DX holds 1 to flag that the function should return coordinates; when the value is 0, the status of the joystick buttons is returned instead (more on this in "Take Digital Input from a Game Port," below). On return, coordinate values are returned in these registers:

```
AX  =   x-axis of joystick A
BX  =   y-axis of joystick A
CX  =   x-axis of joystick B
DX  =   y-axis of joystick B
```

The return values typically range from 0 to about 420.

Of the four compilers discussed in this book, only Microsoft BASIC provides routines for monitoring a game port. The other compilers may call the BIOS interrupt, or set up code to monitor the port directly. See Chapter 2, "Determine the Number and Types of I/O Ports," to learn how to find a game port in any kind of machine.

BASIC

BASIC's *STICK* function returns joystick coordinates specified by the following code numbers:

```
0       X-axis of joystick A
1       Y-axis of joystick A
2       X-axis of joystick B
3       Y-axis of joystick B
```

To find out the X-axis coordinate of joystick A, you would write:

```
COLUMN=STICK(0)
```

Whenever *STICK(0)* is called, it records the settings for the other three coordinates. The functions *STICK(1)*, *STICK(2)*, and *STICK(3)* report these readings without accessing the game port again. This approach means that you will always obtain correct coordinate readings even when time passes between fetching one coordinate and another. But you must always call *STICK(0)* before using any of the other code numbers.

Pascal

This example uses the Turbo Pascal *Intr* procedure to call function 84h of Interrupt 15h:

```
Uses DOS;

var

  Regs: Registers;  {Registers type is declared in the DOS unit}

  JoystickA_X,JoystickA_Y: word;


Regs.AH := $84;    {function number}

Regs.DX := 1;      {subfunction number}

Intr($15,Regs);    {Call the interrupt}

JoystickA_X := Regs.AX;  {get x coordinate of joystick A}

JoystickA_Y := Regs.BX;  {get y coordinate of joystick A}
```

C

In both the Borland and Microsoft compilers, use the *int86* function to call interrupt 15h.

```
#include <dos.h>


union REGS regs;           /* declare the register array */

int joystick_a_x,joystick_a_y;


regs.h.ah = 0x84;          /* function number */

regs.x.dx = 1;             /* subfunction number */

int86(0x15,&regs,&regs);
joystick_a_x = regs.x.ax;  /* get x coordinate of joystick A */

joystick_a_y = regs.x.bx;  /* get y coordinate of joystick A */
```

Assembler

```
;---FIND OUT THE COORDINATES OF JOYSTICK A
        mov   ah,84h           ;function number
        mov   dx,1             ;subfunction number
        int   15h              ;call the interrupt
        mov   STICK_A_X,ax     ;save x coordinate
        mov   STICK_A_Y,bx     ;save y coordinate
```

Low Level Access

In this example, a value for the X-axis of joystick A is taken directly from the game port.

```
;---GET X-AXIS COORDINATE FOR JOYSTICK A:
        mov   dx,201h          ;game port address
        out   dx,al            ;send an arbitrary value to the port
        mov   ah,1             ;will test bit 0
        mov   si,0             ;initialize counter
NEXT:   in    al,dx            ;read the port
        test  al,ah            ;test bit 1
        jz    FINISHED         ;jump ahead when bit clears
        inc   si               ;else increment the counter
        jmp   NEXT             ;loop around
FINISHED:                      ;now SI has X-axis value for stick A
```

Take Digital Input from a Game Port

Game ports monitor the status of up to four buttons on the devices they serve. The status of the buttons is reported by the same port address (201H) that communicates coordinates (discussed in "Take Analog Input from a Game Port," above). The high four bits correspond to the four buttons. A button is "down" when the bit is clear.

bit	button
4	Button #1 of joystick A
5	Button #2 of joystick A
6	Button #1 of joystick B
7	Button #2 of joystick B

It's easy to read the status of individual buttons, but constantly monitoring the buttons can be a complex matter. This is because a program may not always be free to check the buttons, yet a button could be pressed and then released while the program is busy elsewhere. To deal with this problem, special *trapping* routines can be linked into the timer interrupt using the techniques explained in Chapter 5, "Control Real-Time Operations." Such a routine automatically reads the status of the buttons several times per second without the program specifically requesting that this be done. The routine records button presses and releases so that the program may later find out that they have occurred.

BASIC

BASIC uses the STRIG statement to read the status of the buttons. STRIG can trap the occurrence of a button-press without the program immediately concerning itself with the button's status. At any time, the program can ask "has the button been pressed since I last enquired?" This feature is useful in video games, because it allows a program to devote itself to manipulating the screen without constantly needing to check the button status. The feature slows down a program's operation, however, because BASIC is made to check the buttons after *every* instruction. For this reason, STRIG is operational only when it is purposely turned on, and it may be turned on and off as a program requires.

STRIG operates in two ways. First, it can act as a function that reports the current status of the buttons, in the form **X=STRIG(n)**. Here *n* is a code number:

0 Button A1 pressed since last call

1 Button A1 currently pressed

2   Button B1 pressed since last call

3   Button B1 currently pressed

4   Button A2 pressed since last call

5   Button A2 currently pressed

6   Button B2 pressed since last call

7   Button B2 currently pressed

In all cases, the function returns -1 if the description applies, and 0 if not. To report whether button 1 of joystick one is currently down, you could write:

```
IF STRIG(1) = -1 THEN WRITE "BUTTON 1 IS DOWN"
```

The second way in which STRIG is used is in the form where it is set up to automatically switch the program over to a subroutine whenever a button is pressed. Begin by executing an **EVENT ON** statement to enable event trapping. Then execute a separate **STRIG(n) ON** statement for each button you want activated. In these statements, **n** is a button numbered 0, 2, 4, or 6, as in the table above. Then write a subroutine that will be activated when the specified buttons are pressed. Each button may have its own subroutine, if desired. Finally, write **ON STRIG(n)** *GOSUB* statements for each button. Execute **STRING(n) OFF** statements to switch off button trapping.

There is a third option. **STRIG(n) STOP** causes button-presses to be trapped, but no action is taken until the next STRIG(n) ON statement. This feature keeps ON STRIG GOSUB from making undesirable interruptions. A program is still slowed during the STRIG(n) STOP condition. The following lines show the general set-up for **ON STRIG**:

```
EVENT ON              'enable event trapping


ON STRIG(0) GOSUB BUTTONDOWN


'jump to BUTTONDOWN when A1 pressed

   .
STRIG(0) ON           'activate trapping

   .
STRIG(0) STOP         'deactivate trapping, but monitor button

 .
STRIG(0) ON           'reactivate trapping
```

```
        .

    STRIG(0) OFF          'stop checking button status

        .

    'Subroutine to respond to button A1
    ButtonDown:

        .

        .

    RETURN                        'return to wherever left off
```

Pascal

In Turbo Pascal, read the game port button status directly from port $201:

```
    if (Port[$201] And 16) = 0 then Writeln('Button 1 is down');
```

C

Neither Microsoft nor Borland C compilers provide a function for finding game port button settings. Instead, read the value at port 0x201. In Borland's C, write:

```
    if((inportb(0x201) & 16) =-0) printf("Button 1 is down");
```

Microsoft's C uses *inp* instead of *inportb* to access ports:

```
    if((inp(0x201) & 16) =-0) printf("Button 1 is down");
```

Assembler

Function 84h of BIOS interrupt 15h returns the button settings in bits 4-7 of AL. On entry, DX should contain 0; when DX contains 1, the joystick coordinates are returned instead. On return, the carry flag is set if no game port is installed. Unfortunately, this interrupt is not provided in machines with a BIOS date of 11/08/82 or earlier. These machines respond to the function call by setting the carry flag and returning 86h in the AH register.

```
;---TEST BUTTON #2 OF STICK B (BIT 7):
        mov   ah,84h            ;function number
        mov   dx,0              ;request button settings
        int   15h              ;call the function
        jc    NO_JOYSTICK       ;go to error routine if no joystick
        test al,10000000b      ;test bit 7
        jz    BUTTON_DOWN       ;jump if button down
                               ;etc...
```

Low Level Access

To fetch the button settings in any machine, access port address 201h, as described above:

```
;---FIND OUT JOYSTICK BUTTON SETTINGS:
        mov   dx,201h           ;port address of game adaptor
        in    al,dx            ;get the value
        test al,10000b         ;is bit 4 set?
        jz    BUTTON_DOWN       ;if not, button is down
```

10

Managing Disk Drives

- Minitutorial: Disk Types and Allocation
- Set/Check the Default Drive
- Read/Change a Disk's Volume Label
- Determine Available Disk Space
- Read/Write Individual Disk Sectors
- Program Disk Controller and DMA Chips
- Detect and Recover from Disk Errors

Minitutorial: Disk Types and Allocation

All disks, whether diskettes or hard disks, are organized in the same fashion. The surface of the disk is laid out as a series of concentric rings called *tracks*, and the tracks are divided radially into 512-byte *sectors*. Hard disk drives contain several parallel disks, each with a pair of read/write heads to access the two sides. Taken together, all tracks a given distance from the center are referred to as a *cylinder*. Because the heads for all of the disks move in tandem, economy of motion is achieved by filling all tracks in one cylinder before moving inward to the next.

Disk sectors are defined by magnetic information written by the utility that formats the disk. This information includes a number for each sector. Thus, sector #3 on a track is actually labeled as #3. This system lets formatting programs number the sectors noncontinuously. Sector #2 may follow sector #1 by two sectors, and sector #3 would then follow two sectors later. By *interleaving* sectors this way, the drive electronics are given time to finish processing one sector's data before moving on to the next. Fast computers can use a *1:1 interleave* in which sectors are numbered continuously.

A file is divided among as many sectors as are required to hold it. Actually, on all hard disks, and most diskettes, disk space is allocated in *groups* of sectors called *clusters*. Only a few clusters on the outside rim of the diskette are reserved for special purposes. The others are available on a "first-come, first-served" basis. This means that, as the disk is filled with data, available clusters are gradually filled, moving inward toward the center of the disk. When files are deleted, clusters are freed, and with time available, space comes to be scattered around a disk, causing new files to be dispersed and making them slow to read and write.

The first sector of all disks (side 0, track 0, sector 1) holds the disk's *boot record*. The boot record contains code that lets the computer operate the disk drives well enough to start loading DOS. The next sectors holds two copies of the disk's *file allocation table*, which keeps track of the allocation of disk space (the second copy is for safety's sake). And then comes one copy of the *root directory*, which lists files and references to subdirectories and tells where on the disk they begin. Disks used for booting must also contain two small DOS programs, IBMBIO.COM and IBMDOS.COM (or IO.SYS and MSDOS.SYS), which are read at startup, and which give the computer the capability needed to find and load COMMAND.COM so that DOS can take charge of the machine.

Hard disks have a *master boot record* containing a *partition table* by which the disk can be partitioned into two or more *logical drives*, some of which may use a different operating system than DOS. The partition table contains information about where the DOS partition begins on the disk, and the first sector at that partition holds the DOS boot record.

Disks use a *file allocation table* (FAT) to allot disk space to files and to keep track of free sectors. The number of sectors filled by a FAT varies with the size and type of disk. Every position in a file allocation table corresponds to a particular cluster position on the disk. Files usually fill multiple clusters, and a file's directory entry contains the number of the *starting cluster* at which the first part of the file is stored. By looking up the position in the FAT that corresponds to the starting cluster, DOS finds the number of the cluster in which the next part of the file is found. This cluster also has its own corresponding entry in the FAT, which in turn contains the number of the next cluster in the chain. For the last cluster occupied by a file, the FAT holds a special end-of-file value. A zero value fills FAT entries for unused clusters (or deallocated clusters) so that DOS knows they are free for allocation.

Large cluster size tends to waste disk space, but when large disks have a small cluster size, the FAT becomes large. DOS tries to keep as much of the FAT as possible in memory during disk operations, so a large FAT can be a problem. To further complicate matters, the cluster entries in a FAT may be 12 or 16 bits long. The 16-bit fields are used to hold the large cluster numbers required by hard disks larger than 16mb. Figure 10-1 illustrates how a FAT works.

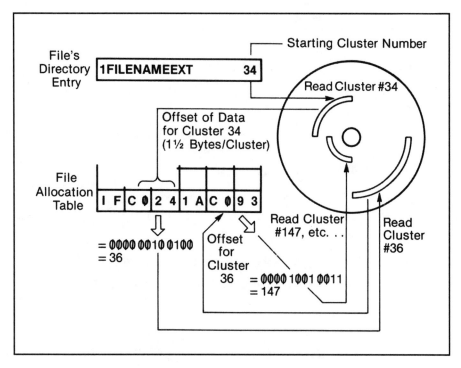

Figure 10-1   A File Allocation Table

Function 1Fh of interrupt 21h provides information that can be used to figure out the size of a disk's file allocation tables and root directory. A program can then access these data objects using direct sector reads and writes ("Read/Write Individual Disk Sectors," below, shows how). There are no DOS functions that give you this kind of access, nor does DOS allow direct access to subdirectories. The reason for these restrictions is obvious. A single error introduced into a FAT or directory can result in massive damage to the file system, in some cases amounting to the loss of all data on the disk. Chapter 11 provides routines for reading and changing nearly every aspect of directory entries. On the other hand, only a few kinds of utility program ever need to read or alter file allocation tables.

Function 1Fh uses no input registers. The function returns with DS:BX pointing to the *drive parameter block* for the default drive. The AL register is nonzero when an error has occurred. The content of the block varies between DOS versions, as follows:

offset	field size	meaning
In ALL DOS versions:		
00h	db	The drive number (A = 0)
01h	db	Number of the drive's device driver
02h	dw	Bytes per sector
04h	db	Sectors per cluster (counted from zero so that 0 = 1 sector, 1 = 2 sectors...)
05h	db	The shift factor
06h	dw	Number of reserved boot sectors
08h	db	Number of copies of the FAT
09h	dw	Number of entries in the root directory
0Bh	dw	Number of the first sector holding data
0Dh	dw	Number of the highest cluster, plus 1
DOS 4.x only:		
0Fh	dw	Number of sectors per FAT (0 to 65535)
11h	dw	Starting sector for the root directory
13h	dd	Address of the drive's device driver
17h	db	The media descriptor byte (See Chapter 2, "Determine the Number and Types of Disk Drives")
18h	db	A flag used by DOS
19h	dd	Address of parameter block of next device
1Dh	dd	Last cluster that has been allocated
1Fh	dd	Reserved
DOS 3.x only:		
1Eh	dw	Starting cluster of the current directory
1Ch	64 bytes	Null-terminated string indicating the current directory path.

offset	field size	meaning
DOS 2.x and 3.x only:		
1Ch	dw	Last cluster that has been allocated
1Eh	dw	Reserved
DOS 2.x only:		
0Fh	db	Number of sectors per FAT (0 to 255)
10h	dw	Starting sector for the root directory
12h	dd	Address of the drive's device driver
16h	db	The media descriptor byte (Discussed in Chapter 2, "Determine the Number and Types of Disk Drives")
17h	db	A flag used by DOS
18h	dd	Address of parameter block of next device

Set/Check the Default Drive

When DOS is asked to perform file operations without a specification for the drive and directory, it accesses the *default directory*. The default directory is the *current directory* of the *default drive*. Thus, to change the default directory, you may need to first set the default drive, and then the current directory for that drive. This section discusses the first operation, and Chapter 11, "Get/Set the Current Directory," explains the second.

BASIC

Microsoft BASIC's *CHDRIVE* statement sets the default drive. It requires a two-byte string parameter that specifies the drive name. To make drive D the default drive:

```
CHDRIVE "D:"                          'make D: the default drive
```

To find out the default drive, use *CURDIR$* to find out the default directory. This function returns the default directory when no drive is specified for which it should report the current directory. In this case, the first two characters of the string give the drive specifier for the default drive, such as **C:** or **D:**. Use *LEFT$* to obtain these two characters.

```
DefaultDir$ = LEFT$(CURDIR$,2)     'get default drive
```

Pascal

The Turbo Pascal *ChDir* procedure changes *both* the current drive and the current directory of that drive. If you want to make B:\BIRDS\SPARROWS the default directory, write:

```
ChDir('B:\BIRDS\SPARROWS');
```

If you were subsequently to call *ChDir* again to make C:\REPTILES\TURTLES the default directory, \BIRDS\SPARROWS would remain the current directory on drive B, although the default drive will have been changed.

Use Turbo Pascal's *GetDir* function to find out the default drive. This function returns a string in which the first two characters are a drive specifier, such as **A:** or **C:**. *GetDir* takes two parameters. The first should be **0** in this case to specify the default drive; the second is a variable in which the path to the current directory is returned. Use the *Copy* function to obtain the first two bytes of the string.

```
var

   PathString: string[80];
```

```
DefaultDrv: string[2];



GetDir(0,PathString);

DefaultDrv := Copy(PathString,1,2);
```

C

The Borland compilers provide the *setdisk* function to set the default drive. The equivalent function in the Microsoft compilers is *_dos_setdrive*. The first parameter in both functions is a drive number, with drive A as 0, drive B as 1, and so on. Microsoft's C, but not Borland's C, takes a second parameter. This is a pointer to an unsigned integer in which the function deposits the number of logical drives in the machine (or the DOS LASTDRIVE setting). Chapter 2, "Determine the Number and Types of Disk Drives," explains a better way of finding out this information. To make drive D the default drive:

```
unsigned num_drives;



setdisk(3);                      /* Borland */
```
or
```
_dos_setdrive(3,&num_drives);  /* Microsoft */
```

Borland's C provides *getdisk*, and Microsoft's C, *_dos_getdrive*, for finding out the default drive. The *getdisk* function takes no parameters and returns the drive number as an integer value. The *_dos_getdrive* function does not return a value, but instead takes a parameter that points to an unsigned integer in which the drive code is written. Both functions count drives from 0, so that drive A is 0, drive B is 1, and so on.

```
unsigned default_drive;



default_drive = getdisk();     /* Borland */
```
or
```
_dos_getdrive(&default_drive);  /* Microsoft */
```

293

Assembler

Function Eh of interrupt 21h sets the default drive. Simply place the drive number in DL and execute the interrupt. The number 0 represents drive A, 1 represents drive B, and so on. Notice that this numbering scheme is different from the one used by most DOS functions, where 0 represents the default drive, 1 is drive A, 2 is drive B, and so on. This function returns the number of logical drives in the machine in the AL register. (Beginning with DOS 3.0, the function returns the DOS LASTDRIVE setting. See Chapter 2, "Determine the Number and Types of Disk Drives," for a better way of counting the drives.) To make drive B the default drive:

```
mov  ah,0Eh        ;function number
mov  dl,1          ;code for drive B
int  21h           ;set B: as the default drive
```

Function 19h of interrupt 21h reports which disk drive is currently the default drive. There are no input registers. AL returns a drive number, using the same numbering system employed by Function Eh (A = 0, etc.). This example tests whether drive C is the default drive:

```
mov  ah,19h        ;function number
int  21h           ;call the function
cmp  al,2          ;drive C?
jne  ChangeDrive   ;change the default drive if not
```

Read/Change a Disk's Volume Label

The disk's volume label is nothing more than a directory entry with a special attribute byte. The label fills the first 11 bytes of the entry, as would a file name and its extension. The directory entry's attribute byte, which is found at offset 11, holds the value 8 (bit 3=1). The date and time fields are also filled in. The label can occupy any position in the directory.

Reading a volume label is easy. It's done by the same function that searches directories for files. This is function 4Eh of interrupt 21h. It, and its corresponding compiler routines, is discussed in Chapter 11, "Read Directories." The function requires two parameters: a file specification and an attribute byte that determines which attributes a file must possess if the function is to return information about it. To find the volume label of drive A, you would make the file specification **A:*.*** (that is, any file in the root directory), and would make the attribute specification **8**. If the disk has a volume label, it is returned as the "file name." Otherwise, the function returns the error message that indicates that no match was found.

Writing a volume label is more difficult. It can only be done using one of the DOS *file control block* file-access routines. In its early incarnations, DOS used data structures called *file control blocks* (*FCBs*) to organize file access. The FCB technique of file access has been superceded, and it is virtually never used today, although DOS continues to support FCBs. There is a special kind of FCB called an *extended file control block*, and this is the data structure required to add, delete, or change a disk's volume label.

To establish an extended file control block, begin by allocating 43 bytes and initializing all to space characters (ASCII 32). Then make the first byte FFh to identify the structure as an *extended* FCB. At offset 06h in the block (that is, at the seventh byte), write 08h. This is the volume label attribute. Then write the number of the drive in which the volume label will be written at offset 07h, using 0 for the default drive, 1 for drive A, 2 for drive B, and so on. Finally, write the volume label starting from offset 08h. It may be up to 11 characters long.

Once the FCB is set up this way, call function 16H of interrupt 21h, which "creates a file" in FCB operations. On entry, DS:DX should point to the data structure. On return, AL will hold 0 if the volume label has been successfully created, or FFh if a volume label is already present. In the latter case, you must remove the existing volume label before the new one can be inserted. This is done by using the same extended FCB set up in the same way, except that all 11 bytes of the volume label field are replaced by the wild card character **?**. Then call function 13h of interrupt 21h, again with DS:DX pointing to the FCB. This function will delete the label, returning 0 in AL if it succeeds, and FFh if it does not. Be sure the proper attribute byte resides at offset 06h, lest the routine delete all files in the root directory. Once the old label is gone, rewrite the new label into the FCB and call function 16h of interrupt 21h again to add the label to the disk.

295

Determine Available Disk Space

Programs should monitor available disk space and inform users of an impending shortage. It's much easier to deal with a disk space shortage *before*, rather than *during*, file operations.

BASIC

Microsoft BASIC does not provide a function that reports free disk space. You'll need to call function 36h of interrupt 21h (discussed below) using BASIC's *Interrupt* routine. On entry, DL holds a drive number, with 0 as the default drive, 1 as drive A, 2 as drive B, and so on. On return, BX reports the number of clusters available, and AX tells how many sectors there are in a cluster. CX gives the number of bytes in a sector, which is always 512 under DOS. This example checks the available disk space on drive C:

```
' $INCLUDE: 'QBX.BI'

DIM regs AS RegType        ' define register array


regs.ax = &H3600           ' function number
regs.dx = &H0003           'select drive C
CALL Interrupt(&H21, regs, regs)
NumClusters = regs.bx
SectorsPerCluster = regs.ax
AvailableBytes = NumClusters * SectorsPerCluster * 512
```

Pascal

In Turbo Pascal, the *DiskFree* function returns a *longint* giving the number of bytes of free disk space. You need only specify the drive number, with 0 as the current drive, 1 as drive A, 2 as drive B, and so on. The function returns -1 when the drive number is invalid. To find out how much space is available on drive C, write:

```
Writeln('Drive C has ',DiskFree(3) div 1024, ' Kbytes free');
```

C

Similar routines for reporting available disk space are found in Borland's C (*getdfree*) and Microsoft's C (*_dos_getdiskfree*). Both functions fill a structure defined in *dos.h*. In the Borland compilers, the structure is called *dfree*:

```
struct dfree
{
    unsigned df_avail:      /* available clusters */
    unsigned df_total;      /* total clusters */
    unsigned df_bsec;       /* bytes per sector */
    unsigned df_sclus;      /* sectors per cluster */
};
```

In Microsoft's C, the structure is named *diskfree_t*:

```
struct diskfree_t
{
    unsigned total_clusters;
    unsigned avail_clusters;
    unsigned sectors_per_cluster;
    unsigned bytes_per_sector;
};
```

Both functions take two parameters, the first being an unsigned integer giving the drive number, with 0 as the default drive, 1 as drive A, 2 as drive B, and so on. The second parameter is a pointer to the structure. In the event of an error, *_dos_getdiskfree* returns a non-zero value. The *getdfree* function reports errors by returning 0xFFFF in the df_sclus field. In this example, *getdfree* checks the number of free clusters on drive C:

```
struct dfree diskstats;


getdfree(3,&diskstats);
printf("There are %d clusters free",diskstats.df_avail);
```

Assembler

Function 36h of interrupt 21h tells how much disk space is free. The only input register is DL, which contains the drive number. The default drive is noted by 0, drive A by 1, and so on. On return, BX reports the number of clusters available, AX tells how many sectors there are in a cluster, and CX tells how many bytes are in a sector. A little multiplication can produce the desired result. However, a large hard disk may have more then 64K sectors. To keep with 16-bit (single-register) arithmetic, it's easiest to work backward by figuring out how many clusters you need and comparing that to the value returned. The following example checks that there is at least 20K of disk space available on drive C.

```
        mov   ah,36h          ;function number
        mov   dl,3            ;drive C
        int   21h             ;go get the disk statistics
        mov   cx,ax           ;keep number of sectors per cluster
        mov   ax,NUMBER_K     ;testing for availablity of this many K
        shl   ax,1            ;multiply by 2 for number of sectors
        sub   dx,dx           ;clear DX, since dividend is in DX:AX
        div   cx             ;divide by number of sectors in cluster
        cmp   dx,0           ;is there a remainder?
        je    NO_REMAINDER   ;jump if not
        inc   ax            ;adjust for rounding down
NO_REMAINDER:
        cmp   bx,ax          ;compare required to available clusters
        jl    NO_ROOM        ;error routine if insufficient space
```

Read/Write Individual Disk Sectors

Reading and writing particular disk sectors is a technique used mostly to access a disk's root directory or file allocation table, where the sectors are always positioned at the same location. While *reading* sectors is harmless enough, *writing* absolute sectors requires that the code be completely accurate the first time it is used. A mistake could make a directory or FAT unreadable, effectively destroying all data on the disk. It's best to work on diskettes until you're sure your code is reliable.

Both the BIOS and DOS offer functions for reading and writing to particular sectors. The main difference is that they number sectors differently. The BIOS routines work with side numbers (counted from 0 upward), track numbers (also counted from 0), and sector numbers (counted from 1). The DOS functions specify sectors using a single *logical sector number.* All sectors on the disk are numbered starting from the side 0, track 0, sector 1, which is considered to be sector 0. Sector 1 is at the next sector on track 0, side 0, and so on. Counting continues along track 0 from side to side until the entire outer cylinder is counted. Then counting continues at sector 1 of track 1 on side 0.

Figure 10-2 compares the BIOS and DOS methods of numbering disk sectors.

The BIOS uses function 2h of interrupt 13h to read sectors, and function 3h of interrupt 13h to write sectors. The processor registers play the same roles in both routines. AL specifies how many sectors should be transferred. DL holds a drive number, with 0 as drive A, 1 as drive B, and so on. In addition, *bit seven should be set in this value when the disk is a hard disk.* DH holds a side (read/write head) number, and CL keeps the sector number. CH holds the track number. When this function is used with a hard disk, the track number is a *ten* bit value. The highest two bits are written at the high end of the CL register. Finally, ES:BX points to the starting point in memory in which the transferred data is deposited, or from which it is taken. On return, AL holds the number of sectors read or written. The carry flag is set when an error occurs, in which case AH returns an error code. Incidentally, these functions sometimes bring about a DMA error condition (error code 9) when a sector's data crosses a memory offset that ends in three zeros, such as **7000h.** Be sure to set ES:BX in a way that this will not happen. Other error codes include 4 when the requested sector was not found, 12 for invalid media, 16 for bad data, 32 and 64 for controller or drive failure, and 128 when the (diskette) drive is not ready.

To access sectors using logical sector numbers, call DOS interrupts 25h and 26h, which respectively read and write absolute sectors. Place the beginning logical sector number in DX, and point DS:BX to the transfer buffer. CX is given the number of sectors to read or write, and AL takes the drive number, where 0 is drive A, 1 is drive B, and so on. The carry flag is set if the function fails.

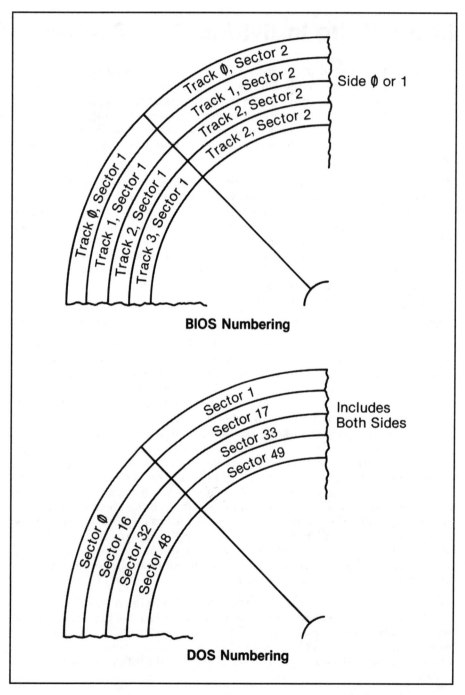

Figure 10-2   BIOS and DOS organization of disk sectors

Starting with DOS 4.0, sector numbers may be 32 bits long. Both of the DOS interrupts will fail when they encounter a disk formatted in this *extended format*, and will return **0207h** in AX. You can access a disk formatted this way by placing −1 in CX instead of the number of sectors to read, and by pointing DS:BX to the following parameter block:

```
offset 00        logical sector number (32 bits)

       04        number of sectors to transfer (16 bits)

       06        pointer to the transfer buffer (32 bits)
```

The flag register remains on the stack when interrupts 25h and 26h return, leaving the stack off balance. Be sure to POP this value off the stack immediately upon return from these functions (the value is arbitrarily POPed into CX in the assembly language example below). This quirk makes these routines hard to use in high-level languages, since they require insertion of assembly language code.

BASIC

Microsoft BASIC provides no routines for reading or writing absolute disk sectors. Use BASIC's *Interrupt* statement instead. You'll need to use the BIOS routine, because the DOS routine requires the addition of an assembly language statement that is unwieldly to create in BASIC. This example reads four sectors from drive A, starting at side 0, track 0, sector 3, and tests the carry flag (bit 0 of the flag register) on return.

```
' $INCLUDE: 'QBX.BI'

DIM REGS AS RegTypeX       ' Define register array

DIM SectorBuffer(1 to 1024) AS Integer


REGS.AX = &H0204           'function number, read four sectors

REGS.CX = &H0003           'track 0, sector 3

REGS.DX = &H0000           'side 0, drive 0 (drive A)

REGS.BX = VARPTR(SectorBuffer)

REGS.ES = VARSEG(SectorBuffer)

CALL InterruptX(&H13, REGS, REGS)

CarryFlag = REGS.FLAGS AND 1

IF CarryFlag = 1 THEN WRITE "SECTOR READ ERROR"
```

Pascal

Turbo Pascal has no routines for absolute sector reads and writes. Instead, use the *Intr* procedure. In this example, Intr uses BIOS INT 13h to read two sectors from drive B, starting on side 1, track 12, sector 0:

```
Uses DOS;

Var

  Regs: Registers;   {Registers type is declared in the DOS unit}

  TransferBuffer: array[1..1024] of Byte;


  Regs.AH := 2;              {function number}

  Regs.AL := 2;              {read two sectors}

  Regs.DH := 1;              {side 1}

  Regs.CH := 12;             {track 12]

  Regs.CL := 0;              {sector 0}

  Regs.DL := 1;              {drive 1 (drive B)}

  Regs.ES := Seg(TransferBuffer);

  Regs.BX := Ofs(TransferBuffer);

  Intr($13,Regs);    {Call the interrupt}

  If Regs.Flags And 1 = 1 then Writeln('Sector Read Error');
```

C

Borland's C offers the *biosdisk* function, and Microsoft's C, the *_bios_disk* function, to read and write absolute sectors. As their names imply, they use the BIOS system of numbering disk sectors. The two functions handle parameters differently. In the Borland compilers, the function takes seven parameters, the first of which is a command number that is 2 for reading sectors and 3 for writing them. The second through sixth parameters are integers giving the drive, side, track, sector, and number of sectors to read. The last parameter is a pointer to a buffer for the data. To read sector 3 from track 2 of side 1 of drive 0 (drive A), write:

```
char disk_buffer[1024]     /* large enough to hold 2 sectors */
int error_code;


error_code = biosdisk(2,0,1,2,3,1,&disk_buffer);
```

See the compiler documentation for a page-long list of error codes returned by this function.

The Microsoft _bios_disk function takes only two parameters. The first is a command number, again either 2 or 3, and the second is a pointer to a structure of type *diskinfo_t*, which is declared in *bios.h*. Its form is as follows:

```
struct diskinfo_t
{
  unsigned drive;
  unsigned head;
  unsigned track;
  unsigned sector;
  unsigned nsectors;
  void _far *buffer;
};
```

Borland's C, but not Microsoft's C, also offers sector-access functions that use the DOS logical sectors numbers. These are the *absread* and *abswrite* functions. They take the same four parameters. The first three are integers: a drive number (0=A), then the number of sectors to write, and then the starting logical sector. The final parameter is a pointer to a buffer large enough to hold the data. The function returns an integer error code that is 0 when all has gone well, or –1 otherwise, in which case the global variable *errno* is given an error code. Again, see the documentation for these codes. This example reads logical sector 0 from the diskette in drive A:

```
char disk_buffer[1024];     /* large enough to hold 2 sectors */
int error_code;

error_code = absread(0,1,0,&disk_buffer);
```

Assembler

Here is an example of the BIOS sector-read routine:

```
;---IN THE DATA SEGMENT:
BUFFER  db 4096 dup(?)      ;create a buffer for 8 sectors
```

```
;---READ SECTORS:
        mov   ax,seg BUFFER   ;point ES:BX to the buffer
        mov   es,ax           ;
        mov   bx,offset BUFFER
        mov   dl,0            ;drive number
        mov   dh,0            ;head number
        mov   ch,0            ;track number
        mov   cl,1            ;sector number
        mov   al,1            ;number of sectors to read
        mov   ah,2            ;function number for "read"
        int   13h
```

And here is an example using the DOS sector-read routine:

```
;---IN THE DATA SEGMENT:
BUFFER  db  4608 dup(?)     ;set up a buffer for 9 sectors
;---READ SECTORS:
        push ds              ;save all required registers
        mov   ax,seg BUFFER   ;point DS:BX to the buffer
        mov   ds,ax
        mov   bx,offset BUFFER
        mov   dx,63          ;logical sector number
        mov   cx,9           ;read whole track of 360K diskette
        mov   al,0           ;drive A
        int   25h            ;DOS function to read sectors
        pop   cx             ;pop flags from stack to any register
        pop   ds             ;restore registers
        jnc   NO_ERROR       ;jump below if carry flag 0
        cmp   ah,3           ;test for write-protected disk
```

```
          .                       ;etc.....

          .

          .

NO_ERROR:                         ;continue...
```

On return, the carry flag will be set if there has been an error, in which case AH and AL contain separate error status bytes. Bit 2 is set in AH when the disk is write-protected, and bit 3 is set when the requested sector is out of range. Bit 2 in AL is set when the drive is not ready. Other error conditions indicate hardware failure.

Program Disk Controller and DMA Chips

Happily, few programmers are subjected to the trials and tribulations of programming disk controller chips and the DMA chips that shunt data back and forth to disk drives. Hardware varies widely, and full coverage of the topic would require a book in itself. Still, it's interesting to see how disk operations are managed at low level. This section shows how a single disk sector is read from a 5 1/2-inch diskette drive on an PC-class machine. These drives use an NEC 765 floppy disk controller (FDC) chip to control the drive motor and heads, and to manage the flow of data to and from disk sectors. A single controller chip can run up to four diskette drives.

The discussion that follows is intended only to get you started. If you want to write useable code for controlling disk drives, you'll need to acquire manufacturer's documentation about the drives. You'll also need full documentation for the disk controller and DMA chips, which also is available from the manufacturer. The BIOS listings found in some IBM Technical Reference Manuals are a good source of programming examples.

The FDC performs 15 operations in all, of which only three are discussed here: seek operations and single-sector reads and writes. Understanding how these operations work will enable you to perform any of the 12 others, providing you have the proper documentation. Reading a file basically entails looking it up in a directory, tracking its disk locations through the file allocation table, and performing a series of single-sector read operations. The example listed below reads a single disk sector. There are six steps in this procedure:

(1) Turn on the motor and wait briefly for it to come up to speed.

(2) Perform the seek operation, and wait for an interrupt that announces its completion.

(3) Initialize the DMA chip to move the data to memory.

(4) Send the read instructions to the FDC and then wait for an interrupt indicating that the data transfer is complete.

(5) Interpret status information about the FDC.

(6) Turn off the motor.

The FDC is operated through only three I/O ports. There are in fact more than three registers on the chip, but most are loaded through a single port address. The three ports are:

```
3F2h        digital output register
3F4h        status register
```

```
3F5h        data register
```

The first step is to access the digital output register. It has the following bit pattern:

```
bits 1-0  selects a drive, where 00 = A
                                 01 = B
                                 10 = C
                                 11 = D
      2   0=reset the floppy disk controller
      3   1=enable FDC interrupt and DMA access
    7-4   1=turn on drive motors D - A (bit 4 = A)
```

This register is write-only, and so all bits must be set at once. The example below uses drive A, and the bit pattern required is **00011100**. This pattern selects drive A, keeps bit 2 set to 1, enables the FDC system, and turns on drive A. *Do not* set bit 2 to 0 at any time, or you will have to recalibrate the drive, an action that is seldom necessary.

To "recalibrate" a drive means to retract its head to track 0. The operation is made by sending a simple command sequence to the FDC chip. The FDC monitors the current head position by keeping track of all changes it makes in the head position from its initial setting at track 0. When the FDC is reset by briefly changing bit 2 of the digital output register to 0, the reading for the current head position is set to 0 no matter at which track the head actually resides, making the recalibration necessary. Ordinarily, an FDC reset is required only after a disk error has occurred that is so serious the current state of the disk controller and drive is unknown.

Note that selecting a drive and turning on its motor are separate actions. The FDC can access only one drive at a time, but more than one motor can turn simultaneously. Motors may be left running for a few seconds after data transfer is complete in anticipation of further disk accesses. This strategy avoids the loss of time that would result from repeatedly waiting for the motor to come up to speed. Conversely, the motor should not be left on all the time or diskettes would wear out prematurely.

The FDC chip operates in three phases: the command phase, the execution phase, and the result phase. In the command phase, one or more bytes is sent to the *data register*. The sequence of bytes is strictly fixed, and it varies by the command. The FDC then undertakes the command, and during that time the FDC is in the execution phase. Finally, during the result phase, a number of status bytes are read from the data register. It is imperative that there be no error in the number of bytes sent to, and read from, the data register during the command and result phases.

The number of command and result bytes varies among the disk operations that the FDC performs. IBM Technical Reference Manuals supply the data for all 15 operations. The first byte of a command is a code that names the desired operation. The code number is held in the low five bits of the byte, and in some cases additional information is encoded in the high three bits. The pattern for these three bits when reading a sector is as follows:

bit	operation	seek	read	write
7	1=multitrack operation	0	0	0
6	1=FM mode (modulation type)	0	1	1
5	1=skip deleted data address marks	0	1	0

In most cases, the second command byte gives the drive number (0-3) in its two lowest bits and the head number (0 or 1) in bit 2; all other bits are ignored by the FDC. In a seek operation, only one more byte is required, and this is the number of the new track. Reading or writing a sector requires seven more command bytes, and they are identical in either case. The third through fifth bytes give the current track number, the head number, and the sector number. And then there follows four bytes of technical data required by the FDC.

The first of the technical data is the number of bytes in a sector, which is coded as 0 for 128, 1 for 256, 2 for 512, and 3 for 1024. Of course, all DOS diskettes use 512-byte sectors. Next is the *end-of-track* (EOT) data, which gives the final sector number of a cylinder; this value is 9 for 360K floppies. Finally, there is a byte that gives the *gap length* (GPL, set to 2Ah), and the *data length* (DTL, set to FFh). The Technical Reference Manuals contain a table that explains other input parameters, such as those used for disk formatting. DOS keeps the four technical parameters in memory in a parameter table called the *disk base*. The disk base is pointed to by interrupt vector 1Eh. The four values are arranged in the order that the FDC requires them, starting from offset 3. The following table shows the command sequence for the three operations shown in the example below. In the bit patterns, X's indicate that the setting of a bit is irrelevant, H stands for the head number, and DD stands for the drive number.

operation	byte #	function	setting for head 0, track 15, sector 1
Seek:	1	code number: 00001111	1Fh
	2	head and drive: XXXXXHDD	00h
Read a Sector:	1	code number: 01100110	66h
	2	head and drive :XXXXXHDD	00h
	3	track number	0Fh

operation	byte #	function	setting for head 0, track 15, sector 1
	4	head number	00h
	5	sector number	01h
	6	bytes in a sector	02h
	7	end-of-track	09h
	8	gap length	1Ah
	9	data length	FFh
Write a Sector:	1	code number: 01000101	45h
	2-9	same as for reading a sector	

You must be sure that the FDC is ready before you send or read a byte from the data register. Bits 7 and 6 of the *status register* provide this information. Here is the bit pattern of the entire register:

```
bits 0-3    1 = disk drive D-A in seek mode
       4    1 = FDC read or write command in progress
       5    1 = FDC in non-DMA mode
       6    1 = FDC data register ready to send data
            0 = ready to receive data
       7    1 = FDC ready to send or receive data
```

Before starting disk operations, it is a good idea to check that bit 6 is set to 0, indicating that the FDC is waiting for a command. If it is waiting to send data then an error has occurred. When a byte of data is sent to the data register, bit 7 of the status register goes to 0; keep reading the register until the bit changes back to 1, and then send the next command byte. Similarly, consult this status bit before reading a status byte from the data register during the result phase. The example below ends with two procedures that perform these functions.

When the seek operation is complete, the FDC invokes INT 6h. During the interrupt, the BIOS interrupt handler sets bit 7 of the *seek status* byte in the BIOS data area, located at 0040:003E. This is the sole result of the interrupt. Keep polling this byte until bit 7 is set, then reset the bit to 0 and continue on to the next step of the sector-read operation.

The next step is the initialization of the 8237 direct memory access chip. This chip transfers data between peripheral devices and memory. PC- and XT-class machines use a four-channel DMA chip. Channel 0 is dedicated to *memory refresh*; it constantly restores the charge in the RAM memory cells. If you operate on this channel, the machine is likely to crash. Channel 2 is dedicated to disk operations, and the other two channels, numbers 1 and 3, are available (via the system board slots) to add-on hardware. Unfortunately, memory-to-memory transfers require two channels, and channel 0 must be one of them, so these transfers are not possible on PC- and XT-class machines.

Before initializing a channel, a program must send a code to the chip telling it whether it is reading from or writing to the floppy disk controller. This one-byte code is **46h** for reading, and **4Ah** for writing. The code must be sent to each of two separate port addresses, numbers 0Bh, and 0Ch.

Each channel of the 8237 chip has three registers. One 16-bit register, the *count register*, is given the number of bytes of data to transfer. This value should be set to 1 less than the number of bytes desired. For channel 2, this register is accessed through I/O port 05h. Send the two bytes of the count in succession, with the least significant byte first.

The other two registers hold the address of the buffer in memory to or from which data is transferred. This address is set up as a 20-bit value, so that, for example, 3000:ABCD is expressed as 3ABCD. The low 16 bits are sent to the *address register*, which for channel 2 is at port address 04h. Send the least significant byte first. The high four bits go to a *page register*, which is at 81h for channel 2. When a byte is sent to this register, only the low four bits are significant. If the buffer is set up in the data segment, you will need to add the values of DS and the buffer offset to derive the 20-bit value. The addition may result in a carry to the page register value. For example, if DS is 1F00h and the buffer offset is 2000h, then the resulting address will be 1F000 + 2000 = 21000h.

Once the three registers are set up, send 2 to port address 0Ah to enable channel 2. This leaves the DMA chip waiting for disk data, and the program should immediately start sending the command codes to the FDC. Here is a summary of the steps in programming the 8237 chip:

(1) Send a read or write code.

(2) Calculate the 20-bit memory address of the buffer to which the data is to be sent, and place it in the channel 2 address and page registers.

(3) Place the value of the number of bytes to transfer (minus 1) in the channel 2 count register.

(4) Enable the channel.

After sending the command bytes, again wait for an interrupt, and monitor it in the same way as for a seek operation. Then read the status bytes. These are as follows:

operation	byte #	function
Seek:	none	--
Read:	1	status byte 0

operation	byte #	function
	2	status byte 1
	3	status byte 2
	4	track number
	5	head number
	6	sector number
	7	bytes/sector code (0-3)
Write:	1-7	same as read

Here are the bit patterns of the three status bytes:

Status byte 1:

bits 7-6		00=normal termination
		01=execution begun, could not complete
		10=invalid command
		11=failed because drive went off line
	5	1=seek operation in progress
	4	1=disk drive fault
	3	1=disk drive not ready
	2	number of selected head
	0-1	number of selected drive

Status byte 2:

bit	7	1=requested sector beyond last sector number
	6	unused (always 0)
	5	1=data transfer error
	4	1=data overrun
	3	unused (always 0)
	2	1=cannot find or read sector
	1	1=cannot write because of write-protection
	0	1=missing address mark in disk formatting

Status byte 3:

	bit	7	unused (always 0)
		6	1=encountered deleted-data address mark
		5	1=cyclic redundancy check error in data
		4	1=track indentification problem
		3	1=scan command condition satisfied
		2	1=scan command condition not satisfied
		1	1=bad track
		0	1=missing address mark

As you can see, much of the status information is devoted to disk formatting, which does not concern us here. There is a fourth status byte, however, that provides useful information:

Status byte 4:

	bit	7	1=disk drive fault
		6	1=disk is write-protected
		5	1=disk drive is ready
		4	1=current head position is known
		3	1=disk is double-sided
		2	number of selected head
	0-1		number of selected drive

You can retrieve this fourth status byte by sending the "Sense Drive Status" command to the FDC. The first byte of this two-byte command is the number **4**, and the second is a byte in which bits 1 and 0 hold the drive number and bit 2 holds the head number. Status byte 3 is the only result value. Note that after every disk operation where you use the BIOS or DOS services, the resulting status bytes are placed in the BIOS data area, starting at 0040:0042. The operating system also keeps a diskette status byte at 0040:0041, where the bit pattern is as follows:

bit pattern	error
80h	attachment failed to respond
40h	seek operation failed
20h	FDC failed
10h	data error (bad CRC) on data read

bit pattern	error
09h	attempt to DMA across 64K boundary
08h	DMA overrun
04h	requested sector not found
03h	tried to write on write-protected disk
02h	address mark not found
01h	bad command sent to FDC

In conclusion, here is a complete disk-read routine, which transfers one sector of data from track 12, sector 1, head 0 of drive A to a 512-byte buffer in the program's data segment. The seven status bytes are also delivered to a holding buffer. Notice the use of **JMP SHORT $+2** statements between successive *OUT* commands directed to the same port address so that the *OUT* commands are not executed too close together. These statements cause the processor to jump two bytes ahead of the position currently pointed to by the IP register. Since the instruction is itself two bytes long, control merely passes on to the next instruction. But a JMP statement causes the processor to clear its instruction queue, resulting in a significant delay.

```
;---IN THE DATA SEGMENT:
BUFFER          db   512 dup(?)
STATUS_BUFFER   db   7 dup(?)


SECTOR_READ   proc
;begin the single-sector read procedure
;---TURN ON MOTOR:
      sti                 ;be sure interrupts are enabled
      mov  dx,3F2h        ;address of digital output register
      mov  al,28          ;set bits 2, 3, and 4
      out  dx,al          ;send the command
;---WAIT FOR MOTOR TO COME TO SPEED (1/2 second delay):
      sub  ax,ax          ;point ES to bottom of memory
      mov  es,ax          ;
      mov  ax,es:[46Ch]   ;get time-of-day count
      add  ax,10          ;10 pulses in one half second
```

313

```
MOTOR_DELAY:
        cmp  ax,es:[46Ch] ;reread time-of-day count
        jne  MOTOR_DELAY  ;loop until match
;---PERFORM SEEK OPERATION:
        mov  ah,15       ;code number
        call OUT_FDC     ;send to FDC
        mov  ah,0        ;drive number
        call OUT_FDC     ;send to FDC
        mov  ah,12       ;track number
        call OUT_FDC     ;send to FDC
        call WAIT_INTERRUPT ;wait for int 6
;---WAIT FOR HEAD TO SETTLE (25 MSEC):
        mov  ax,es:[46Ch] ;get time-of-day count
        add  ax,2         ;target count
WAIT_SETTLE:
        cmp  ax,es:[46Ch] ;reread time-of-day count
        jne  WAIT_SETTLE  ;loop until match
;---BEGIN INITIALIZATION OF DMA CHIP:
        mov  al,46h      ;code to read data from FDC
        out  12,al       ;send the code to 2 addresses
        jmp  short $+2   ;delay between port accesses
        out  11,al       ;
;---CALCULATE ADDRESS OF TRANSFER BUFFER:
        mov  ax,OFFSET BUFFER ;get buffer offset in DS
        mov  bx,ds       ;put DS in BX
        mov  cl,4        ;ready to rotate high nibble of DS
        rol  bx,cl       ;rotate to bottom four bits of BX
        mov  dl,bl       ;copy BL to DL
        and  dl,0Fh      ;blank top nibble of DL
        and  bl,0F0h     ;blank bottom nibble of BX
```

```
        add   ax,bx        ;add BX into AX (DS into offset)
        jnc   NO_CARRY      ;if no carry, DL is page value
        inc   dl           ;but if carry, first increment DL
NO_CARRY:
        out   4,al         ;send low byte of address
        mov   al,ah        ;shift high byte
        jmp   short $+2    ;delay between port accesses
        out   4,al         ;send high byte of address
        mov   al,dl        ;fetch page value
        jmp   short $+2    ;delay between port accesses
        out   81h,al       ;send page number
;---FINISH INITIALIZATION:
        mov   ax,511       ;count value
        jmp   short $+2    ;delay between port accesses
        out   5,al         ;send low byte
        mov   al,ah        ;ready high byte
        jmp   short $+2    ;delay between port accesses
        out   5,al         ;send high byte
        mov   al,2         ;get set to enable channel 2
        jmp   short $+2    ;delay between port accesses
        out   10,al        ;all done, DMA waits for data...
;---GET POINTER TO DISK BASE:
        mov   al,1Eh       ;number of vector that points to table
        mov   ah,35h       ;function that fetches vector
        int   21h          ;now ES:BX points to disk base
;---SEND READ PARAMETERS:
        mov   ah,66h       ;code for single-sector read
        call  OUT_FDC      ;send it
        mov   ah,0         ;head and drive number
        call  OUT_FDC      ;send it
```

```
        mov   ah,12        ;track number
        call  OUT_FDC      ;send it
        mov   ah,0         ;head number
        call  OUT_FDC      ;send it
        mov   ah,1         ;record number
        call  OUT_FDC      ;send it
        mov   ah,es:[bx]+3 ;sector size code (from disk base)
        call  OUT_FDC      ;send it
        mov   ah,es:[bx]+4 ;end-of-track number (from disk base)
        call  OUT_FDC      ;send it
        mov   ah,es:[bx]+5 ;gap length (from disk base)
        call  OUT_FDC      ;send it
        mov   ah,es:[bx]+6 ;data length (from disk base)
        call  OUT_FDC      ;send it
        call  WAIT_INTERRUPT ;wait till INT 6 marks end of transfer
;---READ THE RESULT BYTES:
        mov   cx,7         ;7 result bytes from reading a sector
        lea   bx,STATUS_BUFFER ;place them in a buffer
NEXT:
        call  IN_FDC       ;get a byte
        mov   [bx],al      ;place in buffer
        inc   bx           ;point to next byte of buffer
        loop  NEXT         ;go get next byte
;---TURN OFF MOTOR
        mov   dx,3F2h      ;address of digital output register
        mov   al,12        ;leave bits 3 and 4 on
        out   dx,al        ;send the new setting
        ret                ;end of sector-read procedure
SECTOR_READ   endp


WAIT_INTERRUPT  proc       ;waits for INT 6, resets status byte
```

```
;---MONITOR INT 6 STATUS IN BIOS STATUS BYTE:
        mov  ax,40h          ;segment of BIOS data area
        mov  es,ax           ;place in ES
        mov  bx,3Eh          ;offset of status byte
AGAIN:
        mov  dl,es:[bx]      ;get the byte
        test dl,80h          ;test bit 7
        jz   AGAIN           ;keep looping if not yet set
        and  dl,01111111b    ;reset bit 7
        mov  es:[bx],dl      ;replace status byte
        ret                  ;continue...
WAIT_INTERRUPT  endp


OUT_FDC  proc               ;sends byte in AH to FDC
        mov  dx,3F4h         ;status register port address
KEEP_TRYING:
        in   al,dx           ;fetch value
        test al,128          ;is bit 7 on?
        jz   KEEP_TRYING     ;if not, keep looping
        inc  dx              ;ready, so point to data register
        mov  al,ah           ;value was passed in AH
        out  dx,al           ;send the value
        ret                  ;all done
OUT_FDC  endp


IN_FDC  proc                ;returns byte (in AL) from FDC
        mov  dx,3F4h         ;status register port address
ONCE_AGAIN:
        in   al,dx           ;fetch value
        test al,128          ;is bit 7 on?
        jz   KEEP_TRYING ;if not, keep looping
```

```
        inc  dx          ;ready, so point to data register
        in   al,dx       ;read a byte from the data register
        ret              ;all done
IN_FDC  endp
```

Detect and Recover from Disk Errors

Disk operations are complicated and many kinds of errors can occur. Some disk errors result from inappropriate requests for file access: The file requested may not exist, or disk space may run out before all of a file can be written. Other errors result from faulty hardware. These invoke the *critical error handler*, an interrupt routine pointed to by interrupt vector 24h. Normally, this handler displays the infamous *Abort, Retry, Fail?* message to let the user specify whether DOS should retry a disk operation, continue the program without completing the disk operation, or terminate the program. You can replace this routine with one of your own design. Chapter 4, "Write Your Own Interrupt Service Routine," explains how this is done.

Disk errors that do not invoke the critical error handler are intercepted in various ways by the compilers discussed in this book. The nature and numbering of the returned error codes varies and you must consult the compiler documentation for specifics. This section outlines the approach to error detection and recovery in the four languages discussed in this volume.

BASIC

BASIC uses the ON ERROR GOSUB statement to shift the program to an error recovery subroutine. Chapter 5, "Control Real-Time Operations," provides a full discussion of this construction. The subroutine first finds out the BASIC error code number. Once the routine has decoded the error, the user is prompted to correct the problem. When the user indicates that the problem has been corrected, a RESUME statement sends the program back to the line where the error occurred. Alternatively, the RESUME statement may end with a label that returns the program to the beginning of an entire sequence of disk operations, no matter where the error occurred (note that files do *not* close when an error occurs). The following example recovers from full-disk errors and write-protection errors:

```
ON ERROR GOSUB DiskErrorList   'start up error trapping

   .

   .


StartOfDiskOperations:

   .

   .
```

```
DiskErrorList:

   IF ERR=61 PRINT"Disk Full":GOTO RecoveryMessage

   IF ERR=70 PRINT"Disk Is Write Protected":GOTO
RecoveryMessage

     .

     .


RecoveryMessage:

   PRINT"Correct the problem, then strike any key"

   DO

   LOOP WHILE INKEY$ =   ""

   RESUME NEXT
```

Pascal

To recover from errors in Turbo Pascal, you must begin by disabling the built-in error checking feature that will automatically abort a program if a disk error occurs. This is done by writing **{$I-}** on its own line in the code, and later following it with **{$I+}** to re-enable the feature. If an error occurs during execution of the enclosed code, the corresponding error code will be remembered and can be obtained by calling the *IOResult* function. Here is an example:

```
var ThePathString: string[80];


{$I-}

ThePathString := 'C:\DOS';

ChDir(ThePathString);

if IOResult <> 0 then Writeln('Could not find the directory');

{$I+}
```

C

In C, many disk I/O functions return a value that can in some way indicate that an error has occurred, sometimes by being zero. C programs can also learn that an error has occurred by calling the *ferror* function. This function does not identify the kind of error, and a program must clear the error condition using *clearerr* before calling *ferror* again. For example:

```
FILE *the_stream;


the_stream = fopen("MYFILE.DOC","r");
fgetc(the_stream);
if (ferror(the_stream)){
  printf("A file error has occured");
  clearerr(the_stream);
}
```

Assembler

Each DOS disk function uses only a few of the available disk error codes, or sometimes none at all. In all cases, the carry flag is set to 1 when an error occurs. If there is an error, its code number is placed in AX. Here are the codes relevant to disk operations:

1	Invalid function number
2	File not found
3	Path not found
4	Maximum number of files already open
5	Access denied (hardware error)
6	Invalid file handle
15	Invalid drive was specified
16	Tried to remove the current directory
17	Not same device
18	No more files (when searching directory using global filename characters)

DOS 3.0 introduces *extended error codes*. These are returned in AX by function 59h of INT 21h when the carry flag indicates an error has occurred. Here is a listing of disk-related extended errors:

1	Invalid function
2	File not found
3	File path not found
4	No handles available
5	Access denied
6	Invalid file handle
15	Invalid drive
16	Attempted to remove the current directory
18	No more files
19	Disk is write-protected
21	Drive not ready
22	Unknown command
23	CRC error
25	Seek error
26	Unknown type of media
27	Sector not found
29	Write fault
30	Read fault
31	General failure
34	Invalid disk change
80	File already exists
82	Cannot create directory entry

To diagnose *critical errors*, use function 1 of interrupt 13h, which returns a byte in AL that gives the status of the disk drives. The bit pattern is as follows:

bit 0-1	01=invalid command, or, if bit 3=1, tried to transfer data over 64k boundary
	10=address mark not found
	11=write attempt to write-protected disk
2	1=specified sector not found
3	1=DMA overrun operation (data lost during transfer) or, if bit 0=1, attempted transfer across a 64k boundary

4   1=data was read incorrectly, must try again

5   1=controller failure

6   1=seek operation failure

7   1=drive failed to respond (time-out error)

11

Directory Access

- Minitutorial: How Directories Are Constructed
- Create/Delete a Subdirectory
- Get/Set the Current Directory
- Read Directories
- Move a File to Another Directory
- Determine a File's Size
- Get/Set a File's Time and Date
- Get/Set File Attributes
- Rename Files or Directories
- Delete Files

Minitutorial: How Directories Are Constructed

No matter the type or size of disk, directories are made up of 32-byte entries ("slots"), each holding information for a single file. A 512-byte disk sector can hold 16 entries. The 32 bytes are divided into these fields:

```
bytes 0 - 7  File name
      8 -10  File name extension
         11  File attribute
      12-21  (reserved)
      22-23  Time file last accessed
```

```
24-25   Date file last accessed
26-27   Starting cluster
28-31   File size
```

No period is written between the file name and its three-byte extension. Both parts of a file name are left-justified in their fields, and empty bytes are padded with spaces (ASCII 32). DOS functions combine the two parts into a file name.

The first byte of the file name field is initialized to 0 when a disk is formatted. When a directory slot has been used and its file subsequently deleted, the first byte is marked with **E5h** (the *sigma* character) and the rest of the field goes untouched. In subdirectory files, the file name field may begin with one or two periods (ASCII 2Eh) to mark references to the directory itself (one period) or the parent directory (two periods).

The *file attribute byte* marks a file's special properties, if any. The lower six bits in the byte act as flags telling whether a particular attribute is in effect. The six attributes tell whether the file is a system file, a hidden file, a read-only file, or a subdirectory file, whether the file has been changed since it was last backed up, or whether the directory entry is the disk's volume label. When the byte equals 0 (all bits off), the file is a normal file. Attributes are discussed in "Get/Set File Atributes," below.

The time and date both consist of three values (year/month/day and hour/minutes/seconds) packed into 16-bit fields. "Get/Set a File's Time and Date," below, shows how to access these fields.

Finally, the *starting cluster* refers to a position in a disk's file allocation table (FAT), which is discussed in the Chapter 10 *minitutorial.* The FAT keeps track of free space on the disk, and it assigns the sectors in which a file is written. On most disks, the FAT allocates space in groupings larger than one sector that are called *clusters* (actually, even single-sector allocations are called "clusters"). A file is laid out along a chain of clusters, and the FAT contains a corresponding chain of entries that indicate where the clusters are located on the disk. A directory's *starting cluster* field points to the start of a file's chain of entries in the FAT. Since files usually do not evenly divide into clusters, the *file size* field is required to give the file's exact size in bytes.

Both root directories and subdirectories are structured in the same way. The only difference is that the root directory is always found at particular disk sectors at the outer edge of a partition. Subdirectories, on the other hand, are held in files. Root directories have a fixed size, which varies by the type and size of disk. As files, subdirectories can expand to any size. The only thing that distinguishes subdirectory files from other files is the setting in the attribute byte found in the file's directory entry.

You can access root directories and subdirectories directly, without going through DOS functions. First you must call a DOS function (covered in the Chapter 10 *minitutorial*) to find out the root directory size and location. Then you read and write root directory sectors using absolute sector reads and writes (discussed in Chapter 10, "Read/Write Individual Disk Sectors"). Subdirectory files can then be accessed by temporarily changing their attribute byte and operating on the file as a normal one. Unfortunately, the DOS functions discussed in "Get/Set File Attributes," below, won't change the subdirectory attribute, so a subdirectory's own directory entry must be accessed by a direct sector read and write.

DOS provides routines for operating on nearly every aspect of directory entries. Programs can create files, rename them, or delete them, and file dates, times, attributes, and sizes can be read and changed. Utility software sometimes operates on directories directly, reading directory sectors into memory, changing them, and then writing them back to disk. Utility software takes this route in order to sort directories, unerase files, or move files without physically copying them. This is a risky business, because files are effectively lost when directories are damaged. Direct access also works much more quickly than repeated calls to DOS functions, as when a program searches a directory tree for a file. This is not dangerous so long as a program confines itself to direct sector *reads* (and not *writes*). Keep in mind that operating environments and memory-resident programs can break in while a program modifies directories and attempt to use those very directories.

Create/Delete a Subdirectory

A program can create and delete subdirectories, so long as certain preconditions are met. To create a subdirectory, there must be at least one empty slot in the directory that will be parent to the new subdirectory, and no file in that directory may have the name used by the new subdirectory. To delete a subdirectory, it must be empty of all files and all references to other subdirectories. Note that you cannot delete a subdirectory that is the *current* directory.

BASIC

BASIC uses commands called *MKDIR* and *RMDIR* to create and delete sub-directories. Both commands are followed by a string holding a standard directory path of up to 63 characters. To create a directory called *STORKS* in the subdirectory *BIRDS*, write:

```
MKDIR "C:\MAMMALS\BIRDS\STORKS"
```

To delete the same subdirectory, remove all files and subdirectories from it and execute the statement:

```
RMDIR "C:\MAMMALS\BIRDS\STORKS"
```

Pascal

Turbo Pascal provides procedures named *MkDir* and *RmDir* to make and remove directories. Be sure to disable I/O checking by preceding the calls with **{$I-}** and then use *IOResult* to test that the subdirectory was actually found.

```
var
   ThePathString: string[80];


{$I-}
ThePathString := 'C:\LEVEL1\MYSUB';
MkDir(ThePathString);
if IOResult <> 0 then Writeln('Could not create directory');
```

```
      .

      .

   RmDir(ThePathString);

   if IOResult <> 0 then Writeln('Could not remove directory');
```

Both the Borland and Microsoft compilers use functions called *mkdir* and *rmdir* to create and remove subdirectories. The functions take a single parameter — a string holding the directory path to the subdirectory that will be created or deleted. The functions return an integer error code that is 0 when the function succeeds, or otherwise one of the error codes EACCES (EACCESS in Microsoft's C) or ENOENT. These two examples test for errors as they make and remove a directory and jump to error recovery routines when errors occur.

```
   #include <dir.h>


   char *the_path = "C:\\REPTILES\\LIZARDS";


   if(mkdir(the_path)) dir_creation_failure();


   if(rmdir(the_path)) dir_deletion_failure();
```

Assembler

Function 39h of INT 21h creates directories. Point DS:DX to a null-terminated string giving the drive and path to the directory in which the new directory will reside. The carry flag is set when an error occurs, in which case AX returns 3 (for "path not valid") or 5 (for "access denied"). The latter error can occur when attempting to create a directory in a full root directory.

```
;---IN THE DATA SEGMENT:
PATH  db 'C:\MAMMALS\PRIMATES',0


;---CREATE A SUBDIRECTORY "PRIMATES":
      lea  dx,PATH          ;point DS:DX to path string
      mov  ah,39h           ;function number
      int  21h              ;create the subdirectory
      jc   ERROR_ROUTINE    ;intercept errors
```

Use function 3Ah of INT 21h to remove directories. It is set up just like function 39h, with DS:DX pointing to a string that specifies the directory to be deleted. Again, the carry flag is set if the function fails, and error codes 3 or 5 are returned in AX (code 5 may indicate that the directory is not empty). In addition, the code 16 indicates that the specified directory is the current directory.

```
;---IN THE DATA SEGMENT:
PATH    db   'C:\MAMMALS\PRIMATES',0


;---DELETE THE SUBDIRECTORY "PRIMATES"
        lea  dx,PATH          ;point DS:DX to path string
        mov  ah,3Ah           ;function number
        int  21h              ;remove the subdirectory
        jc   ERROR_ROUTINE    ;intercept errors
```

Get/Set the Current Directory

On any particular disk drive, the *current directory* is the directory DOS accesses when no other directory path was specified. Keep in mind the distinction between a *current directory* and a *default directory*. Every disk drive has its own *current directory*. The *default directory* is the current directory of the *default drive*. (Chapter 10, "Set/Check the Default Drive," explains how to determine the default drive and change it if necessary.)

All four compilers provide ways both to determine the current directory and to change it. When setting the directory, you may optionally include a drive specifier in the path name you provide. By doing so, you can change the current directory for a drive other than the default drive. When no drive specifier is given, you will be changing the current directory of the default drive, and thus will be changing the default directory. Note that it does not matter whether the path you specify is written in lowercase or uppercase letters.

BASIC

BASIC sets the current directory using a *CHDIR* statement. The syntax is:

```
CHDIR directorypath$
```

The path string may be up to 63 characters long, including the optional drive specifier. To make the root directory of drive D the current directory for that drive, write:

```
CHDIR "D:\"
```

Use the *CURDIR$* function to find out the current directory of a particular drive. The drive is specified by a string containing a single character: **A** for drive A, **B** for drive B, and so on. This string is optional; when it is omitted, the current directory of the default drive is returned. To find out the current directory on drive C:

```
CURRENTDIR$ = CURDIR$("C")
```

Pascal

Turbo Pascal uses the *ChDir* procedure to set the current directory. Be sure to disable I/O checking with **{$I–}** and then use *IOResult* to find out whether the specified directory exists:

```
var ThePathString: string[80];
```

```
{$I-}

ThePathString := 'C:\DOS';

ChDir(ThePathString);

if IOResult <> 0 then Writeln('Could not find the directory');

{$I+}
```

GetDir reports the current directory, placing the path in a string variable you have declared. Because every drive has its own current directory, you must specify the drive number, with **0** as the default drive, **1** as drive A, **2** as drive B, and so on. To find out the current directory on drive C, first declare the string variable:

```
var ThePathString: String[80];
```

Then call *GetDir:*

```
GetDir(3,ThePathString);

Writeln('The current path is ',ThePathString);
```

If you specify an invalid drive number, the return string will hold a single backslash, as if for a root directory. To avoid confusion, you must be sure that the drive exists before calling GetDir (Chapter 2, "Determine the Number and Types of Disk Drives," explains how).

C

Both the Borland and Microsoft compilers use the *chdir* function to change the default directory. The function returns an integer value that is **0** when the function succeeds, or **–1** when the specified path is invalid. The only parameter is a pointer to a zero-terminated string giving the directory path. Remember that the backslash character found in directory paths must be doubled in C. To make **C:\DOS** the current directory, write:

```
errorcode = chdir("C:\\DOS");
```

The two compilers have different functions for finding out the current directory of a specific drive:

```
char *getcurdir(int drive, char *path);              /*Borland*/

char *_getdcwd(int drive, char *path, int maxlen); /*Microsoft*/
```

The value for *drive* is **0** for the current drive, **1** for drive A, **2** for drive B, and so on. Borland's C assumes that the memory allocated to *path* will suffice to hold any path; Microsoft's C uses *maxlen* to check that the path fits and returns an error if it does not. To find out the current directory of drive D using Borland's C, write:

```
char thePath[128];


getcurdir(4, &thePath);
```

And now *thePath* holds the path of the current directory. Both compilers also have versions of these routines that will find the *default directory* — that is, the current directory of the default drive. These functions share the same name and syntax:

```
char *getcwd(char *buffer,int bufferlength);
```

Assembler

Function 3Bh of INT 21h sets the current directory. Point DS:DX to a null-terminated string in standard directory-path form. This example makes \BIRDS\PARROTS\POLLY the current directory on drive C.

```
;---IN THE DATA SEGMENT:
PATH   db 'C:BIRDS\PARROTS\POLLY',0


;---MAKE POLLY THE CURRENT DIRECTORY:
     mov   ah,3Bh         ;function number
     lea   dx,PATH        ;point DS:DX to path
     int   21h            ;set the current Directory
     jc    Error Routine  ;carry flag set on error
```

To find out which directory is current, use function 47h of INT 21h. DS:SI points to a 65-byte buffer in which the path will be written. DL is given the drive number, for which **0** is the default drive, **1** is drive A, **2** is drive B, and so on. The function returns a directory path without a drive specifier. AL returns with error code **15** if a nonexistent drive was specified. The directory path begins without a backslash. A 0 byte signals the end of the return string. This example gets the path to the current directory of drive C, placing the path in the buffer named *CURRENT_DIR*.

```
;---IN THE DATA SEGMENT:
CURRENT_DIR   db   65 dup(?)
```

```
;---GET THE CURRENT DIRECTORY:
        mov  ah,47h           ;function number
        lea  si,CURRENT_DIR   ;point to data area
        mov  dl,3             ;drive C
        int  21h              ;place the string at DS:SI
        jc   Error Routine    ;carry flag set on error
```

Read Directories

DOS provides a pair of routines for reading the contents of directories. A program specifies a single file or a group of files to search for. The first routine returns the first file that matches the specification, and the second routine is then called repeatedly for additional matches until no more are found. These routines are the only approved way of reading directories.

The first routine is given the path to the directory that will be searched, with a file name specification that uses wild cards. To find all files in the directory C:\DOGS\SPANIELS, you would specify **C:\DOGS\SPANIELS*.***. A search for all batch files in a directory would be made by specifying ***.BAT**, and a single file could be sought by specifying its name.

You also must specify the file attributes used in the search (file attributes are discussed in "Get/Set File Attributes," below). When the value given for the attributes is **0**, only normal files are returned. When the *hidden* or *system* attributes are set, these files are returned *in addition to* normal files. Setting the subdirectory attribute makes the routines return only information about subdirectories listed in the searched directory, and no files. The same applies to the volume label attribute (which only occurs in a disk's root directory).

The information returned about each file includes its name, time, date, size, and attribute byte. The returned information includes attribute bytes that can be used to figure out what kind of files have been found when a search is made for more than one kind of file.

BASIC

BASIC's *DIR$* function searches directories for both the first and subsequent matches to a file specification. It returns file names as strings, but does not return any information about file times, dates, sizes, or attributes. To find the first instance of a file, provide *DIR$* with a string parameter that specifies the file name and path, with wild card characters in the file name if desired. Then call *DIR$* again without any parameters to find subsequent matches. There is no requirement that you read all instances of a file specification before starting a search for another. This example displays all batch files in the directory C:\PRIMATES\HOMINIDS:

```
TheFile$ = DIR$("C:\PRIMATES\HOMINIDS\*.BAT")

WHILE TheFile$ <> ""

  WRITE TheFile$

  TheFile$ = DIR$

WEND
```

BASIC also offers the *FILES* statement for displaying directory listings. To display all batch files in C:\PRIMATES\HOMINIDS, you would write:

```
FILES "C:\PRIMATES\HOMINIDS\*.BAT"
```

Only file names are displayed, and they are arranged in four columns with a message below telling how much disk space is available. You have little control over the placement of the listings on the screen, nor can you control scrolling when many files are found. For these reasons, the *DIR$* function is the preferred method for displaying file listings.

Pascal

Turbo Pascal provides the *FindFirst* and *FindNext* procedures for searching directories. They use a data structure that is defined in the *DOS* unit. Its form is:

```
type

  SearchRec = record

    Fill: array[1..21] of Byte;

    Attr: Byte;

    Time: Longint;

    Size: Longint;

    Name: string[12];

  end;
```

FindFirst takes three parameters — first the search specification, then the search attributes, and then the *SearchRec* structure shown above. When a match is found, directory information for a file is placed in the structure. Otherwise the function reports errors in the global variable *DosError*, which will hold **3** when the directory was not found and **18** when no match for the file specification was found. To seek additional matches, call *FindNext*. It takes only one parameter, the *SearchRec* structure, and it returns the same information and error codes as *FindFirst*. *FindNext* needs only one parameter because the search specification used in *FindFirst* is stored in the *Fill* field of the *SearchRec* structure. This example displays all matches to the specification C:\REPTILES\TURTLES.*:

```
uses Dos;

var

  DirData: SearchRec;        {Declare a copy of the structure}
```

```
FindFirst('C:\REPTILES\TURTLES.*',0,DirData);
while DosError = 0 do
begin
  Writeln(DirData.Name);
  FindNext(DirData);
end;
```

C

Borland's C offers the *findfirst* and *findnext* functions for searching directories. Microsoft's C provides equivalent routines in *_dos_findfirst* and *_dos_findnext*. Both use a structure declared in *dos.h* for storing the information returned by the functions. Here is the structure in Borland's C:

```
struct ffblk {
    char ff_reserved[21];        /*used by findnext*/
    char ff_attribute;           /*the file's attribute byte*/
    int  ff_ftime:               /*the file's time*/
    int  ff_fdate;               /*the file's date*/
    long ff_fsize;               /*the file's size*/
    char ff_name[13];            /*the file name*/
};
```

And here it is in Microsoft's C:

```
struct findt {
    char reserved[21];           /*used by findnext*/
    char attrib;                 /*the file's attribute byte*/
    unsigned wr_time:            /*the file's time*/
    unsigned wr_date;            /*the file's date*/
    long size;                   /*the file's size*/
    char name[13]                /*the file name*/
};
```

Both *findfirst* and *_dos_findfirst* require three parameters. The first is a pointer to a string holding the file specification. The second and third are a pointer to the above structure and an integer holding the file attributes that should be used for the search. The *findfirst* function takes the structure as its second parameter and the attribute as its third. The *_dos_findfirst* function has the attribute second and the structure last. Both functions return an integer that is 0 when a match was found, and -1 otherwise. Call the *findnext* or *_dos_findnext* functions to search for additional matches. These functions take only one parameter, a pointer to the structure, and they also return 0 when a match is found and −1 when one is not. This example uses Borland's C to display all batch files in the subdirectory D:\PLANTS\FLOWERS. It uses a normal attribute (0) during the search.

```
#include <dir.h>


struct ffblk file_data;
char *dir_path = "D:\\PLANTS\\FLOWERS\\*.BAT";
if(!findfirst(dir_path,&file_data,0)){
  printf("%s\n",file_data.ff_name);
  while(!findnext(&file_data)){
    printf("%s\n",file_data.ff_name);
  }
}
```

Assembler

Function 4Eh of INT 21h finds the first match to a file name. Point DS:DX to a zero-terminated string giving the path to the file. File attributes used in the search go in the low six bits of CX, with all other bits clear. On return, AX holds 0 if a match was found, and 2 if not. When a match is found, directory information for the file is placed in the *data transfer area (DTA)*. The DTA is a 128-byte buffer found at offset 80h in a program's PSP (*program segment prefix*), discussed in the Chapter 1 *minitutorial* . In this application, the first 21 bytes of the DTA are reserved by DOS for searches for more matches. And then the directory information is recorded at the following offsets in the DTA:

offset	content
21	file's attribute byte (db)
22	file time (dw)
24	file date (dw)
26	file size (dd)
30	file name (variable length)

The file name is not reported in the same format as it appears in directory listings. Rather it is given in a variable length string that ends with ASCII 0. A period (ASCII 46) separates the file name and its extension, and neither is padded with spaces.

You can use function 2Fh of INT 21h to find out the DTA address. Besides the function number, there are no input registers. On return, ES:BX holds the segment and offset of the DTA.

While DOS points to the PSP DTA by default, you can move the DTA to any place in memory. This is done by function 1Ah of INT 21h, which informs DOS of the starting address of the buffer it should use as the DTA. It's up to you to see to it that the buffer is large enough; 43 bytes is adequate in this case. Point DS:DX to the new DTA and execute the function. It's considered good programming practice to move the DTA outside of the PSP. A program can use the same DTA for many purposes, or can use many DTAs. It's a good idea to maintain separate DTAs for different functions to avoid interference.

The following example searches for the file TULIPS.DOC in the directory C:\PLANTS\FLOWERS. It uses a DTA set-up in the program's data segment.

```
;---IN THE DATA SEGMENT:
PATH   db  'C:\PLANTS\FLOWERS\TULIPS.DOC',0
DTA    db  43 dup(?)


;---SEARCH FOR THE FILE:
        lea  dx,DTA      ;DS:DX points to DTA
        mov  ah,1Ah      ;function to set DTA
        int  21h         ;set the DTA
        lea  dx,PATH     ;point DS:DX to path string
        mov  ah,4Eh      ;function to find first match
        mov  cx,0        ;normal file attribute
        int  21h         ;search for the file
```

```
        cmp   ax,0          ;found?

        jne   NO_FILE        ;if not, recover

        lea   bx,DTA         ;point BX to DTA

        mov   al,[bx]+21     ;file's attribute byte to AL
```

The next occurrence of the file name (when global characters are used) is found by function 4Fh of INT 21h. This function can only be used *after* 4Eh, with the DTA pointer unchanged. The function has no input registers. This is because the file specification supplied to function 4Eh is maintained in the DTA. When there are no more matches, the carry flag is set and 12h appears in AX.

```
        mov   ah,4Fh         ;function number

        int   21h            ;get the next match

        jc    ALL_DONE       ;no more matches
```

If your program searches an entire directory tree, you'll probably want to write a recursive routine that allocates a new DTA for each directory. These allocations can be made on the stack, but usually it is safer to make dynamic memory allocations (discussed in Chapter 3, "Allocate/Deallocate Conventional Memory") to avoid the danger of stack overflow. Note that the "next" match returned by function 4Fh follows the prior match *for the specified DTA*. You can return to a particular DTA at any time to find out its "next" match. This is possible because function 4Fh searches for the "next" match on the basis of the information stored in the first 21 bytes of a DTA. Thus, your routine can search all file listings in one subdirectory, and then can find the "next" subdirectory listed in the parent directory of that subdirectory, can search all files in that directory, and so on.

Move a File to Another Directory

A file can be moved to another directory on the same drive just by "renaming" the file, giving it the same file name and extension, but a different path. If you wish, you can specify a different file name to rename the file as it is moved. You cannot move files to other disk drives this way. See "Rename Files or Directories," below, for a general discussion of renaming files. All of the examples below move the file BIOMASS.TXT from C:\TREES to C:\FLOWERS.

BASIC

```
NAME "C:\TREES\BIOMASS.TXT" AS "C:\FLOWERS\BIOMASS.TXT"
```

Pascal

```
var  TheFile: Text;


Assign(TheFile,'C:\TREES\BIOMASS.TXT');

Rename(TheFile,'C:\FLOWERS\BIOMASS.TXT');

if IOResult <> 0 then Writeln('Could not move file');
```

C

```
#include <stdio>


char *old_name = "C:\\TREES\\BIOMASS.TXT";

char *new_name = "C:\\FLOWERS\\BIOMASS.TXT";


error_check = rename(old_name,new_name);
```

341

Assembler

```
;---IN THE DATA SEGMENT:
OLDPATH  db 'C:\TREES\BIOMASS.DAT',0
NEWPATH  db 'C:\FLOWERS\BIOMASS.DAT',0


;---CHANGE THE FILE'S PATH:
        lea  dx,OLDPATH          ;point DS:DX to old path
        mov  ax,seg NEWPATH      ;point ES:DI to new path
        mov  es,ax               ;
        mov  di,offset NEWPATH   ;
        mov  ah,56h              ;function number
        int  21h                 ;move the file
        jc   ERROR_ROUTINE       ;go to error routine if carry set
```

Determine a File's Size

A program may need to check a file's size for a variety of reasons. One is to calculate the number of records a file contains. Another is to determine the end-of-file position where the file pointer may be set in order to *append* additional data to a file. File size is *set*, of course, by the DOS functions that write files.

BASIC

In BASIC, the *LOF* (*length of file*) function returns the exact number of bytes allocated to a file. The file must be open. It is referred to by the file number under which it is opened. This number is the only parameter required by the function. To find out how many 64-byte records are contained in a file opened as #3:

```
OPEN"FILENAME" AS #3

FILELENGTH = LOF(3)
```

Pascal

The Turbo Pascal *FileSize* function can return a file's size in bytes. The file must be open. *FileSize* cannot work with files opened as *text* files. If you're working with a text file, first open it as a binary file, get its size, close the file, and then reopen it as a text file for normal access. The *FileSize* function takes only one parameter — the file variable by which the file was opened — and it returns a *long* value giving the file length. This example finds out the size of C:\PRIMATES\GORILLA.TXT:

```
var

  MyFile: File of Byte;

  SizeOfFile: longint;


{I-}          {test for errors}

Assign(MyFile,'C:\PRIMATES\GORILLA.TXT');

Reset(MyFile);

if IOResult <> 0 then

begin

  Writeln('Could not find the file');
```

```
   Halt;
end;
SizeOfFile := FileSize(MyFile);
Writeln('The file size is ',SizeOfFile,' bytes.');
Close(MyFile);
```

C

Both the Borland and Microsoft compilers use the *filelength* function to report a file's size in bytes. The only parameter is the handle under which the file was opened. The function returns a *long* value giving the file length.

```
#include <io.h>
#include <fcntl.h>


int handle;
long the_length;
char *file_path = "C:\\DOS\\FORMAT.COM";


handle = open(file_path,O_RDWR | O_BINARY);
the_length = filelength(handle);
```

Assembler

Using file handles, DOS provides no function that directly reports file size. But it is possible to calculate file size by moving the file pointer from the beginning to the end of the file. When a file is opened, the file pointer is automatically set to the beginning of the file. The pointer can then be moved by function 42h of INT 21h. When you call the function, place the code number **2** in AL so that the pointer is made to move to the end of the file. BX takes the file handle that identifies the file. CX:DX is given the offset from the end of the file to the position at which the pointer is to be set; place 0 in both of these registers so that no offset is made from the end of the file. Then call the function.

On return, DX:AX contains the new position of the pointer as an offset from its prior position — that is, it contains the file length, with DX holding the most significant part. If an error occurs, the carry flag is set and AX returns 1 if the function number was invalid, or 6 if the handle was invalid. Don't forget to reset the pointer to the start of the file, if this is desired. To do this, place 0 in AL, CX, and DX, and call the function again. Here is an example:

```
;---OPEN THE FILE:
        lea   dx,FILE_PATH        ;point DS:DX to path string
        mov   al,0                ;open for reading
        mov   ah,3Dh              ;function to open file
        int   21h                 ;open it
        jc    OPEN_ERROR          ;check for errors
        mov   HANDLE,ax           ;save the file handle
;---FIND THE FILE LENGTH:
        mov   ah,42h              ;function to move pointer
        mov   al,2                ;code to set to end-of-file
        mov   bx,HANDLE           ;file handle in BX
        mov   cx,0                ;0 in CX and DX
        mov   dx,0                ;
        int   21h                 ;move the pointer
        jc    POINTER_ERROR       ;error?
        mov   FILESIZE_HIGH,dx    ;store the file size
        mov   FILESIZE_LOW,ax     ;
```

Get/Set a File's Time and Date

Counting from 0, bytes 22–23 of a 32-byte directory entry hold the time at which a file was last accessed. Bytes 24–25 hold the date. The day of the week is not recorded; DOS calculates the day of the week from the other information when it is required. The two 16-bit values are divided into these bit fields:

```
TIME:   bits 11-15      hours (0-23)

             5-10       minutes (0-59)

             0-4        seconds (0-29 in two-second intervals)
DATE:   bits  9-15      year (0-119, as an offset from 1980)

             5-8        month (1-12)

             0-4        day (1-31)
```

BASIC

In Microsoft BASIC, you'll need to call the DOS interrupt that finds or sets a file's time and date. The file must be opened to do this. The time and date are set or returned in the format shown above, so you must use bit operations to assemble or disassemble the values. In addition, you must tell DOS the *file handle* (file ID number) under which the file was opened. This can be obtained from the *FILEATTR* function. It takes two parameters, the first being the number assigned to the file when it was opened. The second parameter is a code number that should be **2** to make the function return a handle.

This example reads the current time and date using subfunction 0h of function 57h of interrupt 21h. The file handle goes in BX and the time and date are returned in CX and DX, respectively. Then the date is changed to June 21, 1992, without altering the time. This is done with subfunction 1h of function 57h of interrupt 21h, with the registers set up in the same way. The file number used by BASIC is assumed to be **7**.

```
' $INCLUDE: 'QBX.BI'

DIM regs AS RegType       ' Define register array


Day = 21                  '21st day

Month = 6                 'June

Year = 12                 '1992 = 1980 + 12

NewDate = Year * 2^9      'year starts at bit 9
```

346

```
NewDate = NewDate + 2^5   'month starts at bit 5
NewDate = NewDate + Day   'no offset for day field


OPEN "C:\AUTOEXEC.BAT" FOR RANDOM AS #7   'open the file
regs.ax = &H5700          'function &H57, subfunction 0
regs.bx = FILEATTR(7,2); 'file handle to BX
CALL Interrupt(&H21, regs, regs) 'get the time and date
regs.dx = NewDate         'place new date in DX
regs.ax = &H5701          'function &H57, subfunction &H01
regs.bx = FILEATTR(7,2); 'file handle to BX again
CALL Interrupt(&H21, regs, regs); 'go set the file date
```

As you can see, the three bit fields are packed into an integer by multiplying each element by 2 to the power of the element's offset. To unpack fields, placing each element in its own integer, apply the AND operator to zero out all but the field you want, then divide the value to shift the bits to the bottom of the integer. For example, the month is held in bits 5 through 8. Once the integer holding the date is assigned to a BASIC variable, you need to AND it with the bit pattern 0000000111100000 to turn off all bits except those in the relevant field. This number equals &H01E0 in hexadecimal notation. Then divide the integer by 2^5 (32) and the integer will hold the month:

```
Value = regs.dx          'get date returned by the interrupt
Value = Value AND &H01E0 'zero-out fields except for month
Value = Value\32         'shift bit field to bottom of Value
```

Pascal

The Turbo Pascal *GetFTime* procedure returns a file's four-byte time and date stamp as a longint variable parameter. The file must be assigned and opened:

```
var
  TheFile: Text;
  TheTime: longint;


Assign(TheFile,'C:\TREES\BIOMASS.TXT');
```

```
Reset(TheFile);

if IOResult <> 0 then Writeln('Could not find the file');

GetFTime(TheFile,TheTime);

Close(TheFile);
```

Now the time and date stamp is in *TheTime*. You can use *UnpackTime* to disassemble the value and place its components in a predeclared structure called *DateTime* that is found in the *DOS unit*.

```
DateTime = record

  Year, Month, Day, Hour, Min, Sec: Word

end;
```

The file's year is converted to its actual value (1980 is added to it). To display the file's year:

```
var DateAndTime: DateTime;


UnpackTime(TheTime,DateAndTime);

Writeln('The year of the file is: ',DateAndTime.Year);
```

To reverse this process, use *PackTime* to assemble a four-byte time and date stamp, and *SetFTime* to place it in a file's directory entry. Again, the file must be assigned and open. To set the file's time stamp to December 21, 1992 at 5:35:03, write:

```
DateAndTime.Year := 1992;

DateAndTime.Month := 12;

DateAndTime.Day := 21;

DateAndTime.Hour := 5;

DateAndTime.Min := 35;

DateAndTime.Sec := 3;

PackTime(DateAndTime,TheTime);  {Pack the time into TheTime}

SetFTime(MyFile,TheTime);
```

Neither *PackTime* nor *UnpackTime* perform range checking. *GetFTime* and *SetFTime* return an error code in the global variable *DosError*. It will be **0** when all has gone well, or **6** when you haven't specified a valid file.

c

The Borland and Microsoft compilers use the *getftime* and *_dos_getftime* functions, respectively, to fetch the time and date associated with a file, and *setftime* and *_dos_setftime* to set these values. The Borland functions use a structure called *ftime* which is declared in *io.h:*

```
struct ftime {
    unsigned ft_tsec: 5;    /* periods of two seconds */
    unsigned ft_min: 6;     /* minutes */
    unsigned ft_hour: 5;    /* hours */
    unsigned ft_day: 5;     /* day of the month */
    unsigned ft_month: 4;   /* month */
    unsigned ft_year: 7;    /* years since 1980 */
};
```

Both functions require the same two parameters — first, the file number by which the opened file is accessed, and second, a pointer to an *ftime* structure — and both functions return an integer error code. In the following example, the functions provided in the Borland compilers are used to learn the year of an already-opened file and then set the year to 1992.

```
#include <stdio.h>
#include <io.h>


FILE *myfile;
struct ftime the_time;


myfile = fopen("C:\\AUTOEXEC.BAT","wt");
getftime(fileno(my_file),&the_time);
printf("The year is %u",the_time.ft_year + 1980);
the_time.ft_year = 12;    /* 1980 + 12 = 1992 */
setftime(fileno(my_file),&the_time);
fclose(myfile);
```

The Microsoft functions set or return the time and date packed into unsigned integers using the format discussed at the beginning of this section. *Setftime* takes three parameters: the file number, then an unsigned integer holding the date, and then another unsigned integer holding the time. *Getftime* is almost the same, except that it requires pointers to integers in which it will deposit the time and date.

Assembler

Function 57h of INT 21h can both fetch and set a file's time and date. Set AL to **0** to find out the time stamp, or to **1** to set the time stamp. BX holds the file handle. In both cases the date goes in DX and the time in CX using the bit patterns shown in the table above. The carry flag is set if an error occurs, in which case AX returns **1** if the subfunction number in AL was out of range or **6** if the file handle was invalid. The following example finds the hour of the day in a file's time setting:

```
;---IN THE DATA SEGMENT:

PATH  db   'C:\LEVEL1\NEWDATA.BAK',0


;---OPEN THE FILE:
      lea   dx,PATH       ;point to path string
      mov   ah,3Dh        ;function to open file
      mov   al,0          ;open to read
      int   21h           ;open it
      jc    OPEN_ERROR    ;jump to error routine if problem
;---GET THE TIME AND DATA SETTINGS:
      mov   bx,ax         ;move file handle to BX
      mov   al,0          ;code to fetch time
      mov   ah,57h        ;function number
      int   21h           ;go get the file's time
      jc    TIME_ERROR    ;jump to error routine if problem
;---SHIFT 'HOUR' BITS TO BOTTOM OF CH:
      mov   cl,3          ;shift down bits 11-15
      shr   ch,cl         ;hour value is now in CH
```

Get/Set File Attributes

The 12th byte of every directory entry includes an *attribute byte* for assigning special roles to files. Each of the low six bits of the byte flags whether a particular attribute is in effect, as follows:

bit	meaning when the bit is set
0	the file is a "read-only" file
1	the file is hidden from directory listings
2	the file is classified as a "system" file
3	the file is not a file at all, but a volume label
4	the file holds a subdirectory
5	the file has been written to since the last backup

A file may have more than one of these attributes concurrently, but obviously not all. When no attributes are set, the file is a "normal" file. Note the following points:

- The *system* attribute is intended to mark operating system files. Files marked with this attribute are omitted from directory listings, just like *hidden* files.

- *Read-only* files can be read, but not written or deleted. This protection is afforded only by the fact that the DOS file access functions heed the setting of this bit. Programs that access files other ways can change (or damage) read-only files as easily as normal ones.

- The *archive bit* is used by backup programs and by some DOS commands, such as XCOPY. These programs clear the bit after a file has been backed up; DOS resets the bit when the file is written to again. The bit is set even when the file has been rewritten without any changes.

- Subdirectory files can not be read or written by DOS file access functions. Nor will the DOS functions shown in this section change a subdirectory attribute so that you can open a subdirectory file as a normal one.

- The volume label attribute is found only in root directories, where it occurs only once. The functions in this section won't let you alter a file's volume label attribute.

BASIC

In Microsoft BASIC, you must call an interrupt to find out a file's attribute. This is subfunction 0 of function 43h of DOS interrupt 21h. DS:DX points to a path string giving the name and location of the file. Use *VARSEG* and *VARPTR* to get a pointer to the string, and add a zero-byte to the end of the string to convert it to the form required by DOS. On return, CL holds the attribute byte. Clear CH by ANDing the return value with &H00FF.

```
' $INCLUDE: 'QBX.BI'

DIM Regs AS RegTypeX     ' Define register array


PathString$ = "C:\DOGS\POODLES.TXT"+CHR$(0)

Regs.AX = &H4300

Regs.DS = VARSEG(PathString$)

Regs.DX = VARPTR(PathString$)

CALL Interrupt(&H21, regs, regs)

TheAttribute = Regs.CX

TheAttribute = TheAttribute AND &H00FF
```

To set a file's attribute, set up the function in the same way, but place **&H4301** in AL to set the subfunction number in AL to 1. Place the new attribute byte for the file in CL and call the interrupt.

Pascal

Turbo Pascal's *GetFAttr* and *SetFAttr* procedures return and set a file's attribute byte as a *word*-length value with the high eight bits always set to zero. The file must be assigned but *not* opened. To find the attributes for the file C:\CONFIG.SYS:

```
var

  TheFile: Text;

  TheAttribute: word;


Assign(TheFile, 'C:\CONFIG.SYS');

GetFAttr(TheFile,TheAttribute);
```

Now the attribute is in the variable parameter *TheAttribute*. You can test for individual attributes by ANDing the value with any of the following predefined constants found in the *DOS unit: ReadOnly, Hidden, SysFile, VolumeID, Directory, Archive,* and *AnyFile.* For example, to find out if the file is read-only:

```
if TheAttribute and ReadOnly <> 0 then Writeln('Read-only file');
```

The *AnyFile* constant tells you that at least one of the attributes is in effect; otherwise, the file is a normal file.

SetFAttr works just like *GetFAttr*, although in this case the attribute is not a variable parameter. To make the file a normal file by setting its attribute to **0**, write:

```
SetFAttr(TheFile,0);
```

If you want to modify an existing attribute byte, rather than replace it altogether, fetch the attribute byte with *GetFAttr* and then add one or more of the predefined constants mentioned above. For example, if *TheAttribute* holds a file's attribute byte and you want to set the file's archive bit, write this:

```
SetFAttr(TheFile,TheAttribute+ReadOnly);
```

Both *GetFAttr* and *SetFAttr* return error codes in the global variable *DosError*. It will be **0** when all has gone well, **3** when the file path is invalid, and **5** when access to the file failed for some reason.

C

The Microsoft compilers provide the *_dos_getfileattr* and *_dos_setfileattr* functions for getting and setting file attributes. Both functions require two parameters. The first is a pointer to a string holding the file name and path. For *_dos_setfileattr*, the second parameter is an *unsigned int* that holds the attribute. For *_dos_getfileattr* the second parameter is a pointer to this value. The functions return an error code that is 0 when the function succeeds, and otherwise return EACCESS or ENOENT. This example fetches a file's attribute and switches on its archive attribute:

```
#include <dos.h>
char *file_path = "C:\\FELINES\\LEOPARDS.TXT";
unsigned file_attribute,error_code;

error_code = _dos_getfileattr(file_path,&file_attribute);
file_attribute = file_attribute ¦ 32;    /*set archive bit*/
error_code = _dos_setfileattr(file_path,file_attribute); /*reset*/
```

Borland's C does not provide corresponding functions. Instead, use *int86* to call function 0x43 of interrupt 0x21. Place 0 in AL to read a file's attribute and 1 to set the attribute. The attribute byte is placed in CX (that is, in CL with CH zeroed out). This example also switches on a file's archive bit:

```
#include <dos.h>


union REGS regs;          /* declare the register array */
char the_attribute;


regs.h.ah = 0x43;         /* function number */
regs.h.al = 0;            /* subfunction to get the attribute */
int86(0x21,&regs,&regs); /* get the attribute */
regs.h.cl = regs.h.cl & 32; /* set the archive bit */
regs.h.ah = 0x43;         /* function number */
regs.h.al = 1;            /* subfunction to set the attribute */
int86(0x21,&regs,&regs); /* set the attribute */
```

Assembler

Function 43h of INT 21h can both change and find a file's attribute, depending on whether AL holds 1 (to set the file's attribute) or 0 (to read the attribute). In either case, CL holds or receives the attribute byte (with CH zeroed out), and DS:DX points to a string giving the file's path. This example makes the file OVERDUE.DOC a hidden file:

```
;---IN THE DATA SEGMENT:
PATH  db  'C:\ACCTS\OVERDUE.DOC',0


;---TURN ON THE "HIDDEN" ATTRIBUTE BYTE:
      mov  ah,43h          ;function number
```

```
mov   al,0            ;subfunction to get the attribute byte
lea   dx,PATH         ;point DS:DX to the file's path
int   21h             ;place attribute byte in CX
jc    ERROR_ROUTINE   ;on error, jump to recovery routine
or    cx,10b          ;turn on bit 1
mov   ah,43h          ;function number
mov   al,1            ;subfunction to set attribute byte
int   21h             ;and now the file is a hidden file
```

The carry flag is set if an error occurs. In this case, AX returns with 2 if the file was not found, 3 if the path was not found, and 5 if there were other problems ("access denied").

Rename Files or Directories

Files are renamed by changing the 11-character file name field in the file's directory entry. The file itself is untouched. However, DOS can also *move* files to another directory on the same drive by "renaming" it using a different directory path. The directory entry is transferred from one directory to another, but the file itself does not change position on the disk. DOS won't let you move files to other disks (or other partitions on the same disk) in this way. The functions listed in this section can also rename directories. Just specify a directory instead of a file.

BASIC

The NAME command in BASIC renames a file. List the existing name and then the new name for the file, placing them separately in quotes, as in:

```
NAME "C:\LEVEL1\OLDFILE.TXT" AS "C:\LEVEL1\NEWFILE.TXT"
```

Note that the complete path must be given for the new file name. If you were instead to write:

```
NAME "C:\LEVEL1\OLDFILE.TXT" AS "NEWFILE.TXT"
```

the file would not only be renamed, but would also be transferred to the current directory of drive C.

Pascal

The Turbo Pascal *Rename* procedure operates on a file that has been assigned to a file variable, but not yet opened. This procedure takes two parameters. The first is the *file variable* and the second is a string giving the new file name. The global variable *IOResult* returns 0 when the file has successfully been renamed. To rename the text file C:\APES\CHIMPS to C:\APES\GIBBONS:

```
var  TheFile: Text;


{$I-}   {disable error checking}
Assign(TheFile,'C:\APES\CHIMPS.TXT');
Rename(TheFile,'C:\APES\GIBBONS.TXT');
if IOResult <> 0 then Writeln('Could not rename file');
```

Be sure to include a complete directory path along with the new name of the file. The file will be moved to the current directory if you don't.

C

Both the Borland and Microsoft compilers use the *rename* function to rename files or directories. The functions take two parameters. The first is a pointer to the name and path of the file that will be renamed, and the second is a pointer to the new file name, also specified with a full path (otherwise, the file will be moved). The function returns 0 if it renames the file successfully, and a nonzero value otherwise.

```
#include <stdio>


char *old_name = "C:\\REPTILES\\LIZARDS.TXT";

char *new_name = "C:\\REPTILES\\SNAKES.TXT";


error_check = rename(old_name,new_name);
```

Assembler

Function 56h of INT 21h renames (and also moves) files. DS:DX points to a zero-terminated string giving the name and path of the existing file. ES:DI points to a second string giving the new name and path. Use the same path in both strings to rename the file without moving it. On return, the carry flag is set if an error has occurred and AX contains 2 if a file was not found, 3 if a path was not found, 5 if there was a disk error, and 17 if different drives were specified. This example moves ACCOUNTS.DAT from the subdirectory "GAINS" to the subdirectory "LOSSES".

```
;---IN THE DATA SEGMENT:

OLDPATH   db 'C:\GAINS\ACCOUNTS.DAT',0

NEWPATH   db 'C:\LOSSES\ACCOUNTS.DAT',0


;---CHANGE THE FILE'S PATH:

      lea  dx,OLDPATH         ;point DS:DX to old path

      mov  ax,seg NEWPATH     ;point ES:DI to new path

      mov  es,ax              ;
```

```
        mov   di,offset NEWPATH   ;
        mov   ah,56h              ;function number
        int   21h                 ;move the file
        jc    ERROR_ROUTINE       ;go to error routine if carry set
```

Delete Files

When a file is deleted, neither the file's directory entry nor the disk sectors occupied by the file are actually erased. Rather, the sectors and directory slot are deallocated so that they are free for use by other files. The first byte of the deleted file's directory slot, which is occupied by the first character of the file name, is changed to E5h. This code signals to DOS that the directory slot is free for use by a new file introduced to the directory. The deleted file's disk sectors are also freed by altering the disk's File Allocation Table. DOS does this by inserting the code E5h at the FAT positions corresponding to the clusters used by the file. The contents of the deleted file's sectors are not altered in any way when the file is deleted, although any subsequent disk activity may reallocate and overwrite these sectors, thereby destroying the deleted file's data.

A file can be wholly or partially "undeleted" by reclaiming clusters that had been allocated to it. In the simplest case, when both the directory entry and all clusters remain intact, an "undeletion" is performed merely by replacing the first character of the file's name in its directory slot, finding the file's size and starting cluster from the directory entry, calculating the number of clusters required to hold the file, and then reallocating the starting cluster and the required number of clusters from those that immediately follow the starting cluster. Recovery becomes more difficult when the file did not reside on contiguous clusters, or when the file's directory slot has been taken over by another file so that the deleted file's length and starting cluster are lost.

BASIC

BASIC's *KILL* statement deletes files. The file must not be open when it is deleted. The only parameter is a string specifying the file's name and directory path. You can use wild card characters in the file name. Employ the *ON ERROR* facility to detect errors; it is discussed in Chapter 10, "Detect and Recover from Disk Errors." To delete C:\REPTILES\LIZARDS.DOC, you would write:

```
ON ERROR RESUME NEXT

KILL "C:\REPTILES\LIZARDS.DOC"

IF ERR = 0 THEN WRITE "Successful file deletion"
```

Pascal

In Turbo Pascal, the *Erase* procedure deletes files. It operates on a file that has been assigned to a *file variable* (discussed in Chapter 12, "Create, Open, and Close

Files"). The file must not be open when it is deleted. Enable error-checking before calling the procedure and test *IOResult* afterwards. It returns 0 if the operation was successful, and otherwise returns an error code.

```
var   TheFile: Text;
  {$I-}      {disable error checking}
  Assign(TheFile,'C:\FELINES\TIGERS.TXT');
  Erase(TheFile);
  if IOResult <> 0 then Writeln('Could not erase file');
```

C

Both the Borland and Microsoft compilers use the *unlink* function to delete a file. The only parameter is a string specifying the file's name and directory path. Wild card characters are not allowed. The function returns an integer value that is 0 when the file is deleted successfully. Otherwise it returns the error code ENOENT when the path or file was not found, or EACCES (in EACCESS in Microsoft's C) when the file couldn't be erased (normally, because its read-only attribute is set).

```
#include <stdio>


char *file_name = "C:\\REPTILES\\TURTLES.TXT";
int error_check;


error_check = unlink(file_name);
```

Assembler

Function 41h of INT 21h deletes files. Point DS:DX to a null-terminated string that gives the file's path and name. Then call the function. The carry flag is set when the function fails, in which case AX returns **2** if the file was not found or **5** if there was some kind of drive-access problem. Wild card characters are not allowed in the file name you specify; if you want to delete groups of files, you must write code that deciphers the wild cards and then makes the deletions one by one. Here is an example:

```
;---IN THE DATA SEGMENT:
PATH  db 'B:LEVEL1\LEVEL2\FILENAME.EXT',0


;---DELETE THE FILE:
        mov  ah,41h          ;function number
        lea  dx,PATH         ;DS:DX points to the directory path
        int  21h             ;delete the file
        jc   DELETE_ERROR    ;go to error routine if carry flag set
```

12

Reading and Writing Files

- Minitutorial: Approaches to File Access
- Create, Open, and Close Files
- Write to Sequential Files
- Read from Sequential Files
- Write to Random Access Files
- Read from Random Access Files
- Verify Data After Write Operations

Minitutorial: Approaches to File Access

There are two basic ways to access files: sequentially and randomly. Although computer literature commonly refers to "sequential files" and "random files," all files reside on disk in exactly the same way: as a continuous sequence of bytes. There is no indication in the file's directory entry or anywhere else that a particular file is "sequential" or "random." What differentiates the two kinds of files is the layout of data and the corresponding method of access. Ordinarily, random access files have data files that are all the same size, whereas sequential files are comprised of elements of varying length. Nonetheless, any random access file can be accessed sequentially, and any sequential file can be accessed randomly, although there is seldom reason to do so, especially in the latter case.

Sequential files place data items one after the other and separate them with a pair of characters, first the carriage return (ASCII 13) and then the line feed (ASCII 10). High-level languages can add these delimiting characters automatically, but assembly language programs must take the trouble of inserting the characters as each variable is written to the file.

Sequential files usually hold text — that is, a sequence of strings — although any kind of data can be kept in this kind of file. When strings are held in memory, *string descriptors* are used to tell the string length, or a zero-byte is appended to a string to mark its end. Normally, neither string descriptors nor terminating nulls are recorded in sequential files. Instead, the program (or the compiler functions it uses) create these values when strings are read in from a file, and discard them when strings are written to files.

Sequential files can also hold numbers. These are usually recorded as string values that are separated by carriage-return/line-feed (CR/LF) values, just like other data in a sequential file. For example, the number 64 would be recorded in the file as a two-byte string consisting of ASCII 54 ("6") and ASCII 52 ("4"). The value would not be recorded as a *numeric value,* such as a byte value holding the bit pattern for 64 (01000000). In spite of this convention, nothing stops a program from writing numbers into sequential files as numeric values. Anything goes so long as the file will be reread by software that understands the format.

The data items that make up a sequential file vary in length. For this reason, it is impossible to know just where in the file a particular item is located. And so a program must read the file from its beginning to find a particular item, counting the number of carriage-return/line-feed pairs until it encounters the desired item. It is for this reason that files of this format are called "sequential." Generally, the entire file is transferred from disk to memory, placing the component strings into an array.

On the other hand, *random access files* allocate a fixed amount of space to each data item. When a particular data item does not fill the entire space allotted, the excess is filled with spaces. If every item is ten bytes long, then it is easy to look up the 50th item, because a program can calculate that the item starts at the 491st byte of the file (that is, byte #490, since counting begins from 0).

Random access files usually consist of *records* of related items. Each record holds a number of *fields*, which provide a set number of bytes into which to place each data item. For example, a record may have fields for a person's age, weight, and height. The respective fields for each might be one byte, two bytes, and four bytes. Taken together, they would form a record seven bytes long. A random access file could consist of thousands of such records. Each record immediately follows the previous one, with no delimiters like the carriage return/line feed pairs used in sequential files.

Data may be written into random access files in any order. Record 74 can be written even though record 73 has not been. (Disk space would still be allocated for record 73, and in new files the record would contain whatever data happens to be in the sector in which the record resides.) Unlike sequential files, ordinarily only part of a random access file is brought into memory at any one moment.

By far the most common kind of sequential file are *text files*. In DOS, text files are structured with CR/LF delimiters. In addition, the file ends with a Ctrl-Z byte (ASCII 26). Because this character flags the end of the file, it should not occur within the text the file contains. (It is for this reason that numbers are normally written as strings in text files, lest one of the bytes of a numeric value be ASCII 26.) Incidentally, the C language uses only a lone line-feed character as a delimiter in sequential files. So that files generated by programs written in C will be compatable with DOS, the compiler file I/O functions add the carriage-return delimiter as files are written to disk.

Binary files are files that are read by DOS in *binary (raw)* mode. DOS makes no changes to this kind of file as it is moved between memory and disk. Essentially, this means that the files contain no implicit information about the way data is laid out. Programs that use such files need to know the size of the records and fields each file uses (or needs to know where in the file to look for this information). Lacking this information, other programs cannot ordinarily read binary files. Binary files do not end with a Ctrl-Z byte found at the end of many text files. Instead, the *file size* value in the file's directory entry tells DOS where the file ends.

When programs read text files, the file-input functions read the file in nonbinary ("cooked") mode, watching each byte as it passes by to see if it is a carriage-return, line-feed, or end-of-file character. This process takes time. To speed file operations, text files can be accessed in *binary mode* so that their data is read in as an undifferentiated mass. Then the program can sort out the data as required. But while text files can be read as binary files, the reverse is not possible. It makes no sense to read a binary file as a text file because at most there would be only a few incidental CR/LF pairs, and their positions would have nothing to do with the structure of the file's data.

File access is one of the most complicated parts of programming. There are a number of ways to approach it, particular in C compilers, which offer dozens of file-access functions. Compilers may add a considerable amount of code to your programs as they install advanced facilities for processing files. By understanding how files are accessed, you'll be able to make sense of your compiler's I/O library. At bottom, all compiler functions use DOS functions, so it's important to understand how DOS works.

DOS uses a data structure to manage every file it accesses. These structures are created in memory by DOS when a computer is booted. In its early incarnations, DOS used a structure called a *file control block (FCB)*. A program would fill data into this block, including the file's name, and ask DOS to "open" the file. DOS would then fill in other fields in the block, such as the file's size and date, which the program could then access. Thus, the action of "opening" a file consists of nothing more than searching a directory for the file and initializing a data structure for it. The file itself is not read or altered in any way when it is opened.

Once an FCB has been initialized, a program can access the file by calling the appropriate DOS functions and telling it which FCB you want used. The FCB functions move data between disk and a holding area in memory (a *buffer*) called the *disk transfer area* or *DTA*. By default, the DTA is a 128-byte area in the program's *program segment prefix* (PSP), the 256-byte header that begins every program (PSPs are discussed in the Chapter 1 *minitutorial*). However, programs can set up a larger DTA elsewhere in memory.

File control blocks had a short life in DOS. Starting with DOS 2.0, an entirely different method of file access was introduced. It also uses a data structure, but not one that programs directly manipulate. Rather, the DOS function that opens a file returns an identifying value called a *file handle*, and thereafter programs use the handle to refer to the file. DOS functions must be used to access information about the file that is held in the data structure associated with the handle.

In some ways, the FCB functions are easier to use than file handle functions. FCB functions will figure out where a particular record resides in a file, whereas a program must calculate a record's position when file handles are used. Also, using file handles, functions that read or write data must be explicitly told where in memory to find or deposit the data. Still, file handle access is much more flexible, and the FCB method of access is virtually never used today. The only reason you'll ever need the FCB functions is to change a disk's volume label— a topic discussed in Chapter 10, "Read/Change a Disk's Volume Label." Beyond this application, FCB functions are not covered in this book.

DOS keeps a *file pointer* for every file. A file pointer keeps track of the position in a file at which reading or writing will be take place when the appropriate functions are called. When a sequential file is written, the file pointer is initially set to the beginning of the file, and the pointer constantly increments as more and more data are written out to the file. Similarly, when data is appended to a sequential file, the file pointer is initially set to the end of the file.

The file pointer works differently for random access files. When a single record is accessed in a random access file, the location of the record is calculated as an offset from the start of the file, and the pointer is set to that value. Then a record's worth of data is read or written to the file. Again, the pointer is automatically incremented to the end of the data read or written, leaving it at the start of the next record in the file. A program can change the pointer position at any time; this action lets the program move between noncontiguous records in a file.

The file access functions in DOS can do no more than read a specified portion of a file and deposit it byte after byte in memory, or read a specified portion of data and deposit it byte after byte on disk. When a text file is read, a compiler's I/O routines must do the work of separating the constituent strings into a number of string variables. Conversely, when text data is written to a file, the I/O functions must assemble the strings into a continuous series with delimiting characters inserted between the strings. All of this work is done for you in BASIC, Pascal, or C. But in assembly language, the work must be done from scratch.

Typically, a program requires only a small amount of data at once. The program might ask for just one 50-byte record from a random access file. Or, a program might request a single string from a text file, process the string and place it in an array, then ask for the next string, and so on. It would be inefficient for DOS to go to disk for each fragment of data, since disk operations are relatively slow.

Instead, disk data can be *buffered*. This means that a relatively large amount of data is read into memory at once, and then the individual data components are supplied as they are called for. Buffering also applies to writing data to disk.

Because data passes between devices other than disk drives, compilers can generalize the buffer system into a system of *streams* (that is, streams of data). The same functions can manipulate data streams from the keyboard (standard input), to the screen (standard output), to certain other peripherals that are predefined in DOS (LPT1, COM1), and even to memory. In theory, the same buffered I/O functions can manipulate a stream of any kind. In reality, streams are very useful for file I/O, sometimes useful for data display, keyboard input, and printing, and usually impractical for serial communications.

Generally speaking, there are three levels of file access. At the lowest level are the DOS functions that read and write masses of continuous data. Assembly language programmers always work at this level. Compilers also may offer low-level functions that handle data this way. The next level is I/O for which compiler functions provide a certain degree of processing, as when a text file is assembled from string variables. All compilers offer functions that work at this level. Finally, at the highest level is buffered I/O using streams, a feature available in C, but not Pascal or BASIC.

No matter how a file is accessed, the same basic operations must be carried out. First, it must be opened. In doing so, the program is handed some kind of identification number that is subsequently used to refer to the file. When a file is opened, you may specify that it is opened only for reading data, only for writing data, and so on. You also may need to determine where the file pointer is initially set.

Once a file is opened, a program can call functions that read or write data sequentially, or functions that access records of a given length and position. Depending on the language, and on the function used, a program may need to shift the file pointer back and forth as it reads and writes data.

After file operations are complete, the program closes the file. In doing so, it causes the file's directory entry to be updated, and it releases the DOS data structure that monitors the file for use by another file. Closing a file also serves to *flush* buffers associated with the file so that fragments not yet written to disk are saved.

367

Create, Open, and Close Files

To "open" a file means to have DOS verify that the file exists and establish a data structure in memory to manage the file. If a program operates on many files, be sure to keep an eye on how many are open at any one time. The DOS FILES command determines how much memory will be set aside for the data structures that manage files. You may need to open, close, and reopen files in order to avoid exceeding this limit. A program should be prepared to analyze errors that occur when it attempts to open a file and to inform the program user that the FILES setting must be changed.

When a file is closed, the data structure used by DOS to manage the file is freed for use by another file. Closing a file also "flushes" out the data transfer buffer used by the file, sending to disk the last information directed to the file. Files can be lost when a program does not terminate normally, so be sure to close files in your program's Ctrl-Break routine.

BASIC

When BASIC opens a file, it searches the directory for it, and if it is not found, a new file is created with the given name. There are two ways of writing a statement that opens a file, and in most instances one does as well as the other. The only difference is that one form is rather cryptic, while the second comes closer to natural language in its expression. In either statement, you must supply at least three pieces of information. First, the name is required; because it is a string, it is placed within quotes. Second, a number from 1 upward is assigned to the file as the ID number by which the file is referred to thereafter. And third, you must specify for what purpose the file is being opened, that is, whether it is for random access, for a sequential read, or whatever. To open the file C:\LEVEL1\MYFILE.TXT to write to a sequential file ("OUTPUT" or "O"), where the file accessed is the one opened as #2, write either:

```
OPEN "O",#2,"C:\LEVEL1\MYFILE.TXT"
```

or

```
OPEN "C:\LEVEL1\MYFILE.TXT" FOR OUTPUT AS #2
```

Note that in either case the number **#2** refers to file buffer 2. The number may be any value that does not exceed the number of file buffers allowed. If six files are supported simultaneously, the number must be from 1 to 6. However, file buffer #1 does not need to be used before a file can be opened under number #2. BASIC sets the number of files buffers to 8 by default, and you can change the number to any value from 1 to 15. Of these, four are used by BASIC for its own purposes, so that in the default condition only four are available for I/O.

The first form of the open statement shown above uses single letters to designate the kind of file operation desired. There are three options:

```
"O"    output data to a sequential file
"I"    input data from a sequential file
"R"    both read and write data to and
       from a random access file
```

Sequential files cannot be written to while they are opened for reading, and vice versa. Typically, a sequential file is opened, read in its entirety into memory, and then the file buffer is closed. After changes have been made, the file is reopened (via any file buffer) for output, and the file is written back to disk, overlaying the sectors that hold the file and possibly taking up some more.

There are a few things to note about this form of the OPEN statement. The file name should contain a drive specifier if the file is not found on the default drive (the drive from which BASIC was loaded). Also, the file name may be given as a string showing the path to a file located in a subdirectory, as in:

```
OPEN "I",#1,"C:\LEVEL1\LEVEL2\MYFILE.TXT".
```

In addition, note that you can tack on a *record length* specification to the end of the statement, as in;

```
OPEN "R",#3,"B:MYFILE.TXT",52.
```

In this case, every record will take up 52 bytes of disk space. If a FIELD statement does not make use of all 52 bytes, the remainder is wasted. This parameter is essential in random access file operations. Most sequential file operations do not require a record length setting, but you can speed up file operations by setting the record size to 512. The record length may be from 1 to 32,767 bytes, and it defaults to 128.

The second form of the OPEN statement does exactly the same as the first, except that it uses complete words. Rather than write **"O"** or **"I"**, write **OUTPUT** and **INPUT** (without quotes). For random access files, give no such specification at all, as in:

```
OPEN "MYFILE.TXT" AS #2.
```

In addition, you can specify **APPEND** to write data starting from *the end* of a sequential file, without overwriting any of the existing data, as in:

```
OPEN "B:MYFILE.TXT" FOR APPEND AS #3.
```

As with the first form discussed above, the statement also takes an optional specification of record length. Just append **LEN=number** to the end of the statement. For example:

```
OPEN "C:MYFILE.TXT" AS #1 LEN=52
```

opens a random access file with 52-byte records.

To close all open files in BASIC, simply write:

```
CLOSE
```

To close a particular file, or several files , write **CLOSE #1** or **CLOSE #1,#3**, etc. It is important to close *all* files before a program terminates. Data may remain in the buffer that has not yet been output to disk. Note that the END, NEW, RESET, SYSTEM, and RUN commands close all file buffers, but they do not flush the buffers. Once closed, the file can be reopened using any available buffer number.

Pascal

In Pascal, first you must assign a file to a variable by which it is subsequently identified. This is done with the *Assign* procedure. Declare the variable as being of *file* type for binary files, or as *text* type for text files. The Assign procedure takes the file variable as its first parameter, and the file's name and path as the second.

```
var

   File1: File;

   File2: Text;


   Assign(File1,'C:\UTIL\RANDFILE.XYZ');

   Assign(File2,'C:\UTIL\TEXTFILE.TXT');
```

Alternatively, a file may be *typed* so that its data corresponds to a data record declared in the program. For instance:

```
type

   FileRecord = record

      name: string[80];

      age: byte;

      weight: integer;

   end;


var

   TheFile: File of FileRecord;
```

In these declarations, *TheFile* acts as the variable under which a file will be opened. By declaring it as "File of FileRecord," you are telling the compiler that the data in the file will follow the format of the record called *FileRecord*.

370

Once an *Assign* statement has been made, open the file with the *Reset, Rewrite,* or *Append* procedures. *Reset* opens an existing file. *Rewrite* creates a new file, or replaces an existing file. And *Append* opens an existing text file for appending data:

```
Reset(File1);

Rewrite(File2);

Append(File3);
```

To close a file in Pascal, just name the variable under which the file was opened in a *Close* statement:

```
Close(TheFile);
```

C

C uses the *fopen* function to open a file as a stream. The function returns a pointer to type FILE that is subsequently used to identify the file. The *fopen* function takes two parameters. The first is a pointer to a string that gives the file's name and path. The second is a pointer to a string that specifies the mode in which the file is opened. This string is assembled from the following values:

r	Open for reading only.
w	"Create" for writing. Creates a new file when none is found of the speci fied name. Overwrites an existing file.
a	Append data to the end of the file.
r+	Open an existing file for reading and writing.
w+	Create a new file for reading and writing. An existing file is over written.
a+	Open for reading and writing at the end of the file.

Append *t* to the mode string when the file is a text file, and *b* when it is a binary file. When neither of these symbols is specified, the current value of the global variable *_fmode* is used to determine the file type (it can be set to either *O_BINARY* or *O_TEXT*). *Null* is returned when the file could not be opened. This example opens *AUTOEXEC.BAT* for reading and writing:

```
FILE *the_file;


the_file = fopen("C:\\AUTOEXEC.BAT","r+t");

if(the_file == NULL) printf("Couldn't open the file");
```

371

Later, to close the file, use *fclose* to close the file, or *fcloseall* to close all open files (actually, all open streams of any kind). These functions return *EOF* when an error occurs:

```
int result_code;


result_code = fclose(the_file);    /* close the_file */


result_code = fcloseall();         /* close all streams */
```

If you want to open a file without buffering in order to make block transfers between disk to memory, use the *open* function instead. This function takes three parameters, the first of which is a pointer to a string that gives the file's name and path. The second parameter determines the kind of access allowed to the file. There are three basic kinds of access:

O_RDONLY	Open for reading only.
O_WRONLY	Open for writing only.
O_RDWR	Open for reading and writing.

These values are ORed with the following constants:

O_CREAT	Create the file if it does not already exist.
O_EXCL	Return an error if the file already exists (this constant is only ORed with O_CREAT).
O_TRUNC	Truncate the file to 0 length (for rewriting).
O_APPEND	Move file pointer to end of file.
O_BINARY	Used to explicitly open the file in binary mode.
O_TEXT	Used to explicitly open the file in text mode.

When neither *O_BINARY* or *O_TEXT* is used, the file is opened in whatever mode is specified by *_fmode*.

The third parameter used by the *open* function is required only when *O_CREATE* is used in the access specification. This parameter sets access permission for the file, and can be one of the following three values:

S_IWRITE	Permission to write
S_IREAD	Permission to read
S_IWRITE ¦ S_IREAD	Permission to read and write

The *open* function returns an *integer* handle by which the file is subsequently identified. The value **–1** is returned when the file could not be opened, and the global variable *errno* returns a code identifying the error. Here is an example that opens *AUTOEXEC.BAT* to append data:

```
int the_file;


the_file = open("C:\\AUTOEXEC.BAT",O_WRONLY ¦ O_APPEND);

if(the_file == -1) printf("Couldn't open the file");
```

Use the *close* function to close the file. Note that this function does not append *Ctrl-Z* to a file, so your program must output this code if it is required. The function's only parameter is the handle under which the file was opened. It returns an integer result code that is –1 when the file couldn't be closed, in which case the global variable *errno* indicates the error:

```
int  result_code;


result_code = close(the_file);

if (result_code == -1) printf("Couldn't close the file");
```

Assembler

Use function 3Dh of interrupt 21h to open files. Point DS:DX to a string giving the path and file name, with a drive specifier if one is required. The entire string should be no more than 63 bytes long, and it must be terminated by an ASCII 0 byte. Place an "access code" in AL, where **0** opens the file for reading, **1** opens it for writing, and **2** opens it for both. On return, AX holds the 16-bit handle by which the file is thereafter identified. The file pointer is initially set to the beginning of the file and the record size is set at one byte. This function opens both normal and hidden files.

The carry flag will be set if DOS fails to open the file, in which case AX will hold 2 if the file was not found, 4 if the program has attempted to open too many files, 5 if there was a disk access problem, and 12 if the access code placed in AL was invalid. Here is an example:

```
;---IN THE DATA SEGMENT:
PATH   db 'A:LEVEL1\FILENAME.EXT',0


;---OPEN THE FILE FOR BOTH READING AND WRITING:
       mov  ah,3Dh        ;function number
       mov  al,2          ;open for reading or writing
       lea  dx,PATH       ;point DS:DX to path string
       int  21h           ;open the file
       jc   OPEN_ERROR    ;jump to error routine if problem
       mov  HANDLE,ax     ;save a copy of the handle
```

Function 3Eh of interrupt 21h closes files opened under the file handle method. Simply put the handle in BX and execute the function. On return, the carry flag will be set if the function fails, with **6** in the AL register if the file handle was invalid.

```
;---CLOSE THE FILE:
       mov  ah,3Eh      ;function number
       mov  bx,HANDLE   ;place file handle in BX
       int  21h         ;close the file
       jc   CLOSE_ERROR ;go to error routine if carry flag set
```

374

Write to Sequential Files

From the programmer's perspective, high-level languages appear to access sequential files one data item at a time. Actually, entire disk sectors are read and buffered, and the compiler generates code that scans the raw data for the delimiters that define data elements. Nothing stops a program from reading sequential files in blocks and processing the data elements itself. In fact, assembly language programmers always work this way, since assemblers do not ordinarily provide a library of disk I/O routines. Remember that sequential text files may end with a Ctrl-Z byte (ASCII 26). If you read or write sequential text files as raw data, you'll need to consider this terminating byte in designing your algorithms.

BASIC

BASIC prepares to write to a sequential file by opening the file in sequential mode, using the OPEN statement. The statement has two forms, and which to choose is a matter of preference. The formats are:

```
OPEN "MYFILE" FOR OUTPUT AS #1
```

or

```
OPEN "O",#1,"MYFILE"
```

The **"O"** in the second statement stands for "output." The symbol **#1** designates the number 1 as the code number by which to refer to the file in statements that access the file, such as in **WRITE #1** or **INPUT #1**. In both cases, a file named MYFILE is opened and made ready to receive sequential data. If no file by that name is found on disk, the OPEN statement creates one. And if the file already exists, its contents are overwritten, so that when it is closed it contains only the new data written into it. To *append* data to the end of a sequential file without changing its prior contents, open it using the first type of OPEN statement shown above, in the form **OPEN "MYFILE" FOR APPEND AS 1**. See "Create, Open, and Close Files," above, for more information.

Data is written to the file using the INPUT# or WRITE# statements. They share the form:

```
PRINT#1,S$
```

or

```
WRITE#1,X
```

#1 refers to the file ID number (the "file descriptor") assigned by the OPEN statement. The first example writes a string variable to the file, and the second writes a numeric value, but each can write either. Numeric values are written into sequential files in string form, even though they are taken from nonstring variables. For example, 232 is a two-byte integer in numeric form, but if X=232, then **PRINT#1,X** places three bytes in the file, using the ASCII codes for the symbols 2, 3, and 2.

The PRINT# and WRITE# statements differ in how they separate one data item from the next in a file. Which is best depends on the characteristics of the data. The chief difference between the two statements is that WRITE# places extra delimiters around the data items. Consider the case where a statement outputs several variables, in the form **100 PRINT#1,A$,Z,B$** or **100 WRITE#1,A$,Z,B$**. In this case, the carriage-return/line-feed pair is placed in the file only after the last of the three variables (note that string and numeric variables may be mixed). How can the three variables then be distinguished? If PRINT# is used, they cannot. The three items are joined into a continuous string. But when WRITE# is used, each data item is enclosed in quotes, and commas are placed between the items. Later, when the items are read back from the file, BASIC automatically strips away the quotes and commas that were added by the WRITE# statement.

There are a number of minor points to consider. One is that the whole problem of delimitation can be solved by simply writing only one variable in each PRINT# or WRITE# statement. In this case, PRINT# separates all items with the carriage-return/line-feed pair, and WRITE# does the same, but also surrounds the item with quotes (which wastes file space). Further, WRITE# should not be used with strings that contain quotes themselves, since the first internal quote will erroneously signal the end of the variable when the string is read back. Finally, note that when several variables are printed with the same statement, both PRINT# and WRITE# format the data exactly as if it were to be printed on the screen. Thus, **PRINT#1,A$,B$** spaces B$ apart from A$, while **PRINT#1,A$;B$** does not; the file will be padded with spaces accordingly. The PRINT# statement can be used in the form **PRINT#1 USING...**, where all of the usual screen PRINT USING formats are available to format output to the file.

In general it is most economical to use the PRINT# statement, writing only one data item at a time. This method gives over the least amount of file space to delimiters, and it allows a string of any composition to be read back without error. The more complicated delimitation schemes required by writing multiple variables with a single PRINT# or WRITE# statement can lead to trouble, especially when one variable is read as two, so that the correct position in the data sequence is lost.

After all data has been written, simply close the file to secure the data. Write **CLOSE** to close all files that are open, or **CLOSE#1** to close file #1, **CLOSE#1,#3** to close files #1 and #3, etc. Although BASIC is sometimes forgiving of unclosed files, this is not the case here. PRINT# and WRITE# statements output data to the file buffer; the information is written on disk only when the buffer is filled. The last data entered is flushed out to disk by the CLOSE statement. Omitting the statement can result in lost data. Here is an example:

```
OPEN"A:NEWSEQ" FOR OUTPUT AS 1  'open for sequential output
A$="aaaaa"                      'three strings to write
B$="bbbbb"                      '
C$="ccccc"                      '
WRITE#1,A$,B$,C$                'write the strings
CLOSE                           'flush buffer
```

Pascal

After opening the file as a *text* file, use *Writeln* to write strings to the file. This example assumes that the string array *StringArray* holds the data that you want written, and that a null string flags an end of to the data.

```
type
   StringType = string[80];


var
   MyFile: Text;
   StringArray: array[1..100] of StringType;
   ArrayPtr: word;


ArrayPtr := 1;            {point to start of string array¦
Assign(MyFile,'C:\AUTOEXEC.BAT'); {set up the file variable}
Rewrite(MyFile);         {open the file for rewriting}
While StringArray[ArrayPtr] <> '' do
begin
   Writeln(MyFile,StringArray[ArrayPtr]);
   ArrayPtr := ArrayPtr + 1;
end;
```

C

Once a file has been opened by *fopen* as a text file, use *fprintf* to write elements into the file. This function works just like the *printf* function that displays data on the screen, except that its first parameter is the variable under which the file was opened. This example writes out a string array to the file assigned to *the_file:*

```
FILE *the_file;

int array_ptr = 0;


the_file=fopen("C:\\UTIL\\SOMEFILE.TXT","r++t");

if(the_file == NULL) printf("Couldn't open the file");

for(array_ptr = 0;array_ptr <= number_lines;array_ptr++) {

  fprintf(the_file,"%s",string_array[array_ptr]);

}

fclose(the_file);
```

Assembler

To open a file for sequential over-write, use function 3Ch of interrupt 21h (discussed in "Create, Open, and Close Files," above). This function normally *creates* a new file, but if the file already exists, it truncates it to 0 length. To *append* data to a sequential file, however, use the ordinary "open" function, 3Dh of interrupt 21h (also discussed in "Create, Open, and Close Files," above).

Consider first the case of completely overwriting the file. After the file is opened by function 3Ch, the file pointer is set to 0, so there is no need to set its position. Place the file handle in BX and the number of bytes to be written in CX. Then point DS:DX to the first byte of the output data and execute function 40h of interrupt 21h. On return, if the carry flag has been set, there has been an error, and AX holds 5 if there was a disk drive problem, or 6 if the file handle was bad. Otherwise AX holds the number of bytes actually written; if there is a disparity, it is most probably attributable to a full disk. Do not fail to provide error recovery for this situation, since, if the program crashes, the original contents of the disk file are lost (owing to the truncation to 0 length). To check disk space, see Chapter 10, "Determine Available Disk Space." Here is an example:

```
;---IN THE DATA SEGMENT:
PATH          db 'B:FILENAME.EXT',0  ;directory    path
DATA_BUFFER   db 2000 dup(?)  ;or allocate memory for buffer


;---OPEN THE FILE USING THE "CREATE" FUNCTION:
        lea   dx,PATH          ;point DS:DX to directory path
        mov   cx,0             ;file attribute (here, normal)
        mov   ah,3Ch           ;function number
        int   21h             ;truncate file to 0 length
        jc    OPEN_ERROR       ;catch errors
        mov   HANDLE,ax        ;keep copy of handle
;---WRITE 1000 BYTES OUT TO THE FILE:
        mov   ah,40h           ;function number
        mov   bx,HANDLE        ;handle in BX
        mov   cx,1000          ;number of bytes to write
        lea   dx,DATA_BUFFER  ;DS:DX points to data buffer
        int   21h             ;write the data
        jc    OUTPUT_ERROR     ;go to error routine if carry
        cmp   ax,1000          ;1000 bytes successfully written?
        jne   FULL_DISK        ;go to error routine if problem
```

To *append* data to a sequential file, open it with function 3Dh of interrupt 21h, placing 1 in AL if the program will only write data, or 2 in AL if both reading and writing are to take place. The file length is left unchanged, although it will increase as data is appended. The file pointer must be set to the end of the file or else existing data will be overwritten. This is accomplished by function 42h of interrupt 21h. Place the subfunction number 2 in AL to set the pointer to the end of the file, and put the file handle in BX. CX:DX points to the offset from the end of the file at which writing is to start, so place 0 in each. Then execute the function to set the pointer. On return, a set carry flag indicates an error, and AX holds 1 if the function number in AL was invalid, and 6 if the file handle was invalid. Once the pointer is set, the write operation proceeds exactly as above:

```
;---IN THE DATA SEGMENT:
PATH         db   'B:FILENAME.EXT",0   ;directory path
DATA_BUFFER  db   1000 dup(?)          ;or allocate memory for
                                       buffer
;---OPEN THE FILE:
     lea  dx,PATH        ;point DS:DX to directory path
     mov  al,1           ;code to open for writing only
     mov  ah,3Dh         ;function number
     int  21h            ;open the file
     jc   OPEN_ERROR     ;go to error routine if carry
     mov  HANDLE,ax      ;keep copy of handle
;---SET FILE POINTER TO END OF FILE:
     mov  bx,ax          ;file handle in BX
     mov  cx,0           ;CX:DX gives 0 offset from end
                         of file
     mov  dx,0           ;
     mov  al,2           ;code number for end-of-file
     mov  ah,42h         ;function to set file pointer
     int  21h            ;set the pointer
     jc   POINTER_ERROR  ;go to error routine if carry
;---APPEND 300 BYTES TO THE FILE:
     mov  ah,40h         ;function number
     mov  bx,HANDLE      ;handle in BX
     mov  cx,300         ;number of bytes to write
     lea  dx,DATA_BUFFER ;DS:DX points to data buffer
     int  21h            ;append the data
     jc   OUTPUT_ERROR   ;go to error routine if carry
     cmp  ax,300         ;300 bytes successfully written?
     jne  FULL_DISK      ;go to error routine if problem
```

Read from Sequential Files

"Write to Sequential Files," above, explains how sequential files are written. This section continues the discussion, showing how sequential files are read. You should be familiar with the material in the earlier section before consulting the information here.

BASIC

Reading sequential files in BASIC is less complicated than writing them, since there are only two choices about how to go about it, depending on which characters in the file are to be recognized as marking the end of a data item. BASIC reads the files for one data item at a time. The INPUT# statement recognizes commas and quotation marks as data separators, as well as carriage-return/line-feed pairs. The LINE INPUT# statement recognizes only the CR/LF combination, and thus it can read whole lines of text that contain the other delimiters. This capability is essential for text processing.

To read three items with the INPUT# statement, first open the file, as discussed in "Create, Open, and Close Files," above (for example: **OPEN"A:NEWSEQ" FOR INPUT AS 1**). If the file has been opened as #1, then **INPUT #1,X$,Y$,Z$** assigns the first three elements in sequence to the three string variables. When using numeric variables, as in **INPUT #1,X,Y,Z**, be sure that the numeric type of the variable matches the variable found in the file. A double-precision number takes up eight bytes in the file, and it must be read into a variable that is itself double-precision so that it will be large enough to hold eight bytes. An alternative way of reading three data items is to place them in an array:

```
DIM ITEM$(40)        'create 40-element string array
FOR N=0 to 39        'for each element...
INPUT #1,ITEM$(N)    'read it, and place it in the array
NEXT
```

To read the nth item in a sequential file, a program must still read all items that precede it. Simply set up a loop that keeps reading data items, but do not save the data as it arrives.

The LINE INPUT# statement operates in much the same way as INPUT#, except that it can take only one variable at a time, and the variable is always a string. The variable may be up to 254 characters long, which is the longest that a data item can be if it was created by BASIC. A carriage-return/line-feed pair contained in the original data is included in the string that LINE INPUT# returns. This feature enables text files to keep track of paragraph endings.

The EOF ("end of file") function may be used to figure out when all data items in a file have been read. The function returns −1 if the file has been exhausted and 0 otherwise. The buffer number under which the file was opened is required by the function; for example, if the file was opened as #2, then **X=EOF(2)**. The following example reads an entire text file into an array:

```
OPEN "TEXT.AAA" FOR INPUT AS #2   'open for sequential input
DIM TEXT$(500)                    'allow 500 lines
LINECOUNTER=0                     'counts array lines
LINE INPUT #1,TEXT$(LINECOUNTER)  'get 1 line
IF EOF(2) THEN GOTO ALL DONE      'if end of file, quit
LINECOUNTER=LINECOUNTER+1         'increment line counter
GOTO NEXTLINE                     'read next line
ALLDONE:                          'continue...
```

The INPUT$ statement reads a specified number of characters from a sequential file. It is the responsibility of the program to figure out where the various data elements begin and end. The format for a file opened as #1, in which 30 bytes are to be read, is **S$=INPUT$(30,#1)**. Although you can specify the number of bytes to be read, be aware that this number cannot exceed 254 since this is the maximum size of the string variable into which the data is placed. INPUT$ is useful for transferring a body of data into a contiguous memory area. For example, the following code dumps the first 200 bytes of a sequential file into the monochrome display buffer so that it is displayed on the screen, control characters and all:

```
OPEN"A:NEWFILE" FOR INPUT AS #1   'open file
CLS:DEF SEG=&HB000                'clear screen, point to video buffer
FOR N=0 TO 9                      'get 10 groups of 200 bytes
S$=INPUT$(20,#1)                  'get 1 group
FOR M=1 TO 20                     'take each byte and place it at...
POKE N*160 + M*2,ASC(MID$(S$,M,1)) '... even-numbered
                                       positions
NEXT M                            'go get next byte
NEXT N                            'go get next group of 200
```

Pascal

After opening the file as a *text* file, use *Readln* to read strings from the file. Before each read, use the *EOF* (*end-of-file*) function to test whether the file pointer has reached the end of the file. For example:

```
type
  StringType = string[80];


var
  MyFile: Text;
  StringArray: array[1..100] of StringType;
  ArrayPtr: word;


  ArrayPtr := 1;            {point to start of string array}
  Assign(MyFile,'C:\AUTOEXEC.BAT');  {set up the file vari-
able}
  Reset(MyFile);           {open the file}
  While not EOF(MyFile) do {while still data in the file...}
  begin
    Readln(MyFile,StringArray[ArrayPtr]);
    ArrayPtr := ArrayPtr + 1;
  end;
```

C

After a file has been opened by *fopen* as a text file, you can use *fscanf* to read data elements from the file. *Fscanf* works just like the *scanf* function that reads keyboard input, except that its first parameter is the variable under which the file was opened. The *feof* function reports when the end-of-file has been reached. The following example reads strings from a file and displays them.

```
FILE *the_file;
char string_holder[200];
```

```
the_file=fopen("C:\\UTIL\\SOMEFILE.TXT","r+t");
 if(the_file == NULL) printf("Couldn't open the file");
     while(! feof(the_file)) {
     fscanf(the_file,"%s",&string_holder);
     printf("%s\n",&string_holder);
}
  fclose(the_file);
```

Assembler

Function 3Fh of interrupt 21h can read data from a file sequentially. This function is used for all file reading done via file handles, including random access files. The file is opened by function 3Dh of interrupt 21h, with the code number 0 placed in AL for reading only, or 2 for reading and writing. When opened, the file pointer is automatically set to the first byte of the file. The function that reads from the file specifies how many bytes to read, and once that is done the file pointer points to the byte following the last byte read, ready for the next call to the function. Note that the file pointer is unique to the file — operations on other files do not affect its position.

A program may set up a small data transfer buffer, say of 512 bytes, and repeatedly call the read function without attending to the position of the file pointer. Alternatively, a program may in one stroke transfer the entire file directly to the place in memory where it is to reside. In the latter case it is possible to request that the function read more bytes than there are in the file, since reading stops after the last byte of the file. However, it is better to calculate the exact file length so that you know where the data stop in the buffer into which it is read.

Find the file size by moving the file pointer to the end of the file. This is done right after the file is opened, when the file pointer is set to the beginning of the file. Place the code number 2 in AL and call function 42h to move the pointer to the end of the file. Put 0 in both CX and DX, which otherwise would offset the pointer from the end-of-file position by whatever value they hold. On return from this function, DX:AX contains the new position of the pointer as an offset from the start of the file — that is, it contains the file length. Be sure to reset the pointer to the beginning of the file before starting to read; this is done in exactly the same way, except that AL is given 0. If an error occurs in function 42h, the carry flag is set and AX returns 1 if the function number was invalid and 6 if the handle was invalid.

Now the program is ready to read from the file. Put the file handle in BX and the number of bytes to read in CX, then execute the interrupt. On return, AX holds the number of bytes actually read. If AX is 0, then the end of the file has been overrun. For other errors, the carry flag is set to 1 and AX holds 5 if there was a hardware error and 6 if the handle was invalid. The following example reads an entire short file into a memory buffer. For convenience, the buffer is set up in the data segment, which significantly increases the size of the program on disk. It is better for your programs to create the buffer dynamically using the memory allocation techniques discussed in Chapter 3, "Allocate/Deallocate Conventional Memory."

```
;---IN THE DATA SEGMENT:
    PATH        DB  'A:FILENAME.EXT",0  ;directory path string
    DATA_BUFFER DB  1000 DUP(?)         ;buffer
    HANDLE      DW  ?                    ;stores file handle
    FILESIZE    DW  ?                    ;stores file size
;---OPEN THE FILE:
    lea  dx,PATH            ;point DS:DX to directory path
    mov  al,0               ;code to open file for reading
    mov  ah,3Dh             ;function to open file
    int  21h               ;open the file
    jc   OPEN_ERROR         ;go to error routine if carry
    mov  HANDLE,ax          ;make copy of the handle
;---SET FILE POINTER TO END OF FILE:
    mov  ah,42h             ;function to set pointer
    mov  AL,2               ;code for end of file
    mov  bx,HANDLE          ;file handle in BX
    mov  cx,0               ;offset in CX:DX is 0
    mov  dx,0               ;
    int  21h               ;set pointer, DX:AX returns position
    jc   POINTER_ERROR1     ;go to error routine if problem
    mov  FILESIZE,ax        ;store file size (assume < 64K)
```

```
;---RESET FILE POINTER TO START OF FILE:
    mov    ah,42h              ;restore function number
    mov    al,0                ;code for start of file
    mov    cx,0                ;restore CX and DX to 0
    mov    dx,0                ;
    int    21h                 ;set the pointer
    jc     POINTER_ERROR2      ;go to error routine if problem
;---READ THE ENTIRE FILE:
    mov    ah,3Fh              ;function number to read from a
                               ;file
    mov    bx,HANDLE           ;put file handle in BX
    mov    cx,FILESIZE         ;number of bytes to read
    lea    dx,DATA_BUFFER      ;DS:DX points to buffer
    int    21h                 ;read the file
    jc     READ_ERROR          ;go to error routine if problem
;---LATER, CLOSE THE HANDLE:
    mov    bx,HANDLE           ;handle in BX
    mov    ah,3Eh              ;function to close handle
    int    21h                 ;close it
    jc     CLOSE_ERROR         ;check for error
```

Write to Random Access Files

Random access files are not physically different from sequential files; they differ only in the way they arrange data. Random access files assume that all data is organized in records of a fixed size, so that the position of any record of data can be calculated (sequential files must find the nth data element by counting the delimiters between the elements, starting from the beginning of the file). A program calculates a record's position in a file and sets the file pointer to that point. Then a specified number of bytes are read or written. Thereafter, the file pointer is automatically moved to the file position immediately following the last byte that was read or written. For this reason, there is no need to manipulate the pointer when records are accessed in sequence.

Compiler functions may buffer accesses to random access files, and records may lie across sector boundaries on disk. Both of these factors can slow access to individual records. For high performance, sometimes it's better to read in blocks of records — perhaps the entire file — and then calculate the offsets of individual records in memory.

BASIC

"Create, Open, and Close Files," above, explains the format for opening a random access file in BASIC. Unlike sequential files, a single random access file may be read and written to at the same time, without closing and reopening the file in between. The OPEN statement ends with a number giving the size of one record of the file. For example:

```
OPEN "R",1,"NEWDATA",20
```

sets the record size to 20 bytes in the file NEWDATA (opened in file buffer #1).

Once the file is opened, the records can be partitioned into their component variables using a FIELD statement. A FIELD statement tells how many bytes of the record are given to each variable. For example, a 20-byte record might be divided up as:

```
FIELD 1,14 AS LASTNAME$,2 AS DEPOSIT$,4 AS ACCTNUM$
```

In this statement, the initial number 1 indicates that the FIELD statement is defining the layout for the records of the file opened as number #1. The data is placed in the record in exactly the same order as the FIELD statement records it. The RSET and LSET statements move data into the fields, fitting each item against either the right (RSET) or left (LSET) end of the field, and padding unused room (if any) with space characters. For example, in the 14-byte field that is tagged LASTNAME$, the name "SMITH" is inserted by **RSET LASTNAME$="SMITH"**, or, if N$ is given the value "SMITH", then **RSET LASTNAME$=N$**. LSET could as easily be used as RSET. When the data is later

387

read from the field into a variable, the variable is given all 14 characters. If RSET has been used, the program would have to delete the extra spaces from the left of the string variable, but if LSET had been used the excess spaces would be on the right.

Note that all of the variable names in a FIELD statement are for strings. In random access files BASIC treats all variables — numbers included — as strings. A numeric variable must be "converted" to a special form before it is set into its field, and it must be "reconverted" when it is later read back. The word "converted" is written in quotes because BASIC does not actually change the number from the way that it is represented in memory; it just treats the number in a special way. Numeric fields in a FIELD statement require two bytes for integers, four for single-precision numbers, and eight for double-precision numbers — the same number of bytes that these values require in memory. To convert them to "string form," use the MKI\$, MKS\$, and MKD\$ functions, which make the numeric-to-string conversion for variables of integer-, single-, and double-precision type, respectively. Normally, these functions are combined with an RSET or LSET statement, as in **RSET ACCTNUM\$=MKI(X)**, where X is an integer variable if ACCTNUM\$ has been allotted only two bytes in a field statement.

Once all fields have been filled by RSET and LSET statements, the record is written to disk using PUT#. **PUT#1,245** places the data in record number 245 of the file that has been opened as #1. The record number may be omitted, in which case the data is written to the record number that is 1 greater than the last record written to (beginning with record 1). The entire record is written over, even if all fields have not been filled with data. Note that the fields in the buffer are not cleared after a PUT operation, so a data item such as the current date needs to be RSET into the buffer only once, and thereafter it will be written to all records that are accessed in that session. THE LOC function returns the number of the last record written to. If the file is opened under buffer #3, write **X=LOC(3)**.

The LOF (length of file) function returns the length of a file in bytes. Divide this number by the record size in order to determine the number of records contained in the file. Adding 1 to this value gives the record number to use in order to *append* new records to a file. If the file is opened through buffer #2 with a 32-byte record size, write;

```
RECORDNUM=LOF(2)/32+1
```

The following example opens a random access file with a 24-byte record size, and partitions the record into three variables. The program user is prompted for the data for each field, and when it is complete, the record is appended to the file. Line 120 calculates the initial record number. Note that the data may not be physically written to the disk each time a record is PUT. Several records may accumulate in the output buffer before this is done.

```
OPEN "R",1,"A:NEWDATA.DAT",24     'open #1 with 24-byte records

FIELD 1,18 AS LASTNAME$,2 AS
AGE$,4 AS WEIGHT$                 'define records

R=LOF(1)/24+1                     'number of last record + 1

GETDATA                           'clear screen for messages

INPUT"Enter name: ",N$            'get the name (string
                                   variable)

INPUT"Enter age: ",A%             'get the age (integer)

INPUT"Enter weight: ",W!          'get the weight
                                   (single-precision)

RSET LASTNAME$=N$                 'place name in field

RSET AGE$=MKI$(A%)                'place age in field

RSET WEIGHT$=MKS$(W!)             'place weight in field

PUT #1,R                          'write the record

R=R+1                             'point to next record for
                                   next time

PRINT:PRINT"Do another y/n?"      'query user

DO

LOOP WHILE INKEY$=""              'wait for response

IF C$="y" or C$="Y" THEN GOTO GETDATA
                                  'if yes, go do another

CLOSE                             'otherwise close the file
```

Pascal

Use Pascal's *Write* procedure to write individual data items, or whole records, into a file. The expression:

```
Write(MyFile,TheInteger);
```

Writes *TheInteger* into the file that was opened as *MyFile*. For typed files, a single *Write* statement can transfer an entire record into a file. This example assumes that the data elements in the record *ARecord* have been filled with values that are to be written into a file:

```
type
  FileRecord = record
```

389

```
      name: string[80];
      age: byte;
      weight: integer;
    end;


  var

    TheFile: File of FileRecord;
    ARecord: FileRecord;


  Assign(TheFile,'C:\ACCOUNTS\SOMEDATA');
  Reset(TheFile);
  Write(TheFile,ARecord);
```

In this case, only one instance of *FileRecord* is declared in memory. You do not need an array of these records to parallel those in the file. Instead, a program can manipulate the file pointer to direct the single record to any position in the file. This is done by the *Seek* procedure. It takes two parameters: first, a file variable, and then the desired file position expressed in bytes:

```
  Seek(TheFile,800);
```

To move the pointer to the end of the file, write:

```
  Seek(TheFile,FileSize(TheFile));
```

The *FilePos* function returns the current file pointer position:

```
  CurrentPosition := FilePos(TheFile);
```

When many records are stored in memory at once, the best way to write them to a file is by the *BlockWrite* procedure. It writes a given number of bytes to a file, taking them from a buffer you specify. The function takes four parameters, the first of which is the file variable under which the untyped file was opened. Next is a pointer to the buffer from which the data is taken, and then comes a count of how many bytes should be transferred (65,535 bytes, maximum). The last, optional parameter is a *word* variable in which the procedure reports the number of bytes actually written. An error has occurred when this value does not match the number specified. The following example writes out 8,000 bytes from the buffer *TheData*:

```
  BlockWrite(TheFile,TheData,8000,TheResult);
```

See "Read from Random Access Files," below, for a full example.

C

Once a stream has been opened in binary mode for writing (as shown in "Create Open, and Close Files," above), use the *fseek* function to move the file pointer to the appropriate position. It takes three parameters, the first of which is the file pointer associated with the stream (*the_file* in the examples below). The second parameter, a *long* value, gives the offset in bytes at which the file pointer should be positioned. And the third parameter specifies the point in the file from which the offset should be made. It is 0 for the beginning of the file, 1 for the current pointer position, and 2 for the end-of-file. To move to an offset 3,000 bytes from the start of the file, write:

```
fseek(the_file,3000,0);
```

You can learn the current pointer position by calling *ftell*, which returns a *long* value giving the offset from the start of the file:

```
current_offset = ftell(the_file);
```

Then use *fprintf* to write data elements in the file. For example, to write an integer into the file opened as *the_file:*

```
fprintf(the_file,"%d",the_integer);
```

It is convenient to use the *putc* function to write single characters in a file. To write the character *the_char* to the file opened as *the_file*, you would write:

```
putc(the_char,the_file);
```

When a file has been opened for unbuffer I/O using the *open* function (discussed in "Create, Open, and Close Files, above), write to the file using *write*. This function takes three parameters, the first of which is the handle returned by *open* and used to identify the file. The second parameter is a pointer to the data that will be written, and the third is an unsigned integer telling how many bytes to write:

```
write(the_file,&the_data,1024);   /* write two sectors of data */
```

Assembler

Working in assembly language, your program must calculate the location in the file at which any particular record begins and set the file pointer to it. The file pointer is positioned using function 42h of interrupt 21h. Place the file handle in BX and the offset in the file into CX:DX (CX contains the high part of the value). Then put a code number from 0 - 2 in AL. When 0, the pointer is moved to an offset that is CX:DX bytes from the beginning of the file; if 1, the offset is to the point CX:DX bytes higher than the current offset; and if 2, the pointer is moved to the end of the file *plus* the offset (that is, it extends the file). Negative numbers are not allowed for relative offsets. On return DX:AX contains the new pointer location (with DX as the high part of the value). If the carry flag is set to 1, an error has occurred. AX will contain 1 if the code number in AL was invalid, or 6 if the handle was invalid.

Once the file pointer is positioned, a random record is written using the same function used for sequential files, 40h of interrupt 21h. On entry, BX contains the file handle and CX tells how many bytes to write. DS:DX points to the first byte of the data to be written. Upon return, AX holds the number of bytes actually written. If it differs from the number placed in CX, the disk is probably full. As usual, the carry flag is set to 1 if there has been an error. In that case, AX contains 5 if there has been a disk drive problem, and 6 if the file handle was invalid.

The file pointer can be moved around to access particular parts of the data. By carefully manipulating the file pointer in random access file operations, the contents of a particular field of a particular record can singly be taken from the disk and deposited precisely where required in memory.

```
;---IN THE DATA SEGMENT:

    HANDLE        DW   ?              ;stores file handle

    FILEPATH      DB 'A:NEWDATA',0  ;directory path string

    RECORD_BUFFER DB 30 DUP (?)      ;holds record ready for
                                      output


;---OPEN THE FILE:

        mov  ah,3Dh          ;function number

        mov  al,1            ;code to open file for writing

        lea  dx,FILEPATH     ;point DS:DX to path string

        int  21h            ;open the file

        jc   OPEN_ERROR      ;go to error routine if carry flag set

        mov  HANDLE,ax       ;keep copy of file handle

;---CALCULATE THE RECORD POSITION AND SET FILE POINTER:

        mov  ax,30          ;record size is 30 byte

        mov  cx,54          ;write record #54 (55th record)

        mul  cx             ;now DX:AX has record offset

        mov  cx,dx          ;move high word of offset to DX
```

```
        mov   dx,ax                ;move low word of offset to CX
        mov   al,0                 ;sets pointer to start of file
        mov   ah,42h               ;function to set file pointer
        mov   bx,HANDLE            ;handle in BX
        int   21h                  ;set the pointer
        jc    POINTER_ERROR        ;go to error routine if carry flag set
;---WRITE THE RECORD:
        mov   ah,40h               ;function number
        mov   bx,HANDLE            ;file handle in BX
        mov   cx,30                ;record size
        lea   dx,RECORD_BUFFER     ;DS:DX points to record buffer
        int   21h                  ;write the record
        jc    WRITE_ERROR          ;go to error routine if carry flag set
```

Read from Random Access Files

The previous section, "Write to Random Access Files," explains how random access files are written. This section continues the discussion, showing how random access files are read. Reading random access files reverses the process of writing them. You should be familiar with the material in the previous section before consulting the information here.

BASIC

To read a random access file, open it and define the record fields just as was explained for writing random access files. Then use GET# to read a particular record from disk. **GET#1,23** reads record number 23 from the file opened under buffer #1. When the record is read, the variables named in the FIELD statement are automatically given the corresponding values in the record. For example, if the FIELD statement is **FIELD 1,20 AS X\$,2 AS Y\$**, then after the statement **GET#1,23** is executed, X\$ will hold the string in the first 20 bytes of record 23 and Y\$ will hold the second ten bytes. There are no statements corresponding to RSET and LSET that must be used to remove the data from their fields.

In the case of numeric data, recall that they had to be converted to string form using MKI\$, MKI\$, or MKD\$. To reassign these values to proper numeric variables so that they may be manipulated or printed, reconvert them using the corresponding functions CVI, CVS, CVD. If Y\$ holds an integer, then write Y%=CVI(Y\$) and the reconversion is made, with Y% holding the original value of the variable before it was specially processed for random access files. If you were to display the string value of the variable, you would find a number between 0 and 65,535 encoded as two ASCII characters.

This example opens the file created by the example in "Write to Random Access Files," above and displays the data found in any record requested:

```
OPEN "A:NEWDATA" AS 1 LEN=24      'open the file

FIELD 1,18 AS LASTNAME$,
2 AS AGE$, 4 AS WEIGHT$           'partition the records
GET_NEXT:
CLS:INPUT"What is the
record number";R                  'request a record number

IF R*24 > LOF(1) THEN

  BEEP

  PRINT"No such record"
```

```
      GOTO GETNEXT'past end of file?
ENDIF
GET #1,R                             'get the record
PRINT LASTNAME$,CVI(AGE$),
CVS(WEIGHT$)                         'print the data
PRINT:PRINT"Do another y/n?"         'request another?
C$=INKEY$:IF C$="" THEN 170          'loop until keystroke
IF C$="y" OR C$="Y" THEN 120         'go get another if
                                     requested

CLOSE                                'else close the file
```

Pascal

Pascal's *Read* procedure reads data records just as *Write* writes records, as shown in the previous section. This example parallels the one found there:

```
type
  FileRecord = record
    name: string[80];
    age: byte;
    weight: integer;
  end;

var
  TheFile: File of FileRecord;
  ARecord: FileRecord;

Assign(TheFile,'C:\ACCOUNTS\SOMEDATA');
Reset(TheFile);
Read(TheFile,ARecord);
Writeln('The name is ',ARecord.name);
```

For very fast random access operations, a program can use the *BlockRead* procedure. It transfers a specified block of data from a file to memory. A program can then use pointers to access individual records within the mass of data. The procedure requires four parameters. The first is the file variable. Next is a pointer to the buffer where the data will be deposited. Then comes a *word* value that tells how much data to transfer; it must not exceed 65,535 bytes. Finally, the (optional) fourth parameter is a *word* variable in which the procedure reports how many bytes it succeeded in transferring. By monitoring this parameter, you can detect the end of the file, and can learn how much data was in the final block. Note that, when a succession of calls to *BlockRead* are used to read a long file into memory, the value for the second parameter (the address of the buffer) must be changed with each call so that it points to the place in memory where the next block should be placed. This example transfers 512 bytes (data transfers along disk sector boundaries are especially fast):

```
var

   TheBuffer:  array[1..512] of byte;

   TheFile:    File;

   Result:     Word;


Assign(TheFile, 'C:\ACCOUNTS\SOMEDATA');

Reset(TheFile);

BlockRead(TheFile,TheBuffer,512,Result);
```

C

Aftera stream has been opened in binary mode for reading (as discussed in "Create, Open, and Close Files," above), use the *fseek* function to move the file pointer to the appropriate position. This function is discussed in "Write to Random Access Files," above. To move to the position 1,000 bytes from the start of the file, you would write:

```
fseek(the_file,1000,0);
```

Then use *fscanf* to read data elements in the file. For example, to read an integer from the file opened as *the_file*, write:

```
fscanf(the_file,"%d",the_integer);
```

For reading single characters, it's faster to use the *getc* function. To read the character *the_char* from the file opened as *the_file*, you would write:

```
the_char = getc(the_file);
```

When a file has been opened for unbuffer I/O using the *open* function (discussed in "Create, Open, and Close Files"), you can read from the file using *read*. Like its companion function *write, read* takes three parameters, the first of which is the handle returned by *open* and used to identify the file. The second parameter is a pointer to a buffer where the data will be written, and the third is an unsigned integer telling how many bytes to read:

```
read(the_file,&the_data,1024);  /* read two sectors of
data */
```

Assembler

"Write to Random Access Files," above, shows how to *write* random access records using file handles. Set up a random-read routine in exactly the same way, calculating the offset in the file to which to direct the file pointer. Point DS:DX to a buffer into which the record is to be deposited, then execute function 3Fh of interrupt 21h. On entry, CX contains the record size, and BX holds the file handle.

```
;---IN THE DATA SEGMENT:

HANDLE        db   ?               ;stores file handle

FILEPATH      db   'A:OLDDATA',0   ;directory path string

RECORD_BUFFER db   30 dup (?)      ;buffer for 1 record

;---OPEN THE FILE:

      mov  ah,3Dh            ;function number

      mov  al,0              ;code to open file for reading

      lea  dx,FILEPATH       ;point DS:DX to path string

      int  21h              ;open the file

      jc   OPEN_ERROR        ;go to error routine if carry set

      mov  HANDLE,ax         ;keep copy of file handle

;---CALCULATE THE RECORD POSITION AND SET THE FILE POINTER:

      mov  ax,30            ;record size is 30 bytes

      mov  cx,54            ;write record #54 (55th record)

      mul  cx               ;now DX:AX has record offset

      mov  cx,dx            ;move high word of offset to DX

      mov  dx,ax            ;move low word of offset to CX

      mov  AL,0             ;sets pointer to start of file

      mov  ah,42h           ;function to set file pointer
```

397

```
        mov   bx,HANDLE        ;handle in BX
        int   21h              ;set the pointer
        jc    POINTER_ERROR    ;go to error routine if carry set
;---READ A RECORD:
        mov   ah,3Fh           ;function number
        mov   bx,HANDLE        ;handle in BX
        mov   cx,30            ;record size
        lea   dx,DATA_BUFFER   ;DS:DX points to record buffer
        int   21h              ;write the record
        jc    READ_ERROR       ;go to error routine if carry set
;---LATER, CLOSE THE HANDLE:
        mov   bx,HANDLE        ;handle in BX
        mov   ah,3Eh           ;function to close handle
        int   21h              ;close it
        jc    CLOSE_ERROR      ;check for error
```

Verify Data After Write Operations

DOS can verify the accuracy of disk data transfers when data is written. Errors occur so seldom that the verification measure ought ordinarily to be avoided, since it slows down disk I/O. But a program can switch on verification when it is required.

BASIC

BASIC does not provide a way of changing or monitoring verification status. Instead, use BASIC's *Interrupt* statement to call function &H2E of interrupt 21h. Place 0 ("on") or 1 ("off") in AL, and the subfunction number 0 in DL, and call the interrupt. To determine the current status, place 1 in DL instead, and the function returns the status in AL.

```
' $INCLUDE: 'QBX.BI'

DIM REGS AS RegType       'Define register array


REGS.AX = &H2E01          'function &H2E, status = &H01
REGS.DX = &H0000          'function to set verification
CALL Interrupt(&H21, REGS, REGS)   'turn verification on
```

Pascal

Turbo Pascal sets verification by its *SetVerify* procedure. To turn on verification, write:

```
SetVerify(TRUE);
```

Use *GetVerify* to find out the current verification setting. This function's only parameter is a *Boolean* variable in which it deposits the result:

```
var

   VerificationStatus: Boolean;


   GetVerify(VerificationStatus);
```

C

The Borland compilers provide the *setverify* and *getverify* functions for setting and determining the verification status. In these functions, 0 indicates that verification is "off," and 1 indicates that it is "on." Here are examples:

```
setverify(1);       /* turn verification on */


if (getverify()) printf("Verification is ON");
```

The Microsoft compilers do not provide corresponding functions. Instead, use function 0x2E of interrupt 21h to modify the verification status. Place 1 ("on") or 0 ("off") in AL, and the subfunction number 0 in DL, and call the interrupt. When you place 1 in DL instead, the function returns the current status in AL.

```
#include <dos.h>
union REGS regs;           /* declare the register array */


regs.h.ah = 0x2E;
regs.h.al = 1;
regs.h.dl = 0;
int86(0x21,&regs,&regs); /* turn verification on */
```

Assembler

Function 2Eh of interrupt 21h switches verification on and off. Place 1 in AL for "on" and 0 in AL for "off." Also put 0 in DL. Then execute the interrupt. There are no result registers.

```
;---TURN ON VERIFICATION:
        mov   al,1            ;code number
        mov   dl,0            ;required input register
        mov   ah,2Eh          ;function number
        int   21h            ;complete
```

To find out the current verification setting, call function 54h of interrupt 21h. There are no input registers. On return, AL holds 1 if vertification is "on," and 0 if it is "off."

13

Controlling Video Hardware

- Minitutorial: Controlling Video Hardware
- Program a Video Controller Chip
- Set/Check the Screen Display Mode
- Set the Screen Background or Border Color
- Clear All/Part of the Screen
- Scroll a Text Screen
- Switch Between Video Pages
- Set or Find the Cursor Position
- Turn the Cursor On/Off
- Change the Cursor Shape

Minitutorial: Controlling Video Hardware

All major PC video systems are centered upon the Motorola 6845 CRTC (cathode ray tube controller) chip, or on custom chips that share many of the 6845's features. This is necessarily the case, because IBM has preserved most video modes and features from one generation to the next. The 6845 manages a number of technical tasks that are not ordinarily of concern to programmers. But the chip also sets the screen mode, generates and controls the cursor, and manages color. Many of these features are easy to program directly, although operating system routines can handle most operations.

All video systems use buffers in which the data for the screen image is mapped. The screen is periodically updated by scanning this data. In text modes, the buffers begin with the data for the top row of the screen, starting from the left side. The succession of data wraps around from the right end of one row to the left end of the next, as if the screen were really only one very long row.

For an 80-column by 25-row text display, 4,000 bytes are allocated so that there are two bytes for each of the 2,000 screen positions (25 x 80).

The first byte holds the ASCII code of the symbol displayed. Video circuitry converts the ASCII code number to its associated symbol and sends it to the screen. The second byte (the *attribute byte*) holds information about how the character is to appear. In monochrome modes, the attribute byte sets whether the character is shown underlined, intensified, in reverse-image, or as a combination of these attributes. In color modes, the attribute byte sets the foreground and background colors of a character. In all cases, your programs may write data directly to the buffer, a practice that speeds up screen operations considerably.

Graphics modes are more complicated. A certain amount of memory is allocated to every pixel. In a monochrome mode, each pixel uses only one bit in the video buffer, so that a byte of data represents eight pixels. A 16-color scheme takes four bits per pixel, allowing two pixels per byte. A whole byte per pixel is required for 256-color modes.

Graphics data is not generally laid out in memory in so simple a fashion as text data. In CGA modes, alternate display lines are kept in nonadjacent parts of video memory. Likewise, the HGC 720 x 348 2-color mode divides the video buffer into four parts. The more advanced EGA and VGA modes make matters more complicated by setting up a system of *bit planes*. Bit planes are ranges of memory addresses that hold video data. There is one bit plane for each bit needed to hold the data for a pixel. For example, when each pixel requires four bits of data (in 16-color modes), four bytes are maintained at each memory address, with one of the four bits of each pixel residing in each byte. When software writes data to a particular video memory address, it can specify the plane to which the data is directed by manipulating ports on the video hardware.

Bit planes are necessary because, as video systems move to ever higher resolutions supporting more simultaneous colors, more and more memory is needed to hold a single video image. A 256-color 480-by-640 graphics mode requires roughly a third or a megabyte of storage. There is no room within the 1-megabyte real mode address space for a buffer this large. In fact, the PC architecture requires that video buffers be confined to the space between A000 and C000. For this reason, advanced SuperVGA cards employ page switching facilities not unlike those used for expanded memory.

Because some video system modes require much less memory than others, extra video memory may be available for paging. In paging, two or more screens of information are kept in the video buffer at the same time, and a program can decide which to display. Paging is supported in all video systems except a true monochrome display adapter, which contains only enough memory for one character screen. Paging is particularly useful for constructing time-consuming screens out of view; once finished, the screen may be displayed instantly.

One other concern is the cursor. The cursor is generated by video hardware for use in text modes. A hardware-assisted cursor is convenient, because programmers do not need to worry about the cursor overwriting screen data as it is moved around. Software must create its own cursor when working in graphics modes, and this can entail a lot of work.

In text modes, the cursor serves two functions. First, it acts as a pointer to the place on the screen to which program statements send their characters. Second, it provides a visible reference point on the screen for the program user. Only in the latter case does the cursor actually need to be visible. When the cursor is invisible ("turned off"), it still points to a screen position and can be used by video output routines. It's easy to change the cursor's shape. Doing so is a good way of indicating to a program user that a program has entered a particular mode, such as "insert" mode in text editing.

Program a Video Controller Chip

The 6845 video controller chip upon which all IBM video systems are ultimately based has 18 control registers, numbered 0 – 17. The first ten registers fix the horizontal and vertical display parameters. These generally are of no concern to programmers, since the values in the registers are automatically adjusted by the BIOS when the screen mode is changed. It is unwise to experiment with these registers since there is a possibility of damage to the video monitor. The registers are eight bits long, and some are paired to hold 16-bit values. Registers 10 & 11 and 14 & 15 set the shape and location of the cursor. Numbers 12 & 13 handle paging. And numbers 16 & 17 report the light pen position. On early versions of the chip, most registers are write-only; only the cursor address register is read/write, and only the light pen register is read-only. The EGA and VGA have additional registers that are devoted to advanced features.

All registers in the sequence are accessed by the same port address, which is 3B5h on an MDA or HGC, 3D5h on a CGA, and either of these on an EGA or VGA, depending on the screen mode. To write to a register on an MDA, an address register located at port 3B4h (3D4h CGA) must first be sent the number of the desired register. Then the next byte sent to port address 3B5h will be directed to that particular register. Since the registers that concern programmers are used in pairs, you must first write to the address register, then to one register, then again to the address register, and then to the second register. Because the port numbers are adjacent, it is easiest to address them using INC and DEC, as in the following example:

```
;---WRITE TO 6845 REGISTERS 11 & 12 (DATA IS IN BX):
     ;---SELECT THE LOW-BYTE REGISTER:
     mov  dx,3B4h    ;port address of the address register
     mov  al,11      ;select the register for the low byte
     out  dx,al      ;output to 3B5h goes to #11
     ;---SEND THE BYTE:
     inc  dx         ;increase port address to 3B5h
     mov  al,bl      ;put low byte in AL
     out  dx,al      ;put low byte in register #11
     ;---SELECT THE HIGH-BYTE REGISTER:
     dec  dx         ;reset port address to 3B4h
     mov  al,12      ;select the register for the high byte
     out  dx,al      ;now output to 3B5h goes to #12
```

```
;---SEND THE BYTE:
inc  dx          ;again increase port address to 3B5h
mov  al,bh       ;put high byte in AL
out  dx,al       ;now second byte is in place
```

Set/Check the Screen Display Mode

Every new video standard has added more video modes to the repertoire. The BIOS keeps a one-byte variable at 0040:0049 that holds the current mode number. On some — but not all — machines, the byte at 0040:004A gives the number of columns in text modes. Figure 13-1 summarizes the video modes:

Mode	Type	Resolution	Colors	Buffer	MDA	CGA	EGA	MCGA	VGA
0	Alpha	40x25 chars	16	B800		x	x	x	x
1	Alpha	40x25 chars	16	B800		x	x	x	x
2	Alpha	80x25 chars	16	B800		x	x	x	x
3	Alpha	80x25 chars	16	B800		x	x	x	x
4	Graphics	320x200	4	B800		x	x	x	x
5	Graphics	320x200	4	B800		x	x	x	x
6	Graphics	640x200	2	B800		x	x	x	x
7	Alpha	80x25 chars	2	B000	x		x	x	
D	Graphics	320x200	16	A000			x		x
E	Graphics	640x200	16	A000			x		x
F	Graphics	640x350	2	A000			x		x
10	Graphics	640x350	4/16	A000			x		x
11	Graphics	640x480	2	A000				x	x
12	Graphics	640x480	16	A000					x
13	Graphics	320x200	256	A000				x	x

Figure 13-1   Video display modes

One common video mode is not supported by the standard video BIOS. This is the 720 x 348 monochrome graphics mode used by Hercules Graphics Cards (HGCs). To enter this mode, a program must directly address the video controller, as described in "Program a Video Controller Chip," above. Before doing this, relevant parts of the BIOS data area must also be altered. Here are the steps:

(1) Write the following 30 bytes into the BIOS data area starting at 0040:0049 (the values are hexadecimal):

```
07 00 50 80 00 00 00 00 00 00

00 00 00 00 00 00 00 00 00 00

00 00 00 00 00 00 03 B4 0A 00
```

(2) Write the value **1** to port 3BFh to set a configuration switch on the adapter. This action allows you to set the graphics mode via port 3B8h, and also disables the top half of the 64K video buffer (an entire 720-348 image fits in less than 32K).

(3) Write the value **0** to port 3B8h to blank the screen so that no interference appears while the CRT controller is programmed.

(4) Write, in sequence, the following 9 hexadecimal values to port 3B4h:

```
0035 012D 022E 0307 045B 0502 0657 0757 0903
```

These values form nine pairs for programming individual CRT controller registers, with the first byte of each pair specifying a register number.

(5) Finally, start up the new graphics mode by writing **0Ah** to port 3B8h, the mode control register.

BASIC

BASIC uses the SCREEN and WIDTH statements to control the screen mode. SCREEN alone will set a graphics mode. Just follow the command with the mode number, as in:

```
SCREEN 1
```

See the compiler documentation to learn the meaning of each mode number. All modes are initially shown in black and white. A COLOR statement (discussed in Chapter 14, "Set Character Attributes/Color") must be used to set the screen background color. In graphics modes, the color statement alone suffices to change the whole background to the specified color. But for color text screens you must follow the COLOR statement with CLS.

The WIDTH statement sets the number of columns in a text screen. WIDTH 40 gives 40 columns, and WIDTH 80 gives 80. When the WIDTH statement is used with screens set to graphics modes, a WIDTH statement can change the screen resolution.

Pascal

In Turbo Pascal, begin by finding out the value of *Detect* to determine available graphics hardware. *Detect* specifies the appropriate graphics driver:

```
uses Graph;
var
    GraphicsDriver: integer;
    GraphicsMode: integer;
GraphicsDriver := Detect;
```

Then call *InitGraph* to load and initialize the driver:

```
InitGraph(GraphicsDriver, GraphicsMode, '');
```

At this point you can change the default graphics mode to some other mode using the *SetGraphMode* procedure:

```
SetGraphMode(2);
```

Later, to restore the text mode that was in effect before the graphics mode was set, call the *RestoreCrtMode* procedure:

```
RestoreCrtMode;
```

C

In Borland C, start by declaring an integer variable and assigning to it the value of *DETECT*, which results from the compiler's search for video hardware:

```
int graphics_driver = DETECT;
```

Then call *initgraph* to load and initialize the graphics driver:

```
int graphics_mode;


initgraph(graphics_driver,graphics_mode,"");
```

The third parameter optionally specifies a path to the disk directory that holds graphics drivers. Then you can change the default graphics mode to some other one using *setgraphmode:*

```
setgraphmode(3);
```

Finally, return to the original text mode by calling *restorecrtmode:*

```
restorecrtmode;
```

Assembler

Function 0 of interrupt 10h sets the screen mode. AL holds a mode number. To set the screen to mode #4, write:

```
mov  ah,0              ;function number
mov  al,4              ;mode for medium resolution color
int  10h               ;set the mode
```

To find out the current mode, use function Fh of interrupt 10h. The interrupt returns the mode number in AL. It also gives the current page number in BH, and the number of character columns in AH.

```
mov  ah,0Fh            ;function number
int  10h               ;get the screen mode information
mov  MODE_NUMBER,al    ;mode number in AL
mov  NUMBER_COLS,ah    ;number of columns in AH
mov  CURRENT_PAGE,bh   ;current page number in BH
```

Set the Screen Background or Border Color

The border of a text screen may have a different color from the central background color. Graphics screens, on the other hand, do not technically have a border area. When the background color is set in graphics mode, the whole screen including the border area is set to that color. However, functions that draw pixels do not access the border area; if most addressable pixels are changed to a nonbackground color, a border region is effectively created.

For CGA screen modes, the background color may be set by subfunction 0 of function Bh of interrupt 10h. On entry, the subfunction number is placed in BH, and the color code number in BL. The MCGA does not generate a colored border. For EGA and VGA modes, use subfunction 1 of function 10h of INT 10h. Place 10h in AH, 1 in AL, and the color code in BH. There are no return registers.

BASIC

The third parameter of BASIC's COLOR statement sets the border color. The same color code numbers are used that are listed in Chapter 14, "Set Character Attributes/Color." For example, to set the border to light blue, write:

```
COLOR,,8
```

Pascal

This example sets CGA colors by directly calling function $B of interrupt 10h:

```
Uses DOS;

Var
  Regs: Registers; {Registers type is declared in the DOS unit}

Regs.AH := $B;      {the interrupt function number}
Regs.BH := 0;       {subfunction number}
Regs.BL := 1;       {color code}
Intr($10,Regs);     {Call the interrupt}
```

410

C

This example sets border color on a VGA:

```c
#include <dos.h>

union REGS regs;     /* declare the register array */

regs.h.ah = 0x10;    /* function number */
regs.h.al = 1;       /* subfunction number */
regs.h.bh = 7;       /* color code */
int86(0x10,&regs,&regs);
```

Assembler

```asm
;---SET EGA or VGA border color:
        mov   ah,10h      ;function number
        mov   al,1        ;subfunction
        mov   bh,3        ;the color code
        int   10h         ;set the border
```

Low-Level Access

On a CGA, bits 0–3 of port 3D9h (the "Color Select Register") set the border color when the screen is in a text mode. As usual, the ascending order of the bits is *blue, green, red,* and *high intensity.* Because it is a write-only address, another bit in this register must also be set at the same time. This is bit 4, which when set causes all background colors to be displayed in high intensity.

```asm
;---SET THE BORDER COLOR TO LIGHT BLUE:
        mov   al,00001001b    ;bit pattern for light blue
        mov   dx,3D9h         ;address of color select register
        out   dx,al          ;set the border color
```

The border color on an EGA or VGA is set by the *overscan register.* This register is number 11h at port address 3C0h. First *read* port 3DAh to toggle the port to its address register, then send 11h to 3C0h as an index, and then send the data. The number of significant bits depends on the screen mode.

Clear All/Part of the Screen

Clearing the screen is merely a matter of writing the same value again and again in all or part of a video buffer. In graphics modes, sometimes the easiest way to clear the screen is to reinitialize the video mode. In text modes, you can clear the screen by functions 6 or 7 of interrupt 10h, which are designed to scroll the screen. On entry to these functions, the number of lines to scroll is placed in AL, and the screen is cleared when this value is 0. Because the functions can scroll any part of the screen, they may also be used to clear a window. CH is given the window's top row, DH the bottom row, CL the left column, and DL the right column. The coordinates are numbered from 0. In addition, the attribute in which the screen is to be cleared is placed in BH.

BASIC

BASIC provides the *CLS* statement to clear the whole screen:

```
CLS
```

When a *viewport* has been defined, *CLS* clears only that area.

Pascal

Turbo Pascal's *ClrScr* procedure clears the entire screen, or the current window defined by a *Window* procedure. For example:

```
Window(5,5,30,50);

ClrScr;
```

C

Borland C provides the *clrscr* function to clear the screen, or an active window defined by the *window* function:

```
clrscr();
```

In Microsoft C, the *_clearscreen* function clears graphics screens. It takes one parameter that defines what part of the screen to clear. The parameter is a constant defined in *GRAPH.H* that may be **_GCLEARSCREEN, _GVIEWPORT,** and **_GWINDOW**. For example:

```
_clearscreen(_GCLEARSCREEN);
```

Assembler

One way to clear a text screen using operating system functions is to call a routine that scrolls the screen. Function 6 of interrupt 10h does this. You must specify what area should be scrolled, and the number of lines to scroll. When the number of lines is zero, the area is cleared:

```
;---CLEAR THE WINDOW BETWEEN 3,4 AND 13,15:
        mov    ah,6        ;use a scroll routine
        mov    al,0        ;set number of rows to scroll to 0
        mov    bh,7        ;attribute byte for fill
        mov    ch,3        ;top left row
        mov    cl,4        ;top right col
        mov    dh,13       ;bottom right row
        mov    dl,15       ;bottom right column
        int    10h         ;clear the window
```

Another approach is to use function 9 of interrupt 10h, which writes a character and attribute as many times as CX specifies. A value of 2000 clears the screen once the cursor is set to 0,0.

```
;---SET CURSOR TO TOP LEFT CORNER OF SCREEN:
        mov    ah,2        ;function to set cursor
        mov    bh,0        ;page number
        mov    dx,0        ;coordinates are 0,0
        int    10h         ;set the cursor
;---WRITE THE SPACE CHARACTER 2000 TIMES:
        mov    ah,9        ;function number
        mov    cx,2000     ;number of times to write
        mov    al,' '      ;space character in AL
        mov    bh,0        ;page number
        mov    bl,7        ;attribute in BL
        int    10h         ;clear the screen
```

413

Scroll a Text Screen

When a text screen is scrolled upwards by one line, lines 2 through 25 are rewritten upon lines 1 through 24, and the next line of data is taken from memory and written on line 25. Downward scrolling works in like fashion.

Function 6 of INT 10h scrolls any part of the screen upwards, and function 7 scrolls it downwards. In both cases AL holds the number of lines to scroll, and when AL=0, the defined area is cleared instead of scrolled. CH:CL holds the row and column for the top left corner, and DH:DL holds the coordinates for the bottom right. The rows that are scrolled away from are cleared, and they are given the attribute code placed in BH.

Horizontal scrolling is sometimes required for special text processing, such as in program editors. The operating system has no special facilities for it. For this reason it is more complicated than vertical scrolling — but not by much. Consider the case in which you want the screen to scroll leftwards by five columns. The five columns on the left are to be overlaid, the other text is shifted leftward, and the rightmost five columns must be blanked out. Since the video buffer is one long string, if every character in it is moved towards the start of the buffer by ten bytes, the net effect is that the leftmost five characters of every line wrap around to the right edge of the line above. Thus the screen is shifted leftwards by five columns, moving the five discarded columns to the right edge of the screen. All that remains is to blank out the right edge. This is easily done with the vertical scrolling routine discussed above, which can be set up to operate on only part of the screen, and which blanks out that area when it is told to scroll by zero lines. Figure 13-2 illustrates this method.

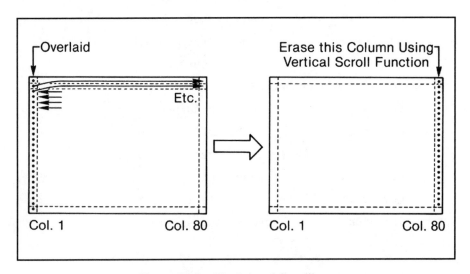

Figure 13-2   Horizontal Scrolling

The following examples all scroll an entire 25-by-80 text screen upward by five rows, using 7 as the attribute for clearing the rows.

BASIC

```
' $INCLUDE: 'QBX.BI'
DIM REGS AS RegType      ' Define register array

REGS.AX = &H0605   'scroll upward five rows
REGS.CX = 0;       'top left corner at 0,0
REGS.DX = &H184F   'bottom left at 79,24 (4F,18 in hex)
Regs.BX = &H0700   'replacement attribute in BH
CALL Interrupt(&H10, REGS, REGS)
```

Pascal

```
Uses DOS;

Var

  Regs: Registers;   {Registers type is declared in the DOS unit}

Regs.AH := 6;      {scroll upwards}
Regs.AL := 5;      {scroll five rows}
Regs.CH := 0;      {top row}
Regs.CL := 0;      {left column}
Regs.DH := 24;     {bottom row}
Regs.DL := 79;     {right column}
Regs.BH := 7;      {replacement attribute}
Intr($10,Regs);    {Call the interrupt}
```

C

```c
#include <dos.h>

union REGS regs;        /* declare the register array */

regs.h.ah = 6;          /* scroll upwards */
regs.h.al = 5;          /* scroll five rows */
regs.h.ch = 0;          /* top row */
regs.h.cl = 0;          /* left column */
regs.h.dh = 24;         /* bottom row */
regs.h.dl = 79;         /* right column */
regs.h.bh = 7;          /* replacement attribute */
int86(0x10,&regs,&regs);
```

Assembler

This example scrolls a screen upward by one line:

```
;---SCROLL UPWARDS ONE LINE:
        mov   ah,6       ;function number to scroll upwards
        mov   al,1       ;number of rows to scroll upwards
        mov   ch,0       ;coordinate of top left row
        mov   cl,0       ;coordinate of top left column
        mov   dh,24      ;coordinate of bottom right row
        mov   dl,79      ;coordinate of bottom right column
        mov   bh,7       ;attribute of cleared line
        int   10h        ;make the scroll
                         ;now fill bottom line with text...
```

Low-Level Access

Scrolling the whole screen vertically is a trivial task, since in memory the right end of one line continues at the left end of the next. Moving everything in the video buffer 160 bytes upwards in memory (80 columns x 2 bytes per character) results in scrolling the screen downwards by one line. If you write your own scroll routine using direct memory mapping, be careful of the screen interference that occurs on a CGA. This problem is discussed in Chapter 14, "Write a Single Character on the Screen." The usual solution is to keep checking a status byte until it gives the go-ahead to write data into the video buffer.

An alternate, less acceptable solution is to turn off the screen entirely during the scroll operation and then instantly restore it. To "turn the screen off" means that the projection of data from the video buffer is disabled, but the buffer itself is untouched. This process is used by the BIOS scroll routine above.

To turn the screen off on a CGA, set bit 3 at port address 3D8h to 0. Changing the bit to 1 instantly turns the screen back on. The port address is for the Mode Select Register on the CGA. This one-byte register is write-only, so a program cannot just read it, change bit 3, and then replace the byte. Rather, you must also determine the settings for the other bits of the register (they are listed in "Program a Video Controller Chip," above).

Here is an example of horizontal scrolling. In this case, the screen scrolls leftwards by five columns. It is easy to modify it to scroll rightwards as well and to move by a specified number of columns. By using direct memory mapping to shift the characters, this technique results in a practically instantaneous scroll.

```
;---SHIFT EVERYTHING DOWNWARDS BY 10 BYTES:
        mov   ax,0B000h    ;point DS and ES to monochrome buffer
        mov   es,ax        ;
        mov   ds,ax        ;
        mov   si,10        ;shift from SI...
        mov   di,0         ;...to DI
        mov   cx,1995      ;move all but 5 of 2000 characters
    rep movsw              ;make the shift
;---BLANK OUT THE RIGHT EDGE:
        mov   ah,6         ;vertical scroll function of INT 10h
        mov   al,0         ;0 lines to scroll blanks out window
        mov   ch,0         ;top left row
```

```
        mov  cl,75        ;top left column
        mov  dh,24        ;bottom right row
        mov  dl,79        ;bottom right column
        mov  bh,7         ;attribute to use for blank
        int  10h          ;clear the window
```

Switch Between Video Pages

All video systems except the MDA have enough memory to hold more than one image in certain video modes. A program can construct several screens and display whichever is required at the moment, or slow graphic fills can be carried out off-screen and then switched into view. The page currently in view is called the *visual page*. The page to which data is written is called the *active page*. The BIOS maintains a one-byte variable at 0040:0062 that tells the current visible page. There is no equivalent value for the active page; rather, the active page is a convention followed by software as it writes to the screen. High-level languages tend to be inflexible in which pages they can write to. When all else fails, a program can write to any page by memory-mapping data directly into the video buffer, adding an offset so that the data is deposited on the desired page (Chapter 14, "Write a Single Character on the Screen," discusses memory-mapping).

The number of pages possible varies by screen mode, by video system, and by how much memory is present on the video adapter. Figure 13-3 compares the various modes and standards.

Mode	MDA	HGC	CGA	EGA	MCGA	VGA
0	1	1	4/8	4/8	8	4/8
1			1	1	1	1
2			1	1	1	1
3		2				
7				8 max		8 max
8				8 max		8 max
9				8 max		8 max
A				8 max		8 max
B					1	1
C						1
D					1	1

Figure 13-3   Numbers of Video Pages

BASIC

BASIC uses the SCREEN command to set the visual and active pages. The third parameter following **SCREEN** sets the active page. For example:

```
SCREEN,,2
```

causes all PRINT or WRITE statements to write upon page 2. The fourth parameter sets the visual page. The statement:

```
SCREEN,,,1
```

causes page 1 to be the one currently shown. Taken together:

```
SCREEN,,2,1
```

writes on screen 2 while displaying screen 1. When the visual page is left unspecified, it automatically becomes the same as the active page.

Pascal

Turbo Pascal's *SetVisualPage* and *SetActivePage* procedures, respectively, determine which page is shown, and which page is operated on by screen output functions. Both procedures take only a single *word* parameter, a page number. Unfortunately, these routines are part of the *Graph* unit, and they operate only in graphics modes. To change the visual page in a text mode, use function 5 of interrupt 10h. The AL register holds the page number on entry. There are no return registers. To make page 2 the active page, write:

```
Uses DOS;


Var

   Regs: Registers;   {Registers type is declared in the DOS unit}


Regs.AH := 5;      {the interrupt function number}

Regs.AL := 2;      {page number}

Intr($10,Regs);    {change the visual page}
```

There is no BIOS function that sets the active page. Instead, all BIOS screen output routines require a page number. Because *Writeln* lacks this flexibility, paging is possible only by memory-mapping text into the appropriate memory positions.

C

Both Borland C and Microsoft C provide the *setvisualpage* and *setactivepage* functions for page switching in graphics modes. They do not operate in text modes. To set the visual page in a text mode, you must call function 5 of interrupt 10h, for which the only input value is the page number placed in AL. There are no return registers. This example makes page 1 the visual page:

```
#include <dos.h>


union REGS regs;          /* declare the register array */


regs.h.ah = 5;            /* function number */

regs.h.al = 1;            /* page number */

int86(0x10,&regs,&regs); /* change the visual page */
```

There is no corresponding function for setting the active page, since BIOS screen routines are always told which page to write on when they are called. Because the C screen output functions lack this flexibility, your program must memory-map data into the pages at the appropriate memory offsets.

Assembler

Function 5 of interrupt 10h selects the visible page. Simply place the page number in AL and call the interrupt:

```
;---SET THE VISUAL PAGE:
        mov   ah,5       ;function number
        mov   al,2       ;page number (numbered from 0)
        int   10h        ;set the page
```

This function does *not*, however, specify the active page. Any of the BIOS interrupts that write on the screen (functions of interrupt 10h) require the number of the active page as an input register. But the DOS screen interrupts all write upon the page currently in view. Thus, for "off-stage" operations you must use interrupt 10h or must memory-map data directly into the video buffer.

To *find* the current page, execute function Fh of interrupt 10h, which gives the video status. The page number is returned in BH.

Low-Level Access

Display pages are chosen by changing the point in video memory from which the monitor receives its data. The point is specified as a 16-bit segment that is placed in video controller registers 12 (high byte) and 13 (low byte). Taken together, the registers are referred to as the *start address*. Before each byte of the address is sent to port address 3D5h, the number of the register it is destined for must be sent to port address 3D4h. A succession of commands can continuously scroll a text screen between pages. The following example sets the start address to B800h.

```
        mov   bx,0B800h      ;the new start address
;
        mov   dx,3D4h        ;output to the address register
        mov   al,12          ;address register 12
        out   dx,al          ;send the request
;
        inc   dx             ;now output to the command registers
        mov   al,bh          ;high word of start address in AL
        out   dx,al          ;send it to register 12
;
        dec   dx             ;back to the address register
        mov   al,13          ;address register 13
        out   dx,al          ;send the request
;
        inc   dx             ;back to the command registers
        mov   al,bl          ;low word of start address in AL
        out   dx,al          ;send it to register 13
```

Be aware that this technique is not without its problems. If a memory-resident program is activated while hardware scrolling is in effect, it will not handle video output properly. Similarly, you must be sure to reset the register settings before quitting the program. Note that the registers can be read in EGA, MCGA, and VGA systems, but not in CGAs. This scrolling feature is not available in MDAs.

Set or Find the Cursor Position

The cursor is generated by video hardware when the hardware operates in text modes. Registers on the video controller chip set the cursor position. The BIOS maintains a cursor position for each video page and changes the cursor to the appropriate position whenever a BIOS function is used to switch pages. The cursor-control functions in high-level languages use the BIOS function, and so they work in the same way, always setting the cursor position for the current page.

The hardware cursor can only reside in one character cell. The *bar cursors* used in many programs are constructed by changing character attribute bytes. The advantage of a hardware cursor over a software-constructed one is that your programs can write on the screen without worrying about obscuring the cursor, or having the cursor change what is displayed. There is no hardware cursor when the computer works in graphics modes; if your program needs a cursor, it must construct one.

BASIC

BASIC's *LOCATE* procedure sets the cursor. It takes up to five parameters, any of which are optional. The cursor row and column are the first two parameters. This example prints a vertical line on the screen:

```
FOR N=1 TO 25      'repeat for each row
LOCATE N,40        'set cursor to row n, column 40
PRINT CHR$(186)    'print line character (no scroll)
NEXT               'next row
```

When several display pages are in use, the LOCATE statement operates on whatever page of memory is currently "active." If the page shown on the monitor is not the active page, the cursor position on the screen does not change.

Pascal

Turbo Pascal's *GotoXY* procedure sets the cursor position. It takes two *byte* parameters, first the column and then the row. To position the cursor at row 15, column 40, write:

```
GotoXY(40,15);
```

This procedure sets the cursor relative to the current window. A *Window* statement like **(Window,3,5,15,20)** will cause the cursor to be placed at coordinates relative to the top left corner of the defined window.

Use *WhereX* and *WhereY* to find out the current cursor position:

```
var CursorRow,CursorCol: byte;


CursorRow := WhereY;
CursorCol := WhereX;
```

C

Borland C provides the *gotoxy* function for positioning the cursor. It takes two integer parameters, the first being the column, and the second the row. To set the cursor to column 12 of row 5, write:

```
gotoxy(12,5);
```

This function sets the cursor relative to the current window. When the *window* function has been called to define a window, *gotoxy* will position the cursor relative to that window's upper left corner.

To find out the current cursor position in Borland C, use *wherex* and *wherey*, which return integer values giving the current cursor column and row:

```
int  cursor_row, cursor_col;


cursor_row = wherey();
cursor_col = wherex();
```

Alternatively, you must call function 2 of interrupt 10h to set the cursor, and function 3 of this interrupt to determine its position. In this function, BH must specify the video page on which the cursor should be repositioned. Normally, this is page 0. DH and DL take the row and column, respectively. This example switches the cursor to row 7, column 52 (note that screen positions are counted from 0, not 1).

```
#include <dos.h>


union REGS regs;     /* declare the register array */


regs.h.ah = 2;       /* function number */
regs.h.bh = 0;       /* video page number */
```

```
regs.h.dh = 7;              /* row (zero-based) */

regs.h.dl = 52;             /* column (zero-based) */

int86(0x10,&regs,&regs);  /* set the cursor */
```

To use function 3 to read the cursor coordinates, place the page number in BH and call the interrupt. On return, DH holds the row and DL the column:

```
regs.h.ah = 3;              /* function number */

regs.h.bh = 0;              /* video page number */

int86(0x10,&regs,&regs);  /* get cursor status information */

cursor_row = regs.h.dh;   /* row (zero-based) */

cursor_col = regs.h.dl;   /* column (zero-based) */
```

Assembler

Function 2 of interrupt 10h sets the cursor belonging to a specified page of memory. The pages are numbered from 0. DH:DL holds the row and column, which also are numbered from 0. The cursor changes its position on the screen only if the cursor setting is made for the page in view.

```
;---SET THE CURSOR TO ROW 13, COLUMN 39

        mov   ah,2           ;function number

        mov   bh,0           ;display page

        mov   dh,13          ;row

        mov   dl,39          ;col

        int   10h            ;position the cursor
```

Use function 3 of interrupt 10h to find out the cursor coordinates for any video page. The only input register is the page number (BH). On return, DH holds the row and DL holds the column:

```
;---FIND CURSOR POSITION ON VIDEO PAGE 0:

        mov   ah,3           ;function number

        mov   bh,0           ;display page

        int   10h            ;get cursor status information

        mov   CURSOR_ROW,dh  ;save the row

        mov   CURSOR_COL,dl  ;save the column
```

425

Low-Level Access

Registers on the video controller chip set the cursor position. When your program changes cursor coordinates by accessing these registers, the BIOS will continue to record the former coordinates in memory. If BIOS screen I/O functions are subsequently called, output may be directed to the old cursor position.

The cursor position is recorded as an offset into the screen. For a 25-by-80 screen, the number ranges from 0 to 1999, corresponding to the 2000 (25 * 80) character boxes. Take care not to confuse this numbering system with the 0-3999 positions in the video buffer, where each character is accompanied by an attribute byte. The high part of the 16-bit offset is written to register Eh, and the low part to register Fh. The registers may be read to find out the current cursor position.

```
;---IN THE PROGRAM:

        mov   bl,24       ;row in BL (0-24)

        mov   bh,79       ;column in BH (0-79)

        call  SET_CURSOR  ;go set the cursor position


;---PROCEDURE TO SET THE CURSOR:

SET_CURSOR    PROC

    ;REQUEST ACCESS TO LOW BYTE REGISTER:

        mov   dx,3B4h     ;port number for 6845 address register

        mov   al,Fh       ;select register Fh

        out   dx,al       ; send the request

    ;CALCULATE THE CURSOR POSITION:

        mov   al,80       ;will multiply number of rows by 80

        mul   bl          ;now rows times 80 is in AX

        mov   bl,bh       ;transfer number of columns to BL

        sub   bh,bh       ;extend BL through BX

        add   ax,bx       ;add the column count to the row count

    ;SEND THE LOW BYTE OF THE RESULT:

        inc   dx          ;next port # is for control register

        out   dx,al       ;send low byte to register 15
```

```
;REQUEST ACCESS TO HIGH BYTE REGISTER:
      mov  al,Eh          ;prepare to send high byte to reg Eh
      dec  dx             ;set port number back to address reg
      out  dx,al          ;send request for register Eh
;SEND THE HIGH BYTE OF THE RESULT:
      inc  dx             ;reset port # to control register
      mov  al,ah          ;put high byte in al
      out  dx,al          ;send the byte
      ret
SET_CURSOR  endp
```

Turn the Cursor On/Off

A cursor can be turned off by "changing its shape" in a way that there is nothing to see. "Change the Cursor Shape," below, explains how a cursor is formed by a *start line* and *stop line*. On an MDA, CGA, or VGA adapter, you can obscure the cursor by setting the start line to 20h. On an EGA, make the stop line 0 and the start line a number greater than or equal to the number of lines in the character matrix. To turn the cursor back on, you'll need to reset the cursor shape. Remember that any changes you make in the cursor form are written into video hardware registers. The settings will be carried over into other programs if you fail to reset them when your program terminates, or when it launches ("EXECs") another program.

BASIC

In Microsoft BASIC, you can turn off the cursor by providing a third parameter to the *LOCATE* statement. When this parameter is 1, the cursor is turned on, and when it is 0, the cursor is turned off. The first two parameters used by *LOCATE* set the cursor position. They can be omitted, but commas must still be written:

```
LOCATE,,1           ;turn on the cursor
```

or

```
LOCATE,,0           ;turn the cursor off
```

The cursor will remain on through successive LOCATE statements without setting the third parameter each time. But note that the *INPUT* and *INPUT$* statements will turn it off when they are finished.

Pascal

You'll need to use an assembly language routine to turn off the cursor in Turbo Pascal:

```
Uses DOS;


Var

  Regs: Registers;   {Registers type is declared in the DOS unit}


  Regs.AH := 1;      {the interrupt function number}
```

```
Regs.CH := $20;      {start line}

Regs.CL := 0;        {stop line}

Intr($10,Regs);      {switch off the cursor}
```

C

Borland C's _setcursortype_ function can switch off the cursor when its only parameter is the constant _NOCURSOR_, which is declared in conio.h:

```
_setcursortype(_NOCURSOR);
```

In Microsoft C, use the _settextcursor function, providing a value like 0x2000 to specify a start line and stop line that shuts off the cursor.

```
#include <GRAPH.H>


settextcursor (0x2000); */ cursor off */

settextcursor (0x0B0C); */ cursor on */
```

Assembler

This examples turns off the cursor:

```
mov   ah,1          ;function number

mov   ch,20h        ;start line

mov   cl,0          ;stop line

int   10h           ;call the function
```

Another way to obscure the cursor is to move it off-screen, such as to "row 26" of a 25-row screen. This approach is unwise, since it is not supported by every BIOS.

Low-Level Access

Bit 6 of register 10 of a 6845 video controller chip (discussed in "Program a Video Controller Chip," below) turns the cursor off when it is 1 or on when it is 0. This register also holds the value for the "start line" for the cursor, which along with the "stop line" found in register 11 determines the thickness of the cursor. Since the shape of the cursor is no concern when it is turned off, simply place 32 in register 10 to set bit 6 to 1. To turn the cursor back on, you must reset the value of the cursor start line. For a normal cursor this value is 11. The stop line for the cursor remains unaffected since it resides in a different register.

```
;---TURN OFF THE CURSOR:
            mov   dx,3B4h      ;port number for 6845 address register
            mov   al,10        ;select register 10
            out   dx,al        ;send the request
            inc   dx           ;next port number accesses registers
            mov   al,32        ;32 turns on bit 6, turning off cursor
            out   dx,al        ;turn off the cursor
;---TURN CURSOR BACK ON:       ;(if necessary, readdress register 10)
            mov   al,11        ;start-line value (bit 6 will = 0)
            out   dx,al        ;turn on the cursor
```

Change the Cursor Shape

The cursor can vary in thickness from a thin line to a character-size block. It is built up out of short horizontal line segments, the topmost of which is referred to as the "start line," and the bottommost as the "stop line." On a 350-line monochrome display,14 lines make up the box in which a character is drawn, numbered 0 to 13, starting from the top. Spacing between characters is provided by the top two lines and the bottom three lines. Most characters fit on lines 2–10, although descenders from some characters reach down to lines 11 and 12. An ordinary cursor fills lines 12 and 13, while underlines occupy line 12 alone.

A cursor may be formed from any combination of adjacent line segments. In a 14-line character matrix, a solid block cursor results when the start line is set to 0 and the stop line to 13 . If the start and stop lines are given the same value, a single-line cursor appears. And when the stop line is a higher number than the start line, the result is a two-part, wrap-around cursor. For example, if the start line is 12 and the stop line is 1, first line 12 is filled, then line 13, then line 0, and, lastly, line 1. The cursor takes on the form of two parallel lines that skirt the top and bottom edges of the row it occupies.

Unfortunately, not all video standards work in the same way. On the EGA, the value given for the stop line should be one more than the actual stop line. On an MCGA, values placed in the cursor-start and cursor-stop registers are automatically doubled to emulate CGA operation. To make matters even more complicated, when the BIOS sets the cursor shape for an EGA or VGA system, it can optionally scale the cursor values. In this mode, it takes start and stop lines in the 0 to 7 range, as if for a CGA, and then scales them when a non-CGA screen mode is in use. This is called "cursor emulation," and the feature is disabled when bit 0 at 0040:0087 is set.

The BIOS data area holds one-byte variables that tell the current start line and stop line settings. The start line is stored at 0040:0060 and the stop line at 0040:0061.

BASIC

In BASIC, the LOCATE command shapes the cursor, as well as positioning it upon the screen, and turning it on and off. The fourth and fifth parameters used by this routine set the start and stop lines, respectively. Other parameters may be omitted so long as the commas that separate them are included. Thus, to create a solid block cursor from lines 2 to 12, write:

```
LOCATE,,,2,12
```

Pascal

Turbo Pascal does not offer a procedure for changing the cursor shape. Instead, call function 1 of interrupt 10h, placing the start line in CH and the stop line in CL. There are no return registers. To create a block cursor between scan lines 2 and 12, write:

```
Uses DOS;


Var

  Regs: Registers;   {Registers type is declared in the DOS unit}


  Regs.AH := 1;     {the interrupt function number}

  Regs.CH := 2;     {start line}

  Regs.CL := 12;    {stop line}

  Intr($10,Regs);   {set the cursor shape}
```

C

Borland C provides the _setcursortype function, and Microsoft C the _settextcursor function, to alter the cursor shape. Its only parameter is a short value in which the high byte holds the start line and the low byte holds the stop line. Borland C declares these three constants in conio.h: _NOCURSOR, _SOLIDCURSOR, and _NORMALCURSOR. To set the cursor from scan lines 6 to 7, write:

```
  _setcursortype(0x0607);    /* Borland C */
```

or

```
  _settextcursor(0x0607);   /* Microsoft C */
```

There are also companion routines for finding out the current cursor shape: _getcursortype in Borland C and _gettextcursor in Microsoft C.

Assembler

Function 1 of BIOS interrupt 10h sets the cursor start and stop lines. CH takes the start line, and CL takes the stop line.

```
;---SET CURSOR START AND STOP LINES:
         mov   ah,1       ;function number
         mov   ch,0       ;start cursor at top line
         mov   cl,7       ;end cursor at eighth line
         int   10h        ;
```

Low-Level Access

Registers 10 and 11 on the video controller chip hold the values for the cursor start and stop lines, respectively. The stop line register, number 11, has no other contents. However, the start line register (#10) indicates by bits 5 and 6 whether or not the cursor is showing. Since the cursor appears when both of these bits are set to 0, placing the line number alone in the register will keep these bits set to zero. The other bits of register 10 are unused.

```
;---SET START LINE:
         mov   dx,3B4h ;access the 6845 address register (MDA)
         mov   al,10   ;select register 10
         out   dx,al   ;send the request
         mov   al,0    ;start line is number 0
         inc   dx      ;next port number accesses ctrl registers
         out   dx,al   ;start line now in register
;---SET STOP LINE:
         mov   al,11   ;select register 11
         dec   dx      ;set port number back to address register
         out   dx,al   ;send the request
         mov   al,7    ;stop line is number 7
         inc   dx      ;reset port number to control registers
         out   dx,al   ;stop line now in register
```

14

Displaying Text

- Minitutorial: Displaying Text
- Set Character Attributes/Color
- Write a Single Character on the Screen
- Write a String of Characters on the Screen
- Read the Character and Attribute at a Given Position
- Create Special Characters

Minitutorial: Displaying Text

It's relatively easy to work in text modes. The standard 25–by–80 character mode is available in all video systems. A hardware cursor is at your disposal. In most video systems there are multiple pages to use. And performance is rarely a problem because so little data needs to be moved to video memory, and the data is laid out in a simple manner. Because all characters are the same size, it's easy to calculate line lengths and design screens. Moreover, compilers provide functions that can elaborately format text.

The operating system provides a variety of routines for writing characters on the screen. Some routines simply place a single character at the current cursor position. Others give control over attributes. There is also an operating system routine that displays entire strings. In all cases, at bottom the machine is doing nothing more than writing ASCII codes (and possibly attribute bytes) at specified positions in the video buffer.

Any program can go around the operating system and write data directly into the buffer, a technique that is called "memory mapping." Memory mapping tends to require a little more programming than other approaches, but it results in much faster screen operations. Programs that require a compiler's formatting capabilities can mix compiler I/O with memory-mapping, depending on the task. Some compilers have screen output functions that can work through either the operating system or memory mapping.

One advantage of memory mapping text is that a program is freed from constantly manipulating the cursor. A cursor is really two things: a pointer to the screen, and a hardware-supported blinking symbol that is normally kept in correspondence with the screen pointer. When a video system operates in a mode that allows several display pages, each page has its own screen pointer; and when you switch between pages, the hardware cursor shifts to wherever it was when the new page was last in view. All operating system screen-output functions use the cursor.

Of course, the disadvantage of text modes is their inflexibility. There is only a limited repertoire of nontext symbols to work with, and placements of symbols are restricted to character-cell boundaries. However, in all video systems except the MDA, you can define special character sets. These may be used as alternate fonts or special symbols. Moreover, several user-defined characters can be assembled into a larger image, such as an icon, or may be combined to form large characters. It can be a lot of work setting up a user-defined character set, but the results can be striking.

Set Character Attributes/Colors

When the display is set to a text mode on any of the video systems, two bytes of memory are given to each row and column position on the screen. The first byte holds the ASCII code number for the character, and the second byte holds the attribute for the character. Of the two original video systems, an MDA is limited to black and white; but it can generate underlined characters, which the CGA cannot. Both systems can create blinking and reversed image characters, and both can create high-intensity characters, although on the CGA the higher-intensity characters are regarded as having a different color (the eight basic colors each have high-intensity versions, making 16 colors in all). The EGA and VGA can do anything that the other systems can, and more. In particular, they can underline color characters, since the higher-resolution character box provides a scan line for this purpose.

Color Text Attributes

Here are the basic color codes used in CGA text mode:

0.	black	8.	gray
1.	blue	9.	light blue
2.	green	10.	light green
3.	cyan	11.	light cyan
4.	red	12.	light red
5.	magenta	13.	light magenta
6.	brown	14.	yellow
7.	white	15.	bright white

The lowest four bits of an attribute byte set the color of the character itself (bit 3 turns on high intensity). The next three bits set the character's background. And, under normal circumstances, the top bit turns blinking on and off. Thus:

```
When bit 0 = 1, blue is included in the foreground color
         1 = 1, green is included in the foreground color
         2 = 1, red is included in the foreground color
         3 = 1, the character is displayed in high intensity
         4 = 1, blue is included in the background color
```

```
5 = 1, green is included in the background color
6 = 1, red is included in the background color
7 = 1, the character blinks
```

Bits 0–2 and 4–6 hold the same color components for the characters and their backgrounds. These three-bit groups allow eight possible combinations. When the high-intensity bit is on, eight more colors are allowed. Each color is given an arbitrary code number, with intensified versions being 8 higher than the base color. The combinations, and their codes, are as follows:

red	green	blue	low-intensity color	high-intensity color
0	0	0	black	gray
0	0	1	blue	light blue
0	1	0	green	light green
0	1	1	cyan	light cyan
1	0	0	red	light red
1	0	1	magenta	light magenta
1	1	0	brown	yellow
1	1	1	white	bright white

It is possible to have 16 background colors as well. In this case, bit 7 must act as a high-intensity bit for background, rather than as a blink bit. On the CGA, this is done by changing bit 5 at port address 3D8h to 0, as shown below. Since the port is write-only, all other bits must be reset at the same time. This feature is relevant in only two cases: 80- and 40-column text modes. For 80-column text, send 9 to the port. For 40-column text, send 8. To switch back to blinking, add 32 to either of these values.

The EGA and VGA also can enable/disable the blink bit, although in this case the relevant port address is 3C0h. First *read* port 3DAh to access the address register at 3C0h. Then send 10h to 3C0h to index the proper register. Finally, write the data to the same address. The register is write-only, so all bits must be set. Blinking is turned on by setting bit 3 and turned off by changing it back to 0. All other bits will be 0 when in a color text mode.

Unlike the CGA, the EGA and VGA use palette registers. They are accessed through port address 3C0h and are numbered from 00–0Fh. First *read* port 3DAh to toggle the port to its address register, then send the palette register number to 3C0h, and then the data. When the dip switches on an EGA card are set to enhanced mode (for the IBM Enhanced Color Display), the palette may be selected from 64 colors. In this case, the palette register settings are six bytes long, in the format **R'G'B'RGB**. The RGB bits produce dark colors, and the R'G'B' bits produce brighter ones. When both R and R' are set, for example, a very bright red results. Bits are mixed to produce new hues. Should the palette registers be set up for 64 colors when the EGA is not in enhanced mode, bits 4 & 5 of the registers are ignored, and their contents are treated as an ordinary IRGB pattern. Because the EGA and VGA use palette registers, the number of background colors available is not limited by enabling bit 7 of an attribute byte as the blink bit.

Monochrome Text Attributes

Monochrome characters are idiosyncratic in their use of attribute bytes. As with color attributes, bits 0–2 set the foreground color, and bits 4–6 set the background color. These "colors" may only be white or black, of course, and they result from the following bit patterns:

bit 6 or 2	bit 5 or 1	bit 4 or 0	foreground attrib	background attrib
0	0	0	black	black
0	0	1	underlined white	white
0	1	0	white	white
0	1	1	white	white
1	0	0	white	white
1	0	1	white	white
1	1	0	white	white
1	1	1	white	white

Normal mode is white on black, so bits 0–2 are set to 111 and bits 4–6 are set to 000. Reverse image is created by reversing these assignments. The characters are given high-intensity by setting bit 3 to 1; there is no way to give high-intensity to the background when a character is displayed in reverse image, nor is underlining allowed in reverse image. In all cases, setting bit 7 to 1 sets the character blinking. All in all, there are ten possible combinations that create visible characters. Most of the combinations can be obtained from a variety of bit settings. Here is one setting for each attribute:

attribute	bit pattern	hex	decimal
normal	00000111	7	7
intense	00001111	F	15
normal underlined	00000001	1	1
intense underlined	00001001	9	9
reverse image	01110000	70	112
blinking normal	10000111	87	135
blinking intense	10001111	8F	143
blinking normal underlined	10000001	81	129
blinking intense underlined	10001001	89	137
blinking reverse image	11110000	F0	240

Note that there is no underlining in reverse image. This limitation does not apply to the EGA or VGA. Use the same bit patterns as for the monochrome card, but program palette registers 0 and 1 to change black to white and white to black.

BASIC

BASIC sets character attributes by the COLOR statement. All PRINT or WRITE statements that follow a particular COLOR statement are executed with the specifications of that statement. The background color is changed only for the characters subsequently written, not the whole screen. A new COLOR statement has no effect on what has already been written.

Except on an MDA, **COLOR 3,4** sets a character's foreground color to #3 (cyan) and its background color to #4 (red). The foreground color codes range from 0–31; numbers 0–15 correspond to the colors listed in the table above, and numbers 16–31 result from adding 16 to any of these values, which produces the same color but causes the character to blink. (In blinking, the foreground alternates between background color and foreground color while the background itself remains unchanged.)

Note that when you start out in color text modes, the screen is in black and white. To set the entire screen to a background color, write a COLOR statement like **COLOR,2** for green background, and then clear the screen using CLS. Whenever you clear the screen during a program, be sure that the most recent COLOR statement has set the current background color to the one with which you want the whole screen filled.

Monochrome attributes are set in much the same way. 0 represents black, and any of the numbers from 1 to 7 represent white. Thus, **COLOR 0,7** makes for black on white ("reverse image"), while **COLOR 7,0** results in white on black (the standard attribute). There is one exception: 1, as a foreground color, gives an underlined character. Adding 8 to any of the foreground values leads to an intensified image. Adding 16 to any of the values from 0 to 15 causes the character to blink. Thus $7 + 8 + 16 = 31$ gives a blinking, intense, white foreground. Background values range only from 0–7.

Pascal

In Turbo Pascal, use the *TextColor* procedure to set foreground text color, and *TextBackground* to set background color. Both procedures take a single *byte* parameter, the code for the desired color:

```
TextColor(5);

TextBackground(1);
```

These routines make changes in a global variable called *TextAttr*, which is the actual attribute used in screen operations. You can alter this global directly.

C

In Borland C, use the *textcolor* and *textbackground* functions to set text foreground and background colors. The only parameter for either function is the color code, and neither function returns a value:

```
textcolor(7);

textbackground(3);
```

Microsoft C's *_settextcolor* routine sets the current text color. It takes only one parameter, the color code.

Assembler

The BIOS and DOS interrupts are poorly equipped to handle color text. Only function 9 of interrupt 10h takes an attribute byte when it writes a character. Function A of interrupt 10h writes single characters without specifying a color or attribute; it simply places the character in the video buffer without touching the adjoining attribute byte, so that the current attribute remains. Function D of interrupt 10h, the "teletype" routine, also leaves the current attribute bytes alone. All of these functions are discussed in the next section, "Write a Single Character on the Screen." The DOS routines of interrupt 21h that write on the screen *always* write in monochrome attributes.

Write a Single Character on the Screen

All operating system functions that write characters on the screen place the character at the current cursor position and automatically forward the cursor one space, and all wrap the cursor from the end of the line. An important difference between the functions is that some write a character's attribute along with the character, while others do not.

In any programming language, characters can be placed on the screen without using the usual print operations. Rather, direct *memory mapping* is performed, in which the codes for a character and its attribute are directly placed in the memory locations of the video buffer that correspond to a particular cursor position on the screen. The buffer begins at B000:0000 in monochrome text modes, and at B800:0000 in color text modes. Even-numbered positions (starting from 0) hold the ASCII character codes, and odd numbered positions hold the attribute bytes. Figure 14-1 illustrates this layout. The cursor does not follow these operations, and it may be turned off if desired.

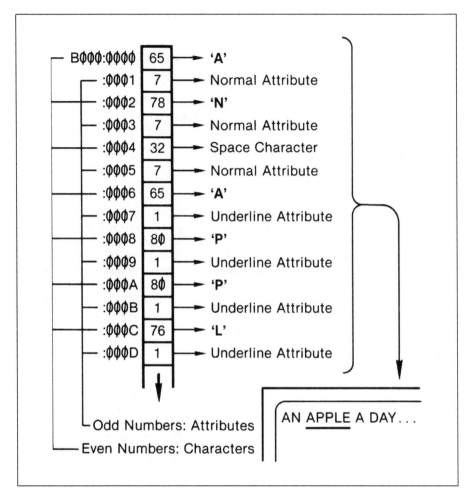

Figure 14-1   Memory mapping on an MDA

BASIC

BASIC writes both single characters and whole strings with the same statements, either PRINT or WRITE. PRINT is used most; WRITE is a variant with special, seldom used formatting characteristics. PRINT functions with data in three forms. It displays the contents of both string and numeric variables, as in **PRINT S$** or **PRINT X**. It displays characters inserted (within quotes) in the PRINT statement itself, such as **PRINT"These words are printed"**. And it displays the characters that correspond to ASCII codes that appear within the PRINT statement in the form of CHR$ statements, as in **PRINT CHR$(65)**, which writes **A** (ASCII code #65) on the screen.

A single PRINT statement can hold many data items, and any of the three forms of data may be intermixed. The data items are delimited using commas or semicolons. Commas set each subsequent data item at the next tab position on a line. Semicolons cause the items to be printed together on the screen with no intervening spaces. (Note that PRINT adds a space before any numeric variables it displays; WRITE does not.) Normally, a PRINT statement automatically makes a carriage return at its end, so that the next such statement will begin writing on the following line on the screen. To avoid this carriage return, place a semicolon at the end of the PRINT statement, as in **PRINT S$;**.

Memory mapping considerably speeds up screen writing operations in BASIC. First set the memory segment pointer to &HB000, then use POKE to place each byte in memory. Horizontally adjacent character positions are two bytes apart, with attribute codes in between. On 80-column screens, vertically adjacent positions are 160 bytes apart (two bytes for each character and attribute that make up the 80 columns of a row). The following two examples draw a box around the circumference of the screen using the double-line graphics characters. The first case mostly uses PRINT statements, and the second case exclusively uses memory mapping. Note how the first case still requires memory mapping at the last columns of rows 24 and 25 to avoid automatic scrolling. In either case, you'd need to add antisnow code (discussed below) if your program is to be used with CGAs.

Using PRINT:

```
CLS:KEY OFF              'blank the screen
DEF SEG=&HB000           'access buffer for 24,80 and 25,80
LOCATE 1,1:PRINT CHR$(201)   'corner character at 1,1
LOCATE 1,80:PRINT CHR$(187)  'corner character at 1,80
LOCATE 1,24:PRINT CHR$(186)  'the loop below misses this char
LOCATE 1,25:PRINT CHR$(200)  'corner character at 1,25
POKE 3838,186            'column 80 of row 24
POKE 3998,188            'column 80 of row 25
FOR N=2 TO 79            'print the horizontals
```

```
LOCATE 1,N:PRINT CHR$(205):LOCATE 25,N:PRINT CHR$(205)
NEXT               '
FOR N=2 TO 23           'print the verticals
LOCATE N,1:PRINT CHR$(186):LOCATE N,80:PRINT CHR$(186)
NEXT               '
```

Using Memory Mapping:

```
CLS:KEY OFF                    'blank the screen
DEF SEG=&HB000                 'point to monochrome buffer
POKE 0,201                     'top left character
POKE 158,187                   'top right character
POKE 3840,200                  'bottom left character
POKE 3998,188                  'bottom right character
FOR N=2 TO 156 STEP 2          'insert horizontals
POKE N,205:POKE N+3840,205     'both top and bottom
NEXT               '
FOR N=160 TO 3680 STEP 160     'insert verticals
POKE N,186:POKE N+158,186      'both left and right
NEXT               '
```

Pascal

Use Pascal's *Write* command to display single characters:

```
Write('A');
Write(chr(254));
Write(TheCharacter);
```

The Mem array will memory map characters directly into the buffer. This example writes 'A' at 0,0 on a color screen and then adds the attribute byte, 47:

```
Mem[$B000:0000] := 'A';
Mem[$B000:0001] := 47;
```

C

In C, use the *putch* function to write single characters. Its only parameter is an integer value specifying the character:

```
putch('A')

putch('\n');

putch(the_character);
```

Use a far pointer to memory map into the video buffer. This example writes 'Z' at the top left corner of a monochrome display, using normal attribute (ASCII 7):

```
char far *vbuffer = 0xB0000000;


*vbuffer = 'Z';

vbuffer++;

*vbuffer = 7;
```

Assembler

The operating system offers six routines that write on the screen — three in the BIOS and three in DOS. They differ mostly by whether or not they move the cursor after writing a character, whether they cause scrolling, whether they set the character's attribute or color, and which control codes they interpret (some see the backspace character, for example, as just another symbol, which others actually make a backspace on the screen). The six routines are:

```
            INT 10h:

function 9  writes character with attribute

         A  writes character without attribute

         E  "teletype" routine (treats screen like

            a printer)

            INT 21h:

function 2  writes character without attribute

         6  writes character without attribute

         9  writes string of characters
```

Functions 9 and A of interrupt 10h do not interpret any control codes at all. The DOS functions interpret those in the following table. Function E of interrupt 10h interprets all codes in the table except ASCII 9.

```
ASCII   7   beep

        8   backspace

        9   tab

        10  line feed

        13  carriage return
```

The first two functions of interrupt 10h do not move the cursor after they write a character. Function 9 of this interrupt writes with an attribute, and function A writes without one, so that the current attribute of a particular position remains. On entry, AL holds the character, and BL takes the attribute. The page number is in BH. It must be set even for the MDA, which, of course, has only one page of memory for the screen to use. In this case, set it to the *first* page, which is numbered as page 0. A special feature of these two BIOS functions is that they print the character as many times as is specified in CX. Ordinarily CX is given 1, but a whole line of characters may be easily printed using a higher count — a useful feature for block graphics. Note that even when multiple characters are written, the initial cursor position remains unchanged. When the line of characters exceeds the space below the cursor, the line wraps around to the top of the screen.

```
;---WRITE A CHARACTER IN REVERSE IMAGE:
    mov   ah,9              ;function to write with attribute
    mov   al,THE_CHARACTER  ;character in AL
    mov   bl,112            ;attribute in BL
    mov   bh,0              ;page 1
    mov   cx,1              ;write the character just once
    int   10h
```

Rather than constantly restore the count in CX, the BIOS interrupts also offer a "teletype" routine that is more suitable for outputting strings of characters. This is performed by function E. It is set up the same as function A above, but without placing a value in CX. Strings are written simply by changing the character in AL and recalling the interrupt. When used in a graphics mode, the palette color is set in BL; otherwise the current attributes remain.

```
;WRITE A STRING USING THE TELETYPE ROUTINE:
        mov  ah,0Eh            ;teletype function number
        mov  bh,0              ;page number
        lea  bx,STRING         ;point BX to the string
NEXT_CHAR:
        mov  al,[bx]           ;move a character to AL
        cmp  al,'$'            ;is it '$' (end of string)?
        je   ALL_DONE          ;if so, quit
        int  10h               ;write the string, cursor forwards
        inc  bx                ;point to next char
        jmp  short NEXT_CHAR    ;go get next character
ALL_DONE:
```

The DOS functions are generally more useful, since they all forward the cursor and cause the screen to scroll after the bottom line is accessed, as well as interpreting some of the common control codes. The functions write to whatever page has been set by function 5 of interrupt 10h, which is covered in Chapter 13, "Switch Between Video pages." There are two functions designed to write a single character, numbers 2 and 6. The former senses Ctrl-Break; the latter does not. (When Ctrl-Break is entered from the keyboard, the Ctrl-Break routine ordinarily does not execute until a function that can detect it is used.)

Both functions write characters in white on black. In general, you need only place the character in DL, place the function number in AH, and invoke interrupt 21h. However, function 6 is special in that it has a second life as a keyboard input function. It acts in this role only when it is given the character FF in DL. In all other cases, it writes on the screen whatever is in DL. In this example, function 6 alternates between receiving and printing a character:

```
        mov  ah,6              ;function number
NEXT:   mov  dl,0FFh           ;if FF in DL, gets keystroke
        int  21h               ;execute the interrupt
        jz   NEXT              ;if no character, keep trying
        cmp  al,13             ;got a character, is it CR?
        je   END_INPUT         ;if so, quit
        mov  dl,al             ;otherwise, move the character to DL
        int  21h               ;now function 6 prints the character
        jmp  short NEXT        ;go get the next
```

Low-Level Access

At bottom, all output to the monitor is memory mapped. The technique is discouraged so as to sustain compatibility through generations of machines, but IBM has gone to lengths to see to it that the video buffers of its microcomputers are structured the same and positioned in memory at the same range of addresses. Because the buffers are structured so that attributes are interleaved with character bytes, character data cannot be moved from memory to the buffer using a simple MOVSB instruction, since the pointer to the buffer must increment by 2 after each one-byte transfer. Still, screen operations are *much* faster using this technique. Note that memory mapping does not work when writing characters in graphics modes. In this case the BIOS *draws* each character, pixel by pixel.

```
;---IN THE DATA SEGMENT:

 SAMPLE_STRING        db    'PRINT THIS STRING$';data string ends
 with $ terminator


;---WRITE OUT THE STRING:

        mov   ax,0B000h           ;monochrome monitor

        mov   es,ax               ;point to video buffer

        lea   bx,SAMPLE_STRING    ;BX points to the string

        mov   di,CURSOR_START     ;starting point in buffer for
                                  string

NEXT:   mov   al,[bx]             ;get a character

        cmp   al,'$'              ;is it end of string?

        je    ALL_DONE            ;if so, quit

        mov   es:[di],al          ;else put the char in the buffer

        inc   di                  ;increase buffer pointer by 2

        inc   di                  ;

        inc   bx                  ;increase string pointer by 1

        jmp   short NEXT          ;go get next character

ALL_DONE:                         ;move on
```

The CGA presents special problems in memory mapping. When its video memory is written to at the same time as it is read for display, interference occurs on the screen. The problem is avoided by waiting for an "all clear" signal before beginning to write. Continuously read the value of port address 3DAh. When bit 0 equals 1, it is safe to begin writing.

```
;---WAIT UNTIL ALL CLEAR:
     mov  dx,3DAh          ;port address for status register
CHECK_AGAIN:
     in   al,dx            ;get the value
     test al,1             ;is bit 0 equal to 1?
     jne  CHECK_AGAIN      ;if not, keep trying
;---NOW WRITE THE MESSAGE
```

Writing takes place during *blanking intervals* — the moments when the CRT's electron beam sweeps back to the start of the next line ("horizontal blanking") or back to the top of the screen ("vertical blanking"). On many machines only 2 characters can be written during horizontal blanking. To accomodate the slowest machines, data must be readied in advance and should be transferred with a MOVSW instruction. Several hundred bytes can be moved during vertical blanking.

Write a String of Characters on the Screen

Routines that display whole strings of characters are useful, but they can impose restrictions on the content of the string. Pay attention to which *control codes* (tab, space, etc.) are interpreted and which are not. Original IBM PCs and early XTs did not have a BIOS function to display strings, although DOS always has provided one. The BIOS function offers more control over character attributes.

BASIC

BASIC writes strings the same way that it writes individual characters. Simply use **PRINT S$**, where S$ is any string up to 255 characters that the program has constructed or transported into memory. Ten of the *control codes* are interpreted. They include:

```
ASCII   7   beep
        9   tab
       10   line feed
       11   cursor home
       12   form feed (erases screen, cursor home)
       13   carriage return
       28   cursor right
       29   cursor left
       30   cursor up
       31   cursor down
```

All other codes appear as symbols on the screen.

Pascal

Pascal's *Write* procedure displays strings at the current cursor position:

```
Write('The one and only string');
```

or

```
var
  TheString: string;
```

```
TheString := 'The one and only string';

Write(TheString);
```

The *Writeln* precedure can be used instead, in which case the cursor automatically wraps to the start of the next line after the string has been displayed:

```
Writeln('The one and only string');
```

Either procedure can take multiple arguments:

```
Writeln(String1,String2,String3);
```

In this case, *Writeln* wraps the cursor only after all arguments have been printed. No space is left between the arguments in any case. When nonstring variables are named, they are converted to string form:

```
var

  TheYear: word;


  Writeln('The year is: ',TheYear);
```

These procedures display most command codes as symbols, rather than interpreting them. Tabs are treated this way. Two command codes that *are* interpreted are the *line feed* (ASCII 10) and the *carriage return* (ASCII 13). The line feed sends the cursor to the line below without changing its column. The carriage return sends the cursor back to the start of the current row. Used together, the two codes wrap the cursor to the beginning of the next line.

C

C's *printf* function displays strings at the current cursor position, and converts and formats numeric data into string form. The function takes only one argument nested in quotation marks:

```
printf("This string will be displayed");
```

Symbols preceeded by the % sign represent substrings. For example, the symbol **%d** represents any nonfloating point number, and the expression:

```
printf("The year is: %d",the_year);
```

substitutes the integer variable *the_year* for the %d symbol, converting the variable to string form, so that the result might look like:

```
The year is 1992
```

Other symbols include:

%c	a value displayed as a single character
%e	a number displayed using exponential notation
%f	a number displayed in floating pointer format
%s	a value displayed as a string
%o	a number displayed in octal notation
%u	a number displayed as an unsigned decimal number
%x	a number displayed in lowercase hexadecimal format
%X	a number displayed in uppercase hexadecimal format

Many such symbols may be placed between the quotation marks, with the corresponding variable for each listed in order thereafter. The quotation marks may be empty except for these symbols:

```
printf("%s%d%s",string1,integer1,string2);
```

Add the symbol \n at any point between the quotation marks, and any number of times, to wrap the cursor to the next line:

```
printf("Here's line 1\nline2\nline3\n");
```

This function can format data elaborately. To specify a field width for an element, insert between the % sign and the element's symbol the number of characters that should be allotted to the element. For instance, to display an integer in an eight-character-wide field, with the integer right-justified, write:

```
printf("%8d",the_integer);
```

Precede the specification with a minus sign to left-justify the integer:

```
printf("%-8d",the_integer);
```

For floating point value, include a specification for both sides of the decimal point. For example, when you write:

```
printf("%5.3f",the_float);
```

The number will be displayed with three characters to the left of the decimal point (with zeros added, if necessary), and five to the right of the decimal point (with leading spaces).

Printf has a number of other formatting features. Consult the compiler documentation to learn about them. These same features also apply to companion functions like *fprintf,* which can be used to format output to files or to a printer.

Assembler

Function 9 of interrupt 21h displays a string. DS:DX points to the first character of the string. The string must end with the $ character, which means that $ itself cannot be part of the string. The string may be any length. The function does not automatically send the cursor to the start of the next line after the string is displayed; to cause this, append 0Ah (line feed) and 0Dh (carriage return).

```
;---IN THE DATA SEGMENT:
FIRST_STRING  db 'This is the first string in
memory',0Ah,0Dh,'$'

SECOND_STRING db 'And this is the second string$'


;---PRINT THE STRING:
    mov  ah,9                ;function number to print string
    lea  dx,FIRST_STRING     ;load the offset of FIRST_STRING in
                             DX
    int  21h                 ;prints string at cursor position
    lea  dx,SECOND_STRING ;load pointer to SECOND_STRING
    int  21h                 ;write 2nd string at start of new
                             line
```

The following control codes are interpreted:

```
ASCII  7    beep
       8    backspace
       9    tab
      10    line feed
      13    carriage return
```

DOS function 40h of interrupt 21h is also useful for writing strings on the screen. It requires that you know the length of the string, since the string requires no terminating character. This function was designed primarily for output to files. It requires a *handle*, which is an ID number assigned to a particular file or peripheral. The video display has a ready-made handle, number 1. Place the handle in BX and the number of bytes in the string in CX. Then point DS:DX at the string. The function writes text with a normal (white-on-black) attribute. Note that there is no need to "open" the video display the way you must open a file in order to use this function. Here is an example:

454

```
;---OUTPUT 1000 BYTES OF TEXT:
     mov   ah,40h          ;function number
     mov   bx,1            ;handle for video display
     lea   dx,STRING       ;point DS:DX at the string
     mov   cx,1000         ;number of bytes to display
     int   21h
```

Except on early PCs and XTs, function 13h of BIOS interrupt 10h displays a string. Point ES:BP to the string, and place the length of the string in CX. DH and DL hold the starting row and column for the string. BH takes the page number. Finally, place a code number from 0–3 in AL to specify how the string is to be displayed:

AL=0	string is all characters, cursor is not moved
AL=1	string is all characters, cursor is moved
AL=2	string alternates characters and attributes, and cursor is not moved
AL=3	string alternates characters and attributes, and cursor is moved

When AL=0 or 1, place the attribute in BL. All characters will be written in this attribute. The backspace, carriage return, line feed, and bell (ASCII 7) codes are interpreted as commands by this function, rather than as printable characters.

Read the Character and Attribute at a Given Position

A BIOS function reads the character and attribute at a particular screen position; otherwise they can be found by reading the values directly from video memory. To find the character and attribute at row 0, column 39 in 80-column mode, add 0 * 160 plus 39 * 2 and take the two bytes at that offset in the video buffer. See Chapter 13, "Switch Between Video Pages," if offsets for paging are required. Also, keep in mind that CGAs display "snow" when data is read from their video buffers, exactly as when data is written. "Write a Single Character on the Screen," above, explains how to set up code to avoid snow. For simplicity, the examples below do not include antisnow code.

BASIC

BASIC uses the SCREEN function to find a character or attribute: **SCREEN 5,10** retrieves the ASCII code (0–255) of the character at row 5, column 10 (rows and columns are numbered starting from 1). To retrieve the characters' attribute byte instead, add 1 as a third parameter, as in **SCREEN 5,10,1**. When used in a graphics mode, 32 is returned if the indicated screen position does not hold a character.

Pascal

To find out the character and attribute at a particular screen position, read them directly from the screen buffer. For example, to find out the character and attribute at 0,0 in a CGA text mode, write:

```
var

  TheChar,TheAttribute: byte;


TheChar := Mem[$B800:0];

TheAttribute := Mem[$B000:1];
```

C

Read the character and attribute directly from the video buffer. This example reads text cell 0,0 in a CGA color text mode:

```
char far *vbuffer = 0xB8000000;

char the_char,the_attribute;


the_char = *vbuffer++;

the_attribute = *vbuffer;
```

Assembler

Function 8 of interrupt 10h returns the character and attribute at the current cursor position. Place in BH the value of the current display page (numbered from 0, and always 0 for the monochrome adaptor). The character code is returned in AL, and its attribute byte in AH. This function is so versatile it can read characters in graphics modes, reporting the palette color in AH. It works even for user-defined characters. This example checks the character and attribute at 0,39 on page 2:

```
;---SET THE CURSOR POSITION:

        mov   ah,2      ;function to set cursor

        mov   dh,0      ;set cursor row

        mov   dl,39     ;set cursor column

        mov   bh,0      ;set the page number

        int   10h       ;position the cursor

;---FIND THE CHARACTER AND ATTRIBUTE:

        mov   ah,8      ;function to find character/attribute

        mov   bh,2      ;page 2 (always 0 on monochrome card)

        int   10h       ;now AH:AL holds attribute:character
```

Low-Level Access

After calculating a character cell's offset, read its value directly from video memory. Add a page offset if required. This example gets the character and attribute at 7,39 on page 2 in an 80 x 25 text mode. (For simplicity, the example doesn't include "antisnow" code for CGA cards, as discussed in "Write a Single Character on the Screen," above).

```
;---FIND THE CHARACTER AND ATTRIBUTE AT 7,39 IN PAGE 1:
     mov   ax,0B800h ;address of graphics buffer
     mov   es,ax              ;ES points to first byte of buffer
     mov   di,1000h           ;page offset
     mov   al,80              ;multiply number of rows by 160
     mov   bl,7               ;place row number in BL
     mul   bl                 ;now AX has (rows-1) times 160
     mov   ax,39              ;place column number in AX
     add   bx,ax              ;add rows and columns
     shl   bx,1               ;double number for attribute bytes
     mov   ax,es:[bx][di]   ;now AH:AL holds attribute:character
```

Create Special Characters

Only the monochrome adaptor cannot display characters of the programmer's own design. The other video standards allow different numbers of user-defined fonts. On the CGA, the ROM BIOS contains data for drawing only the first 128 characters of the ASCII set (numbers 0–127). The second 128 characters are not available for your use unless you re-create them using the technique explained here. DOS (starting with version 3.0) provides the GRAFTABL command to supply the required data for the second 128 characters. All other video standards have all characters on board.

CGA characters:

Characters on a CGA are designed within a cell that is 8x8 pixels. Eight bytes hold the data for each character. Each byte holds the settings for a row of pixels, starting with the top row, and the high bit (number 7) corresponds to the leftmost pixel of the row. When the bit equals 1, the pixel shows. To design a character, you must determine the bit patterns for the eight bytes and place them in sequence in memory.

One hundred twenty-eight characters together require 1024 bytes, although there is no requirement that all characters be set up in memory. An interrupt vector is set to point to what would be the first byte for the first character of the extended set, that is, to character number 128. When the code 128 is sent to a character position in the video buffer, these first eight bytes are looked up and displayed. If the character is 129, the ninth through sixteenth bytes are displayed, and so on.

The interrupt vector is number 1Fh, which is located at address 0000:007C. Place the address of the offset in the low word (low byte first), and the address of the segment in the high word (again, low byte first). Note that you can create higher code numbers without setting aside memory for lower ones; simply adjust the vector to some lower address that is actually outside of the block that contains the character data.

The EGA and VGA are more complicated and more versatile. When a text mode is initialized, one of the two character sets (8x8 or 8x14) is copied from the onboard ROMs onto bit map 2 of the video buffer. This part of the buffer is treated as if it were broken into blocks, and the standard character set is placed in block 0. Provided that the adapter is equipped with adequate memory, three more blocks of character data may be set up. The size of a block depends on the number of scan lines used in the character. Characters that are 8x8 need 8 times 256, or 2,048 bytes. When more than one block of characters is enabled, bit 3 of the attribute byte of a character determines which block the character data will be taken from.

459

Which block is used depends on the settings of bits 3–0 in the *character map select register,* which is located at port address 3C5h. First send 3 to 3C4h to index the register. Bits 1–0 give the number of the character block that is enabled when bit 3 of an attribute byte is 0, and bits 3–2 do the same for when bit 3 is 1. When the pattern is the same in both pairs of bits, the dual character set feature is disabled, and bit 3 of attribute bytes reverts to setting character intensity. In this case, only block 0 is enabled. Nothing stops you from placing your own characters at whatever positions you choose within this block, however. And if you overwrite the standard character set, you can replace it at any time using the ROM data.

Assembler

On the CGA, use function 25h of interrupt 21h to set the pointer kept in position 1Fh in the interrupt vector table. On entry, DS:DX points to the first byte of the data block. See Chapter 4, "Write Your Own Interrupt Service Routine," for more information on this topic. The example creates two characters, numbers 128 and 129. They are mirror images of each other, and written in sequence they form a small rectangle.

```
;---IN THE DATA SEGMENT:

CHARACTER_DATA     db 11111111B,10000000B,10000000B,10000000B
                   db 10000000B,10000000B,10000000B,11111111B
                   db 11111111B,00000001B,00000001B,00000001B
                   db 00000001B,00000001B,00000001B,11111111B


;---SET UP THE INTERRUPT VECTOR:
     push ds                  ;save DS
     lea  dx,CHAR_DATA        ;offset of character data in DX
     mov  ax,seg CHAR_DATA    ;segment of character data in DS
     mov  ds,ax               ;
     mov  ah,25h              ;interrupt to set vector
     mov  al,1Fh              ;number of the vector to change
     int  21h                 ;set the vector
     pop  ds                  ;restore DS
;---PRINT THE CHARACTER:
     mov  ah,2                ;DOS function to write single char
```

```
mov   dl,128              ;first character
int   21h                ;write it
mov   dl,129              ;second character
int   21h                ;write it
```

On an EGA or VGA, function 11h of interrupt 10h manipulates the character sets. This function can be quite complex when it is used to create special screen modes, but its basic application is straightforward. There are several subfunctions. When AL is 0, user-defined data is transferred from elsewhere in memory into a special character block. When AL is 1 or 2, the 8x14 and 8x8 ROM data sets are respectively copied into a block. And when AL is 3, the function sets the block assignments in the character map select register, as described above. In the latter case, simply place the relevant data in BL and call the function. To load the ROM data, place the block number in BL and execute the function. To load your own data, point ES:BP to it and place the number of characters to transfer in CX, the offset (character number) in the block at which to begin the transfer in DX, the number of bytes per character in BH, and the number of the block in BL. Then call interrupt 10h. Here is an example:

```
;---INSTALL 128 USER DEFINED CHARACTERS AT TOP END OF BLOCK 0:
      mov   ax,seg CHARACTER_DATA      ;point ES:BP to the data
      mov   es,ax                      ;
      mov   bp,offset CHARACTER_DATA   ;
      mov   cx,128                     ;number of characters
      mov   dx,128                     ;starting offset
      mov   bl,0                       ;block number
      mov   bh,8                       ;8x8 character box
      mov   al,1                       ;subfunction number
      mov   ah,11h                     ;function number
      int   10h                        ;transfer the data
```

461

15

Displaying Graphics

- Minitutorial: Displaying Graphics
- Set the Colors for Graphics Modes
- Draw a Pixel (CGA, MCGA, HGC)
- Draw a Pixel (EGA, VGA)
- Find the Color at a Point on the Screen

Minitutorial: Displaying Graphics

Graphics data consist of code numbers corresponding to the colors that are displayed in individual pixels. In the earliest graphics system, the CGA, there is very little control over the correlation between codes and colors. Starting with the EGA, however, the codes act as indexes into *palette registers*. This sequence of registers holds data describing actual colors. When the code **3** (for example) is written into the video buffer, the color value found at offset 3 in the palette register is used to determine the color. Changing the color specification in a palette register causes all associated pixels to instantly change their hue.

Unlike text data, in modes 4–6 and 8, A graphics data is subdivided as it is laid out over a video page. In most of these modes, the data is split in two; and the first half of the buffer holds data for the even-numbered lines of the screen, and the second half keeps data for the odd-numbered lines (the lines are numbered downwards from the top of the display). In four-color modes, the first byte in the buffer gives the leftmost horizontal dots on line 0, with the highest bits holding the information for the leftmost pixel. The next byte holds data for the next segment of the line, and so on. Eighty bytes are typically required per line. The 81st byte keeps the information for the left end of *line 2*. Sixteen-color modes use roughly the same arrangement, but 160 bytes are required for a line, and each part of the buffer holds data for only half as many lines. On the CGA, even lines stretch from offset 0000 to 1F3Fh and the odd lines from 2000h to 3F3Fh. The gap between 1F3Fh and 2000h is ignored.

The MCGA uses two non-CGA graphics modes, a 640-by-480 2-color mode, and a 320-by-200 256-color mode. Both are mapped in the 64K memory block starting from A000:0000. Unlike the CGA video buffer, this map is linear, with the bytes of data ordered as they appear on the screen, starting from the top left corner.

The video buffer of the Hercules Graphics Card (HGC) starts at address B000:0000. The 720-by-348 screen resolution uses one bit per pixel with the buffer divided into two parts. Data for the top row begins at B000:0000, at :2000 for the second row, at :4000 for the third row, and at :6000 for the fourth row. The fifth row falls in the first block, starting at B000:005A, the sixth row is at B000:205A, and so on. This standard has been copied in many clones that often go by the name "monographics adapter."

Memory is organized quite differently starting with screen mode Dh on the EGA and VGA. It is split into one, two, or four *bit planes*, in which a single plane is organized with each bit corresponding to a pixel on the screen, laid out as a horizontal segment with bit 7 leftmost. Imagine four such bit planes, residing side by side at the same address in the video buffer. This leaves four bits for each pixel, which provides for 16 colors. Figure 15-1 shows the various ways graphics memory is organized.

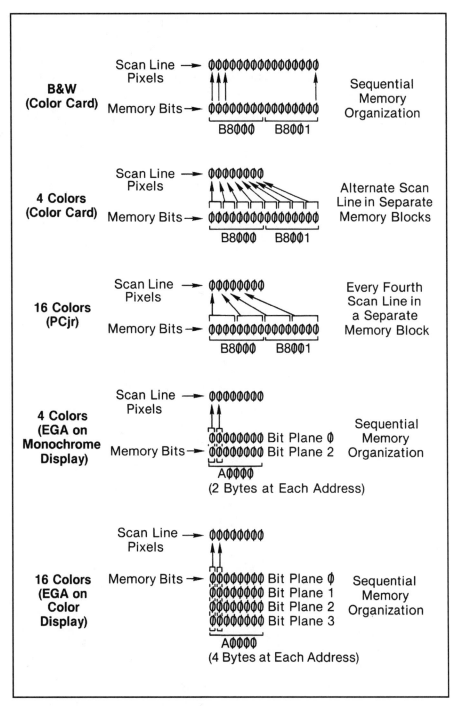

Figure 15-1   Pixel mapping in the various video standards

Characters may be written while in graphics mode. However, they are not created in the same way as in text mode. Rather, the BIOS draws characters dot by dot without changing the background color. For this reason, characters do not have *attributes* in graphics mode. Every pixel must be modified when a character is shown in reverse-image in a graphics mode, or is made to blink. Nor is there a hardware cursor at your disposal in graphics mode. If a cursor is required, your program must construct it and maintain the screen image as the cursor traverses the display.

Set the Colors for Graphics Modes

On a CGA, four colors are allowed in medium-resolution graphics. Two bits out of each byte in the video buffer are given over to each pixel. The four possible bit combinations represent one background color and three foreground colors. The background color may be any of the 16 listed for the EGA and VGA below. The three foreground colors, however, must be chosen from one of two palettes that are limited to three predetermined colors each. They are:

code number	bit pattern	palette 0	palette 1
0	00	background color	background color
1	01	green	cyan
2	10	red	magenta
3	11	yellow/brown	white

A program can change between palettes at any time; the screen colors will instantly change accordingly. The only way to use colors from outside of the two palettes is by artificially treating one of the palette colors as the background color, which requires filling the whole screen in that color whenever the screen is cleared (use memory mapping for this). Then the true background color can "show through" as a foreground color. This technique results in a screen border like that of text screens. Graphics screens do not otherwise set a special border color because the whole screen is set to the background color, even though the border-area pixels are not addressable. Note that the BIOS keeps a one-byte variable in its data area that holds the current palette number. It is located at 0040:0066h. Changing this number does not change the palette setting.

The EGA and VGA have greater flexibility in their use of color, no matter which video mode they operate in. In 16-color graphics, the four bits laid down in memory for a particular dot on the screen give a bit pattern that is not directly translated into a corresponding color. Rather, the number refers to one of 16 *palette registers*. Each of these registers holds the bit pattern for the color that will actually be displayed. If all 16 registers are given the pattern 0100, then no matter what attribute is used in memory for a pixel, it is displayed in red. The value in register 0 is used as the background color. In two- and four-color modes, only the first two or four palette registers are relevant. Here are the default values:

code number	bit pattern	color
0	0000	Black
1	0001	Blue
2	0010	xGreen
3	0011	Cyan
4	0100	Red
5	0101	Magenta
6	0110	Brown
7	0111	Light Gray
8	1000	Dark Gray
9	1001	Light Blue
10	1010	Light Green
11	1011	Light Cyan
12	1100	Pink
13	1101	Light Magneta
14	1110	Yellow
15	1111	White

The palette registers let a program change everything displayed in one color to another color without making any changes in the video buffer. What's more, objects can be caused to magically disappear and reappear. This is done by changing to background color the value found in the palette register that corresponds to the attribute in which the objects are drawn. For example, say that the background color is black (0000) and that an object is drawn using the attribute 1110, so that it appears in whatever color is given in palette register 15 (yellow is the default value for this register). By changing register 15 to 0000 (the black background color) the object disappears from view. But the object is still defined in memory by virtue of being written with the attribute 1110, rather than the attribute 0000, as would be used by all background dots. The object can be made visible again by changing palette register 15 back to 1110. Not all yellow objects would need to disappear, since some could be drawn using a different attribute that also corresponds to a palette register containing the code for yellow.

BASIC

When the CGA operates in a graphics mode, BASIC treats the COLOR statement differently than for a text mode. First comes the background color as a number from 0 to 15, and then the palette number is given, either 0 or 1. For example, COLOR 2,1 sets the whole screen to the background color green (#2) and activates palette 1. Thereafter, the three foreground colors are specified by their palette numbers.

For the EGA and VGA, there are special statements to set the contents of palette registers: PALETTE and PALETTE USING. PALETTE sets the color corresponding to any attribute. PALETTE 9,11, for example, causes dots drawn with palette color 9 (normally light blue) to be shown in color 11 (light cyan). To change all palette registers back to their initial settings, so that register 0 contains 0, register 12 contains 12, etc., simply write PALETTE. Note that in the modes SCREEN 4 and SCREEN 6 the palette registers are initialized so that the attributes of colors 1–3 are the same as those of palette 1 on the color graphics card. This is done for the sake of compatibility.

All 16 palette registers may be set by a single statement, PALETTE USING. PALETTE USING dumps the contents of a 16-element integer array into the palette registers. By keeping several such arrays, a program can quickly switch back and forth between various color schemes. Each element of the array must be a number from 0 to 15, or else -1, in which case no change is made in the contents of the corresponding register. For example, to reverse the usual color scheme, create an array where ARRAYNAME(0)=15, ARRAYNAME(1)=14, etc. Then write PALETTE USING ARRAYNAME(0), and the contents of ARRAYNAME are dumped into the palette registers. The 0 indicates the starting position in the array from which the data for the registers is taken. Longer arrays may be used, with the data taken from any starting point so long as there are 16 elements between it and the end of the array. PALETTE USING ARRAYNAME(12) would take data starting from the 12th byte of the array. Note that PALETTE USING operates for both text and graphics modes. Here is an example:

```
DEF INT A-Z             'all variables integers
DIM SCHEME1(16)         'array for color scheme #1
DIM SCHEME2(16)         'array for color scheme #2
DATA 3,5,9,2,4,12,15,1,6,7,14,13,8,11,10,0
DATA 0,11,13,7,1,12,2,5,10,8,14,6,15,4,9,3
FOR N=0 TO 15           'for each palette register
READ Q                  'read color code
SCHEME1(N)=Q            'place in the array
```

469

```
NEXT N                   'go get next
FOR N=0 TO 15            'repeat for second array...
READ Q                   '
SCHEME2(N)=Q             '
NEXT N                   '
PALETTE USING SCHEME1(0) 'set the registers

   .

   .

PALETTE USING SCHEME2(0) 'change them mid-program
```

Pascal

In Turbo Pascal, use the *SetAllPalette* procedure to initialize the palette registers. The procedure takes only one parameter: a pointer to a variable length structure. The first byte of the structure tells the length of the palette, and the next *n* bytes replace the current palette colors. The values may range from -1 to 15, with -1 indicating that the particular palette entry is not to be changed. Changes made are immediately reflected in the screen colors. Here is an example:

```
var
   ThePalette: PaletteType;


with ThePalette do
begin
   Size:= 3;
   Colors[0] := 3;
   Colors[1] := 2;
   Colors[2] := 7;
   SetAllPalette(ThePalette);
end;
```

To change a single palette entry, use the *SetPalette* procedure. There are companion routines for determining the current palette settings, *GetAllPalette* and *GetPalette*. For VGA 256-color modes, use *SetRBGPalette*.

C

Borland C uses the *setallpalette* function to set some or all of the palette entries. The function's only parameter is a pointer to a structure of *palettetype* that is declared in *graphics.h*. The first element is a *char* telling how many elements the variable-length structure contains. The remaining *char* elements are palette codes, counted from zero upward. This example initializes the first three palette elements:

```
struct palettetype thepal;

thepal.size = 3;

thepal.colors[0] = 12;

thepal.colors[1] = 7;

thepal.colors[2] = 3;

setallpalette(&thepal);
```

Use the *setpalette* function to set individual elements in a palette. Its first parameter is the palette position, and the second is a color code:

```
setpalette(7,12);
```

There are parallel functions for finding out current palette settings: *getallpalette* and *getpalette*. For 256-color VGA modes, use the *serrgbpalette* function.

Assembler

Function BH of interrupt 10h sets both background and palette colors—but not at the same time. To set the background, place 0 in BH, and then put a color code from 0–15 in BL. To set the palette, place 1 in BH, and put either 0 or 1 in BL. This example sets the background to cyan and chooses palette 0:

```
;---SET BACKGROUND AND PALETTE COLORS:

        mov   ah,0Bh      ;function to set graphics colors

        mov   BH,0        ;first, choose background color

        mov   BL,3        ;code for cyan background

        int   10h         ;set the color

        mov   BH,1        ;now set the palette

        mov   BL,1        ;choose palette 1

        int   10h         ;set the palette
```

Low-Level Access

On the CGA, port address 3D9h accesses the "Color Select Register." The register operates in graphics modes differently than for text modes. Bits 0–3 hold the background color information in the usual format (respectively, the blue, green, and red components, and intensity). Bit 5 selects the palette; when the bit is 0, the palette is number 0. In graphics modes no other bits are significant. The register is write-only, so you must include both the background and palette bits when making a change in either.

```
mov  dx,3D9h          ;color select register address

mov  al,00100110B     ;bit pattern for cyan, palette 1

out  dx,al            ;send it
```

Because they use palette registers, the above example does not apply to the EGA or VGA. Instead, simply load the desired values into these registers. The palette registers are at 3C0h, and they are numbered from 00 to 0Fh. Read port 3DAh (not 3C0h) to be sure an index is awaited.

Draw a Pixel (CGA, MCGA, HGC)

Because of the organization of graphics information in the video buffer, drawing a pixel entails changing individual bits within memory. The two-, four-, sixteen-, and 256-color modes require that one, two, four, and eight bits, respectively, be changed to set a single pixel. These operations can consume a tremendous amount of processor time, as evidenced by how slowly much graphics software operates. Careful forethought often leads to ways of setting all of the bits of a particular byte at once, rather than accessing the same byte more than once.

BASIC

BASIC provides the PSET and PRESET statements to change the color of individual dots. The names stand for PointSET and PointRESET. Both are followed by the column and row coordinates of the dot, placed in parentheses. Note that coordinates are given in the order x,y — that is, first the column and then the row; this is the reverse of the row-column order by which the LOCATE statement positions text on the screen. **PSET(50,80)** or **PRESET(50,80)** set the dot color at column 50, row 80. PSET may be followed with a color code that is in the range permitted by the current screen mode. When no color is given, the highest number code that the screen mode allows is used. PRESET, on the other hand, names no color. It always returns the dot to background color (code 0). For example:

```
PSET (100,180),3   'set dot at 100,180 to palette color 3

PRESET (100,180)   'change the dot back to background color
```

PSET and PRESET ordinarily use a coordinate system where the top left corner of the screen is numbered 0,0. The WINDOW statement lets you redefine the coordinate system so that, for example, the top left corner is –100,100, center-screen is 0,0, and the bottom right corner is 100,–100. In this instance, the statement would be written as **WINDOW(–100,100)-(100,–100)**. The first number in each of the pairs of parentheses gives horizontal, x-axis coordinates. They could both be positive or negative, so long as they are not identical. The left edge of the screen is always assigned the smallest number (which may be the largest *negative* number). Thus, even by reversing the coordinates of the example to **WINDOW(100,–100)-(–100,100)** the value –100 is given to the left end of the x-axis.

The second number of each coordinate pair gives the vertical boundaries of the screen. Again, whichever value is smallest is given to the bottom edge of the screen, no matter which coordinate pair it is matched with. The largest positive value (or smallest of two negative values) is assigned as the value of the y-axis at the top line of the screen. The direction of increasing value can be reversed so that the largest value is at the bottom of the screen and vice versa. Simply add the word SCREEN to the statement, as in **WINDOW SCREEN (–100,100)-(100,–100)**.

A program may direct points to be set at areas outside of the screen coordinate system. For example, a circle could be centered off-screen, so that only an arc of it is in view. Note also that the coordinates given by WINDOW statements may be continuously changed to "zoom" or "pan" an image. The image must be redrawn, and sometimes erased, each time the WINDOW coordinates are changed.

The PMAP statement converts coordinates between the usual *physical* system and a *world* system set up by a WINDOW statement. PMAP uses four code numbers:

```
0        convert x from world to physical

1        convert y from world to physical

2        convert x from physical to world

3        convert y from physical to world
```

The statement takes the form **PMAP(position,code)**. For example, say that you have set up a system of world coordinates using WINDOW. The top left corner of the screen is given (–100,100), and the bottom right is given (100,–100). What is the pixel position of the center point of the screen (0,0) using the usual 320 x 200 physical system, where the top left is 0,0? To find X, write **X=PMAP(0,0)**, and to find Y, write **Y=PMAP(0,1)**. X will be given the value 160, and Y will be 100.

Pascal

Turbo Pascal's *PutPixel* procedure draws a pixel. The procedure's first two parameters are the x and y coordinates of the pixel, and the third is the color code for the pixel:

```
PutPixel(25,50,6);
```

C

Borland C's *putpixel* function takes three parameters: first, the x and y coordinates for the pixel, and then its color code:

```
putpixel(150,300,15);
```

In Microsoft C, use the *_setpixel* function to set a pixel in the *current color*. This color is set by the *_setcolor* function. For example:

```
_setcolor(12);              /* color code is 12 */

putpixel(150,300);          /* set the pixel at 150,300 */
```

474

Assembler

Function CH of interrupt 10h sets a dot. DX holds the row, and CX the column, both counted from 0. The color code is placed in AL, and the video page number is BHO.

```
;---PRINT A DOT AT 100,180:
        mov   ah,0Ch           ;function to set dot
        mov   al,3             ;choose palette color 3
        mov   cx,100           ;row
        mov   dx,180           ;column
        mov   bh,0             ;page number
        int   10h             ;draw the dot
;---"ERASE" THE DOT:
        mov   ah,0Ch           ;replace function (AX destroyed)
        mov   al,0             ;use background color to "erase"
        mov   dx,100           ;row
        mov   cx,180           ;column
        mov   bh,0             ;page number
        int   10h             ;erase the dot
```

While the palette color is placed in the low bits of AL, the top bit is also significant. When it is equal to 1, the color is exclusive-ORed (XORed) with the color currently in place. Recall that in the XOR operation a bit equals 1 solely in the case where, of two bits compared, only one is presently turned on. If both of the bits compared are 1, or if neither is 1, then the bit is set to 0. In two-color modes this means that XORing a bit reverses its setting. The whole screen can be reversed by XORing every pixel. In four- or 16-color modes, on the other hand, areas of the screen can be made to change their colors. For example, say that in four-color medium resolution an area is entirely covered by pixels of either palette code 1 (bit pattern 01b) or palette code 2 (10b). When every pixel in the area is XORed with 11B, 01b becomes 10b, and 10b becomes 01b—the colors are reversed.

Low-Level Access

The following example sets one pixel in a CGA four-color mode:

```
;---IN THE DATA SEGMENT:
PALETTE_COLOR db    2
;---CALL THE ROUTINE:
        mov  ax,0B800h       ;point to graphics buffer
        mov  es,ax           ;
        mov  cx,100          ;row in CX
        mov  dx,180          ;column in DX
        call SET_DOT

            .

            .


;---FIGURE NUMBER OF BYTES IN ROWS PRIOR TO PIXEL'S ROW:
SET_DOT  proc
        test cl,1            ;is it an odd numbered row?
        jz   EVEN_ROW        ;if not, then jump ahead
        mov  bx,2000h        ;put offset for odd rows in BX
        jmp  short CONTINUE  ;jump ahead
EVEN_ROW:
        mov  bx,0            ;put offset for even rows in BX
CONTINUE:
        shr  cx,1            ;half the number of rows
        mov  al,80           ;multiply by 80 bytes per row
        mul  cl              ;now AX holds bytes up to prior row
;---FIGURE POSITION OF 2 BITS WITHIN THE BYTE:
        mov  cx,dx           ;copy the column count
        not  cl              ;reverse bits
```

```
        and   cl,00000011b       ;now CL has bit position 3-0
        shl   cl,1               ;CL x 2 gives bit position of 1st bit
;---TALLY NUMBER OF BYTES IN COLUMN OFFSET:
        shr   dx,1               ;divide number of columns by 4
        shr   dx,1               ; (keep bottom 2 bits)
;---FIGURE OFFSET OF THE BYTE THAT NEEDS CHANGING:
        add   ax,dx              ;add column offset to row offset
        add   bx,ax              ;add above to buffer offset
;---CHANGE THE BITS:
        mov   ah,es:[bx]         ;get the byte at that position
        ror   ah,cl              ;mov relevant bits to bottom of byte
        and   ah,11111100b       ;blank out the bottom 2 bits
        mov   al,PALETTE_COLOR   ;palette color in AH
        or    ah,al              ;change the bits to the palette color
        rol   ah,cl              ;rotate bits back to correct position
        mov   es:[bx],ah         ;replace the byte
        ret
SET_DOT  endp
```

Draw a Pixel (EGA, VGA)

This section is concerned with low-level access to EGAs and VGAs. For operating system-level access, see the discussion in the previous section, "Draw a Pixel (CGA, MCGA, HGC)."

Graphics in the EGA and VGA advanced video modes are complicated. From the CPU's point of view, screen modes 0 through 7 operate exactly as on a CGA, but modes Dh through 10h are completely different. The memory organization of these memory modes varies, depending on how many colors are used, and how much RAM is installed on the card.

In modes D, E, and 10h, memory is organized in four *bit planes*. A single plane is organized as in the CGA's high-resolution black and white mode. When a byte of data is sent to an address in the video buffer, each bit corresponds to a pixel on the screen, laid out as a horizontal segment with bit 7 leftmost. Picture four such bit planes, residing side-by-side at the same address in the video buffer. This leaves four bits for each pixel (giving 16 colors), where each bit is in a separate byte on a separate bit plane.

But how can you write four different bytes of data when they are at the same memory address? The answer to this question is *not* that four bytes are sent in sequence to the address. Rather, one of three *write modes* can alter all four bytes on the basis of a single byte of data received from the CPU. (The VGA adds a fourth write mode that is not very useful and will not be discussed here.) The effect of the CPU data depends on the settings of several registers, including two mask registers that determine which bits and which bit planes are to be affected.

To understand these registers, you must first know about the four *latch registers*. These hold the data from each of the bit planes at whatever memory position was last accessed. (Note that the term *bit plane* is used to refer to both the entire extent of the video buffer, and to the one-byte swatches of the buffer temporarily held in these latch registers). When the CPU sends data to a particular address, that data may change or entirely replace the latch register data, and then it is the latch register data itself that is written into the video buffer. *How* the latch registers are influenced by the CPU data depends on which write mode is used and how certain other registers are set up. Whenever a video memory address is *read*, the latch register is filled by the four bytes from the four bit planes at that location. The latch registers are easily manipulated so that their contents may be ORed, ANDed, XORed, or rotated, greatly facilitating fancy graphics and scrolling.

The bit mask register and map mask register act on the latch registers, protecting particular bits or bit planes from being changed by the CPU data. The *Bit Mask Register* is a write-only register at port address 3CFh. First send 8h to 3CEh to index the register. Setting a bit in this register masks out a bit across all four bit planes, so that the corresponding pixel on the screen is immune to change. The hardware still operates in byte-size units, however, so the "unchanged" bits are in fact *rewritten* into the four bit planes. The data for these masked-out bits is whatever resides in the latch registers, and so the program must be sure that the current contents of the latch registers are those of the relevant memory address. For this reason, the memory address is read before being written to.

The *Map Mask Register* is at port address 3C5h. The register is write-only. Before sending data, send 2 to port 3C4h as an index. Bits 0–3 of this register correspond to bit planes 0–3; the high four bits of the register are not used. When bits 0–3 are 0, the corresponding plane is unaffected by write operations. This feature is used in different ways by the various write modes, as you will see below.

The three write modes are set by the *mode register,* a write-only register at 3CFh that is indexed by first sending 5h to port 3CEh. The write mode is set in bits 0 and 1 as a number from 0 to 2. Bit 2 should be 0, as should bits 4 through 7. Bit 3 sets up one of two modes for reading from the video buffer. The bit may be set to either 1 or 0. The EGA and VGA BIOS initializes the write mode to 00.

Write Mode 0: In the simplest case, write mode 0 copies the byte of CPU data into each of the four bit planes. For example, say that 11111111b is sent to a video memory address when all bits and all bit planes are enabled (that is, none are masked out using the registers discussed above). Every bit in all four planes is set to 1, so that the bit pattern for each of the corresponding pixels is 1111b. This means that the eight pixels are shown in color code 15, which is initialized to bright white, although the palette registers allow it to be any other color, of course.

Now, consider the same case, but sending the value 00001000b. The bit pattern for pixel 3 is 1111, and for the others it is 0000, which corresponds to black (at start-up). And so in this case only pixel 3 would appear on the screen (again as bright white), and the other seven pixels would be "off." Even if the other seven pixels were already set to display a color, they would all be switched to 0000.

Next, consider using a color other than 1111b. If you send the palette code of the desired color to the map mask register, the register will mask out certain bit planes in a way that creates that color. For example, if you want the color code to be 0100, send 0100 to the map mask register. Bit planes 0, 1, and 3 will then be immune from changes. When you send 11111111b to the address, that value will be placed only in bit plane 2, and the bit patterns for each pixel will be 0100. If you send 00001000b to the address, pixel 3 will have the pattern 0100B, and all other pixels will be 0000b.

There is a complication, however. The map mask register *disables* bit planes, but it does not zero them. Say that bit plane 0 is filled with 1s, and that bit planes 1 and 3 are filled with 0s. If you disable these three planes and then write 11111111b to the video address, bit plane 2 will be filled by 11111111B, and bit plane 0 will keep its 1s, so that the resulting color code for each pixel will be 0101b. There are cases where you may wish to use this feature as a means of adjusting screen colors. But generally it is necessary to *clear* all four bit planes (that is, all four latch registers) before writing in any color other than 1111b or

0000b. This is done simply by sending 0 to the address. Be sure that all four bit planes are enabled when doing this.

The discussion up to now has concerned writing eight pixels at once. What about writing fewer pixels? In this case, existing pixel data must be preserved, of course, and this is done by seeing to it that the current contents of the video address are stored in the latch registers. Then the *bit map register* is used to mask out those pixels that are not to be changed. When a bit is set to 0 in this register, the data sent from the CPU for that bit is ignored, and instead the data for the bit that is found in the latch registers is used. Whether the bit in the CPU data is a 1 or a 0 makes no difference; if you are changing only bit 2 and all others are masked out, the data you send to the CPU could be 0FFh, or 4h, or any other value in which bit 2 is turned on. If bit 2 is off, 0 is placed in that position in all enabled bit planes.

Generally, a program must first *read* any memory position to which it is about to write fewer than eight pixels. There are two read modes (discussed in "Find the Color at a Point on the Screen," below) and it does not matter which is selected. The read operation "primes" the latch registers with the four bytes of data from that memory address. The data returned to the CPU by the read operation may be discarded.

All of this comprises only the most *basic* functioning of write mode 0. You can make matters much more complicated if you like. One option is to modify the latch contents before writing, using logical operations. The *data rotate register* uses the following bit pattern to provide these services:

```
bits   2-0   rotate count

4-3    00     data unmodified

01     data ANDed with latch contents

10     data ORed with latch contents

11     data XORed with latch contents

7-5    unused
```

The data rotate count, from 0 to 7, sets how many bits the data is rotated before it is placed in the latch. Normally the value is 0. Similarly, bits 4–3 are 00 except when the data is to be ANDed, ORed, or XORed. By clever manipulation of these features, the same data can result in different colors and images, all without any additional CPU processing. The data rotate register is indexed by sending 3 to port address 3CEh; then send the data to 3CFh.

Finally, write mode 0 can be made to operate completely differently by enabling the *set/reset* feature. Here, a particular color is kept stored in the low four bits of the *set/reset register* (also located at 3CFh, and indexed by sending 0 to 3CEh). There is a corresponding register, the *enable set/reset register* which enables any or all of these four bits by setting its own low bits to 1. When all four bits in the set/ reset register are enabled, they are placed in all eight locations of the bit plane when data is received from the CPU, and the CPU data is completely discarded. When fewer than all four of the set/reset bits are enabled, the CPU data is placed in the unenabled bit maps. Note that the bit mask register will prevent the set/reset data from being written to certain pixels, but that the map mask register setting is ignored by the set/reset feature. BIOS initializes the enable set/reset register to zeros so that it is inactive. It is located at 3CFh and is indexed by sending 1 to 3CEh.

Write Mode 1: Write mode 1 is for special applications. In this mode, the current contents of the latch register are written to the specified address. Recall that the latch registers are filled by a read operation. This mode is extremely useful for rapidly transferring data during scroll operations. The bit mask register and map mask register have no effect on this operation. Nor does it matter what value it is that the CPU sends to the particular memory address — the latch contents are dumped without alteration.

Write Mode 2: Write mode 2 provides an alternate way of setting individual pixels. The CPU sends a value in which only the four low bits are significant, and these four bits are taken as a *color* (palette register index). This is to say that the bit pattern is inserted *across* the four bit planes. The pattern is replicated across all eight positions at that memory address unless the bit mask register has been set up to protect certain pixels from being changed. The map mask register is active, as in write mode 0. Of course, the CPU must send a whole byte to the memory address, but only the low four bits are significant.

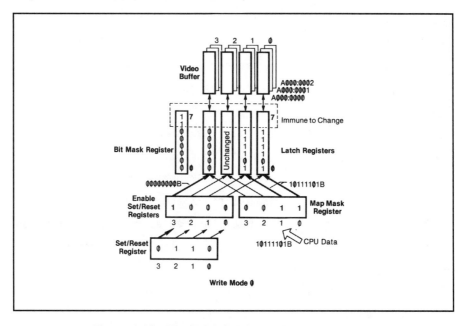

Figure 15-2   The EGA/VGA graphics write modes

Section 15.2 shows how pixels are set through functions provided by BASIC, Pascal, and C. The examples below show how to program the video controller directly.

BASIC

First, you need to set the write mode. This example sets write mode 2:

```
OUT &H3CE,5        'index the mode register
OUT &H3CF,2        'select mode 2
```

The original write mode should also be restored when the program is finished. Here are samples of code that perform the actual memory mapping:

Write Mode 0:

```
'draw red pixel at top left corner of the screen:
DEF SEG=&HA000          'point to the video buffer
OUT &H3CE,8             'address the bit mask register
OUT &H3CF,128           'mask out all bits but 7
X=PEEK(0)               'read current contents into latches
POKE 0,0                'clear
OUT &H3C4,2             'address map mask register
OUT &H3C5,4             'set red as the color
POKE 0,&HFF             'draw the pixel
```

Write Mode 1:

```
'copy top scan line to the scan line below:
DEF SEG=&HA000          'point to video buffer
FOR N=0 TO 79           'for all 80 bytes in the line
X=PEEK(N)               'fill the latches
POKE N+80,Y             'empty latches at scan segment below
NEXT                    'go do next scan line segment
```

Write Mode 2:

```
'draw a red pixel at the top left corner of the screen:
DEF SEG=&HA000          'point to the video buffer
```

```
OUT &H3CE,8                    'address the bit mask register
OUT &H3CF,128                  'mask out all but bit 7
X=PEEK(0)                      'fill the latch registers
POKE 0,4                       'send red as the color
```

Pascal

First, set the write mode. These lines set write mode 2:

```
Port[$3CE] := 5;              {index the mode register}
Port[$3CF] := 2;              {select mode 2}
```

Here are examples of write modes 0–2:

Write Mode 0:

```
{draw red pixel at top left corner of the screen}
Port[$3CE] := 8;              {address the bit mask register)
Port[$3CF] := 128;            {mask out all bits but 7)
X := Mem[$A000:0];            {read current contents into latches)
Mem]$A000:0] := 0;            {clear)
Port[$3C4] := 2;              {address map mask register)
Port[$3C5] := 4;              {set red as the color)
Mem[$A000:0] := $FF;          {draw the pixel)
```

Write Mode 1:

```
{copy top scan line to the scan line below)
for N := 0 TO 79              {for all 80 bytes in the line)
begin
  X := Mem[$A000:N];          {fill the latches)
  Mem[$A000:N+80] := Y;       {empty latches at scan segment below)
end;                          {go do next scan line segment)
```

Write Mode 2:

```
{draw a red pixel at the top left corner of the screen)
Port[$3CE] := 8;              {address the bit mask register)
```

```
Port[$3CF] := 128;          {mask out all but bit 7)
X := Mem[$A000:0];          {fill the latch registers)
Mem[$A000:0] := 4;          {send red as the color)
```

C

These examples use the Borland C *inportb* and *outportb* functions. In Microsoft C, use *inp* and *outp* instead. Begin by setting the write mode, in this case to write mode 2:

```
outportb(0x3CE,5);                  'index the mode register
outportb(0x3CF,2);                  'select mode 2
```

Write Mode 0:

```
/* draw red pixel at top left corner of the screen */
char far *buffer = 0xA0000000;
outportb(0x3CE,8);       /* address the bit mask register */
outportb(0x3CF,128);     /* mask out all bits but 7 */
x = *buffer;             /* read current contents into
                            latches */
*buffer = 0;             /* clear */
outportb(0x3C4,2);       /* address map mask register */
outportb(0x3C5,4);       /* set red as the color */
*buffer = 0xFF;          /* draw the pixel */
```

Write Mode 1:

```
/* copy top scan line to the scan line below */
char far *buffer = 0xA0000000;


for(i=0;i <= 79;i++){ /* for all 80 bytes in the line */
  x = *buffer;         /* fill the latches */
  *(buffer+80) = y;    /* empty latches at scan segment below */
}                      /* go do next scan line segment */
```

484

Write Mode 2:

```
/* draw a red pixel at the top left corner of the screen */
char far *buffer = 0xA0000000;

outportb(0x3CE,8);      /* address the bit mask register */
outportb(0x3CF,128);    /* mask out all but bit 7 */
x = *buffer;            /* fill the latch registers */
*buffer = 4;            /* send red as the color */
```

Assembler

Use function Ch of interrupt 10h. On entry, DX holds the row, and CX the column, both counted from 0. The color code is placed in AL.

```
;---DRAW A PIXEL AT 50,100:
        mov   ah,0Ch        ;function to set dot
        mov   al,12         ;choose palette register 12
        mov   cx,100        ;column
        mov   dx,50         ;row
        int   10h           ;draw the dot
```

Low-Level Access

Examples of the three write modes are given below. Before using them you must set a screen mode that uses the video buffer at A000:0000. Use the ordinary BIOS function; for example, to set mode D:

```
        mov   ah,0          ;function to change mode
        mov   al,0Dh        ;choose mode D
        int   10h           ;change the mode
```

Be sure to restore the prior mode when finished. You will also need to set the write mode. Here is an example that sets write mode 2:

```
        mov   dx,3CEh       ;point to address register
        mov   al,5          ;index register 5
```

```
        out   dx,al              ;send the index
        inc   dx                 ;point to mode register
        mov   al,2               ;choose write mode 2
        out   dx,al              ;set the mode
```

Finally, here are examples of the three write modes:

Write Mode 0:

```
;---DRAW RED PIXEL AT TOP LEFT CORNER OF SCREEN:
        mov   ax,0A000h          ;point ES to buffer
        mov   es,ax              ;
        mov   bx,0               ;point to first byte of the buffer
;---MASK ALL BITS BUT BIT 7:
        mov   dx,3CEh            ;point to address register
        mov   al,8               ;register number
        out   dx,al              ;send it
        inc   dx                 ;now point to data register
        mov   al,10000000b       ;the mask
        out   dx,al              ;send the data
;---CLEAR CURRENT LATCH CONTENTS:
        mov   al,es:[bx]         ;read contents in
        mov   al,0               ;get ready to clear
        mov   es:[bx],al         ;clear it
;---SET UP MAP MASK REGISTER FOR RED:
        mov   dx,3C4h            ;point to address register
        mov   al,2               ;map mask register index
        out   dx,al              ;set the address
        inc   dx                 ;point to data register
        mov   al,4               ;color code
        out   dx,al              ;set the color
;---DRAW THE PIXEL:
        mov   al,0FFh            ;send any value with bit 7 on
        mov   es:[bx],al         ;pixel written
```

<u>Write Mode 1:</u>

```
;---COPY A SCAN LINE TO THE SCAN LINE BELOW:
        mov   cx,80           ;eighty bytes in a scan line
        mov   bx,0            ;start from first byte of buffer
        mov   ax,0A000h       ;buffer address
        mov   es,ax           ;point ES to it
NEXT_BYTE:
        mov   al,es:[bx]      ;fill latch registers with data
        mov   es:[bx]+80,al   ;empty latch at scan segment below
        inc   bx             ;point to next byte
        loop NEXT_BYTE        ;go do next
```

<u>Write Mode 2:</u>

```
;---DRAW RED PIXEL AT TOP LEFT CORNER OF SCREEN:
        mov   ax,0A000h       ;point ES to buffer
        mov   es,ax           ;
        mov   bx,0            ;point to first byte of the buffer
;---SET UP BIT MASK REGISTER:
        mov   dx,3CEh         ;point to address register
        mov   al,8            ;bit mask register
        out   dx,al           ;address the register
        inc   dx             ;point to data register
        mov   al,10000000b    ;mask out all bits but bit 7
        out   dx,al           ;send the data
;---DRAW A RED PIXEL:
        mov   al,es:[bx]      ;fill the latch registers
        mov   al,4            ;red
        mov   es:[bx],al      ;draw the pixel
```

Find the Color at a Point on the Screen

For the graphics modes of the CGA, finding the color of a pixel at low-level entails no more than reversing the procedures that write one: A program reads from video memory and isolates the relevant bits. The EGA and VGA, however, cannot be accessed this way in modes Dh – 10h, since there are two or more bytes of memory at any particular address. There are two *read modes* to deal with this situation. Keep in mind that once you find the color code for a pixel, you still must check the current palette register setting for that code in order to find the color it is associated with.

Any programming language can access the two read modes. Mode 0 returns the byte found at any one of the bit planes at the particular address. Mode 1 seeks a specified color code and returns a byte in which a bit is set to 1 when the corresponding pixel has that color. Bit 3 of the *mode register* determines which read mode is in effect (0=mode 0). This register is at port address 3CFh, and you must first send 5 to 3CEh to select the register. Ordinarily, all other bits in this write-only register are set to 0, except for bits 0 and 1, which set the write mode. Since the BIOS sets these two bits for write mode 0 (so that they are both 0), normally you need only send 0 to the register to bring about read mode 0, or send 8 to invoke read mode 1.

Read mode 0 requires that you first set the *map select register*. The sole purpose of this register is to set which bit map is to be read. So send a number from 0 – 3 to it. The register is at port address 3CFh, and 4 must first be sent to 3CEh to index the register.

Read mode 1 is more complicated. First the *color compare* register must be given the bit pattern of the color code you are seeking. The code is placed in the bottom four bits of the register; the high four bits are not significant. The register is at port address 3CFh, and it is indexed by first sending 2 to 3CEh. When the memory position is read, a byte is returned with 1s for every pixel that matches that color. However, by using the *color don't care* register, one or more bits of the color code can be ignored when the comparison is made. Normally the four low bits of this register are set to 1; zeroing one of these bits causes the contents of the corresponding bit plane to be ignored. For example, ordinarily if the bit pattern for pixel #3 (bit 3) at a particular address is 0110, and the color compare register contains the value 0010, it will return a byte in which bit 3=0 when the color don't care register is all 1s. But if the color don't care register contained 1011, bit 3 would be set to 1 in the byte returned to the CPU. The color don't care register is at 3CFh, and it is indexed by sending 7 to 3CEh. The high four bits are not significant.

Neither of the two read modes can quickly tell the color of a particular pixel. In read mode 0, four separate reads are required, one for each bit plane, and then the relevant bits must be masked out of each byte. In read mode 1, on the other hand, it could take up to 16 reads before a 1 is returned for a particular pixel, showing that it is the specified color.

BASIC

BASIC provides the POINT function to return the color of a pixel. The palette color of the pixel at column 200, row 100 is found by **Q=POINT(200,100)**. The value given to Q is an ordinary color code number. If a point off-screen is named, POINT returns –1. When the coordinate system of the screen has been changed by a WINDOW statement, the POINT statement observes the new system.

POINT can also report the position of the last pixel drawn. Using the ordinary coordinate system where 0,0 is the top left corner of the screen, **Q=POINT(1)** gives to Q the x coordinate of the pixel, and **Q=POINT(2)** gives the y coordinate. If a WINDOW statement is in effect, **Q=POINT(3)** and **Q=POINT(4)** provide the respective x and y coordinates in the specified coordinate system. When no WINDOW statement is operational, the second two statements operate like the first two.

Pascal

Turbo Pascal's *GetPixel* function returns the value of a pixel at specified coordinates. The return value is of *word* type. To find the color of the pixel at **33,77**, write:

```
var

  ThePixel: word;


ThePixel = GetPixel(33,77);
```

C

Borland C's *getpixel* function, and Microsoft C's *_getpixel*, return the value of a specified pixel as an unsigned integer. The function takes two parameters: first the horizontal pixel position, and then the vertical position:

```
unsigned the_pixel;


the_pixel = getpixel(33,77);
```

Assembler

Function D of interrupt 10h returns the color code of a specified pixel. Place the row number (counting from 0) in DX, the column number (also from 0) in CX. The result is returned in AL.

```
;---FIND THE PALETTE CODE OF 100,200:
        mov   ah,0Dh         ;function number to read dot
        mov   dx,100         ;row number
        mov   cx,200         ;column number
        int   10h            ;and now the palette code is in AL
```

Low-Level Access

For CGA or MCGA graphics modes, simply reverse the memory mapping process by which a pixel is set, as shown in "Draw a Pixel (CGA, MCGA, HGC)," above. Use the same example found there, but end it this way:

```
;---CHANGE THE BITS (starting point for the change):
        mov   ah,es:[bx]     ;get byte from correct position
        ror   ah,cl          ;move 2 relevant bits to bottom of AH
        and   ah,00000011b   ;make out other bits
        ret                  ;and now AH holds the palette code
```

For EGA and VGA modes that use bit planes, manipulate the registers discussed above. The following example reads bit plane 2 at memory address A000:0012.

```
;---SET THE READ MODE:
        mov   dx,3CEh        ;index register
        mov   al,5           ;address the mode register first
        out   dx,al          ;send the index
        inc   dx             ;point to the register itself
        mov   al,0           ;all bits off for read more 0
        out   dx,al          ;set the mode
;---SET WHICH BIT PLANE TO READ:
```

```
        dec   dx                ;point back to index register
        mov   al,4              ;address the map select register
        out   dx,al            ;send the index
        inc   dx                ;point to the register itself
        mov   al,2              ;request bit map 2
        out   dx,al            ;send the value
;---READ THE BIT MAP:
        mov   ax,0A000h         ;buffer starts at A000:0000
        mov   es,ax            ;point ES to the buffer
        mov   bx,12            ;offset in buffer
        mov   al,es:[bx]       ;read bit plane 2
```

Finally, here is an example that seeks color code 0010 or 1010 using read mode 1:

```
;---SET THE READ MODE:
        mov   dx,3CEh           ;index register
        mov   al,5              ;address the mode register first
        out   dx,al            ;send the index
        inc   dx                ;point to the register itself
        mov   al,8              ;set bit 3 for read mode 1
        out   dx,al            ;set the mode
;---SET THE COLOR COMPARE REGISTER:
        dec   dx                ;return to index register
        mov   al,2              ;address of color compare register
        out   dx,al            ;send the index
        inc   dx                ;point to the register itself
        mov   al,0010b          ;the color code
        out   dx,al            ;send the code
;---SET THE COLOR DON'T CARE REGISTER:
        dec   dx                ;back to the index register
        mov   al,7              ;address of color don't care register
```

```
        out  dx,al              ;send the index
        inc  dx                 ;point to the register itself
        mov  al,0111b           ;accept either 1010 or 0010
        out  dx,al              ;send the value
;---SEEK THE COLOR:
        mov  ax,0A000h          ;buffer starts at A000:0000
        mov  es,ax              ;point ES to the buffer
        mov  bx,12              ;offset in buffer
        mov  al,es:[bx]         ;read the buffer position
        cmp  al,0               ;any bits set?
        jnz  FOUND_IT           ;if so, go find out which ones
```

16

Controlling a Printer

Minitutorial: Controlling a Printer

There are two major classes of printers: *line printers* and *page printers*. A line printer is one that prints out data line by line starting from the top of the page. Page printers, on the other hand, receive all data for an entire page before printing it. Dot-matrix printers and inkjet printers are line printers; laser printers are page printers. Despite the differences in their functioning and quality of output, programming is similar for the two kinds of printers. By default, the printers expect to receive a stream of text, which they print just as if the text were sent to the video display, starting a new line when the ASCII codes for carriage-return (and line-feed) appear, or wrapping automatically when a line exceeds the page width.

Special codes are sent to a printer to set the many specifications for page format, type style, and so on. These codes are transmitted to the printer like any other data. Some are no more than one-byte codes from the first 32 bytes of the ASCII character set, the *control codes* (they are listed in Chapter 17, "Look Up a

Communications Control Code"). However, most print specifications are sent as *escape sequences*, where one or more code bytes follow the escape character (ASCII 27). The escape character informs the printer that the characters that follow are to be interpreted as commands, rather than as data. Such escape sequences generally have no terminating character, since the printer "knows" the length of each sequence. Only when the escape sequence is of variable length is a terminating character required.

HP LaserJet printers have a special format for escape sequences. Various symbols follow the initial escape character to specify the nature of the command and to supply parameters that it uses. The final symbol in the sequence is normally an uppercase alphabetic character, while prior characters are written in lowercase, as in **Esc & a 7 L**. Here, the final "L" specifies a page's left margin. Another command, **Esc & a 4 5 M**, sets the right margin. Similar commands can be reduced to a single escape sequence by combining the variable final parts of the commands, but capitalizing only the last character. In this case, the composite command would be **Esc & a 7 l 4 5 M**. Notice that numbers are written in decimal form; the value **45** is expressed as the two ASCII characters representing "4" and "5," not as the single value, ASCII character #45.

In many instances, the specifications made by escape sequences stay in effect until they are explicitly undone. Once the code for underlining is received, for example, underlining continues indefinitely until the code that stops underlining is sent. The same goes for the selection of a font or the type size. The printer's buffer may be cleared without affecting the specifications. But if there is a printer error and the printer is reset, then all specifications are cleared and they must be sent to the printer once again.

Most codes that set print specifications are interspersed throughout the data they affect. For example, data for a word that is to be boldfaced is preceded by an escape sequence that turns boldfacing on and followed by an escape sequence that turns it off. Since there is no universal standard for the various codes, sophisticated printing requires that printer drivers be written for every printer that is to be supported. Each driver converts instructions generated by the print routine into the protocol used by the particular printer. Writing printer drivers is arguably the greatest hardware-compatability nightmare in the IBM PC world.

Graphics are normally printed by sending a command sequence that sets the printer in a graphics mode. Most dot-matrix printers provide a number of graphics modes that vary in the resolution at which they draw dots on the page. One mode might draw 80 dots per inch, another mode might draw 240. The image that is to be drawn is then sent to the printer. This is done by reducing the image to a bit pattern. In many printers, the top eight rows (bits) of the image are converted into a sequence of bytes with each row corresponding to a bit in each byte. Then, following a carriage return, the next eight rows of the image are printed, and so on.

Once a dot-matrix printer is set to a graphics mode, it treats incoming text as if it were bit patterns from a graphics image. Although the printer can be switched

494

back and forth between graphics and text modes, it can be difficult to align graphics and text objects, particularly when they are side by side on the same lines. So it may be necessary to set up fonts as graphics images and print text as a kind of graphic too. Unfortunately, printers take longer to print a page when working in graphics modes. In a text mode, a single ASCII character is converted by the printer into the image of a character. In a graphics mode, every dot of every character must be sent from the computer, and this takes time.

Laser printers make it much easier to mix graphics and text. Because they are page printers, a program can send data for the various parts of the page in any order. When text is printed to the right of a graphic, a program can send the entire graphic, and then the text. By comparison, output to a dot-matrix printer would need to output a horizontal strip of first the graphic and then the text, then the next strip, and so on.

Laser printers are also placed in a graphics mode when they print graphics. Escape sequences announce the dimensions and placement of a graphic that is about to arrive. Then the graphics data is output, reduced to a bit image just as for a dot-matrix printer. Text is transmitted as one-byte ASCII characters, and the printer draws the characters in whatever typeface, style, and size is currently specified. The printer maintains a pointer to the page — a sort of cursor that can be manipulated by escape sequences — and text is printed at this position. When the entire contents of the page have been output, a final command code is issued and the printer proceeds to print the page and eject it.

Most laser printers operate at a 300-dots-per-inch (dpi) resolution. While dot-matrix printers may nominally provide a similar resolution (their dots are much larger than a laser printer's), they offer such accuracy only along the horizontal axis. The vertical resolution of dot-matrix printers is much lower. This means that when graphics are transmitted to a dot-matrix printer, much less data is required than for the same graphic on a laser printer.

To limit the time and processing required for sending graphics, laser printers may have built-in graphics generating capabilities. A single command sequence from the computer tells the printer to draw a graphic of particular shape and dimensions. In the simplest case, a laser printer may offer a small library of graphics functions, including the ability to draw a variety of lines and rectangles, and to fill them with standard patterns.

At the other extreme, the printer may incorporate a graphics generation language like *PostScript*. In this case, application software sends programs written in this language to the printer, and the printer interprets the programs and generates the corresponding graphics. Obviously, software must be specially designed to use a language like *PostScript*, since the program's own internal representation of graphics must complement their description in *PostScript*. This can create problems when the graphics must also be displayed on a (*non-PostScript*) screen.

As you can see, programs treat data differently when using line printers and page printers. Although laser printers are a little harder to program than dot-matrix printers for simple text output, they make graphics much easier. When text and graphics are mixed, a program normally needs to create separate printer-output routines for the two kinds of printers.

To make matters more complicated, there are four basic printer standards in the IBM PC world, and many variants. These standards are:

- ***The Diablo standard.*** Named for the American company that developed it, this is the earliest and most primitive of the standards. It is oriented toward daisy-wheel printers. Its only graphics capability is in striking the page repeatedly with the period symbol. So much business software supports this standard that many printers provide an operating mode in which they emulate it.

- ***The Epson standard.*** This is the dot-matrix standard found in the printers offered by IBM for the first PCs. It was developed by a Japanese company, *Epson*, and its basic commands are found in most Japanese printers. Lots of bells and whistles have since been added to this standard. More printers support this standard than any other.

- ***The ISO standard.*** Formulated by the *International Standards Organization*, the ISO standard is essentially a superset of the Epson standard. It's advanced features include the ability to rotate and invert fonts, and to report certain kinds of information, such as font widths, to the program using the printer.

- ***The PCL standard.*** The PCL ("Printer Control Language") standard was developed for the Hewlett-Packard LaserJet printers. This "language" is really nothing more than a system of escape sequences. The LaserJet printers normally operate as text-oriented page printers that can handle graphics on part of the page (or all of the page in some recent models). Hewlett Packard has made the *PostScript* language an option in its newest printers.

Hewlett-Packard's *LaserJet* printers so dominate the IBM PC laser printer market that programs can safely support this laser printer standard alone. Other manufacturers have cloned these printers, and even radically different laser printers, such as the PostScript-oriented Apple *LaserWriter* printers, provide LaserJet emulation modes. As Laserjet printers have evolved, so has PCL, and today there are three main "levels" (versions) of the language:

- **PCL 3.** Found in the earliest LaserJets, it does little more than print high-quality text and handle simple graphics.

- **PCL 4.** Level 4 is used in the LaserJet Plus and the immensely successful LaserJet II printers. It adds support for downloaded fonts. More advanced models of the LaserJet II add a few extensions to this standard, such as the ability to choose paper trays. PCL4 is the *de facto* laser printer standard for PCs. It serves the vast majority of LaserJet printers in use.

- **PCL 5.** PCL5 was introduced with the LaserJet III printers. PCL is radically revised in this version, with the addition of a powerful graphics language called *HP-GL/2* that supports *scalable fonts* (fonts that can be drawn in nearly any point size). Programming HP-GL/2 is a complicated topic that requires a book of its own. We won't discuss it here.

This chapter shows the basic commands by which pages are formatted, fonts are chosen and manipulated, and graphics are constructed in each of the four printer standards. You'll find that good printer routines require a lot of work and a lot of cleverness. The more printers your software supports, the harder the job becomes. Because many printers deviate from the standards, a programmer is confronted with the prospect of needing to test software with hundreds of printers. In reality, software must be limited both in what it attempts to do with printers, and in how many printers it supports. Often, programs are crafted to support a dozen mainstream printers, and adjustments are then made as users report problems in using the program with their particular printers.

Initialize the Printer Port/Reinitialize the Printer

Traditionally, PCs have interacted with printers through parallel ports. For this reason, DOS names the parallel ports *LPT1* (for "line printer #1"), *LPT2*, and so on. However, many printers, particularly laser printers, operate through serial ports. Printers work in the same way no matter which kind of port they use. Programs send the same sequences of codes and data in either case. This chapter concerns itself with parallel ports. See Chapter 17 to learn about serial communications.

Every parallel device connects to its own port. A parallel port is manipulated through three I/O registers, and the I/O addresses of these registers are different for each port. The BIOS data area contains the base address of each adaptor. A *base address* gives the lowest address of the group of three port addresses. The base address for LPT1 is at 0040:0008, for LPT 2 it is at 0040:000A, and so on. A base address is initialized to 0 when no corresponding adaptor is installed. A program can swap base addresses to change the printer represented by LPT1.

The *data output register* is the port address to which each byte of data is sent on its way to the printer. The *status register* reports a variety of information about the printer. The CPU may continuously monitor this register to find out when it is all right to send data. The status register also reports when a printer error has occurred. The *control register* initializes the printer and controls the output of data. It also can set up a port for interrupt operations so that the printer will interrupt the CPU when it is ready for more data, freeing the CPU for other tasks. Here are the bit patterns in the status and control registers:

Control Register:
```
bit   0    0=normal setting, 1=initiates output of byte of data
      1    0=normal setting, 1=automatic line feed after CR
      2    0=initialize printer port, 1=normal setting
      3    0=deselect printer, 1=normal setting
      4    0=printer interrupt disabled, 1=interrupts enabled
     5-7   unused
```

Status Register:
```
bit 0-2  unused
     3   0=printer error, 1=no error
```

```
4    0=printer not on line, 1=printer on line

5    0=printer has paper, 1=printer out of paper

6    0=printer acknowledges receipt of character, 1=normal

7    0=printer busy, 1=printer not busy
```

Refer to "Test that a Printer Is On-line," which follows, for examples of how the status register is used, and "Output Data to a Printer," below, to see how the registers are manipulated to transmit data.

Because printer status information is always available, there is no good reason for any program to lack the error recovery routines needed to deal with printer problems. A well-written program should begin by checking that a printer is on-line. If more than one printer is connected, the program should let the user choose the one he prefers. And the print routine should be able to recover from printer errors of any kind, preferably without requiring that the entire document be redone.

Programs can initialize each printer port prior to its first use, or after a printer error condition is corrected. Do not confuse printer port initialization with the initialization of the printer itself. Printer initialization occurs automatically within a printer when the printer is turned on. Most printers can be reset by buttons on the printer, or by a code sent from the computer. Some printers, including Epson and IBM printers, respond to the initialization of a printer port by resetting themselves. Many other printers do not respond to port initialization. A few printers are actually disrupted by port initialization.

Programs can reinitialize *all* printers in the sense that they can restore the printer's default settings by returning the printer to a standard text-input mode and cancelling special settings for fonts, tabs, and so on. It is good programming practice to reset a printer this way when a program has finished with it. Keep in mind that virtually all printers have buffers that hold incoming data. In certain situations, a program may terminate before the last data it placed in the buffer has been printed. When another program starts using the printer, the lingering data may be printed. To avoid this problem, always clear the buffer before starting to print.

HP LaserJet printers are reinitialized by the sequence:

```
<Esc> E              (0B 45)
```

Besides returning a printer to its default settings, this command causes the printer to print out any data left in its buffer.

Function 1 of BIOS interrupt 17h initializes a printer port and returns a byte giving the port's status. On entry, DX holds the port number, counted from 0 upward. The printer status byte discussed in "Test that a Printer Is On-line," which follows, is returned in AH. None of the compilers discussed in this book has a printer initialization routine. Instead, you must call interrupt 17h.

BASIC

```
' $INCLUDE: 'QBX.BI'
DIM REGS AS RegType                   ' Define register array

REGS.AX = &h0100                      'function number
REGS.DX = &H0000                      'LPT 1
CALL Interrupt(&H17, REGS, REGS)      'initialize the port
```

Pascal

```
Uses DOS;
Var
   Regs: Registers;   {Registers type is declared in the DOS unit}

Regs.AH := 1;     {function number}
Regs.DX := 0;     {LPT 1}
Intr($17,Regs);   {initialize the port}
```

C

```
#include <dos.h>
union REGS regs;            /* declare the register array */

regs.h.ah = 1;              /* function number */
regs.x.dx = 0;             /* lpt1 */
int86(0x17,&regs,&regs);   /* initialize the port */
```

Assembler

```
;---INITIALIZE LPT1:

      mov   ah,1        ;function to initialize printer

      mov   dx,0        ;LPT1

      int   17h         ;make the initialization
```

Low-Level Access

The output control register of each printer adaptor has a bit that causes the parallel port to initialize. This register is located at the port address that is 2 higher than the base address of the adaptor. Recall that the base address for LPT1 is kept at 0040:0008, for LPT2 it is at 0040:000A, and so on. Only the low five bits of the output control register are significant. Bit 2 is the printer initialization bit, and ordinarily it is set to 1. To initialize the printer, set this bit to 0 for 1/20th second using the BIOS time-of-day count (as explained in Chapter 5, "Time or Delay Program Operations"). Only bit 3 ("printer selected") needs to be set at this time. So send 8 (00001000) to the port, make the delay, and then send the usual (noninterrupt) initialization value to the register, which is 12 (00001100).

This example initializes LPT1:

```
;---INITIALIZE LPT1:

         mov   ax,40h       ;point ES to BIOS data area

         mov   es,ax

         mov   dx,es:[8]    ;move base address to DX

         inc   dx           ;add 2 to the base address

         inc   dx           ;

         mov   al,8         ;initialization value

         out   dx,al        ;start the initialization

         push  dx           ;save register address

         mov   ah,0         ;function to read time-of-day

         int   1ah          ;time-of-day now in DX:CX

         add   dx,2         ;use just the low word

         mov   bx,dx        ;save in BX

DELAY:   mov   ah,0         ;get ready to call function again
```

```
        int    1ah              ;get new time-of-day reading
        cmp    dx,bx            ;compare to target reading
        jne    DELAY            ;loop till time arrives
        pop    dx               ;restore register address
        mov    al,12            ;normal value for the control register
        out    dx, al           ;end initialization
```

Test that a Printer is On-line

A program should always test that a printer is on-line before transmitting data. It is easy to ascertain that a printer is not ready since bit 3 of the printer status register is set in this case. But it is more difficult to find out exactly *why* the printer is not ready: whether it is (a) turned off, (b) deselected, or (c) out of paper. This is because printers of different manufacture bring about different bit patterns in the status register even when they are in an identical state. Although the status register has bits that should show the three printer states, the bit patterns that actually occur with these conditions may not be in accord. In theory, bit 3 should show that the printer is turned off, bit 4 that it is deselected, and bit 5 that paper has run out. If any values are "standard," they should be those of the original IBM/Epson printers:

value	bit pattern	interpretation
223	11011111	printer ready
87	01010111	printer not ready
119	01110111	printer out of paper
247	11110111	printer turned off

The input status register is located at the port address that is one greater than the *sa* of the printer. The base address for LPT1 is kept at 0040:0008; it is at 0040:000A for LPT2, and 0040:000C for LPT3. Keep in mind that if the printer was turned off, it will take a while to self-initialize once it is switched on. Do not begin printing until the input status register indicates that the printer is on-line and ready to receive data.

Function 2 of interrupt 17h returns the printer port status byte in the AH register. On entry, DX contains 0 for LPT1, 1 for LPT2, and so on. This function turns off the three unused bits of the byte, and it XORs two others, so the bit patterns differ from those listed above:

bit	meaning when bit is set
0	timeout
1	(unused)
2	(unused)
3	I/O error
4	printer is selected
5	printer is out of paper

bit	meaning when bit is set
6	printer is acknowledged
7	printer is *not* busy

Again, be aware that the behavior of this status byte differs from printer to printer. Note that, starting with the IBM AT, this function calls function 90h of interrupt 15h when bit seven is clear, indicating that the printer is busy. This feature lets a PC wait for networked printers, instead of returning an error message; it is of concern only to operating system designers.

The examples below call interrupt 17h to test whether LPT1 is ready.

BASIC

```
' $INCLUDE: 'QBX.BI'
DIM REGS AS RegType                  ' Define register array

REGS.AX = &H0200                     'function number
REGS.DX = &H0000                     'LPT 1
CALL Interrupt(&H17, REGS, REGS)     'get status byte
Result = REGS.AX \ 256 AND 8
If Result = 8 THEN WRITE "Printer not ready"
```

Pascal

```
Uses DOS;
Var
  Regs: Registers;  {Registers type is declared in the DOS unit}
Regs.AH := 2;      {function number}
Regs.DX := 0;      {LPT 1}
Intr($17,Regs);    {get status byte}
if Regs.AH = and 8 = 8 then Writeln('Printer not ready');
```

C

```c
#include <dos.h>
union REGS regs;              /* declare the register array */

regs.h.ah = 2;                /* function number */
regs.x.dx = 0;                /* lpt1 */
int86(0x17,&regs,&regs);      /* get status byte */
if (regs.h.ah 88) printf("Printer not ready\n");
```

Assembler

```
;---INITIALIZE LPT1:
        mov   ah,2        ;function to initialize printer
        mov   dx,0        ;LPT1
        int   17h         ;make the initialization
        test  ah,1000h    ;compare printer ready value
        jz    READY       ;jump if printer is ready
```

Low-Level Access

This example takes a simpler route by checking the "on-line" bit of the status register, using the base address of LPT1 to get the status byte.

```
;---IN THE DATA SEGMENT:
MESSAGE DB 'Printer not ready -- strike any key when OK$'

;---CHECK TO SEE IF ON LINE:
        mov   ax,40h      ;point ES to BIOS data area
        mov   es,ax       ;
        mov   dx,es:[8]   ;get the base address
        inc   dx          ;offset to status register
```

```
        in   al,dx        ;put status byte in AL
        test al,1000b     ;test bit 3
        jnz  GO_AHEAD     ;jump ahead if printer on-line
;---PRINT ERROR MESSAGE AND WAIT FOR KEYSTROKE:
        mov  ah,9         ;function to display string
        lea  dx,MESSAGE   ;DS:DX points to message
        int  21h          ;print the error message
        mov  ah,7         ;function to wait for keystroke
        int  21h          ;wait for keystroke (no echo)
GO_AHEAD:                 ;program continues...
```

Output Data to a Printer

Printers receive data one byte at a time. Working in a text mode, a printer checks each byte as it arrives to see if it is an escape character. If so, it begins interpreting the data as a command sequence. The printer knows how long each command is, and when as many bytes have been read as are required, the printer reverts to interpreting the data as text. Graphics commands normally include a specification of how many bytes of graphics data will follow. This sequence of data is not scanned for the escape character, since the binary pattern that represents Esc is a legitimate form of graphics data.

High-level languages usually provide two kinds of routines for outputting data to a printer. One kind simply sends the data; the second kind adds a carriage-return/line-feed pair (ASCII 13 and 10) after the data has been transmitted. The latter kind of routine is useful for simple "text dumps," but sophisticated printer output routines usually explicitly transmit the CR/LF. When a string is printed that is as long as the line length or longer, the print head wraps around, effectively performing a carriage return/line feed. This means that when the string length exactly matches the line length, a second line feed is made if the string is followed by a carriage-return/line-feed pair. Programs should watch for strings that would cause this to happen and avoid inserting the unnecessary CR/LF.

Be aware that many printers can be configured to perform a carriage return and line feed when only a carriage-return character is received. In this case, a CR/LF pair will leave text double-spaced. A program's documentation can warn the user of this eventuality and explain how to change dip switches to reconfigure the printer.

The printer output functions provided by high-level languages normally require data in *string* form. Thus, your programs must assemble command sequences into strings of whatever form a language requires. Single characters are output by making up strings that are only one byte long. Languages like BASIC and C, which write strings within quotation marks, can't readily handle a string that *contains* a quotation mark. Similarly, Pascal has trouble with apostrophes within strings, because Pascal strings are written between apostrophes. In all cases, you must insert the character into the string using its ASCII number instead of its ASCII symbol.

The standard printer-output routines send data to parallel port #1 (LPT1). The user can type in a DOS MODE command to redirect this output to COM1. Programs can also access a printer by "opening" it as if it were a file, and then outputting data using normal file output functions. This approach lets the program use any parallel or serial port. The file must be opened in *binary mode* so that DOS does not translate outgoing data (for example, the carriage-return character) that is intended to be used in some other way, typically as raw graphics data.

A program can devote its full attention to sending data to the printer, or it may print "in the background" by using the printer interrupt. Background printing is useful, because in most instances the mechanical process of printing does not proceed nearly as quickly as the computer can feed data to a printer. Whenever a printer is ready to receive more data, it can invoke the routine pointed to by IRQ#7 (the LPT1 interrupt). The routine in turn takes data from a holding buffer and outputs it. Meanwhile, the program that sets up the interrupt must see to it that the buffer is constantly fed new data. Interrupt service routines are discussed in Chapter 4, "Write Your Own Interrupt Service Routine." An alternative approach to background printing is to tie a printer output routine to the computer's timer interrupt, which is discussed in Chapter 5, "Set or Read the BIOS Time-of-Day Count." It is invoked 18.2 times per second. Each time the interrupt is activated, it can be made to test whether the printer is ready for more data, and to send data if so.

BASIC

BASIC provides the *LPRINT* and *PRINT#* statements for sending data to a printer. *LPRINT* needs no special preparation, but *PRINT#* requires that the printer be opened just like a file, using statements like **OPEN "LPT1" AS #1**, or **OPEN "LPT3" AS #2**. The LPRINT statement always addresses LPT1, whereas PRINT# can address any printer number. A carriage-return/line-feed pair is automatically inserted after every LPRINT and PRINT# statement, unless the statement is followed by a semicolon.

A single LPRINT statement may contain several data items in a variety of forms. The information can be written into the statement itself, as in:

```
LPRINT"The Rain In Spain"
```

or it may be referred to by variable names, as in:

```
X$="The Rain In Spain":LPRINT X$
```

Special characters may be included by using CHR$. Control sequences are normally sent this way; for example, **LPRINT CHR$(10)** sends a line-feed control code to the printer. All kinds of data can be combined in the same statement. Place semicolons between the items to have the items printed adjacent to one another, or use commas to have each item begin at the next tab position. This is to say that an LPRINT statement is printed exactly as a similarly formatted PRINT statement would be displayed on the screen. Here are some examples:

```
LPRINT S$;" and ";Y$     'combines three strings
LPRINT X,Y,Z             '3 numbers spaced as on screen
LPRINT "The total is ";X 'combines string and numeric values
```

```
LPRINT"The";CHR$(27);CHR$(45);CHR$(1);"real";CHR$(27);CHR$(45);CHR$(0);"thing."
     'underlines the middle word
```

The PRINT# statement can use the same data types as LPRINT, and it also can include many data items in one statement and can mix data of different types. Semicolons and commas operate in the same fashion. Here are some examples that parallel those above:

```
OPEN "LPT1:" AS #2
PRINT#2,S$;" and ";Y$
PRINT#2,X,Y,Z
PRINT#2,"The total is ";X
PRINT#2,"The ";CHR$(27);CHR$(45);CHR$(1);"real";
          CHR$(27);CHR$(45);CHR$(0);" thing."
```

Pascal

Use Turbo Pascal's *Write* or *Writeln* procedures to send data to a printer using the reserved word *lst*. To output the string, "The rain in Spain," write:

```
Write(lst,'The rain in Spain');
```

or

```
Writeln(lst,'The rain in Spain');
```

In the second case, the four words would be printed and then a carriage-return/line-feed pair would be transmitted. The *Write* command does not add these characters at the end of the line and subsequent *Write* statements would continue printing on the same line. For this reason, a *Write* command may have no obvious effect on a line printer until a full line of characters are output, or until the CR/LF pair is transmitted by using *Writeln*, or by writing the two characters into a *Write* statement.

This method always outputs data to LPT1. To write to a printer other than LPT1, explicitly "open" the printer as if it were a file and then, instead of *lst*, use the file variable in *Write* and *Writeln* statements:

```
Uses printer;
var
  ThePrinter: Text;


Assign(ThePrinter,'LPT2');  {set up the file variable}
```

```
Rewrite(ThePrinter);          {get ready to print}
Writeln(ThePrinter,'Here is some data');  {output some data}
```

C

In C, use the fprintf function to output data to a printer. To make it direct the data to the printer instead of the screen, use the expression *stdprn:*

```
fprintf(stdprn,"Something to print.\n");
```

The function can format output just like a screen-oriented p*rintf* statement:

```
char *the_string = "The winning number is: ";
int the_number;


fprintf(stdprn,"%s%d\n",the_string,the_number);
```

This approach to printing is convenient, but it only works with LPT1. If you need to send data to a different parallel port, open it as a stream (as if it were a file), and use *fprintf* to output data in the same way. This example sends data to LPT2 (the "w" symbol indicates that the printer is opened for "writing"):

```
FILE *myhandle;


myhandle = fopen("LPT2","w");
fprintf(myhandle,"Hello from printer number 2!\n");
```

Assembler

Function 0 of interrupt 17h sends one character to the printer. Place the character in AL and the parallel port number in DX (0 = LPT1). On return, AH holds a status register that should constantly be monitored to detect printer errors. "Test that a Printer Is On-line," on earlier pages explains how to do this. To output a stream of data, set a pointer to the buffer holding the data, and write a routine like this one:

```
j---IN THE DATA SEGMENT
      string db   '1234567890',10,13
;---OUTPUT DATA TO LPT1:
      mov   cx,12             ;CX counts number bytes output
      mov   dx,0              ;choose LPT1
```

```
            mov   bx,offset string  ;point BX to the string
NEXT_CHAR:
            mov   ah,0               ;function to send 1 byte to printer
            mov   al,[bx]            ;get a character
            int   17h                ;send the character
            test  ah,8               ;test error bit
            jnz   PRNTR_ERROR        ;if problem, jump to recovery routine
            inc   bx                 ;increment data pointer
            loop  NEXT_CHAR          ;go get next byte
```

The standard DOS function for printer output is function 5 of interrupt 21h. Simply place the character in DL and call the function. This function always accesses LPT1, and there are no return registers.

```
;---OUTPUT DATA TO LPT1:
            mov   ah,5               ;DOS function number
            mov   dl,CHAR            ;move output character to DL
            int   21h                ;send it
```

Another way to output data to the printer is by function 40h of INT 21h. This function uses *handles* (identification numbers) to access a file or device. In this case, the function uses a predefined handle for PRN. The handle is 0004h, and it is placed in BX. The function only accesses LPT1. DS:DX points to the output data, and CX holds the number of bytes to send. For example:

```
;---OUTPUT 120 BYTES OF DATA TO LPT1:
            mov   ah,40h             ;function number
            mov   bx,4               ;predefined handle for printer
            mov   cx,120             ;number of bytes to send
            lea   dx,PRTR_DATA       ;point DS:DX to the data
            int   21h                ;send the data
            jc    PRTR_ERROR         ;jump to recovery routine if error
```

On return the carry flag is set if there has been an error, in which case AX holds 5 if the printer was off line, or 6 if you used the wrong handle number. Note that there is no need to *open* a device when a predefined handle is used.

Low-Level Access

A byte of data is sent to the printer by placing it in the *output data register*, the port address of which is the same as the base address for the printer. Remember that the base addresses for LPT1–3 are the port addresses found at offsets 8, 10, and 12 in the BIOS data area (beginning at 0040:0000). Once the data is sent to the register, briefly turn on the *strobe* bit of the output control register, which is located at the port address that is 2 higher than the data register. The strobe bit is number 0, and it needs to be set to 1 only very briefly to initiate transmission of the data in the data register. The print routine may immediately change the strobe bit back to 0.

Once the byte of data is sent, the program must wait for the printer to signal that it is ready for another. This is done in two ways. When ready, the printer briefly pulses the *acknowledge bit* of the input status register. This register is located at the port address that is 1 greater than the base address of the printer. The acknowledge bit is number 6, and it normally is set to 1. The acknowledge pulse sets the bit to 0 long enough that an assembly language program is sure to catch it if it constantly monitors the register.

An alternative way of knowing that the printer is ready for another byte of data is to constantly monitor bit 7 of the status register, which is set to 0 when the printer is busy and to 1 when it is free to receive data. Use this method if you write a low-level print routine in interpreted BASIC or some other very slow language.

The following example checks the BIOS data area for the base address of LPT1, and then it writes data from a buffer pointed to by BX. The program monitors the status register for its busy signal, and at the same time it checks bit 3 to see if there has been a printer error.

```
;---GET READY:
        mov   ax,40h            ;point ES to bottom of BIOS data area
        mov   es,ax             ;
        mov   dx,es:[8]         ;put base address of LPT1 in DX
        lea   bx,DATA_START     ;BX points to data buffer
        mov   cx,DATA_LENGTH    ;number bytes to be printed
;---PREPARE TO FIND A CHARACTER:
NEXTCHAR:
        mov   al,[bx]           ;place character in AL
        out   dx,al             ;send the character
        inc   dx                ;point DX to output control register
```

```
        inc  dx                ;
        mov  al,13             ;bit pattern to pulse strobe line
        out  dx,al             ;send the strobe signal
        dec  al                ;normal bit pattern for control reg
        out  dx,al             ;turn off strobe signal
;---CHECK FOR ERRORS, WAIT TILL PRINTER READY:
        dec  dx                ;point DX to status register
NOT_YET:
        in   al,dx             ;get status byte
        test al,8              ;error?
        jnz  PRTR_ERROR        ;jump to error routine if a problem
        test al,80h            ;print busy?
        jz   NOT_YET           ;if so, loop
        inc  bx                ;printer ready, increment data pointer
        dec  dx                ;point DX to data register
        jmp  NEXTCHAR          ;go print next character
```

The printer interrupt is enabled by setting bit 4 of the printer control register. When interrupts are used, a program does not have to wait for a "not busy" signal from the printer by continuously monitoring the printer status register. Instead, a program may send a character to the printer and then go about some other business. When the printer is ready for more data, it sends an acknowledge signal (bit 6 of the status register is briefly set to 1), and the printer interrupt is automatically invoked. The interrupt handler then sends more data to the printer and returns. Chapter 4, "Write Your Own Interrupt Service Routine," shows how to set up an interrupt handler.

Control Page Layout on a Line Printer

Most line printers can print on any part of the page except for two narrow strips along the sides of the paper. Left margins are formed by printing space characters at the start of each line. Right margins are created by using an appropriate line length for the text that is printed.

To form margins at the top and bottom of the page, software must feed paper forward. When a program starts functioning, it assumes that the paper is properly aligned in the printer at the "top of form" position. There is no way for a computer (or even a printer) to tell whether the perforation between pages is properly set. When printing has proceeded to the lowest position it will occupy on a page, the program sends a "form-feed" command to the printer (ASCII 12). This action causes the printer to forward the paper to the same position on the next page that it started at on the current page. Because the form-feed command is synchronized with rotations of the printer's paper feed tractor, the top-of-form position remains consistent even when many pages are printed.

Figures 16-1 through 16-3 list escape sequences used for page layout in the three line-printer standards.

```
#7              Beep the printer speaker
#8              Backspace
#9              Horizontal tab
#10             Line feed
#11             Vertical tab
#12             Form feed
#13             Return to start of current line
#17             Select printer
#19             Deselect printer
#24             Clear the printer's buffer
Esc 1 #         Set the left margin
Esc Q #         Set the right margin
Esc @           Reinitialize the printer
Esc C #0 #      Set the page length to # inches
Esc C #         Set the page length to # lines
Esc N #         Skip over paper perforation by # lines
Esc O           Cancel the skip over performations
Esc 3 #180      180 line spacing
Esc 3 #216      216 line spacing
Esc A #60       60  line spacing
Esc A #72       72  line spacing
Esc 0           8 lines per inch
Esc 1           10 lines per inch
Esc 2           6 lines per inch
Esc B #,#, #0   Set vertical tab positions
Esc e 1 #       Set vertical tab increment
Esc f 1 #       Vertical skip
Esc D #,#…      Set horizontal tab positions
Esc e #0 #      Set horizontal tab increment
Esc f #0 #      Horizontal skip
Esc J #         Forward paper by # 180ths or 216ths inches
Esc j #         Reverse paper by # 216ths inches
Esc S # #       Set absolute print position
Esc \ # #       Set relative print position
Esc U 1         Turn on unidirectional printing mode
Esc U 0         Turn off unidirectional printing mode
Esc s 1         Select slow speed mode
Esc s 0         Cancel slow speed mode
Esc V # (data)  Repeat the data # times
Esc V #0        Cancel data repetition
Esc 6           Use 80h—9Fh as control codes
Esc 7           Use 80h—9Fh as characters
Esc #25 #0      Disable cut sheet feeder
Esc #25 #1      Select cut sheet Bin 1
Esc #25 #2      Select cut sheet Bin 2
Esc #25 #4      Enable cut sheet feeder
Esc #25 R       Eject cut sheet
Esc 9           Enable the out-of-paper sensor
Esc 8           Disable the out-of-paper sensor
```

Figure 16-1   Epson page layout commands

```
        #7              Bell
        Esc <           Soft reset (clears data)
        Esc c           Reinitialize (equivalent to power on)
        #155 z          Eject all pages held in the printer buffer
        #155 # v        Make X copies
        #155 #;#;#p     Set page orientation (landscape/por trait), page
                        length, page width.
        #155 # d        Move to absolute vertical position #
        #155 # '        Move to absolute horizontal position #
        #155 # a        Relative move rightward by #
        #155 # j        Relative move leftward by #
        #155 # k        Relative move vertically backwards by #
        #155 # c        Relative move vertically forwards by #
        #136            Set horizontal tab at current position
        #138            Set vertical tab at current position
        #9              Horizontal tab
        #11             Vertical tab
        #13             Return to start of line
        #10             Line Feed (without carriage return)
        #133            Combination of line feed and carriage return
        #8              Backspace
        #12             Form feed
        #139            Move to subscript position
        #140            Move to superscript position
```

Figure 16-2   ISO page layout commands

```
Esc #13 P         Reset printer
Esc #25 #         Select paper feed option
Esc 6             Print current line backward
Esc /             Select automatic backward printing
Esc \             Cancel backward printing
Esc 5             Cancel backward printing (same as above)
Esc ?             Enable automatic wrap
Esc 9             Set left page margin at current position
Esc 0             Set right page margin at current position
Esc C             Clear both top and bottom page margins
Esc T             Set top of page at current position
Esc L             Set bottom of page at current position
Esc #12 #         Number of lines per page
Esc !             Truncate text when lines too long
Esc #30 #         Set line spacing
Esc #11 #         Move to line #
Esc U             Move down 1/2 line for subscript
Esc D             Move up 1/2 line for superscript
Esc #10           Move up by one line
Esc #9 #          Relative move by # characters
Esc 1             Set horizontal tab at current position
Esc 8             Clear horizontal tab at current position
Esc -             Set vertical tab at current position
Esc 2             Clear all tabs
Esc #8            Backspace
Esc #9            Jump to next horizontal tab
Esc #10           Line feed
Esc #11           Jump to next vertical tab
Esc #12           Form feed
Esc #13           Move to start of current line
```

Figure 16-3   Diablo page layout commands

Control Page Layout on an HP LaserJet Printer

In HP LaserJet printers, there is an absolute margin of about 1/6th of an inch on the sides of a page, and 1/5th of an inch at the top and bottom, where the printer is physically unable to print. The area within these margins is called the *printable area*. All positions in the page are measured from the "top left corner." This position coincides with the left edge of the printable area and the actual physical edge at the top of the page, even though the printer cannot actually reach the top position. A program can optionally specify a top margin, in which case all page measurements are made from the intersection of this margin and the left edge of the printable area.

However it is defined, the top left corner corresponds to the coordinates **0,0**. Offsets within the coordinate system vary depending on the settings of the *horizontal motion index (HMI)* and the *vertical motion index (VMI)*. Normally, these two values are set to represent a character width in a fixed-pitch type, and the height of a line occupied by the type. The units of measurement can be changed to suit the task at hand. The coordinate system can be used to set left and right margins for printing text. There also are commands for defining top and bottom margins for text. A "cursor" moves within the defined boundaries, and software can position it to write anywhere on the page, just as software can write anywhere on the video display.

Figure 16-4 lists the various LaserJet page layout commands.

```
Esc E              Printer reset
Esc & 1 # A        Select paper size #
Esc & 1 # H        Select paper source #
Esc & 1 # X        Print # copies of each page
Esc & a # L        Set left margin to column #
Esc & a # M        Set right margin to column #
Esc & 1 # P        Set to # lines per logical page
#8                 Backspace
#9                 Horizontal tab
#10                Move cursor down by one line
Esc =              Half line feed
#12                Move cursor to start of next page (eject)
#13                Move cursor to beginning of the current line
#32                Move cursor one position to the right
Esc 9              Reset right and left margins to maximum
Esc & 1 # E        Set top margin to # lines
Esc & 1 # F        Set number of text lines on a page as #
Esc & k # H        Set horizontal motion index to # 1/120ths
Esc & 1 # C        Set vertical motion index to # 1/48ths
Esc & 1 # D        Set line spacing to # lines per inch
Esc & a # C        Move cursor to column #
Esc & a # R        Move cursor to row #
Esc * p # X        Move cursor horizontally by # dots
Esc * p # Y        Move cursor vertically by # dots
Esc & a # H        Horizontally position cursor relative to edge
                   of page in decipoints (1/720ths of an inch)
Esc & a # V        Vertically position cursor relative to top
                   margin in decipoints (1/720ths of an inch)
Esc & f 0 S        Push cursor position
Esc & f 1 S        Pop cursor position
```

Figure 16-4   LaserJet page layout commands

Select Line Printer Fonts

All printers provide at least some control over fonts. At the minimum, a daisy-wheel printer can underline text. At the other extreme, most dot-matrix and ink-jet printers can change fonts, can produce italics and boldface versions, and may even be able to scale fonts to many sizes. Dot-matrix printers typically have only one font that they can manipulate into the various type styles. For example, italic characters are created by differentially shifting the character matrix to the right, and boldface is made by printing each dot twice. Fonts are controlled in much the same way in all printers. A program sends a sequence of commands that set the font, font size, and font style. All text input is then written to these specifications until further commands are received. Figures 16-5 through 16-7 provide the most important font control commands in the three line-printer standards.

```
      Esc 4          Select italic style
      Esc 5          Cancel italic style
      Esc - 1        Select underline style
      Esc - 0        Cancel underline style
      #20            Cancel expanded style
      Esc E          Select emphasized style
      Esc F          Cancel emphasized style
      Esc G          Select doublestrike style
      Esc H          Cancel doublestrike style
      #15            Select condensed style
      Esc #15        Select condensed style
      #18            Cancel condensed style
      Esc #18        Cancel condensed style
      Esc W 1        Select expanded style
      Esc W 0        Cancel expanded style
      Esc w 1        Select double height style
      Esc w 0        Cancel double height style
      Esc S 0        Superscript
      Esc S 1        Subscript
      Esc T          Cancel super- or subscript
      Esc x 1        Near letter quality mode
      Esc P          10 characters per inch
      Esc M          12 characters per inch
      Esc g          15 characters per inch
      Esc p 1        Select proportional spacing
      Esc p 0        Cancel proportional spacing
      #14            Expand all on current line
      Esc #14        Expand all on current line
      Esc q 0        Select normal character style
      Esc q 1        Select outline character style
      Esc q 2        Select shadow character style
      Esc q 3        Select combined shadow/outline character style
      Esc ! #        Select style, for which the bit pattern in # is:
                        0 = Pica
                        1 = Elite
                        2 = Proportional
                        4 = Condensed
                        8 = Emphasized
                       16 = Double-Strike
```

continued

```
                       32 = Double-Width
                       64 = Italic
                      128 = Underline
    Esc k 0    Use Roman typeface
    Esc k 1    Use San Serif typeface
    Esc k 2    Use Courier typeface
    Esc k 3    Use Prestige typeface
    Esc k 4    Use Script typeface
    Esc k 5    Use OCR typeface
    Esc x 0    Draft mode
    Esc r #    Select color, for which 0 = black, 1 = red,
                 2 = blue, 3 = Violet, 4 = yellow, 5 = orange,
                 6 = green
    Esc t 0    Select Italic character set
    Esc t 1    Select Epson graphics character set
    Esc t 2    Remap user defined symbols to characters 80h through FFh

    Esc R #    Select international character set,
               for which 0 = USA, 1 = France, 2 = Germany,
                 3 = Denmark I, 4 = Sweden, 6 - Italy,
                 7 = Spain, 8 = Japan, 9 = Norway,
                 10 = Denmark II, 11 = Spain II, 12 = Latin America
    Esc m 4    Select HX-20 graphic symbols
    Esc m 0    Deselect HX-20 graphic symbols
```

Figure 16-5   Epson font control commands

```
    #155 # y        Specify typeface
    Esc ( ##        Select graphic set ## as the primary set
    Esc ) ##        Select graphic set ## as secondary set
    #155 # C        Select character point size
    Esc ( #         Specify graphic set # as primary
    Esc ) #         Specify graphic set # as secondary
    #155 # #32 K    Characters per inch
    #155 # m        Set character attributes
    #155 # #32 L    Lines per inch for text
    #155 #;# #32 G  Set spacing increment:
                       # space width
                       # distance to advance paper after blank line
    #155 #;# w      Proportional character offset:
                       # offset size
                       # sign of offset
```

Figure 16-6   ISO font control commands

```
        Esc #29          Select first character set on print wheel
        Esc #25          Select second character set on print wheel
        Esc #31 #        Set alternate character pitch
        Esc S            Return to primary character pitch
        Esc P            Select proportional spacing
        Esc Q            Cancel proportional spacing
        Esc #17 #        Change proportional spacing width by #
        Esc O            Select boldface mode
        Esc W            Select boldface mode (same as above)
        Esc &            Cancel boldface mode
        Esc E            Select underline mode
        Esc R            Cancel underline mode
        Esc A            Change color (by lifting ribbon)
        Esc B            Return to primary color
```

Figure 16-7   Diablo font control commands

Select and Download HP LaserJet Fonts

When printing text, LaserJet printers work much like line printers. Sending the ASCII code for a character to the printer causes the character to be printed at the current cursor position (analogous to the current print head position in line printers). The cursor automatically wraps to the next line when insufficient room is left to print the character. A carriage-return/line-feed pair (ASCII 13, 10) sends the cursor to the next line. An automatic form-feed occurs when a page fills. Figure 16-8 lists the escape sequences that let you select fonts, type sizes, and type styles.

```
Esc ( s # V        Set point size for primary symbol set in 1/72nds.
Esc ) s # V        Set point size for secondary symbol set in 1/72nds.
Esc ( s # H        # characters per inch if fixed, primary set.
Esc ) s # H        # characters per inch if fixed, secondary set.
Esc & k 2 S        Select compressed pitch.
Esc & k 0 S        Return to standard pitch.
Esc ( s # S        Select style.
                      0 = upright
                      1 = italic
Esc ( s # B        Select stroke weight.
                      -3 = light
                      0 = medium
                      3 = bold
Esc ( s # T        Select typeface, including:
                      0 = Line Printer
                      3 = Courier
                      4 = Helvetica
                      5 = Times Roman
                      6 = Gothic
                      8 = Prestige Elite
Esc ( s # P        Selecting spacing.
                      0 = proportional
                      1 = fixed
Esc ( 0 U          Select US ASCII symbol set.
Esc ( 8 U          Select Roman-8 symbol set.
Esc ( 0 E          Select Roman Extension symbol set.
Esc ( 1 U          Select legal symbol set.
Esc ( 0 F          Select French symbol set.
Esc ( 0 G          Select German symbol set.
Esc ( 1 S          Select Spanish symbol set.
Esc ( 1 E          Select UK symbol set.
Esc ( 0 I          Select Italian symbol set.
Esc ( 0 D          Select Danish/Norwegian symbol set.
Esc ( 1 S          Select Swedish/Finnish symbol set.
Esc ( 0 B          Select Line Draw symbol set.
Esc ( 8 M          Select Math8 symbol set.
Esc ( 3 @          Select default font as primary font.
Esc ) 3 @          Select default font as secondary font.
Esc * c # D        Specify Font ID.
Esc ( # X          Designate font # as primary.
Esc ) # X          Designate font # as seoondary.
Esc ( s # W        Download Character. # = data length. Followed by
                   character data.
Esc ) s # W        Create Font.  # = data length. Followed by
                   character data.
Esc * c # F        Delete soft fonts from memory, as follows:
                      0 = delete all
                      1 = delete only temporary soft fonts
                      2 = delete last specified font
                      3 = make last specified font temporary
                      4 = make last specified font permanent
```

Figure 16-8   LaserJet font control commands

524

Fonts are made available to LaserJet printers in three ways. First, a number of fonts reside on ROM within the printer. Second, additional ROM-based fonts can be installed by inserting a cartridge into the printer. And third, fonts may be downloaded by the computer, moving the font from a disk file to RAM inside the printer. These are called so*ft fonts.*

Soft fonts are kept in files that follow the format shown in Figure 16-9. Escape sequences are found at the beginning of the file and at many places within the file. By including these sequences within files, the files can be directly transmitted to the printer. The printer sees the initial escape sequence and understands that a font is being downloaded. Subsequent escape sequences mark the beginning of each character and give information about it.

```
Overall Format of a Font File:
            Esc ) s # W
            Font Descriptor (see below)

            Esc * c # E
            Esc ( s # W
            Character Descriptor for first character (see below)
            Character Bitmap

            Esc * c # E
            Esc ( s # W
            Character Descriptor for second character
            Character Bitmap
                  .
                  .
                  .
            Esc * c # E
            Esc ( s # W
            Character Descriptor for last character
            Character Bitmap
```

Format of a Font Descriptor:

Field Name	Data Type	Purpose
Font Descriptor Size	U Int	The size of the font descriptor in bytes.
Font Type	U Byte	The range of values used by the font: 0 = 0—127. 0—31 unprintable. 1 = 0—255. 0—31, 128—159 unprintable. 2 = 0—255. 0, 7—15, & 27 unprintable.
Baseline Distance	U Int	Distance in dots from baseline to top of character cell.
Cell Width	U Int	Maximum character cell width in dots.
Cell Height	U Int	Maximum character cell height in dots.
Orientation	U Byte	The font's orientation. 0 = portrait and 1 = landscape.
Proportional Spacing	Byte	0 = fixed width font. 1 = proportionally spaced font.
Symbol Set	U Int	Selects symbol set for the font. Normally 341.
Default Pitch	U Int	The distance between characters in mono-spaced fonts, or the width of a space in proportionally spaced fonts.

continued

Design Height	U Int	The font height expressed in quarter-dots. (For use when selecting font by point size)
X Height	U Int	Height of a lowercase 'x' in quarter-dots.
Width Type	S Byte	Used for variable proportional spacing: -2 = Condensed -1 = Semicondensed 0 = Normal 1 = Semiexpanded 2 = Expanded
Style	U Byte	The font style. Upright = 0 and Italic = 1.
Stroke Weight	S Byte	The font's stroke thickness, from -7 to +7 for thinest to thickest. Normal = 0 and boldface = 3.
Typeface	U Byte	The typeface code number. Common fonts include Courier (=3), Helvetica (=4), Times Roman (=5), and Letter Gothic (=6).
Serif Style	U Byte	Styles for both serif and sans serif fonts: 0 = Sans serif, square 1 = Sans serif, round 2 = Serif, line 3 = Serif, triangular 4 = Serif, swath 5 = Serif, block 6 = Serif, bracket 7 = Rounded bracket 8 = Flair stroke
Underline Distance	S Byte	Distance in dots from top row of underline to character cell baseline. Positive value is above baseline, negative value is below.
Underline Height	U Byte	Underline thickness in dots. (Three dot fixed value in LaserJet II.
Text Height	U Int	Recommended value for spacing between lines in quarter-dots. Used by software, not the printer.
Text Width	U Long	Recommended value for character spacing in quarter-dots. Used by software, not the printer.
Pitch Extended	U Byte	An increment to the font's pitch field, expressed in 1/1024th-dots.
Height Extended	U Byte	An increment to the font's height field, expressed in 1/1024th-dots.
Font Name	16 Bytes	The font name in ASCII. Field may be extended to hold other information, such as a copyright message.

Format of a Character Descriptor:

Field Name	Data Type	Purpose
Descriptor Format	U Byte	A code indicating the descriptor format. The LaserJet II uses 4.
Continuation Flag	Byte	0 = the following data is a character descriptor. 1 = the following data is a continuation of the bitmap used by the prior descriptor.
Descriptor Size	U Byte	The size of this record, minus the first two fields, that is, 14 bytes.

continued

Data Class	U Byte	Format of the character's bitmap. Always set to 1.
Character Orientation	U Byte	Matches the font descriptor's orientation field so that 0 = portrait and 1 = landscape.
Left Offset	S Int	The offset, in dots, from the left edge of the character bitmap to the character's reference point.
Top Offset	S Int	The offset, in dots, from the top edge of the character bitmap to the character's reference point.
Character Width	U Int	The character bitmap width in dots. (Bitmap width is rounded upward to the nearest byte.)
Character Height	U Int	The character bitmap height in dots.
Delta X	S Int	The number of quarter-dots the cursor is forwarded after printing the character. Used only with proportionally spaced fonts.
Character Bitmap	Byte	The bitmap is organized in *scan lines* so that you first encounter data for the top line of the image of all characters, then data for the next row, and so on. Bitmap size is calculated from the Character Width and Character Height fields above.

Figure 16-9   File format for soft fonts

The user can download a font file using the DOS COPY command. The file named HELV010.SFP is sent to LPT1 by the command:

```
COPY HELV010.SFP /B LPT1:
```

Notice the use of the **/B** (for "binary") switch in the command. It tells DOS not to translate Tab and Ctrl-Z characters, which are present as graphics data in character bit maps. Alternatively, software can download fonts by opening the font file for reading and the printer for writing, and then passing one character at a time between disk and printer ("Output Data to a Printer," on earlier pages, explains how to open the printer for writing).

As Figure 16-10 shows, characters are positioned relative to an imaginary line called a *baseline*. Baselines are analogous to the lines drawn on ruled notebook paper. Characters like "A" or "a" rest just on top of the baseline, while other characters, such as "g" and "p", extend their *descenders* below the baseline. Any particular font has a maximum *ascent distance* — the farthest a character will ascend above the baseline — and a corresponding maximum *descent distance*. These two values are added together to obtain the *character height*. Character height gives the maximum vertical space required by any character in a font. Thus "a" and "A" and "g" nominally have the same height, even though the actual vertical extent of the three characters differs. Of course, space is left between lines of text so that characters do not touch. This spacing is called *leading* (rhymes with *heading*).

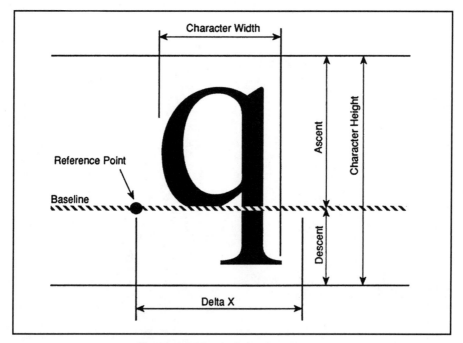

Figure 16-10   Soft font structure

While all characters in a font have the same character height, their widths normally differ, since most fonts use proportional spacing. Like the height, the width includes not just the space taken up by the character itself, but also additional space to the right and left used to separate the character from its neighbors. The character is positioned relative to a point on the baseline called the *character reference point.* Space between this point and the right edge of the character is referred to as the *left offset.* The space occupied by the character proper is called the *character width,* and it is followed by a *right offset.* These three measurements taken together give a value termed *Delta X,* and it is this value that is the character "width" that your programs will concern themselves with when they calculate line lengths for formatting, wordwrap, and so on. You can construct a font width table as you download a font, taking the DeltaX values from the offsets shown in Figure 16-9. It is your responsibility to see to it that all font parameters, including line and character spacing, make sense. Otherwise, characters and lines may overlap.

Print Graphics on a Line Printer

Line printers always operate in text mode unless specially placed in a graphics mode. The command that invokes a graphics mode must state how many bytes of graphics data follow, and once that number of bytes has been interpreted as a graphics image, the printer returns to text mode. For this reason, these printers do not have commands that turn on text mode. Figures 16-11 through 16-12 list the most important graphics control commands for two of the three line-printer standards (Diablo graphics capabilities are negligible).

```
Esc K (counter) (data)    Selects 60 dpi graphics mode. Counter
                          is two-byte (16-bit) value specifying how
                          many bytes of graphics data follow.
Esc L (counter) (data)    120 dpi.
Esc Y (counter) (data)    120 dpi high speed.
Esc Z (counter) (data)    240 dpi.
Esc ^ 0 (counter) (data)  60 dpi.
Esc ^ 1 (counter) (data)  120 dpi.
Esc * # (counter) (data)  As above, but # selects the graphics
                          mode, for which:
                          0 = 60 dpi
                          1 = 120 dpi
                          2 = 120 dpi high speed
                          3 = 240 dpi
                          4 = 80 dpi
                          5 = 72 dpi
                          6 = 90 dpi
                          7 = 144 dpi
                          32 = 60 dpi
                          33 = 120 dpi
                          38 = 90 dpi
                          39 = 180 dpi
                          40 = 360 dpi
```

Figure 16-11   Epson graphics commands

```
#155 # & z              Set graphics resolution

#155 #; #; # . r        Specify data in binary form
#155 #; #; # / r        Specify data in hexadecimal form
                        # data length
                        # image width
                        # resolution

#155 #; # s             Specify start position for shading
#155 #; # r             Specify end position for shading
                        # shading density
                        # position

#155 #; #; # {          Specify start of line
#155 #; #; # }          Specify end of line
                        # line width
                        # line type: solid or dotted
                        # position
```

Figure 16-12   ISO graphics commands

Print Graphics on an HP LaserJet Printer

LaserJet printers can create graphics in three ways: by using built-in graphics routines, by drawing pictures dot by dot ("raster graphics"), or by sending commands to a built-in graphics language. The latter option is only found in the most recent LaserJet printers and is beyond the scope of our discussion here.

Built-in Graphics

A LaserJet's built-in graphics options consist of nothing more than the ability to draw rectangles. Rectangles may be solid black, or can be filled in a number of cross-hatch patterns or shadings, or a combination of these. There are no separate routines for drawing lines; rather, lines are drawn as very thin rectangles. This approach allows a number of line styles, since lines can also be drawn using shades or cross-hatching.

Rectangles are drawn by first placing the cursor at what will be the upper left corner of the rectangle. The cursor will remain in this position after the rectangle is drawn. To specify the rectangle's horizontal and vertical dimensions in dots, use the escape sequences:

```
Esc * c # A     (width)

Esc * c # B     (height)
```

where # is the number of dots. A rectangle 100 dots wide and 500 dots tall would be defined by:

```
Esc * c 100 A

Esc * c 500 B
```

Alternatively, use:

```
Esc * c # H     (width)

Esc * c # V     (height)
```

to specify the dimensions in decipoints.

Once the rectangle dimensions have been set, you draw the rectangle by the escape sequence:

```
Esc * c # G
```

The symbol # is filled with a number from the following table that tells how the rectangle should be filled:

```
0        black
1        white (erase)
2        shaded fill
3        cross-hatched fill
4        current-pattern fill
```

For a solid black rectangle, you'd write:

```
Esc * c 0 G
```

By specifying 1 instead, all pixels in the defined area would be "turned off" so that the area is effectively erased.

Cross-hatching is performed in any of six built-in patterns:

```
1        horizontal lines
2        vertical lines
3        lines sloping downward to the left
4        lines sloping downward to the right
5        a grid of horizontal and vertical lines
6        a screen of small white dots on a black back-
```
ground

After specifying that a cross-hatched fill is to be used, you set the fill pattern by the escape sequence:

```
Esc * c # G
```

in which # is a number from the table. Thus, to draw the rectangle with a grid pattern, you would write:

```
Esc * c 5 G
```

It is this sequence that actually draws the rectangle. It may be repeated using a different number to superimpose one cross-hatching pattern upon another.

If instead you specify that the rectangle should be shaded by the command

```
Esc * c 2 P
```

then you must set the shading percentage using the

```
Esc * c # G
```

escape sequence. The value for # can be anywhere from 1 to 100. However, the printer can create only eight levels of shading and a range of shading values applies to each. The lightest level is for 1 (2% shading), then 3 (10%), 11 (20%),

21 (35%), 36 (55%), 56 (80%), 82 (99%), and finally, 100% for solid black. In reality, all percentages above 35% are "solid" black, although the actual printing may be mottled, particularly when large areas are filled. Best results are usually obtained on new printers using new cartridges and high-quality paper.

Raster Graphics

Graphics data is organized just like in line printers. The image that will be printed is reduced to a grid that may be regarded as a series of horizontal lines. Each dot in each line is either "on" (black) or "off" (white — that is, unprinted). The first byte of graphics data holds the settings for the first eight dots of the topmost line, starting from the left. Thus, if the first four dots are black and the next four are white, the first data byte is 11110000 in binary arithmetic (F0 in hexadecimal, or 240 decimal). The succeeding data byte holds settings for the next eight dots, and so on to the end of the line. Then data is sent for the next line. When the line width is not an even multiple of eight, part of the final byte holding data for the line goes unused, with its empty positions set to 0.

Raster graphics are the most time-consuming of all graphics operations because your program must transmit data for every dot that is printed. Just to fill a 1-inch by 1-inch square at 300 dots-per-inch requires 90,000 bits of data! For this reason, raster graphics should only be used when the printer's built-in rectangle routines can't do the job, and the two techniques should be combined when suitable.

To reduce the time required by raster graphics, you can ask the printer to draw dots at a lower resolution than the 300 dots-per-inch in which text is always printed. You can opt for 75 dpi, 100 dpi, or 150 dpi. The printer continues to print in 300 dpi resolution, but instead draws dots as miniscule squares having 4 x 4 dots (75 dpi), 3 x 3 dots (100 dpi), or 2 x 2 dots (150 dpi). Using the same graphics data, an image drawn in 75 dpi will be four times wider and taller on the page than one drawn in 300 dpi. Use this escape sequence to set the resolution:

```
Esc * t # R
```

writing the dots-per-inch value in place of #. The four possibilities are:

```
75 dpi       Esc * t 75 R        1B 2A 74 37 35 52

100 dpi      Esc * t 100 R       1B 2A 74 31 30 30 52

150 dpi      Esc * t 150 R       1B 2A 74 31 35 30 52

300 dpi      Esc * t 300 R       1B 2A 74 33 30 30 52
```

Before printing a graphic, a program must position the cursor and specify the graphics dimensions. Then the printer is set to raster-graphics mode. Once in this mode, the printer accepts only graphics data and a few graphics control sequences. There are a few other graphics control sequences that the printer simply ignores when in graphics mode. Any other escape sequence causes the printer to exit graphics mode. Use this escape sequence to enter raster graphics mode:

```
Esc * r # A
```

In this sequence, # may be either 0 or 1. When it is 1 (the usual case) the graphic is drawn with its upper left corner at the current cursor position. When 0, the graphic is instead drawn at the left margin. A program then issues the command:

```
Esc * b # W
```

in which # is the number of bytes of graphics data that will follow.

Figure 16-13 summarizes the LaserJet graphics commands.

```
     Esc * t # R          Set graphics resolution in dots per inch.
                              # = 75, 100, 150, or 300.
     Esc * r # A          Set the starting point for a graphic.
                              0 = left margin
                              1 = current position
     Esc * c # V          Rectangle height in 1/720ths inches.
     Esc * c # B          Rectangle height in 1/300ths inches.
     Esc * c # H          Rectangle width in 1/720ths inches.
     Esc * c # A          Rectangle width in 1/300ths inches.
     Esc * c # P          Start drawing a rectangular element.
                              0 = solid black
                              2 = shaded fill
                              3 = pattern fill
     Esc * c # G          Set shading pattern density.
     Esc * b # W          Specify that there are # bytes in a row of coming
                          graphics data.
     Esc * r B            End of graphics data transfer.
```

Figure 16-13   LaserJet graphics commands

17

Serial Communications

- Minitutorial: How Serial Data Is Transmitted
- Program a Serial Communications Chip
- Initialize a Serial Port
- Monitor the Status of a Serial Port
- Initialize and Monitor a Modem
- Transmit Data
- Receive Data
- Send/Receive Data by Communications Interrupts
- Look Up a Communications Control Code

Minitutorial: How Serial Data Is Transmitted

In asynchronous communications, the computer sends or receives bytes of information one bit at a time. The timing between the bytes of data is not important, but the timing of the sequence of bits that make up a byte is critical. The signal on the communications line goes high and low, corresponding to logical 1s and 0s. The line is said to be *marking* when the level is high (=1) and to be *spacing* when the level is low (=0).

The line is held in the marking condition whenever it is not transferring data. At the onset of the transmission of a byte of data, the signal drops to 0 during the *start bit*. Then the eight bits of data (sometimes fewer) follow as a pattern of highs and lows. The last data bit is optionally followed by a *parity bit* used in error detection, and then the sequence concludes with one or more stop bits, which are comprised of a high signal. These stop bit(s) begin the marking state that continues until the transmission of the next byte of data begins; the number of stop bits used is significant because they set the minimum amount of time that must pass before the next start bit. Figure 17-1 diagrams this sequence.

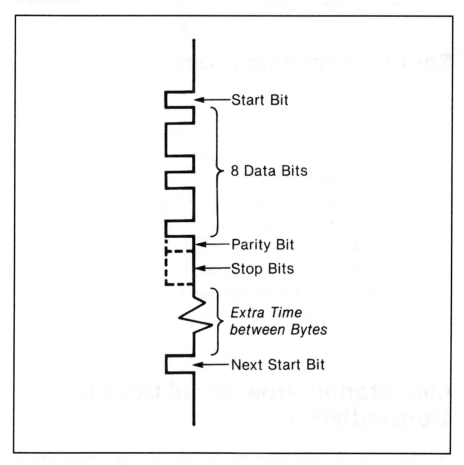

Figure 17-1   The transmission of one byte of serial data

Of course, both the transmitting and receiving stations must use the same protocol for these bit patterns, and they must operate at the same transmission Errors can easily occur, and the serial hardware offers a variety of status information, both for the port itself and for the modem that the port is connected to. The modem's job is to convert the signal generated by the serial port into an acoustic signal that can be transmitted across phone lines. Most modems also provide a number of advanced communications features, such as automatic dialing and answering, most of which are not supported by the serial port itself.

Full-blown, "bullet-proof" communications programs are complicated beasts. They require the use of protocols, error detection codes, and modem control that are beyond the scope of this book. The examples given here are useful for writing simple routines for tasks like sending data to a serial printer. For more advanced information, consult the *C Programmer's Guide to Serial Communications* by Joe Campbell.

Program a Serial Communications Chip

Serial communications is so complicated that special chips have been designed to do the work of forming and timing the strings of bits that comprise serial data. Such a chip is called a *universal asynchronous receiver transmitter*, or *UART*. Without UARTs, communications programming would be extremely complicated. IBM PCs use variants of the Intel 8250 UART.

From the programmer's point of view, a communications chip consists of a series of registers that correspond to a sequence of port addresses. The first address in the series is the *base address*. The base address for COM1 is kept at 0040:0000, for COM2 it is at 0040:0002, and so on. Usually, COM1 starts at port address 3F8h and COM2 at 2F8h. For convenience, the discussion here refers to the sequence of registers numbered 3Fxh.

The 8250 UART has ten programmable one-byte registers used to control and monitor the serial port. Most are devoted to initializing the port, a process that can be rather complicated. The ten registers are accessed through seven port addresses, numbers 3F8h–3FEh (or 2F8h–2FEh). In five cases, the register accessed at a particular port address depends on how bit 7 is set in the *line control register*, which is the only register at port 3FBh. Here are the registers:

```
3F8h (OUT, bit 7=0 at 3FBh)    Transmitter Holding Register

3F8h (IN,  bit 7=0 at 3FBh)    Receiver Data Register

3F8h (OUT, bit 7=1 at 3FBh)    Baud-Rate Divisor (low byte)

3F9h (IN,  bit 7=1 at 3FBh)    Baud-Rate Divisor (high byte)

3F9h (OUT, bit 7=0 at 3FBh)    Interrupt Enable Register

3FAh (IN)                      Interrupt Identification
                               Register

3FBh (OUT)                     Line Control Register

3FCh (OUT)                     Modem Control Register

3FDh (IN)                      Line Status Register

3FEh (IN)                      Modem Status Register
```

Of the ten registers, only six are necessary for simple serial communications. The *transmitter holding* register holds the byte of data about to be sent and the *receiver data* register keeps the most recently received byte of data. The *line control* and *line status* registers initialize and monitor the serial line, using the baud rate placed in the two baud-rate divisor registers. Of the remaining four registers, the *modem control* and *modem status* registers are used only for modem communications, and the two interrupt-related registers are used only in interrupt-driven routines.

Interrupts are used in communications for reasons of efficiency. Simple communications routines constantly monitor the line status register, waiting for an incoming character, or waiting until the register indicates that it is all right to transmit another byte of data. Because the CPU operates very quickly relative to the 2,400 or 9,600 bit-per-second rate at which serial data typically move, this method can be wasteful of CPU time that might otherwise be devoted to processing the incoming/outgoing data. For this reason, a serial communications chip may be set up to bring about an interrupt whenever a character arrives, an error occurs, etc. The interrupt momentarily brings into action a procedure in your program that would, say, output the next character from a communications buffer.

The remaining sections in this chapter provide examples in which an 8250 UART is programmed. DOS provides functions for this purpose, but they are not interrupt driven and cannot exceed 1,200 bps. Nor do DOS functions provide the level of error checking and recovery required by most serial I/O.

Initialize a Serial Port

When a communications port is initialized ("opened"), all of the parameters by which it operates are set. These parameters include the word length, the number of stop bits, the parity setting, and the baud rate. The *word length* is the number of bits that form the basic data unit. While we are accustomed to working in eight bits, seven bits is adequate for standard ASCII files (where all characters are below ASCII 128).

BIOS function 0 of interrupt 14h initializes the serial port. DX is given the number of the communications channel (COM1=0, COM2=1, etc.). AL takes a byte that gives the initialization data, as follows:

```
bits 1-0    Word length. 10=7 bits & 11=8 bits.

      2     Number of stop bits. 0=1 & 1=2.

    4-3     Parity. 00 or 10=none. 01=odd & 11=even.

    5-7     Baud rate.  000=110 bps

                        001=150

                        010=300

                        011=600

                        100=1200

                        101=2400

                        110=4800

                        111=9600
```

BASIC

BASIC opens the communications channel as a file, and as such it must be given a file identification number:

```
OPEN"COM1: ............" AS #1
```

Placed within the quotation marks is all the information required to initialize the serial port, each entry separated from the prior by a comma. The initialization data is always entered in the following order:

- **Baud rate** given as an integer: 75, 100, 150, 300, 600, 1200, 1800, 2400, 4800, or 9600 bits per second. Defaults to 300 baud.

- **Parity** given as a one-character code: O for ODD parity; E for EVEN parity (the default); N for NONE (no parity); S for SPACE, where the parity bit is always 0; and M for MARK, where the parity bit is always 1. If eight data bits are used, specify N; if four bits are used, do *not* use N.

- **Data bits** given as the integer 4, 5, 6, 7, or 8, with 7 as the default value.

- **Stop bits** given as the integer 1 or 2, with 2 as the default for 75 and 110 bps, and 1 for all others. When the number of data bits is 4 or 5, 2 stands for 1-1/2 stop bits. "1-1/2" bits is possible because in communications a bit is a *unit of time,* and hence it is divisible.

The statement **OPEN "COM1:1200,O,8,1" FOR INPUT AS #1** opens COM1 for 1200 bps communications with odd parity, eight-bit characters, and one stop bit. Note that you can end one of the OPEN statements with the expression **LEN = number**, where the number sets the maximum block size by which GET and PUT instructions may handle data (128 bytes is the default). There are a number of modem-control commands that optionally may be included with these specifications ("Initialize and Monitor a Modem," below, explains the special terminology found here):

- **RS** Suppresses the "Request To Send" signal. If this command is omitted, OPEN"COM... turns on RTS.

- **CS** Causes the "Clear To Send" line to be checked. This command may optionally be followed by a value (from 0–65535) that gives the number of milliseconds to wait for the signal before a "Device Time-Out" error occurs — for example, **CS500**. The default value is 1000, unless RS is specified, in which case it is 0.

- **DS** Causes the "Data Set Ready" line to be checked. An optional parameter is allowed, as for CS above. The default value is 1000.

- **CD** Causes the "Carrier Detect" line to be checked. An optional timing parameter is allowed, as for CS above. The default value is 0.

- **LF** Causes a line feed (ASCII 10) to automatically follow every carriage return (ASCII 13). Used for serial output to a printer.

- **PE** Enables parity checking, causing a "Device Time-Out" error if a parity error occurs.

These special commands may be placed anywhere in the OPEN"COM... statement and in any order. Note that normally the CTS and DSR signals must be turned on or the OPEN statement will fail and a "Device Time-Out" error will occur. In summary, here is an OPEN"COM... statement that includes all parameters except RS and LF:

```
OPEN"COM1:1200,O,7,1,CS2000,DS2000,CD,PE" AS #1 LEN=256
```

Pascal

Turbo Pascal offers no functions for initializing a serial port. Instead, you must call function 0 of interrupt 14h.

```
Uses DOS;


Var

  Regs: Registers;   {Registers type is declared in the DOS
                      unit}


Regs.AH := 0;      {the interrupt function number}

Regs.AL := 0 Or WordLength Or StopBits Or Parity Or BaudRate;

Regs.DX := 0;      {select COM 1}

Intr($14,Regs);    {initialize the port}
```

C

Borland C's *bioscom* function, and Microsoft C's *_bios_serialcom* function, can initialize a serial port. Both functions take three parameters, the first of which is a code that is 0 to initialize the port. In *bioscom*, the second two parameters are a *char* value giving the initialization parameters, and then a serial port number, for which 0 is COM1, 1 is COM2, and so on. The Microsoft C function reverses the order of the second and third parameters. Here is an example of the Borland C function:

```
char init_byte;


init_byte:= 0 ¦ WordLength ¦ StopBits ¦ Parity ¦ BaudRate;

bioscom(0,init_byte,0)    ;initialize COM1
```

Both functions return a complicated status word that is discussed in "Receive Data," below.

Assembler

This example initializes the port to an eight-bit word length with one stop bit and even parity. The baud rate is 1200 bps.

```
;---ASSIGN VALUES TO THE PARAMETER VARIABLES:
        mov     WORDLENGTH,00000011b    ;8-bit word length
        mov     STOPBITS,00000000b      ;1 stop bit
        mov     PARITY,00011000b        ;even parity
        mov     BAUDRATE,10000000b      ;1200 baud
;---INITIALIZE COM1:
        mov     al,0                    ;clear AL
        or      al,WORDLENGTH           ;initialize the bits from 4
                                        variables
        or      al,STOPBITS             ;
        or      al,PARITY               ;
        or      al,BAUDRATE             ;
        mov     ah,0                    ;function to initialize serial
                                        port
        mov     dx,0                    ;select COM1
        int     14h                     ;initialize the port
```

Low-Level Access

Whether for input or output, minimally four registers of the 8253 chip must be initialized for serial operations. These are the two baud-rate divisor registers, the line control register, and the interrupt enable register.

Baud-rate initialization

The *baud-rate divisor* is a number that divides the rate of the system clock (1190000 cycles/second) to give a result that equals the desired baud rate. For example, for 1200 bps the baud-rate divisor would be 96, since 119000/96 equals roughly 1200. The larger the divisor, the slower the baud rate. Baud rates of 300 and under require a two-byte number for the divisor, and for this reason the 8250 chip needs two registers to hold the divisor. The high byte is sent to 3F9h (or 2F9h), and the low byte to 3F8h (2F8h). In both cases, bit 7 of the line control register at 3FBh (2FBh) must be set before sending values; otherwise these two addresses direct the values to other registers (see "Program a Serial Communications Chip," above). Here are some values required by common baud rates:

baud rate	3F9h	3F8h
110	04h	17h
300	01h	80h
600	00h	C0h
1200	00h	60h
1800	00h	40h
2400	00h	30h
3600	00h	20h
4800	00h	18h
9600	00h	0Ch

Always set the baud rate divisor registers first since they are the only ones that require that bit 7 be set in the line control register. Then initialize the line control register, clearing bit 7 so that all subsequent register accesses are correct. Since the line control register is write-only, there is no way to reset bit 7 without redoing all of the bits in the register.

Line Control Register Initialization

The bit settings for the line control register at 3FBh (or 2FBh) are as follows:

```
bits 1-0   Character length. 00=5 bits, 01=6 bits
             10=7 bits, 11=8 bits.

       2   Number of stop bits. 0=1. 1=1.5 if the
             character length is 5, else =2.

       3   Parity. 1=parity bit is generated, 0=not.

       4   Parity Type. 0=odd, 1=even.

       5   Stick Parity. Causes parity to always be 1 or 0.
             0=disabled.
             1=always 1 if bit 3=1 & bit 4=0,
             or 1=always 0 if bit 3=1 & bit 4=1
             or 1=no parity if bit 3=0.
```

> 6   Set Break. Causes output of string of 0s as signal to remote station. 0=disabled, 1=break.
>
> 7   Toggles port addresses of other registers on chip.

Ordinarily bits 5 – 7 are set to 0. The others are given the values of the desired communications protocol.

The Interrupt Enable Register

Even when interrupts are not used, you should access the interrupt enable register to be sure that interrupts are disabled. Simply place 0 in the register. The interrupt identification register may be ignored.

The remaining initialization registers are concerned with modems. Modems, of course, are required only for distant communications and not for the control of nearby devices such as a serial printer. "Initialize and Monitor a Modem," below, explains how to program the modem control register.

In this example, the base address of COM1 is found in the BIOS data area and the various registers are initialized for 1200 baud, seven-bit data, even parity, and one stop bit.

```
;---GET BASE ADDRESS OF COM1:
        mov   ax,40h          ;point ES to BIOS data area
        mov   es,ax           ;
        mov   dx,es:[0]       ;get base address for COM1
;---INITIALIZE THE BAUD RATE DIVISOR REGISTERS FOR 1200 BPS:
        add   dx,3            ;point to line control register
        mov   al,10000000b    ;turn on bit 7
        out   dx,al           ;send the byte
        dec   dx             ;point to MSB of baud rate divisor
        dec   dx             ;
        mov   al,0            ;MSB for 1200 bps
        out   dx,al           ;send the byte
        dec   dx             ;point to LSB of baud rate divisor
        mov   al,60h          ;LSB for 1200 bps
        out   dx,al           ;
;---INITIALIZE THE LINE CONTROL REGISTER:
        mov   al,0            ;initialize AL to 0
```

```
        or    al,10b          ;7-bit data length
        or    al,000b         ;1 stop bit
        or    al,1000b        ;parity bit generated
        or    al,10000b       ;even parity
        add   dx,3            ;point to line control register
        out   dx,al           ;send the initialization value
;---INITIALIZE THE INTERRUPT ENABLE REGISTER:
        dec   dx             ;point to interrupt enable register
        dec   dx             ;
        mov   al,0           ;disable all interrupts
        out   dx,al           ;send the byte
        .                    ;continue
        .
```

Monitor the Status of a Serial Port

The *line status* register of the 8250 UART sets up the communications protocol. This register is located at the port address that is 5 higher than the base address for the particular COM channel. Ordinarily it is constantly monitored during communications activity. During data transmission, the register tells when the last-received character has been sent off, lest the program write the next character on top of it. In data reception, the register informs the program when a character arrives, so that the program can remove it before it is overlaid by the one that follows. The contents are as follows:

```
bit 0    1 = a byte of data has been received

    1    1 = received data has been overrun (prior
             character was not removed in time)

    2    1 = parity error (probably from line noise)

    3    1 = framing error (transmission is out of sync)

    4    1 = break detect (a long string of 1s has been
             received, indicating that the other station
             requests an end to transmission)

    5    1 = transmitter holding register empty (this
             register is given output data)

    6    1 = transmitter shift register empty (this
             register takes holding register data and converts
             it to serial form)

    7    1 = time-out (off-line)
```

Function 3 of BIOS interrupt 14h returns the contents of the line status register in AH (AL receives the modem status register, which is discussed in "Program a Serial Communications Chip," above). On entry, DX holds the number of the communications port that is accessed (COM1 = 0, COM2 = 1, and so on). All of the examples below fetch the status register through this function.

BASIC

```
' $INCLUDE: 'QBX.BI'

DIM REGS AS RegType       ' Define register array

REGS.AX = &H0300          'function number
REGS.DX = 0               'select COM1
```

549

```
CALL Interrupt(&H14, REGS, REGS)
LineStatusRegister = REGS.AX AND &H00FF
```

Pascal

```
Uses DOS;

Var

   Regs: Registers;  {Registers type is declared in the DOS
   unit}

   LineStatusRegister: byte;


Regs.AH := 3;        {the interrupt function number}
Regs.DX := 0;        {select COM1}
Intr($14,Regs);      {Call the interrupt}
LineStatusRegister := Regs.AL;
```

C

```
#include <dos.h>

union REGS regs;     /* declare the register array */
char line_status_register;

regs.h.ah = 3;       /* function number */
regs.x.dx = 0;       /* choose COM1 */
int86(0x14,&regs,&regs);
line_status_register = regs.h.al
```

Assembler

This example checks for the *break detect* condition:

```
mov   ah,3            ;function number
mov   dx,1            ;choose COM2
int   14h            ;fetch the status byte
test  ah,10000b      ;break detect?
jnz   BREAK_DETECT   ;jump to break routine if so
```

Low-Level Access

This example reads the base address of the COM2 channel from the BIOS data area, adds 5, and fetches the status byte directly from the port.

```
mov   ax,40h         ;point ES to bottom of BIOS data area
mov   es,ax          ;
mov   dx,es:[2]      ;get COM2 base address
add   dx,5           ;add offset of 5 for status register
in    al,dx          ;get the status byte
test  al,10000b      ;bit 5 set?
jnz   BREAK_DETECT   ;if so, jump to break routine
```

Initialize and Monitor a Modem

There are six lines by which modems communicate with the computer (sophisticated modems may have extra lines through the RS232 interface). Here are their names, abbreviations, and functions:

From computer to modem:

Data Terminal Ready (DTR)   informs modem that computer is powered up and ready for communications.

Request To Send (RTS)   informs modem that computer wants to send data.

From modem to computer:

Data Set Ready (DSR)   informs computer that modem is powered up and ready.

Clear To Send (CTS)   informs computer that modem is ready to begin data transmission.

Data Carrier Detect (DCD)   informs computer that modem has connected with another modem.

Ring Indicator (RI)   informs computer that the phone line the modem is connected to is ringing.

First, software turns the data *terminal ready* signal on, and then it instructs the modem to dial the remote station. Once the modem has established a connection, it turns on the *data set ready* signal. This informs software that the modem is ready for communications, and at that point a program can turn on the *request to send* signal. When the modem replies with *clear to send*, transmission can begin.

The two standard lines by which the computer controls the modem may be accessed through the m*odem control register* on the 8250 UART chip. This register is located at an address that is 4 greater than the base address for the COM channel in use. Here is the bit pattern in the register:

Modem Control Register:

bits 7-5   (always 0)

4   1=UART output looped back as input

3   auxiliary user designated output #2

```
        2        auxiliary user designated output #1

        1        1="request to send" is active

        0        1="data terminal ready" is active
```

Ordinarily, bits 0 and 1 of the modem control register are set to 1, and the others are set to 0. Bit 2 is set to 0 unless a modem's manufacturer has given it a special use. Bit 3 is set to 1 only when interrupts are used. Finally, bit 4 is a special feature that is useful for testing communications programs without actually going on line. The output signal from the UART is looped back so that the UART receives it as serial input. This feature may be used to test whether the chip is functioning properly. Loop-back is not available through the BIOS interrupt 14h communications routines.

The four lines by which the modem sends information to the computer are monitored through the *modem status register*. This register is located at the port address that is 6 higher than the base address of the communications adaptor in use. Here is the bit pattern:

Modem Status Register:

```
    bit  7        1="data carrier detect"

         6        1="ring indicator"

         5        1="data set ready"

         4        1="clear to send"

         3        1=change in "data carrier detect"

         2        1=change in "ring indicator"

         1        1=change in "data set ready"

         0        1=change in "clear to send"
```

Programs constantly monitor these bits during communications operations. Note that the four low bits parallel the four high bits. These bits are set to 1 only when a change has occurred in the status of the corresponding high bit *since the last time the register was read*. All four low bits are automatically restored to 0 after the read operation. Programs can read the register directly. Alternatively, function 3 of BIOS interrupt 14h returns the contents of the modem status register in AL (the line status register contents appear in AH). On entry to this function, DX must hold the number of the COM channel (0 or 1).

Most modems have many more capabilities than the two modem-related registers reflect. Features like autodial and autoanswer are controlled by *control strings*. These strings are sent to the modem as if they were data being transmitted. The modem extracts the strings from the data by watching for a special character used only to signal the start of a control string. This character may be predefined (often it is ASCII 27, the ESCape character) or it may be user-selectable. The modem is able to determine how long each sequence must be, so that beyond the end of the string it again treats the transmission outflow as data. Every modem has its own set of commands. Figure 17-2 lists some common commands used by Hayes-standard modems.

```
    Command              Function


  A T         Marks beginning of any command.


  A /         Repeat prior command.


  A           Specify that answer be made without waiting for ring.

  B #         Set protocol mode. 0 = CCITT v.22/v.22bis.

  C #         Carrier State.  0 = off and 1 = on.

  D #         Dial. # = the telephone number.

  E #         Specify that modem commands should be echoed. 0 = no, 1 = yes.

  F #         Set duplex setting. 0 = half duplex, 1 = full duplex.

  H #         Set status of "hook."  0 = on hook (hang up), 1 = off hook.

  L #         Set speaker volume. 0 = low, 1 = low, 2 = medium, 3 = high.

  M #         Specify speaker mode. 0 = off, 1 = on, 2 = always on,
              3 = speaker is disabled when carrier is received.

  P           Specifies that modem should use pulse dailing.

  Q #         Specifies command state. 0 = commands are sent, 1 = not sent.

  S           Dial stored number.

  S # = ##    Set S-Register # to the value ##.

  S # ?       Display the value of S-register #

  T           Specifies that modem should use tone dialing.

  V #         Select method of returning result codes. 0 = use digits, 1= words.

  W           Wait for access tone or a second dial.

  X #         Enables extended features for mode setting and returning result
              codes.  0 = basic services used at 300 bps. 1 = no detection
              of busy signal or dialtone. 2 = Detection of dialtone but not
              busy signal. 3 = Detection of busy signal but not dialtone.
              4 = Detection of both busy signal and dialtone.

  Y #         Specifies status of automatic disconnection after 1.6 second
              break. 0 = disabled, 1 = enabled.

  .           Pause during dialing sequence.
```

```
!          "Flash" (hangs up for one half second).

;          Specifies that should return to command mode after dialing.

& C #      Sets handling of data carrier detect. 0 = DCD kept on.

& D #      Sets DTR handling. 0 = DTR ignored. 1 = assumed command state
           when DTR is triggered. 2 = modem goes off hook when DTR off.
           3 = modem initialized when DTR off.

& G #      Select guard tone.  0 = no guard tone. 1 = 550 Hz tone. 2 =
           1800 Hz tone.

& M #      Set communications type. 0 = asynchronous. 1 = synchronous with
           asynchronous dialing. 2 = synchronous with stored number dialing.
           3 = synchronous with manual dialing.

& P #      Set pulse dialing parameters. 0 = US standard. 1 = alternate
           standard.

& R #      Set handling of RTS and CTS. 0 = CTS tracks RTS. 1 = RTS ignored.

& S #      Set handling of DSR. 0 = DSR switched on at start up. 1 = DSR
           follows EIA specifications.

& Z #      Store telephone number #.
```

Figure 17-2   Hayes Modem Commands

In response to a *query* command, the modem returns status information, sending it to the serial communications chip like incoming data. All in all, a good deal of documentation is required to properly use a modem's command sequences and status information. The examples below give only the bare framework by which modem connections are established.

BASIC

```
OUT BASEADDRESS+4,1      'turn on "data terminal ready"

'''now send control string to modem to dial number and establish

'''connection -- this code varies by the modem

    .

    .

FirstLoop:

  X=INP(BASEADDRESS+2)      'get modem status register value

  IF X AND 2 <> 2 THEN GOTO FirstLoop 'loop until bit 1 is set
```

555

```
   OUT BASEADDRESS+4,3                'turn on "request to send" bit as well
SecondLoop:
   X=INP(BASEADDRESS+2)               'get modem status register value
   IF X AND 1 <> 1 THEN GOTO SecondLoop  'loop until bit 0 is set
   '''now begin sending data...
```

Pascal

```
   Port[BaseAddress+4] := 1;    {turn on "data terminal ready"}
   {now send control string to modem to dial number and estab-
lish connection -- this code varies by the modem}

   .

   .

FirstLoop:
   X := Port[BaseAddress+2]; {get modem status register value}
   If X And 2 <> 2 Then Goto FirstLoop;
                             {loop until bit 1 is set}
   Port[BaseAddress+4] := 3;    {turn on "request to send" bit also}
Second Loop:
   X := Port[BaseAddress+2]; {get modem status register value}
   If X And 1 <> 1 Then Goto SecondLoop {loop until bit 0 set}
   {now begin sending data}
```

C

This example uses the Borland C inpor*tb* and *outportb* functions. In Microsoft C, use *inp* and *outp* instead.

```
   outportb(baseaddress+4,1); /*turn on "data terminal ready"*/

   /*now send control string to modem to dial number and estab-
lish connection -- this code varies by the modem */

   .

   .
```

556

```c
first_loop:
  x = inportb(baseaddress+2);/*get modem statusregister value*/
  if(x & 2 != 2) goto first_loop; /*loop until bit 1 set*/
  outportb(baseaddress+4,3);/*turn on "request to send" bit*/
second_loop:
  x = inportb(baseaddress+2); /*get modem status register value*/
  if(x & 1 != 1) goto second_loop; /*loop until bit 0 set*/
  /*now begin sending data...*/
```

Assembler

```asm
;---TURN ON THE "DATA TERMINAL READY" SIGNAL:
        mov     dx,BASE_ADDRESS ;start with base address
        add     dx,4            ;point to modem control register
        mov     al,1            ;turn on bit 1
        out     dx,al           ;turn on DTR
;---SEND CONTROL STRING TO MODEM TO DIAL NUMBER...
                .               ;this code is modem-dependent
                .

;---THEN WAIT UNTIL "DATA SET READY" SIGNAL IS ON"
        inc     dx              ;point to modem status register
        inc     dx              ;
TRY_AGAIN:
        in      al,dx           ;get contents
        test    al,10b          ;see if bit 2 is on
        jz      TRY_AGAIN        ;don't continue until it is
```

```
;---TURN ON "REQUEST TO SEND":
        dec   dx                ;return to modem control register
        dec   dx                ;
        mov   al,3              ;turn on RTS, leaving DTA on
        out   dx,al             ;send the new bit setting
;---WAIT FOR "CLEAR TO SEND"
        inc   dx                ;return to modem status register
        inc   dx                ;
ONCE_MORE:
        in    al,dx             ;get the status byte
        test  al,1              ;ready to send?
        jz    ONCE_MORE         ;don't go on if not
;---NOW BEGIN SENDING DATA...
```

Transmit Data

Transmitting data is simpler than receiving it, because a program has complete control over the composition of the data, and over the rate at which it is sent. Still, transmission routines can become elaborate if they process data as they send it. And timing can be a problem when communications protocols are used. For example the XON/XOFF protocol uses ASCII characters 17 (XON) and 19 (XOFF) to signal to the transmitting station that the receiver wants the transmission flow temporarily interrupted. To accommodate the protocol, a program must constantly watch for incoming characters while it transmits. (In the *full duplex* mode in which most modems operate, signals simultaneously flow both ways across the telephone line.) Similarly, to detect that the remote station has sent a string of 0s and has brought about a *break* condition, the transmitting status must intermittently monitor the status of the break bit (number 4) of the line status register (discussed in "Program a Serial Communications Chip," above). Figure 17-3 shows how the data transmission routine interacts with the data reception code.

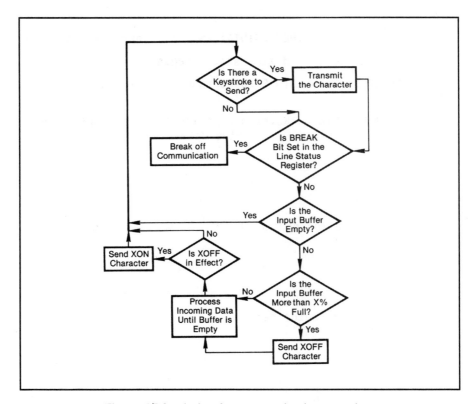

Figure 17-3   A simple communications routine

Because of these considerations, the presentation here of an isolated transmission routine is somewhat artificial. But it can be combined with the data reception routine shown in "Receive Data," below, to create a general framework. Obviously, a tremendous amount of elaboration is required to form a workable routine, particularly by way of error checking and recovery.

BASIC

In BASIC, use *PRINT#*, *PRINT#USING*, and *WRITE#* to send characters out an opened communications port. The latter two statements have special formats that parallel those of the *PRINT USING* and *WRITE* statements used for video operations. Generally *PRINT#* is used. This example sends data taken directly from the keyboard. It assumes that COM1 has already been opened, as shown in "Initialize a Serial Port," above. The routine monitors the break bit of the line status register.

```
    .

    .

  C$=INKEY$:IF C$<>"" THEN PRINT#1,C$ 'if a keystroke, send it

  X=BASEADDRESS+5     'read line status register

   IF X AND 32=32 THEN GOTO BreakRoutine 'if bit 5 set then
BREAK

 IF EOF(1) THEN GOTO GetKeystroke'if input buffer empty, check
for     keystroke 'else, go receive data...

    .

    .

    .


      (data reception routine here)

    .

    .


  BreakRoutine:

  '''BREAK routine begins here

    .

    .
```

Pascal

In Turbo Pascal, assign COM1 (or some other serial port) to a variable, just as if you were opening a file. Then use the variable in *Write* procedures to output data, again, just as if the data were directed toward a disk drive.

```
var

  SerialPort: Text;


Assign(SerialPort, 'COM1');

Rewrite(SerialPort);

Write(SerialPort,'Here is some data');

  .

  .

Close(SerialPort);
```

C

In C, open a stream, specifying the COM port that you want to use. Then write formatted data using *fprintf*:

```
FILE *the_stream;

char the_char;


the_stream = fopen("COM1","r+");

fprintf(the_stream,"Hello big wide world out there!");
```

Alternatively, write single characters using *putc:*

```
putc(the_char,the_stream);
```

These functions are appropriate for simple serial communications that is not very error-prone, such as output to a serial printer. For modem communications, you'll (at the very least) need to turn to the Borland C *bioscom* or Microsoft C *_bios_serialcom* functions. These call the assembly language routines discussed in this section and the next.

Assembler

Function 1 of BIOS interrupt 14h sends the character in AL out the serial port. On entry, DX holds the COM port number, counted from 0 upward. On return, AH holds a status byte in which bit 7 is set if the operation failed. In this case, the following bits are significant:

```
bit 4    Break detect (the receiving station signals "stop!")

    5    Transmission shift register empty

    6    Transmission holding register empty
```

DOS has an asynchronous communications function that transmits the character placed in DL. The function, number 4 of interrupt 21h, offers no advantage over the BIOS interrupt; indeed, it does not return status information, and it does not allow you to designate which COM port to use (it always addresses COM1).

In DOS it's also possible to output strings of data using function 40h of interrupt 21h. This is the common output function for all files and devices under the *file handle* method of access. Be warned that this method is not reliable, but may occasionally be suitable for "quick and dirty" programs. COM1 uses a predefined handle, number 0003. Place the handle in BX and the number of bytes to output in CX. Then point DS:DX to the output data buffer and call the function.

```
mov  ah,40h          ;function number

mov  bx,3            ;predefined COM handle

mov  cx,50           ;output 50 bytes

lea  dx,DATA_BUFFER  ;point DS:DX to the data buffer

int  21h             ;send the data

jc   COM_ERROR       ;jump if there has been an error
```

Note that there is no need to "open" a predefined handle. If an error occurs, the carry flag is set, and AX returns 5 if the communications port was not ready and 6 if the handle number was wrong.

Low-Level Access

When a character of data is placed in the 8250's *transmitter holding register*, it is automatically output to the serial line via the *transmitter shift register*, which serializes the data. There is no need to pulse a strobe bit to initiate the transfer, as is required on the parallel adaptor. Bit 5 of the *line status register* tells whether the transmitter holding register is free to receive data. The register is constantly monitored until bit 5 becomes 1. Then one byte of data is sent to the transmitter holding register, from where it is instantly output. Bit 5 changes to 0 while the byte is output, and only when it again becomes 1 may the next character be sent to the transmitter holding register. This process is repeated as long as required.

The following example gives the basic set-up of such a routine. The example assumes that the serial port and modem have already been initialized, as shown in "Intialize a Serial Port" and "Initialize and Monitor a Modem," above. The first part is a loop that keeps checking for errors and received characters. "Receive Data," below, gives the code for the data reception routine.

```
;---WAIT UNTIL ALL RIGHT TO SEND A CHARACTER:
 KEEP_TRYING:  mov  dx,BASE_ADDRESS  ;base address from prior
code
     add  dx,5           ;point to line status register
     in   al,dx          ;get status byte
     test al,00011110b   ;test for error
     jnz  ERROR ROUTINE  ;jump to error routine if a problem
     test al,00000001b   ;test whether data received
     jnz  RECEIVE        ;go to receive routine (next section)
     test al,00100000b   ;test if ready to transmit character
     jz   KEEP_TRYING    ;if not, loop around
;---TRANSMIT A CHARACTER (GET IT FROM THE KEYBOARD):
     mov  ah,1           ;BIOS function to check if keystroke
     int  16h            ;BIOS keyboard interrupt
     jz   KEEP_TRYING    ;return to loop if no keystroke awaits
     mov  ah,0           ;BIOS function to get a keystroke
     int  16h            ;keystroke now in AL
     sub  dx,5           ;point to transmitter holding register
     out  dx,al          ;send the character
     jmp  SHORT KEEP_TRYING ;return to loop
```

Receive Data

A communications program is ready to receive data once a communications port has been initialized and contact has been established with the remote station. Data reception is never entirely separate from data transmission, since a program may need to send a protocol code such as an XOFF signal (ASCII 19) to stop the data flow if data is received faster than it can be processed. XON (ASCII 17) tells the remote station to recommence transmission.

Depending on the complexity of the data protocol, the incoming data may require only a little, or a good deal, of interpretation. Any of the various control codes listed in "Look Up a Communications Control Code," below, might be received. Those that signal data boundaries are more often found in *synchronous* communications. When displaying the incoming data on the screen, consider the effect of line feed characters (ASCII 10), since some languages automatically insert a line feed after a carriage return. In this case, eliminate the incoming line feed characters to avoid double-spacing on the screen. Figure 17-3, found in "Transmit Data," above, diagrams the basic communications routine, including the transmission code that is discussed in that section.

BASIC

For communications routines written in interpreted BASIC, time is of the essence. Processing is slow, and if the input routine is improperly designed, the input buffer can fill (that is, *overflow*) while the program is still busy interpreting the prior data received. An obvious solution to this problem is to make the buffer extremely large. When BASIC is loaded the input buffer size is set by appending a **/C:** command. **BASICA/C:1024** creates a 1K buffer, and this is the minimum size for 1200 baud (4096 bytes may be required by complex routines). The default value is 256 bytes, and this buffer size has the advantage that when BASIC reads from the buffer it can fit the entire contents into a single string variable. Use it only at 300 baud or below.

BASIC reads from the buffer using the INPUT$ statement (INPUT# and LINE INPUT# also work, but INPUT$ is the most flexible). This statement is in the form **INPUT$(numberbytes,filenumber)**. For example, **INPUT$(10,#1)** reads ten bytes from the communications channel opened as #1. If the buffer size is under 256 bytes, it is most convenient to read the entire contents of the buffer at once. LOC tells how many bytes of data currently reside in the buffer. So write **S$=INPUT$(LOC(1),#1)** and S$ is given all the data received since the buffer was last accessed. Of course, if **LOC(1)=0** then the buffer is empty, and the routine must keep looping until data is received. Note that **EOF(1)** also reports on the buffer contents, returning -1 if empty, and 0 if there are any characters.

Once data is given to S$, the program seeks whatever control codes are of concern. The INSTR function performs this task most quickly. Recall that INSTR is followed by first the position in the string from which to begin searching, and then the name of the string, and finally the character (or string) that is sought. To find the XOFF character (ASCII 19) the statement would be **INSTR(1,S$,CHR$(17))**. To find a second occurrence of a control code, search the string again, starting from the character following the position at which the first was located.

Ordinarily the input routine eliminates most control codes from the incoming data so that it appears properly on the display. Then the data is displayed, shunted around memory, and sometimes written to disk or dumped on to a printer. In the midst of all this, the program must constantly return to look for more data. If the buffer turns out to be filling too quickly, the program can send an XOFF character to the transmitting station, halting the data flow. Then the flow may be re-enabled after the received data has been decoded. Of course, XON and XOFF must be supported by the protocol in use. Programs written in interpreted BASIC usually can use XON/XOFF for "speed-matching" when they receive data; but usually such programs cannot respond quickly enough when they *receive* an XOFF signal while they are transmitting.

```
     .

     .

'''transmission routine here (see "Transmit Data," above)
TRANSMIT:

     .

     .

READ_DATA:
IF LOC(1)>100 THEN XOFF=1:PRINT#1,CHR$(19) 'if buffer filling,
             'turn XOFF status on by sending ASCII 19
C$=INPUT$(LOC(1),#1)         'read the contents of the buffer
'''filter the data for special characters:
IF INSTR(1,C$,CHR$(19))>0 THEN GOTO XOFF_Routine 'XOFF
character received?
IF INSTR(1,C$,CHR$(17))>0 THEN GOTO XOFF_Routine 'XON
character received?

     .

     .    (delete unwanted control codes)

     .
```

```
PRINT C$;                       'display the string
IF LOC(1)>THEN GOTO READ_DATA   'if more data arrived, go
get it
IF XOFF=1 THEN XOFF=0:PRINT#1,CHR$(17)   'switch off XOFF
GOTO TRANSMIT           'goto start of transmission routine

   .

   .

XOFF_ROUTINE:

   .

XON_ROUTINE:

   .

   .
```

When applied to a communications port, the LOF (length of file) function returns the amount of free space remaining in the input buffer. For example, if the COM port was opened as #1, then **LOF(1)** reports the amount of free space. This feature may be useful for telling when the buffer is nearly full. But note that the LOC statement returns the location of the buffer pointer, and this value can be used for the same purpose. For example, for a COM port opened as **#3**, in which the buffer size is 256 bytes, so long as LOC(3) does not return 256, the buffer is not full.

Pascal

In Turbo Pascal, a serial port is read by treating it like a file. Assign COM1 (or some other serial port) to a variable and open the port with *Reset*. Then use the variable in *Read* commands to read data, again. This example reads a single character:

```
var
  SerialPort: Text;
  IncomingByte: Byte;


  Assign(SerialPort, 'COM1');
  Rewrite(SerialPort);
  Read(SerialPort,IncomingByte);
```

```
    .

    .

Close(SerialPort);
```

As always, you can check for errors by writing **{$I-}** before the I/O commands are executed and testing *IOResult* afterwards to see if it is nonzero (in which case an error has occurred).

C

Serial data may be read as a *stream* in C. Use *fopen* to open the stream, specifying COM1 (or some other serial port). Then read single characters using *getc:*

```
FILE *the_stream;

char the_char;


the_stream = fopen("COM1","r+");

the_char = getc (the_stream)
```

For greater control, use the Borland C *bioscom* or Microsoft C *_bios_serialcom* functions. These provide access to the BIOS serial communications routines. They take a command number that is 0 for setting communications parameters (more on this in "Initialize a Serial Port," above); 1 for sending a character, 2 for receiving a character, and 3 for reporting status information. In Borland's C, the second parameter is the character that is data input to the function, and the third is the serial port number (0 = COM1). For example:

```
bioscom(0, com_settings,status_word);
```

The Microsoft function reverses the second and third parameters. In all instances, these functions return an integer providing the following status information:

bit	meaning when bit is set
15	Time out
14	The transmit shift register is empty
13	The transmit holding register is empty
12	Break detect
11	Data framing error

bit	*meaning when bit is set*
10	Parity error
9	Overrun error
8	Data ready

For command 0, bit 15 is set when the function fails. When a byte is received using command 2, the byte is returned in the low eight bits of the status word and now bit is set in the high byte of the word. When the command is 0 or 3, these bits are also set:

7	Received line signal detect
6	Ring indicator status
5	Data set ready
4	Clear to send
3	Change in the receive line signal detector
2	Trailing edge ring detector
1	Change in data set ready
0	Change in clear to send

Assembler

BIOS function 2 of interrupt 14h waits for a character from the serial port, places it in AL when one is received, and then returns. On entry, place the COM port number (counted from 0 upward) in DX. On return, AH holds 0 if no error has occurred. If AH is not 0, then a status byte has been returned in which only five bits are significant. These bits are:

bit 1	overrun error (new character before prior one removed)
2	parity error (probably from a transmission line problem)
3	framing error (start and stop bits not as they should be)
4	break detect (received a long string of 0 bits)
7	time out error ("data set ready" signal not received)

DOS also offers an asynchronous communications function that receives single characters, number 3 of interrupt 21h. The function waits for a character from COM1 and places it in AL. Note that there is no matching function to initialize the port, and so it must be done via the BIOS routine, or directly, as shown in "Initialize a Serial Port," above. The default initialization is 2400 baud, no parity, with one stop bit, and eight-bit characters. This interrupt offers no advantages over the BIOS routines.

Low-Level Access

When receiving data without the use of the communication interrupt, a program must constantly monitor the line status register, which is located at the port address that is 5 greater than the base address of the serial adaptor in use. Bit 0 of this register is set to 0 so long as no character has been received in the *receiver data register*. When bit 0 changes to 1, the character must immediately be removed from the register in order to avoid being overrun by the next character to arrive. Once the character is removed, bit 0 immediately returns to 0, and it stays 0 until another character is received.

Although not shown here, be aware that communications routines usually set up a *circular buffer* to collect the incoming characters. In a circular buffer, two pointers keep track of the beginning and end of the data, and the data wrap around from the "end" of the buffer to the "beginning." You also should know that if the incoming data is directed to the screen, the BIOS scrolling routine (discussed in Chapter 13, "Scroll a Screen Vertically") may not act quickly enough, and an overrun will occur. An easy solution to this difficulty is to rely on communications interrupts, which are examined in "Send/Receive Data by Communications Interrupts," below.

The following example duplicates part of that shown in the prior section, where characters are transmitted. What is shared is the infinite loop that begins the code. Combine the two routines along with the initializiation routines found in "Initialize a Serial Port" and "Initialize and Monitor a Modem," above, for a complete serial I/O routine.

```
KEEP_TRYING:

    mov  dx,BASE_ADDRESS  ;base address from prior code

    add  dx,5             ;point to line status register

    in   al,dx            ;get status byte

    test al,00011110b     ;test for error

    jnz  ERROR_ROUTINE    ;jump to error routine if a problem

    test al,00000001b     ;test whether data received

    jnz  RECEIVE          ;go to receive routine

    test al,00100000b     ;test if ready to transmit character

    jz   KEEP_TRYING      ;if not, loop around
```

```
                            ;else, transmit a character...

        .
     ;---(transmission routine here --see "Transmit Data,"
         above)

        .

        .


;---RECEIVE DATA AND DISPLAY ON SCREEN:
RECEIVE:
     mov   dx,BASEADDRESS ;base address=receiver data register
     in    al,dx          ;get the newly arrived character
     cmp   al,19          ;check for XOFF, etc
     je    XOFF_ROUTINE   ;
                          ;etc...
                          ;
     mov   dl,al          ;prepare to display the character
     mov   ah,2           ;DOS interrupt to display character
     int   21h            ;display the character
     jmp   short KEEP_TRYING ;return to loop
```

Send/Receive Data by Communications Interrupts

Elaborate communications programs have too much to do to devote themselves full time to I/O operations. Incoming data must be analyzed, outgoing data must be gathered, and large blocks of data may need to be moved to and from disk. Communications interrupts let a program spend no more time in I/O operations than is required. For example, by setting up an interrupt, control is transferred to a data transmission routine only when the transmitter holding register is empty, and control reverts to the program once a byte of data is sent, allowing the program to continue until the transmitter holding register is ready again. Be sure to be familiar with the discussion of interrupts in the Chapter 4 *minitutorial* before reading on.

IBM PCs allot two hardware interrupt channels for communications, numbers 3 (COM1) and 4 (COM2). The 8250 UART for each channel allows four classes of interrupts, using the following binary code numbers:

```
00        change in modem status register

01        transmitter holding register empty

10        data received

11        reception error, or break condition received
```

These codes are contained in bits 2–1 in the *interrupt identification register*, which is located at the port address that is 2 greater than the base address of the serial port in use. Bit 0 of this register is set to 1 when an interrupt is pending; the other bits are not used, and are always set to 0.

To select one or more interrupts, program the *interrupt enable register*, which is located 1 higher than the base address. The bit pattern is:

```
bit 0    1=interrupt when data received

    1    1=interrupt when transmitter holding register
         empty

    2    1=interrupt when data reception error

    3    1=interrupt when change in modem status register

  4-7    unused, always 0
```

A hardware interrupt is invoked when one of these events occurs. The interrupt routine transfers control to whatever code is pointed to by the associated interrupt vectors. Because this is a hardware interrupt, it can be masked out (see Chapter 4, "Allow/Disallow Hardware Interrupts"). Remember that the interrupt routines you provide must end with the standard exit code for hardware interrupts **MOV AL,20h/OUT 20h,AL**. Figure 17-4 illustrates the communications interrupt.

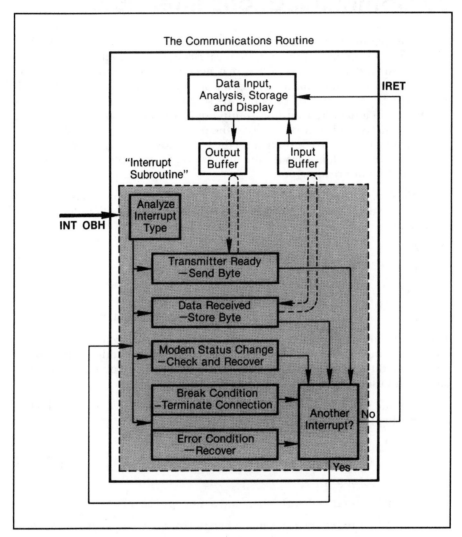

Figure 17-4   A communications interrupt

Any number of interrupt types may be enabled simultaneously, but when this is the case, the routine must begin by checking the interrupt identification register to find out which it is. More than one interrupt can occur simultanously, and for this reason bit 0 of the identification register tells whether additional interrupts are pending. When two or more occur at the same instant, they are processed in the order shown in the table below. The additional interrupts must be processed before the interrupt routine returns. The prior interrupt condition is "undone" by taking the action shown in the righthand column of the table.

code	type	action for "reset"
11	error or break	read line status register
10	data received	read receiver data register
01	transmitter ready	output character to transmitter holding register
00	modem status change	read modem status register

Assembler

Here is the general form of a communications interrupt handler:

```
;---SET UP THE COMMUNICATION INTERRUPT VECTOR:
        PUSH DS               ;DS changed by function
        mov  dx,offset IO_INT ;point DS:DX to COM routine
        mov  ax,seg IO_INT    ;
        mov  ds,ax            ;
        mov  al,0Ch           ;vector number for COM1
        mov  ah,25h           ;function to change vector
        int  21h              ;change vector
;---INITIALIZE THE INTERRUPT-ENABLE REGISTER (COM1):
        mov  ax,40h           ;point DS to BIOS data area
        mov  ds,ax            ;
        mov  dx,ds:[0]        ;get base address for COM1
        inc  dx               ;point to interrupt enable register
        mov  al,3             ;enable both receive and transmit INTS
        out  dx,al            ;send the byte
        pop  ds               ;restore DS
                              ;the program continues...
```

```
;---HERE IS THE INTERRUPT ROUTINE—FIND OUT TYPE OF INTERRUPT:
IO_INT proc    far
NEXT_INT:
        mov  dx,BASEADDRESS   ;base address for COM1
        inc  dx              ;
        inc  dx              ;point to interrupt identification
        reg
        in   al,dx           ;read the value
        test al,10b          ;transmitter?
        jnz  TRANSMIT        ;go transmit a character
                             ;else, must be receive interrupt:
RECEIVE:
        .                    ;begin character/line reception

        .

        .
        jmp short ANOTHER    ;go see if another interrupt pending
TRANSMIT:                    ;begin routine to transmit a character

        .

        .


;---BEFORE EXITING, CHECK THAT NO OTHER INTERRUPT REQUESTS
PENDING:
ANOTHER:
        mov  dx,BASEADDRESS  ;base address of COM1
        inc  dx              ;point to interrupt identification reg
        inc  dx              ;
        in   al,dx           ;read the value
        test al,1            ;request pending?
        jnz  NEXT_INT        ;if so, jump back to start of routine
```

```
        mov   al,20h            ;else, send end-of-interrupt code
        out   20h,al            ;
        iret                    ;quit
IO_INT  endp                    ;end of interrupt procedure
```

Look Up a Communications Control Code

This table gives the 32 ASCII control codes that are used in communications or to operate printers or other devices. An extra code is added, ASCII 127 (DEL), because it is normally used as a control code, although there is no Ctrl key combination to produce it. The applications of some of these codes are invariant, such as the carriage return. But most are given a wide range of interpretations, much to the detriment of hardware compatibility.

decimal	hex	symbol	code	mnemonic	purpose
00	00	(null)	^@	NUL	Spacing character (meaningless, so also useful for delays).
01	01	☺	^A	SOH	Start Of Heading. Begins transmission of data block or new file.
02	02	●	^B	STX	Start Of Text. Marks beginning of text following header data.
03	03	"	^C	ETX	End Of Text. May mark beginning of error checking data.
04	04	u	^D	EOT	End Of Transmission. Sign-off code, but sometimes only marks end of file.
05	05	¤	^E	ENQ	Enquiry. Requests status information from remote station.
06	06	♠	^F	ACK	Acknowledge. Verifies the success of communications between stations.
07	07	•	^G	BEL	Bell. Beeps the speaker, signalling need of attention.
08	08	◘	^H	BS	Backspace.
09	09	O	^I	HT	Horizontal Tab.

576

decimal	hex	symbol	code	mnemonic	purpose
10	0A	◙	^J	LF	Line Feed.
11	0B	♂	^K	VT	Vertical Tab.
12	0C	♀	^L	FF	Form Feed.
13	0D	♪	^M	CR	Carriage Return.
14	0E	♫	^N	SO	Shift Out. Changes character set.
15	0F	☼	^O	SI	Shift In. Changes character set.
16	10	►	^P	DLE	Data Link Escape. Modifies meaning of subsequent characters (like Esc).
17	11	◄	^Q	DC1	Device Control 1. Used as XON to signal remote station to transmit.
18	12	↕	^R	DC2	Device Control 2. General purpose toggle signal.
19	13	‼	^S	DC3	Device Control 3. Used as XOFF to signal remote station to not transmit.
20	14	¶	^T	DC4	Device Control 4. General purpose toggle signal.
21	15	§	^U	NAK	Negative Acknowledge. Signals transmission failure.
22	16	▬	^V	SYN	Synchronous Idle. Used between data blocks in synchronous communications.
23	17	↨	^W	ETB	End Of Transmission Block. Variant of ETX.
24	18	↑	^X	CAN	Cancel. Usually signals transmission error.

decimal	hex	symbol	code	mnemonic	purpose
25	19	↓	^Y	EM	End Of Medium. Signals physical end of data-source.
26	1A	→	^Z	SUB	Substitute. Replaces characters that are invalid or impossible to display.
27	1B	←	^[	ESC	Escape. Marks following characters as a control sequence.
28	1C	⌞	^/	FS	File Separator. Marks logical boundary between files.
29	1D	↔	^]	GS	Group Separator. Marks logical boundary between data groups.
30	1E	▲	^^	RS	Record Separator. Marks logical boundary between data records.
31	1F	▼	^_	US	Unit Separator. Marks logical boundary between data units.
127	7F	⌂	none	DEL	Delete. Eliminates other characters.

Index

B

C

pull-down menus, 242
putch C function, 446
putpixel C function, 474
PutPixel Pascal procedure, 474

R

RAM, *see* random-access memory
random files, 363-364
random access files
  reading, 394
  reading from, 394-398
  writing to, 387-391, 396
random-access (RAM) memory, 58
raster graphics, 534
re-entrant interrupts, 93
read modes, 488
read-only (ROM) memory, 58
Read-only files, 351
reading
  attributes, 456-458
  characters, 456-458
  dates, 131-133
  directories, 335-340
  from random access files, 394-398
  from sequential files, 381, 383, 384, 386
  joystick coordinates, 278-281
  random access files, 394
  real-time clock, 134-135
  sectors, 299-305
  time, 127
  volume labels, 295
ReadOnly constant, 353
reads sector, 327
real-time
  clock, 117-118
    accessing low-level, 137-138
    alarm, 135
    reading, 134-137
    setting, 134-137
  operations, 120, 143-147
  programming, 166
recalibrating drives, 307
receiver data register, 540, 569
receiving data, 564-570
recording times and dates, 346-350
records, 364
rectangles, drawing, 532-533
registers

address, 310
AH, 244
AL, 289
AX, 244, 257, 270, 276, 279
bit mask, 478
BX, 245, 270, 276, 279
command, 120
control, 498
count, 310
counter, 119
CX, 245, 257, 260, 263-265, 270, 279
data, 307
  output, 498
  rotate, 480
DI, 276
DX, 245, 257, 260, 263-265, 270, 279
input status, 503
interrupt
  enable, 547-548
  identification, 571
latch, 119, 478
line control, 540
  initializing ports, 546
line status, 540, 549, 562
map
  mask, 478
  select, 488
mod, 479
modem
  control, 541, 552
  status, 541, 553
output data, 512
page, 310
receiver data, 540, 569
SI, 263, 276
status, 309, 498
transmitter
  holder, 540
  holding register, 562
  shift, 562
reinitializing printers, 498-502
relocation process in EXE program, 20
Rename procedure, 356
renaming
  directories, 356-358
  files, 356-358
reporting positions, 244
request to send signal, 552
RESET command, 370
Reset procedure, 371
resources of system, assessing, 25
return registers, 92